Jewels of Authority

Jewels of Authority

Women and Textual Tradition in Hindu India

EDITED BY
LAURIE L. PATTON

OXFORD
UNIVERSITY PRESS
2002

OXFORD
UNIVERSITY PRESS

Oxford New York
Athens Auckland Bangkok Bogotá Buenos Aires Cape Town
Chennai Dar es Salaam Delhi Florence Hong Kong Istanbul Karachi
Kolkata Kuala Lumpur Madrid Melbourne Mexico City Mumbai Nairobi
Paris São Paulo Shanghai Singapore Taipei Tokyo Toronto Warsaw

and associated companies in
Berlin Ibadan

Published by Oxford University Press, Inc.
198 Madison Avenue, New York, New York 10016

Library of Congress Cataloging-in-Publication Data

Patton, Laurie L., 1961–
Jewels of authority: women and textual tradition in Hindu India /
edited by Laurie L. Patton.
p. cm.
Includes bibliographical references and index.
ISBN 0-19-513478-8
1. Women–India–Social conditions. 2. Hindu women–India–History.
3. Women–Religious aspects–Hinduism. 4. Hinduism–Social aspects. 5. Women's rights–Religious aspects–Hinduism. 6. Dowry–India–History.
HQ1742.P39 2000
305.42'0954–dc21 99-053416

1 3 5 7 9 8 6 4 2

Printed in the United States of America
on acid-free paper

In memory of S. S. Janaki
who taught so many of us, so well

Foreword

It is no news that, in an earlier genre of writing on women in India, women were the objects of study and, in Cartesian fashion, were viewed as the "other" by knowing subjects, who were men. The voices of the women themselves were muted, and they were present more as functions of a particular literary or religious situation than as functions of authority in their own right. Earlier books, such as Altekar's *The Position of Women in Hindu Civilization from Prehistoric Times to the Present Day* or Shakuntala Rao Shastri's *Aspirations from a Fresh World*, are not of much help in a reconstruction of a sociohistorical account of the lives of women. As Laurie Patton mentions in the introduction to this book, these works are inventories, designed to give us a certain amount of data.

Jewels of Authority belongs to a new genre, developed painstakingly by women scholars through careful hermeneutics. The contributors to this volume are interested in retrieving truthfully and reconstructing faithfully a sociohistorical perspective in which women exercise authority in the different periods they are investigating. This work is representative of the new genre in Women's Studies and Gender Studies, where women are no longer under the gaze of men. They are also the subjects who study themselves as the objects and not as the other. Thus they are able to approach the topic in a critical and differently empathetic way. This book is a collection of essays on women, based on textual and documented material that covers a vast spectrum of topics, ranging from Vedic to contemporary times. While the material spans many historical periods, the focus captures the vicissitudes of women's interaction within a brahminical ideology.

How is this interaction between women and brahmins described in the pages of *Jewels of Authority* in a way that honors indigenous categories? One of the criticisms of colonial Indological research was the transference of some ideas and interpretations from a western perspective into an alien context. The authors in this book are careful not to fall into that trap. To reach their findings, they use the tools of interpretation given in the Hindu tradition itself, such as that of *mīmāṃsā* hermeneutics or the sociolegal approach of the Dharma Śāstras. This book is thus a unique attempt to critique prevailing modes of social behavior from the tradition's own perspective.

Moreover, there are some special problems that only a scholar working in Hindu texts faces. Because ancient Indian texts lack a definite chronology, the study of the

Sanskrit and other texts of the ancient and medieval periods leaves one with a sense of frustration. One works constantly with the suspicion that one is extrapolating only from available texts, which may not all represent the whole culture. This suspicion can always lead to the guilty feeling that there may be more there than what meets the eye. The break between theory and practice, and the related truism that what prevails in society does not generally conform to the norms set forth in the texts, is perhaps even more applicable to these Hindu contexts. In the study of Sanskrit texts, for instance, one must work with many texts within a single period, without a corresponding sense of their relative dating. The historical difficulty of dating some of the important texts like the Vedas, the Epics, the *Manu Smṛti*, the Dharma Sūtras, the various Dharma Śāstras, and many other texts is well known. In addition, because of this lack of genuinely historiographical material in the early texts, we have not been able to glean much useful information on women as figures of authority. Because of these limitations, scholars working on sociohistorical problems, especially in the case of women in Hinduism, work against great odds. It is the measure of their dedication that this work finally yields results.

To be sure, the challenges that face scholars working in Women's Studies and Gender Studies are daunting in all cultures. But, in addition to the general problem of dating Hindu texts mentioned above, Women's Studies in Hinduism has some additional hurdles with which to contend. First, the literature covered in this field is indeed vast—ranging from the ancient to the modern, which by any standards can cover at least four thousand years to date. Second, any scholar working in this field needs a mastery of at least one of the languages of India, depending on the period in which she or he is working. For those working in the ancient and medieval periods, competency in Sanskrit, in both its Vedic and classical forms, is indispensable. For a medieval scholar, and one dealing with modern Indian material, competency in at least one regional language like Marathi, Bengali, Hindi, or Tamil would also be an asset. These demands on scholars working in these areas of Hinduism can be quite intimidating and have certainly hindered the progress of sophisticated studies in Hinduism. Added to all this, one must also realize that, in general, until a few years ago, good scholars in Sanskrit, Tamil, and so on, especially women, would not be those trained in modern sociohistorical research methodology. And those who did have the research skills would not have the language competency. If both were found somehow in the same person, they would not be inclined to work on "Women's Studies," as this was not a favored research area until recently. It is therefore heartening to see that scholars contributing to this volume are precisely those who have those necessary skills. They are well known for their expertise; they have the latest research skills and have been able, in the respective topics they have chosen, to retrieve and present the women hidden behind these texts as women of authority having voices of their own.

Aside from these general technical issues, a particular conceptual problem also emerges in the study of women in ancient and medieval India: the lack of multiple voices on women's issues. When one deals with Hindu texts concerned with sociological issues, like the position, authority, or autonomy of women, these topics come within the purview of the Dharma Sūtras/Dharma Śāstras, and perhaps also the Epics. Amazingly, in these very texts we tend to encounter a single, uniform ideology about women. It is well known that "the power of patriarchy" the world over was not genuinely challenged till the feminist movements came on the scene. But what is difficult to understand is that, in India, almost all the Dharma Śāstra texts that deal directly with society, and therefore with women, seem to depict one kind of social ideology in presenting the picture of women in particular. For instance, while one need not accept totally the glorified picture of women in the Vedic period, by the same token it is difficult to believe that she had fallen to such a pathetic state without a voice of her own, as we see in the Smṛtis. Women composed hymns in the Vedic period; there were philosophers in the Upaniṣadic times; there were women poets and writers of *kāvya* in the *kāvya* period; and there were *saṃnyāsinīs* mentioned right up to the time of Bhavabhūti. Therefore it is a bit surprising to see that there is not a single woman writer of a Dharma Śāstra text available to us today. Is it possible that, like the Tamil Tirukkōnēri Dāsyai commentarial text discussed by Vasudha Natayanan in this volume, a woman did write or compiled a Dharma Śāstra work in this period, but unlike the Tirukkōnēri Dāsyai work, it somehow never saw the light of day? This seems plausible when one sees that the works of Smṛti writers like Bṛhaspati, Prajāpati, and Kātyāyana, whose views from citations from other works seem more sympathetic to widows with regard to inheritance, are also all lost and unavailable now. Scholars like Julia Leslie have cited a lawbook written by a woman named Lakshmīdevi, called *Bālambhatti* (ca. 1800). This is a late text and it is generally sympathetic to women. But its authorship is also attributed to Lakshmīdevi's son who supposedly used her name in order, perhaps, to escape censure for his lenient views concerning women.

While this age seems to be particularly weighted against women, in a sociohistorical context, facts are not just black or white. There can be many gray areas in between, and it may be in these gray areas that we have our only clue to such multiple voices. For instance we are all too familiar with the statement from Manu that a woman does not merit freedom (*na strī svātantryamarhati*). There are other statements in the *Manu Smṛti* which are not so condemnatory toward women. We find another saying, also well known, that only such a society can thrive in which women are respected (*yatra nāryastu pūjyante ramante tatra devatah* 3.56). Then again we are told by Manu that a mother is more worthy of respect than a thousand *ācāryas*, or teachers (2.145). Manu also gives a woman full rights over her *strīdhana*. He even mentions that, rather than be married to a man having no good qualities, a daughter should not be given in marriage at all (9.89). He then has a whole set of verses in the fifth and ninth chapters that look upon women as depraved. What is one to make of all these conflicting statements in the same book? Are these all written by the same Manu or by a number of people and compiled by one Manu much in the manner of Patañjali's *Yoga Sūtras*? It is difficult to believe that one and the same Manu could have had such different views, both of an extreme nature, on women. More to our purposes in this volume, the contradictory statements in Manu hint at the different possible perceptions of women prevalent in society, as well as the attempt to paint all those images with a single color in keeping with a single ideology, mentioned earlier.

Jewels of Authority also shows many other new, intriguing patterns and possible readings of early Indian history. In the brahminical culture, which values its individuals because they have the competency or *adhikāra* to perform Vedic rituals, the ultimate act of demonizing women is to take away from her this right. Whether this was done deliberately or because of circumstances will be anybody's guess. But what was her right, as shown by Mary McGee in this book, was denied to her by the time of the Smṛtis. One of the necessary conditions of a person to have this *adhikāra* being that he or she has to be in a state of marriage effectively ruled out widows having this right. But the point to be noted is that women had the right to remarry after being widowed, and this right is expressly stated in many a text. The Vedic literature definitely allows it. The Epics are full of such stories. The Jātaka tales in Buddhism sanction it. The explicit statement in the Artha Śāstra of Kauṭilya (3.2.19–32) leaves no doubt in anybody's mind that widow remarriage was not looked down upon. All the Smṛtikāras are familiar with its existence (Manu, Gautama, Vasiṣṭha, Viṣṇu) and reluctantly admit its sanction although they qualify it with many caveats. It is in the Dharma Śāstras that the opposition to widow remarriage is building up.

By the time of the medieval period, as we all know, women were not allowed to study the Vedas. Here also, we can point out intriguing ambivalences and possibilities in interpretation. That this harsher view of women was not the view of Jaimini has been pointed out in one of the chapters of this volume. Yet Jaimini remains an authority in the medieval period, with that part of his philosophy ignored. One is reminded of Śaṅkarācārya, of Advaita fame, interpreting the famous *Bṛhadāraṇyaka Upaniṣad* passage (Br. Up.6.4. 17), which advocates the birth of a daughter who would be a scholar by reciting certain *mantras* (. . .*icched duhitā me panditā jāyeta*). In his interpretation, Śaṅkarācārya states that this mantra recitation is not applicable to Vedic learning. He writes that the passage only means that "one be skilled in household work" and not Vedic learning. For someone who advocated the oneness of Brahman in the neuter gender (Brahman) (*sarvamidam khalu brahma*), with no gender bias at all, the compulsion to conform to the norms of the Dharma Śāstras must indeed have been great for him to so interpret this passage like the ignoring of certain key passages of Jaimini. One can imagine the depths to which this social engineering was undertaken. What the compulsions were to do this we do not know, but we cannot doubt that the position of women was undermined deliberately and texts were written to promote that same ideology.

Let us follow the same ambivalences and possibilities and look at another question: women who want to follow the spiritual path without going through the *vivāha*/ marriage *saṃskāra*/ ritual. We are led to believe that personalities like Gārgī and Maitreyī are not relevant any more in the medieval period. But we do find examples like Sulabhā in the *Mahābhārata*, which is more or less in the same period as the *Manu Smṛti*. We also have the famous Ātreyī in the *Uttararāmacaritam*, and *Kāmandakī* in the *Mālatīmādhavam* of Bhavabhūti of the seventh century of the Common Era. We also find in the *Yatidharmasamuccaya* of Yādavaprakāśa (putatively assigned to the eleventh century of the common era) that a *saṃnyāsin* is asked not to accept alms from a woman who is independent, one who is naked, one who lives as she pleases, one who is without a husband, or a woman who has married a second time (*Yatidharmasamuccaya*, 6, 143–146).

Who are these naked women and who are these independent women? Do these refer to some *saṃnyāsinī* groups or women who follow the Tantra form of worship? We do know that women like Mahādeviakka in the South and Lal Ded in Kashmir are both described as naked. Are we then witnessing an existing ascetic sect in this period that allows even women to roam around naked? Is it possible to connect them with the Tantric women who were, all along, part of the spiritual landscape but do not figure much in the Dharma Śāstra works? Tantra did not find favor with the early

Sanskritist researchers because of so many misunderstandings. While some of the Tantric practices look unusual from our contemporary standpoint, there were other practices that were generally favorable to women. The medieval period reveals these Tantric practices existing side by side with other belief systems, and one cannot afford to ignore these juxtapositions if one has to arrive at some understanding of that age.

Finally, as Paola Bacchetta points out some of the intriguing possibilities for the idea of *saṃnyās* for women in the contemporary period, we can see these patterns in earlier history as well. A comparison with other literature, such as Buddhist, Jaina, Ājīvika, and Tamil texts, definitely argues for the existence of women *saṃnyāsinīs* in this period. The prejudice of the brahminical ideology comes into sharp focus in the area of whether women can become *saṃnyāsinīs* or not. There is a concerted effort to decry women taking up *saṃnyāsa*, although there are plenty of examples both in the Epics and in literary works that tell us of the presence of women *saṃnyāsinīs*. Dhṛtavratā, Śrutavatī and Sulabhā did not marry and pursued a spiritual life. Records from the Kuṃbhamelas, calendrical events that occur every twelve years, show the presence of women *saṃnyāsinīs* who come to take part in the mela, both as individuals and as members of institutions. This is an ancient tradition, and it is a travesty of history to deny it to women. Dilip Kumar Roy and Indira Devi, in their book *Kuṃbha: India's Ageless Festival,* record their meeting with such women who proclaim their tradition as very old. In addition, we get useful information on the topic of women *saṃnyāsinīs* in the chronicles of the Buddhist and Jaina nuns and *sādhvīs*. Tamil literature has the famous example of Avvaiyyār who, according to some, is a generic term for a woman *saṃnyāsinī*.

With the end of the colonial chapter India has emerged from its "petrified" state to face a world that has, at least in theory, allowed its women to develop their potency to the full. Falk and Gold show the ways in which such theory and practice sometimes exist in significant but creative tension. In this context one needs to answer the question as to the relevance of *Jewels of Authority* in today's world. The chapters in this book substantiate Gadamer's view about the past being "an effective history" that therefore opens up its texts. In the Hindu context, the festivals and narratives of the past invite the possibility of new interpretations by those competent to do so. *Jewels of Authority* has also set a new methodological approach by looking at women through a single lens (interaction with brahminical ideology) and thus has the advantage of being very well focused. This book can very well set the trend for researches of a similar nature in future.

T. S. Rukmani
Concordia University

Acknowledgments

This volume began as a thought experiment: what would happen if some of the leading women Sanskritists in the country gathered to talk about their work and concerns about gender? Since graduate training with several women Sanskritists in America and India, my fledgling thought experiment became an increasingly important dream. In 1993, at Columbia University, the dream moved out of the realm of *svarga*, or heaven, and into the *laukika*, or everyday, world. In April of that year we gathered for the first time to think about gender and Vedic authority, supported by the Southern Asian Institute and the Dharam Hinduja Indic Research Center at Columbia University. It became clear at that initial exchange of papers that the world of women's studies and Sanskrit was, by nature, interdisciplinary. We immediately felt the need for ethnographic and historical, as well as textual, information—in languages other than Sanskrit. Moreover, we immediately felt the need to broaden the circle to include other colleagues and graduate students who might be interested in this conversation.

For the next four years, as the Working Group on Gender and Authority in Indic Traditions, we continued to broaden our focus and reach, even while keeping women's textual production and brahminical authority about women as our main focus. We were able to hold conferences on women and domestic violence; masculinity in Indic traditions, women and activism, and the role of Sītā in the religious lives of women, as well as many other smaller projects such as the sponsoring of art exhibits and a cross-cultural exchange on women and traditional healing practices in Bangalore, India. The meetings of that group spun off into a myriad of projects that included colleagues from all over the globe. The meetings were, for many of us, the pinnacle of scholarly collegiality and enthusiasm. Although textual work remained at the center of our priorities, we were able to integrate it into a variety of concerns in the study of Indic traditions because of the true intellectual generosity of the environment in which we were working.

The chapters in this volume reflect that generosity to a very large extent. They are culled mostly from the first and second meetings of our working group, but in their revised form they represent the ongoing research as our own conversations have moved forward, and outward, across the spectrum of scholars in India and Europe with whom we shared our work. Although our working group has moved on to other projects, it remains for many of us one of the happier scholarly gatherings in our collective memory.

Scholars regularly involved in this ongoing conversation are especially appreciated: Julia Leslie, Linda Hess, Martha Selby, Lucy Bullet, Rachel McDermott, Gary Tubb, Kenneth Zysk, Nadine Berardi, Carla Petrovich, Kusumita Peterson, Ruth Katz, Fran Pritchett, David Magier, Natalia Lidova, Jim Hartzell, Sunita Vase, Timothy Lubin, Susham Bedi, Uma Chakravarty (University of Delhi), Uma Chakravarty (Cotton College, Assam), Medha Lotwal Lele, Simrita Singh, and Gayatri Chatterjee. Lesley Gray and Harry Cahill of the Hinduja Foundation were always quiet, helpful, and interested presences. S. P. Hinduja and his family deserve special credit for supporting a group of scholars with whose opinions they did not necessarily always agree. Without Jack Hawley's ongoing attendance, support, and enthusiasm the meetings would never have taken place; without Nancy Braxton's indefatigable good humor and efficiency our conferences would not have been as pleasant and productive as they invariably were; without the inspiration and energy of Mary McGee, our intellectual and administrative goals would never have been met.

In the production stages here at Emory, I am indebted to several graduate students and colleagues for their support: Deepika Petraglia Bahri, Joyce Flueckiger, Tara Doyle, Paul Courtright, Bobbi Patterson, Wendy Farley, Barbara Deconcini, and Deborah Lipstadt have provided much needed intellectual encouragement. The dedication of one particular group of graduate students made the final stages of preparation an unexpectedly rich and rewarding experience: David Mellott, Chris Noble, Arlene Robie, Linda Sherer, and Kevin Jaques were a cheerful army of editorial and formatting assistants. My partner Shalom Goldman, as always, provided his own unreplaceable kind of inspiration and support during particularly fallow moments.

The contributors to this volume are the model of interdisciplinary collegiality and efficiency. They have remained, in the years of editing and revising, a group of scholars on whom I can depend for insight, wisdom, and humor. The depth of their knowledge of India, their insistence that text and context are productively married, and their own eagerness to think outside of their disciplinary boundaries, have constituted a gathering of the minds unlike, any I have previously encountered. Gargī and Maitreyī would indeed be proud.

Atlanta, Georgia L. L. P.
August 2000

Contents

PART III
REFORM AND CONTEMPORARY ARGUMENTS

Contributors

PAOLA BACCHETTA earned her Ph.D. in Sociology at the Sorbonne in Paris, was a research affiliate at the Delhi School of Economics of Delhi University for two years, and currently has a joint appointment in the Department of Geography and the Women's Studies Program at University at Kentucky at Lexington. She is the author of *The RSS and the Nation: Gendered Discourse/Gendered Practice* (New Delhi: Kali for Women, forthcoming) and contributing co-editor of *Right-Wing Women across the Globe* (New York: Routledge, forthcoming). She has published numerous book chapters and articles in professional journals (in the United States, India, and England) on Hindu nationalist women and men, gender, and sexuality over the past eight years.

NANCY AUER FALK is Professor of Comparative Religion and Women's Studies at Western Michigan University of Kalamazoo, Michigan. She was trained initially in History of Religions at the University of Chicago, with specialization in the religions of South Asia. For many years her principal research interest has been the study of women's religious lives and roles, both in South Asia and cross-culturally, and she has written on aspects of women's lives and practice in both Hindu and Buddhist traditions of South Asia. Most recently she has published a third edition of the book *Unspoken Worlds: Women's Religious Lives,* with co-editor Rita M. Gross (2000) and *Women and Religion in India: An Annotated Bibliography of Sources in English,* 1975–92 (1994).

ELLISON BANKS FINDLY is Professor of Religion and Asian Studies at Trinity College in Hartford, Connecticut. She has degrees from Wellesley, Columbia, and Yale and is the author of numerous articles on Vedic, Mughal, and Buddhist topics. She has co-edited *Women's Buddhism, Buddhism's Women* and is the author of *Nur Jahan: Empress of Mughal India* and the forthcoming *Giving and Getting: Relations between Donors and Renunciants in Early Buddhism.*

ANN GRODZINS GOLD holds a Ph.D. in Anthropology from the University of Chicago and is a professor in the Department of Religion at Syracuse University. Gold's extensive work in the North Indian state of Rajasthan has included studies of pilgrimage, performance, world-renunciation, women's expressive traditions, and oral histories of environmental change. Among her publications are articles on spirit possession, semiotics of identity, the practice of ethnography, women's ritual storytelling, children's environmental perceptions, moral interpretations of climate change, memories as history, and three books (all published by the University of California Press): *Fruitful Journeys: The Ways of Rajasthani Pilgrims* (1988) *A Carnival of Parting: The Tales of King Bharthari and King Gopī Chand* (1992) and *Listen to the Heron's Words: Reimagining Gender and Kinship in North India* (co-authored with Gloria Raheja, 1994). Gold's most recent writing, co-authored with Bhoju Gujar, explores nature, power, and memory in a Rajasthani kingdom.

STEPHANIE JAMISON received her Ph.D. in linguistics from Yale University and has taught historical and Indo-European linguistics as well as Sanskrit at the University of North Carolina, Yale University, and Harvard University. She is the author of numerous publications dealing with Indo-Iranian and Sanskrit linguistics, poetics, and religion including *The Ravenous Hyenas and the Wounded Sun: Myth and Ritual in Ancient India* and *Sacrificed Wife/Sacrificer's Wife: Women, Ritual, and Hospitality in Ancient India.* She is currently Gardner Cowles Associate Professor of Sanskrit and Indian Studies at Harvard University.

MARY MCGEE is a Senior Fellow at the Heyman Center for the Humanities and Adjunct Professor of Hinduism in the Department of Religion at Columbia University. As a former director of Columbia's Dharam Hinduja Indic Research Center, she oversaw the scholarly work, outreach, and conferences of the DHIRC's working groups, including the working group on Gender in Indic Traditions that generated this volume of essays. Her research and publications focus on issues related to gender, ritual, and ethics in India; her most recent publication is *Invented Identities: The Interplay of Gender, Religion and Politics in India* (Oxford University Press, 2000), co-edited with Julie Leslie, in which McGee authored the title essay. She is currently at work on a translation of the *Yājñavalkya Smṛti*, a preeminent work of Hindu law.

VASUDHA NARAYANAN is Professor of Religion at the University of Florida. She has written and edited five books and over sixty articles, chapters in books, and encyclopedia entries. Her research has been supported by grants and fellowships from numerous organizations, including the National Endowment for the Humanities and the John Simon Guggenheim Foundation. She is the past president for the Society for Hindu Christian Studies and currently the president-elect of the American Academy of Religion.

LAURIE L. PATTON's interests are in interpretation of early Indian ritual and narrative, comparative mythology, and literary theory in the study of religion. In addition to twenty-five articles in these fields, in 1994 she edited and published *Authority, Anxiety, and Canon: Essays in Vedic Interpretation.* Her authored work, *Myth as Argument: The Bṛhaddevatā as Canonical Commentary*, was published in 1996 as the forty-first volume in the series Religionsgeschichtliche Versuche and Vorarbeiten. Another edited volume, co-edited with Wendy Doniger, *Myth and Method*, was published in 1996. She is also completing a book on the use of poetry in Vedic ritual, *Bringing Ritual to Mind* and another edited volume, *The Indo-Aryan Controversy: Evidence and Evocation* (with

Edwin Bryant), on the debates about early Indian origins. Her translation of the *Bhagavad Gita* is forthcoming in 2003. She serves as chair of the Department of Religion, Emory University.

T. S. RUKMANI holds a Ph.D. and a D.Litt. in Sanskrit from Delhi University—the first woman to receive a doctorate in Sanskrit from that institution. She has taught at Indraprastha College; Miranda House at Delhi University; and at the University of Durban Westville, South Africa. Since 1996 she has acted as Professor and Chair for Hindu Studies at the Department of Religion, Concordia University in Montreal, Canada. She has published a four-volume work on Vijñanabhikṣu's *Yogavārttika*, and a two-volume translation of *Yogasūtrabhāṣyavivaraṇa* of Śaṅkara. She was the editor of *Hindu Diaspora: Global Perspectives*. She acted as president of the University Women's Association of Delhi and presently serves on the Concultative Committee of the International Association for Sanskrit Studies.

KATHERINE YOUNG has written on gender in a comparative context in her introduction to *Feminism and World Religions*, edited by Arvind Sharma and Katherine K. Young, and in her introductions to *Women Saints in World Religions, Today's Woman in World Religions, Religion and Women*, and *Women in World Religions* (all edited by Arvind Sharma). With Sharma she has edited five volumes of the *Annual Review of Women in World Religions*. Young has written chapters on women in Hinduism for several of the books and in numerous articles on women in Hinduism, especially Śrīvaiṣṇavism, her area of specialization.

Abbreviations

AB	Aitareya Brāhmaṇa
AGS	Āpastamba Gṛhya Sūtra
AN	Aṅguttaranikāya
ĀpDS	Āpastamba Dharma Sūtra
ĀPŚS	Āpastamba Śrauta Sūtra
AS	Arthasaṅgraha of Laugāksi Bhāskara
ĀśGS	Āśvalāyana Gṛhya Sūtra
ĀśŚS	Āṣvalāyana Śrauta Sūtra
AV	Atharva Veda
BĀU	Bṛhadāraṇyaka Upaniṣad
BD	Bṛhaddevatā
BDS	Baudhāyana Dharma Sūtra
Cār	Cārudatta of Bhāsa
CU	Chāndogya Upaniṣad
DN	Dīghanikāya
GDS	Gautama Dharma Sūtra
GGS	Gobhila Gṛhya Sūtra
HGS	Hiraṇyakeśin Gṛhya Sūtra
JB	Jaiminīya Brāhmaṇa
JGS	Jaiminīya Gṛhya Sūtra
JM	Mīmāṃsā Sūtra of Jaimini
KA	Kauṭilya's Artha Śāstra
KāmSū	Kāma Sūtra
KB	Kauṣītaki Brāhmaṇa
KBU	Kauṣītaki Brāhmaṇa Upaniṣad
KhādGS	Khādira Gṛhya Sūtra
KS	Kāthaka Saṃhitā
KSS	Kātyāyana Śrauta Sūtra
Kum	Kumārasaṃbhava
Māl	Mālavikāgnimitra
Mālatīm	Mālatīmādhava
Manu	Manu Smṛti

MBh	Mahābhārata
MGS	Mānava Gṛhya Sūtra
MDŚ	Manava Dharma Śāstra
MN	Majjihimanikāya
MNP	Mīmāṃsānyāyaprakāśa of Āpadeva
Mṛcch	Mṛcchakaṭika
MS	Maitrāyaṇī Saṃhitā
NS	Nirṇayasindhu of Kamalākarabhaṭṭa
PārGS	Pāraskara Gṛhyra Sūtra
PM	Pañcaviṃśa Brāhmaṇa
Ragh	Raghuvaṃśa
RV	Ṛg Veda
SB	Jaiminīya Mīmāṃsābhāṣya of Śabarasvāṃī
ŚB	Śatapatha Brāhmaṇa
ŚBM	Śatapatha Brāhmaṇa Mādhyaṃdina
ŚGS	Śāṅkhāyana Gṛhya Sūtra
ŚN	Śamyuttanikāya
TB	Taittirīya Brāhmaṇa
TM	Trikāṇḍamaṇḍana of Bhāskara Miśra
TS	Taittirīya Saṃhitā
VGS	Vārāha Gṛhya Sūtra
VāsDS	Vāsiṣṭha Dharma Sūtra
VDS	Vāsiṣṭha Dharma Sūtra
Vik	Vikramorvaśī
Vin	Vinaya Piṭakam
ViSmṛ	Viṣṇu Smṛti
Yāj Smṛ	Yājñavalkya Smṛti

Note on Transliteration and Citation

Every effort has been made to be consistent throughout this volume in the transliteration and citation of Sanskrit, Hindi, and Tamil. However, individual authors may differ slightly in their references to individual texts and names.

Jewels of Authority

Introduction

LAURIE L. PATTON

The pages of this book glitter with the images of jewelry. Yet its chapters are not concerned only with the colorful worlds of Indian myth, epic, and poetry. They are also the ritual manuals of the ancient Indian sacrifice, the legal texts of the Dharma Śāstras, the Tamil commentaries of medieval Vaiṣṇavas, and the Hindi manuals of contemporary organizations of Hindu nationalists. Why does jewelry bring together such disparate topics?

If there is any one thing that symbolizes the relationship between women and the brahminical textual tradition of India, it is their jewelry. Passages in the *Atharva Veda* and the Upaniṣads specify gold ornaments as the specific property of the wife, her *strīdhana*, which she herself gave as part of the offering in the Vedic sacrifice. The courtesans of ancient India were not free persons but had full authority over their assets, which consisted of their jewelry and other payments they received from lovers. One early Buddhist benefactress established a monastery with gifts of her jewelry. The Vedic mantras used to heal a miscarrying woman are recited over an amulet made especially for her. The *Laws of Manu*[1] classify jewelry as one of the main types of women's property, which (if she has the right to give anything) she has the right to give to her offspring or bring to her marriage.

The classical period of India is no less rich in the use of jewels to illustrate the highly charged link between women and textual authority. *Dharma-nibandhas*, or lawbooks, of the medieval period specify important kinds of ownership for a woman, such as "the ornaments a woman inherits from her mother." In Bhāsa's Sanskrit drama *Cārudatta*, the jewels of Vasantasena, Cārudatta's courtesan, are stolen from Cārudatta's house. To rescue his honor, his own wife gives him her necklace. As in the *dharma-nibandhas*, the jewels are what are in the wife's power to give. And, on a more literary level, the medieval commentator Tirrukōnēri Dāsyai names her entire commentary a "Garland of Words," and she arranges her scholarly output as one would a necklace. It is the most powerful metaphor she can choose for her writings. So, too, the necklace that a married woman wears is, in the same Tamil Vaiṣṇava tradition, the symbol that a devotee also dons to declare the purity of his devotion to god.

In the contemporary period, the goddess Aṣṭabhūja, used as an inspirational model for Hindu nationalist women, holds a rosary as the quintessence of feminine qualities, "to remind women of their own qualities." And in village Rajasthan, the offerings to please female power connect visibly with female desires—and here the imagery of jewelry is prevalent. In hymn to Sītalā, women promise to put a jewel in her forehead. In the brahmin ritual of Tīj Mother, women's jewelry is held up to the reflection in a polished platter, as a sign of auspicious wifehood.

As the brahmin textual tradition has it, the jewels of women are both a source of independence and a source of bondage. Jewels signify her authority in giving as a wife or as a courtesan; they also act as evidence of her lack of religious realm, the married authority in her marriage as they designate her as property herself. In the women's necklace is a paradigm of all devotees' purity, whether male or female. It is also the chosen metaphor for one of the few female commentators known in Indian history. Pendants are desired by, and offered to, the goddess herself, whether in the form of Sītalā or Aṣṭabhūja. They are the quintessence of femininity and resistance at the same time.

Like jewels, individual texts in the Indian tradition act as very particularized mirrors of the roles and status of women in different periods of history. It is the purpose of this volume to honor the specificity of these texts and the specificity of women's attitudes toward them as producers and audience, in the village and in the city.

Setting the Stage

Much of the excellent, groundbreaking work on gender and the Hindu tradition in the last two decades has been, of necessity, at a fairly general level. The basic questions about power relations between the sexes, the codification of gender behavior, conflicts over gender behavior, and so forth needed to be raised before the more detailed work could be done.

Yet the scenario we are frequently confronted with—a kind of sweeping time line that moves from the Vedic golden age to the age of brahminical repression to the more hopeful era of Hindu reform— is becoming less and less helpful in our classrooms and in our scholarship. Other work in this area contents itself with an inventory of references to and about women but eschews any larger, theoretical implications for gender studies as a whole. This, too, is important inventorial work, but it needs to be supplemented with theoretical analysis. Our own perspective is that close textual or ethnographic analyses are not incompatible with theoretical sophistication. As contributors to this volume, we are presented with a unique opportunity to put these emphases together in the context of South Asian studies, as well as in the larger context of gender studies.

The Postcolonial Challenge and the Role of Gender Studies

A single example should suffice to illustrate the difficulty: When previous authors have written on women in the Ṛg *Veda*, they have usually included human, semidivine, and divine figures in a single category. Bhagwat Saran Upadhyaya's book, *Women in Ṛg Veda* (1974), is a case in point: a potpourri of female *ṛṣis*, Apsarases, and goddesses, such as Vāc, Uṣas, and others, is mingled together in a single category, with only a superficial typological treatment of differences between these figures. Shyam Kishore Lal's early *Female Divinities in Hindu Myth and Ritual* (1980) does the same. This very tendency to create a single, inventorial category of "female," which distinguishes only sketchily between various kinds of "female," is inherently problematic. The move is similar to the tendency of colonialist writers to create a unified Hinduism, whereas, as Fryckenberg, Prakash, and many others have recently pointed out, no such Hinduism existed.[2] The assumption made is that because women, human, semidivine, or divine, are all essentially different from men, they must all have the same characteristics.

Despite the difficulties inherent in such a task, scholarship on women in early India would do well to avoid the dangers of ghettoizing women in a single intellectual category. Instead, we might recognize gender identity as a necessary point of departure, but always as a construction in and of itself. Following the lead of several feminist writers on colonial India,[3] we might move beyond the large, unwieldy, and confusing category of "the female" in ancient India as well. The study of women in Hindu religious practice is no different from any other arena of South Asian studies: we are challenged to avoid creating an "essence" where none exists but to focus instead on a complex set of social relations, referring to a changing set of historically variable processes.[4]

The Case for Close Studies of Women and Traditional Authority

Many of the chapters in this volume build on such postcolonial insights to think through their very specific cases of women and brahminical, textual authority. Like many postcolonial and feminist authors, these authors assume that knowledge is indeed constructed by particular ideologies and that brahmin ideology in particular needs to be examined in its own right as a form of effective intellectual and social critique.

However, the interest in this volume is not solely in the colonial construction of such knowledge about women and the brahminical collusion therein. Instead, the authors expressly advocate rereading ancient, medieval, and contemporary cases with a closer, finer lens—a jeweler's lens, if you will. One particular way to address these historically variable processes involves the close reading of situations in which women are given or denied authority in ritual and interpretive situations in India. This approach involves not only how women are represented by Indian texts (how they wear their jewels) but also several other perspectives: how the particular strategies of debate about women are carried on (who owns those jewels and when), how women are depicted as negotiating certain kinds of authority; and how women might resist particular kinds of traditional authority in certain colonial and postcolonial situations (how they use their jewels to subvert or to resist). Such a view necessitates smaller studies of individual debates about women and brahminical textual authority and how such arguments and negotiations change over time.[5]

Jewels of Authority focuses on just these kinds of particularities of textual and ethnographic debate. First, the chapters discuss the details of particular debates about women, such as that in the Vedic mīṃāṃsā (McGee) and medieval Vaiṣṇava (Young) traditions. Second, the contributors examine particular textual and ethnographic problems about the agency of women, such as women's gift giving in Vedic, epic, and poetic sources (Findly and Jamison) or the cure for problematic childbirth (Patton). This approach yields a more complex picture of what options are depicted as being available to women in ancient and classical India. Finally, the volume examines historical situations in which women appropriate authority for themselves in relationship to brahminical authority:

in village Rajasthan (Gold), the colonial reform period in Calcutta (Falk); or the conservative wing of the Hindu nationalist movement, the RSS (Bachetta).

None of these debates, nor the sweep of the volume in general, is meant to be exhaustive but rather suggestively representative of problems and possibilities within a particularly focused lens. For purposes of clarity and coherence, the perspectives of the chapters remain focused on a single theme—that of brahmin authority—and do not attempt to move beyond that intellectual axis. This emphasis is not an attempt to stress brahminical discourse in relation to women but rather to examine its historical vicissitudes and manifestations more carefully. The hope is that this volume's insights will suggest other kinds of focused studies: women and *kṣatriya* ideology, the vexing identification between women and *śudras* (touched on by Young in this volume but deserving a volume in its own right), the depiction of Dalit women by brahmin women and vice versa, and the role of women in the merchant (*vaiśya*) class, to name just a few possibilities.

Part I introduces themes from the earliest period of Indian history—ones that have only begun to be examined in full detail, such as gift giving, the rights to participate in sacrifices, and own property, and so on. These are themes that are introduced and puzzled over by the ancient texts themselves and will remain constant throughout the historical sweep of the book.

In the first chapter, Ellison Banks Findly begins with the early Indian concern over women as symbols of household plenitude and charity; in "The Housemistress at the Door: Vedic and Buddhist Perspectives on the Mendicant Encounter," she focuses on the contrast between the Vedic and Buddhist models for gift giving. Although Vedic texts women become masters of the household, controlling wealth and becoming representatives of the household, they are not able to be agents of gift giving on their own. Pali Buddhist texts, however, reflect a context in which women have their own property, separate from men, and where the intention of the giver, either male or female, is stressed.

Also focusing on the late Vedic period, examine the relationship between the Vedic ideology of mantra and womb imagery in "Mantras and Miscarriage: Controlling Birth in the Late Vedic Period." Whereas the late Vedic emphasis on the rituals of childbirth seems to reflect an alliance between canonical mantra and the domestic world of childbirth, the opposite is the case. Examination of the *Ṛg Vidhāna* (a. 4th c. B.C.E.) and other texts reflect not alliance but control over the gestating female body through mantric utterance. As the brahmin becomes the sole representative and carrier of Vedic knowledge, so, too, he must control the sphere of its reproduction—the womb that produces the male child. Thus, womb imagery is not simply an expression of fertility but also a depiction of the reproduction of knowledge itself, to be controlled by the brahmin at a distance from the female body.

In her chapter, "Ritual Rights: The Gender Implications of *Adhikāra*," Mary McGee picks up on the theme of the autonomy of women, looking at the topic of *adhikāra*, meaning right or authority and referring specifically in the *mīṃāṃsā* school on an individual's ability to perform sacrifices. McGee goes on to investigate some of these issues, arguing that some texts say that women do have the right to perform sacrifices; others modify their views by adding that this right is not independent but shared with her husband. If a woman is in fact dependent on her husband, such a question of *adhikāra* immediately raises questions about ownership within the household.

Part II examines classical and medieval debates about some of these very same issues—only within the structure of the newly emergent forms of literature: the drama, *kāvya* poetry, the Purāṇas, and the devotional commentaries of South India. In many ways, the debates are more complex in that the Vedic antecedents still hold sway in much of the literature, but the universalism of *bhakti* has raised the question of women's participation in what were traditionally male, brahmin roles.

In "Giver or Given? Some Marriages in Kālidāsa," Stephanie W. Jamison complicates the usual picture of women's gift-giving practices in the Vedic and classical periods. Using episodes from Kālidāsa, the *Mahābhārata*, and Dharma Śāstras, she argues that, whereas much of the *śāstric* tradition prohibits it, the epic and poetic literature does indeed portray women as gift givers. The interesting twist, however, is that this act of autonomy is usually couched in terms of religious practice and spiritual austerity.

In "*Om*, the Vedas, and the Status of Women with Special Reference to Śrīvaiṣṇavism," Katherine K. Young traces the history of women's right to chant mantras through the Vaiṣṇava *ācāryas*. She argues that the relatively conservative position that emerged out of the previously liberal Vaiṣṇava position was achieved by a deft interpretation of Pāñcarātra Āgamas. This interpretive move prohibited women and *śūdras* from the chanting of the sacred syllable, yet also kept the *ācāryas* clearly in line with the earlier Vaiṣṇava theological positions. She speculated that these interpretive changes also occurred in times of great stress within society, and a clear identity needed to be maintained against external threats, such as that of the Muslims during the time of Vedāntadeśika.

Vasudha Narayanan follows up on the theme of medieval textual authority with an exploratory chapter on the work of the female commentator Tirukkōnēri Dāsyai, "Casting Light on the Sounds of the Tamil Veda." Tirukkōnēri's composition, "Garland of Words," has not received the kind of scholarly attention it deserves. Narayanan describes some of the intriguing features of this commentary, including its emphasis on word play as a form of devotional praise. She also speculates about the reasons for Tirukkōnēri's obscurity, citing perhaps her usage of Tamil, and the historical problems involved in placing her in the strict line of interpreters of the *Tiruvāymoḻi*.

In Part III Nancy Auer Falk continues the focus on the obscurity of women in "By What Authority? Hindu Women and the Legitimization of Reform in the Nineteenth Century," which looks at the differences between male and female ways of teaching the conclusions of the nineteenth century. The men ground themselves in an authority that is primarily intellectual, creating carefully reasoned arguments based in part on new approaches to India's heritage of *śāstric* and Vedic scripture. Falk then shows thatafter an initial period of simple deference to male authority that had always in the past governed their lives, the women involved in Hindu reform discovered the painful and potent authority of their own experience.

Also in this part, Paola Bacchetta examines the ideology of the Samiti, or women's wing of the RSS, a Hindu nationalist organization. In "Hindu Nationalist Women: On the Use of the Feminine Symbolic to (Temporarily) Displace Male Authority," Bacchetta focuses particularly on the women's perspectives on feminine models and textual authority. She argues that the ideology of the RSS Samiti contains fierce femininity more powerful than any form of masculinity. She goes on to examine the operability of these models in actual political events involving the RSS in India. In one case, the women of the RSS argue that Muslim women were ex-Hindu women who were not defended by

Hindu men against Muslim men; in another, RSS women argued that the presence of a mosque on the landscape of India was tantamount to a rape of mother India—again a failure of Hindu men to protect Hindu femininity.

In the final chapter, "Counterpoint Authority in Women's Ritual Expressions: A View from the Village," Ann Grodzins Gold considers the question of traditional authority from an anthropological point of view. She shows the ways in which some modern Hindu women in a large Rajasthan village contradict through performance some of the culturally posited disadvantages of being female. In a study of several particular rituals (Holī, Sītalā, Tīj, and others), Gold develops the idea of women's "counterpoint" authority, discussing how women's ritual influence, although articulate in these festivals, does not exist in a realm independent of male authority. Rather, this kind of women's power sends both complementary and contradictory messages.

The Context of Emerging Studies on Women in South Asia

From the perspective of continuing theoretical sophistication in gender studies, and also from the perspective of the growing interest in gender in South Asian studies, scholarship on Hindu women in South Asia is now beginning to be refined and modified along the lines discussed in my introduction: close textual and ethnographic analysis has begun to replace the rather sweeping schemata mentioned above. I might cite here Julia Leslie's (1991) edited volume, *Roles and Rituals for Hindu Women*; Nita Kumar's (1994) *Women as Subjects*; Stephanie Jamison's (1996) *Sacrificed Wife/Sacrificer's Wife*; Lindsay Harlan and Paul Courtright's (1996) *On the Margins of Hindu Marriage*; Gloria Raheja and Ann Gold's (1994) *Listen to the Heron's Words*; Anne Pearson's (1996) *"Because It Gives Me Peace of Mind"*; and Joyce B. Flueckiger's (1996) *Gender and Genre in the Folklore of Middle India*. Although not solely focused on Hinduism, Rajeswari Sunder Rajan's *Signposts* (1999) contains exemplary essays.

Jewels of Authority contributes to this growing literature in several important respects. First, whereas several of these works involve either a close textual or ethnographic study, as does *Jewels of Authority* also attempts a broader overview in its arrangement of the chapters from the early to the contemporary periods. Thus, the reader might see a mosaic of themes and motifs throughout various periods of Indian religious history.

Women and Idealized Practice

Several important points of commonality emerge. First, traditional debates about women tend to focus not only on the "essence" of women's nature but also on the relationship between women and social roles that they may or may not occupy in an idealized practice. The ideal *adhikāra* of women to perform rites in the Mīṃāṃsā debates is bound up with their ability to own property (McGee); the question of whether women can recite mantras is bound up with Śrīvaiṣṇavas' attempts to establish authoritative lines of tradition based on both popular and Sanskritic norms (Young). Second, textual depictions of female authority tend to be couched in terms that stress ideal modes of brahminical authority: the *dāna* of women in epic and poetic sources, even when performed in royal, more "secular" contexts, is given the religious language of self-sacrifice

(Jamison); the textual tradition created by the RSS in their teachings is couched in language in which it is more dharmically correct to appropriate female authority in the face of a threat to the entire Hindu nation (Bacchetta). Third, the discourse of female authority is never created within a world totally separated from male brahminical authority, and it is under constant threat of either being silenced or of reappropriated even as it emerges into the public sphere. Thus, some of the chapters point to the relative silence of women on Vedic authority in colonial India (Falk); the transformation of the imagery of *garbha* from a female to a male concept in late Vedic commentary (Patton); and the "counterpoint" authority of the women's celebrations in a Rajasthani village—an authority that constitues a kind of "soft claim," which must constantly reassert itself in the larger brahminical environment of which it is a part (Gold).

Leaving Room for Unpredictability

Even within their emphasis on the links between women and idealized brahminical practice, these chapters reveal that the relationship can be surprising and not always predictable. *Jewels of Authority* treats the relationship between women and traditional authority as a dynamic point of debate, one that gets argued and reargued in specific historical contexts, which have their own, sometimes startling, characteristics. For instance, it is clear that historians are not the only ones who must discover and analyze changing attitudes toward women; in almost all of the chapters specific debates within the Hindu tradition are coping with their assessments of the changing perspectives on women *within their own framework*. *Mīṃāṃsā* must cope with *sadācāra*, or traditional practice; Buddhists change the entire framework of intentionality in which women in the late Vedic period might donate their wealth; the Śrīvaiṣṇavas must contend with differing commentarial traditions about who has access to the syllable Auṃ; the colonial reformers and the postcolonial RSS leaders must contend with Western ideas about women as they reassert Hindu identity; and so on. In other words, this volume places the origin of debate not within the scholarly world but within the world of historical India itself.

To take another example, the chapters also reveal that there is a kind of surprising interplay between the women idealized by brahmin authority and the women's voices themselves. Even in the elite Tamil and Sanskrit traditions (epic, *kāvya*,and *śāstric*) composed by men, many of the women's practices are depicted as a set of ingenious, indirect strategies for dealing with ubiquitous brahmin authority, not unlike those of the actual village women whom Ann Gold describes. In the legal and ritual traditions about women, particularly those of *mīṃāṃsa* and Śrīvaiṣṇava, there is a clear understanding of individual cases, exceptional cases, and changing circumstances that require new rules. Moreover, in the Tamil commentarial tradition of Tirukkōnēri Dāsyai that Vasudha Narayanan describes, it is not even entirely clear that the gender of the writer matters at all.

The surprises of the colonial period are equally intriguing; Nancy Falk reveals the emerging scholarship on individual women who resisted the colonial attempt to create the ideal Indian woman, about whom so much has been written in the recent postcolonial context. And in the contemporary period that Bacchetta describes, one cannot help but notice that the relationship between national rhetoric and feminist discourse takes a very different tone than in the colonial period: in the late twentieth-century nationalist ideal, there is an emerging place for celibacy and militarism in women's public lives.

In its attempt at breadth, as well as specificity, *Jewels of Authority* also attempts to be interdisciplinary in its scope: social history, textual study, and contemporary ethnography are all fields that are engaged in the service of a deeper analysis of women and traditional authority in Hindu India. This interdisciplinary perspective is not simply an attempt to be inclusive; it is also based on a commitment to the idea that the question of women's authority in India can and should be approached from a number of different angles. However, the chapters are also cooperatively interdisciplinary; the ethnographic chapters explicitly refer to textual authority, and the textual works attempt, insofar as possible, to take into account social and historical realities.

The volume's contributors are some of the leading scholars in the field of gender and South Asia today. In these and many other works, they have produced groundbreaking ideas, which have shaped the framework within which scholars pursue their studies in this area. Gathered together, they are a garland of authoritative voices, which we hope will engage textualists, ethnographers, and historians of South Asia alike.

Notes

1. *Laws of Manu,* Wendy Doniger with Brian K. Smith, Trans. (London: Penguin, 1991).

2. See Robert Fryckenberg's "The Emergence of Modern 'Hinduism' as a Concept and as an Institution: A Reappraisal with Special Reference to South India," in *Hinduism Reconsidered,* Gunther Sontheimer and Hermann Kulke, Eds. See also Subaltern Studies I: "Subaltern Identity *Subalter, Studies 10,* Ranajit Guha, Ed." (1989); C. A. Bayly, "Rallying Around the Subaltern," *Journal of Peasant Studies* 16.1 (1988): 110–20; Gyan Prakash, "Can the 'Subaltern' Ride?: A Reply to O'Hanlon and Washbrook" (1992). More recently, works are Ronald Inden, *Imagining India* (Oxford: Blackwell, 1990); Bernard Cohn, *An Anthropologist Among the Historians and Other Essays* (Delhi: Oxford University Press, 1991); Partha Chatterjee, *The Nation and its Fragments: Colonial and Postcolonial Histories* (Princeton, N.J.: Princeton University Press, 1993); Carol A. Breckenridge and Peter Van Der Veer, Eds, *Orientalism and the Postcolonial Predicament: Perspectives on South Asia* (Philadelphia: University of Pennsylvania Press, 1993); Gyan Prakash, Ed. *After Colonialism: Imperial Histories and Postcolonial Displacements* (Princeton, N.J.: Princeton University Press, 1995); Henry Schwarz, *Writing Cultural History in Colonial and Postcolonial India* (Philadelphia: University of Pennsylvania Press, 1997); *Representing Hinduism: The Construction of Religious Traditions and National Identity,* Vasudha Dalmia and Heinrich von Stietencron, Eds. (New Delhi: Sage, 1995).

3. See Partha Chatterjee's "Colonialism, Nationalism and Colonized Women: The Contest in India," *American Ethnologist* 16.4 (1989): 634–660, and Chandra Mohanty's "Under Western Eyes: Feminist Scholarship and Colonial Discourses," in *Third World Women and the Politics of Feminism,* Chandra. T. Mohanty, Ann Russo, and Lourdes, Torres, Eds. Bloomington: Indiana University Press, (1984, pp. 337–38) for a comparison of the ways in which Western feminism imitates colonial discourse in its depiction of "third-world women" under a homogeneous category.

4. See Jane Flax's "Postmodernism and Gender Relations in Feminist Theory," *Signs* 12.4 (1987): 621-643, for a fuller theoretical elaboration of this idea for feminist theory.

5. As Flax (1987, p. 629) puts it, "From the perspective of social relations, men and women are both prisoners of gender, although in highly differentiated but interrelated ways." To the extent that feminist discourse defines being a woman as problemactic, it, too ironically exempts the man from being determined by gender relations.

Part I

ANCIENT ARGUMENTS

1

The Housemistress at the Door

Vedic and Buddhist Perspectives on the Mendicant Encounter

ELLISON BANKS FINDLY

It has been said that within the broad parameters of *dānadharma* (the duty of the gift), "the utmost importance is given to the gift of food."[1] In the period of the Vedic age in its maturity, the gift of food by the householder, in particular by the householder wife, to renunciant petitioners at the household door is a common feature of the early Indian landscape. From this time, the undertaking of *bhikṣā*, petitioning or seeking alms, by a *bhikṣācara*, a mendicant, is a ritual of tremendous "sacramental character"[2] and belongs to several religious institutions: Vedic studenthood *(brahmacarya)*, both ritualized in the initiatory Upanayana and habitualized in the patterns of the student's daily life; the ascetic wanderings of the *saṃnyāsin* as prescribed in later formulations of the Vedic *āśrama* system; Buddhist *piṇḍapāta/piṇḍacāra*, or alms gathering, enjoined on every *bhikkhu* and *bhikkhunī* who has gone forth from the home; and similar institutions of other non-Vedic *śramaṇas*, such as the Jains, for whom mendicancy is obligatory. The urgency behind the various forms of this ritual is due in part to the renunciant being normally prohibited from using the cooking fire and from storing edibles, and being thus dependent on a daily round of door-to-door petitioning to procure his serving of cooked food.[3]

When a renunciant of any of these four traditions comes to the door, the representative of the household the renunciant most often encounters is the housemistress, the wife of the householder, who is normally the one to put cooked food into the waiting bowl. Although passages codifying guest etiquette, particularly for brahmin guests, explicitly or obliquely describe a joint hosting of the guest (i.e., by both the husband and the wife), prescriptions for the ritual transaction of *bhikṣā* are formulated with the assumption that the normal householder donor is the wife.[4] Whereas rules for this "threshold" encounter often raise issues that differ tradition to tradition, there is enough common ground to use these rules as a way of eliciting a tradition's peculiar view on the nature and social role of women. If we recognize fully that the traditional forms and values of *dāna* emerge from the early sacrificial ritual,[5] and that one of the features present in the threshold encounter of housemistress and renunciant is a range of "hospitality anxieties" that are rendered manageable in ritual form,[6] three issues emerge from the texts. Of varying mutual concern to the Vedic and Buddhist traditions, then, are (1) the reciprocal obligations of the *bhikṣā* relationship (i.e., the nature of the "contract" under which food is given), (2) a woman's economic life, and (3) a woman's sexuality.

We will not focus here on strict chronological or geographical distinctions and influences among aspects of the mendicant encounter. Rather, mindful of O'Flaherty's comment that there is "such constant interaction between Vedism and Buddhism in the early period that it is fruitless to attempt to sort out the earlier source of many doctrines [and practices as] . . . they live . . . in one another's pockets,"[7] we will see the mendicant encounter as one example, among others,[8] of a Vedic form reconfigured in other settings. Given "that the main features of the renunciatory life are by and large uniform across all the traditions," we will look instead at how each tradition may have "modified them to suit its own needs"[9] and, in the particular case of the housemistress role, at how each tradition uses prescriptions for this encounter to reflect prevailing understandings and values about women.

Whereas the practice of *bhikṣācarya* is known in such texts as the *Bṛhadāraṇyaka* and *Kauṣītaki-Brāhmaṇa Upaniṣads*,[10] systematic standards for the *bhikṣā* ritual between renunciant and donor have their clearest expression in the institution of the Vedic student *(brahmacārin)*[11] as it is incorporated into the *āśrama* system, thus providing an "obligatory mode . . . suitable for different periods of an individual's life."[12] In the *Śatapatha Brāhmaṇa*, for example, the young student entering the *brahmacārin's* life during the Upanayana is obliged to petition alms according to prescribed rules for the initiation and then to continue petitioning alms until the final ceremonial bath, which marks the end of studenthood.[13] The Gṛhya and Dharma Sūtras then require, more exactingly, that the young boy[14] who is undertaking initiation vows live by certain practices (e.g., tending the teacher's ritual fire, petitioning alms, sleeping on the ground, doing the teacher's bidding, and studying the Veda)[15] and that *bhikṣā* continue as a daily practice; the food may be petitioned from a number of houses that belong to any but the very-low caste families and is then brought back to the residence for announcement to the teacher, who gives permission to eat.[16]

In the case of the *saṃnyāsin*, *bhikṣā* prescriptions are a function of the rite of passage in which he renounces the sacred fires, depositing them in himself *(ātmasamāropa)*, and renouncing as well the ritual implements used in connection with these fires.[17] Now the obligations of his lifestyle belong to its peripatetic nature, as he has renounced a dwelling place, as well as fire; as a *bhikṣu*, he is to live on alms gathered morning and evening (or by some accounts, once a day) as he goes from village to village to randomly or to accidentally selected houses. Thus, with a fully concentrated mind, he is to "continue to obtain alms" *(bhikṣāṃ liseta)* and, without eagerness, to accept only that amount of food needed to sustain life.[18]

In similar fashion the Buddhist *bhikkhu/bhikkhunī* is obliged by virtue of his or her admission into the Saṅgha to take up the bowl and outer robe and to beg food *(piṇḍa)* once a day during the period before noon.[19] The Pali accounts of the *piṇḍapāta/piṇḍacāra*, like those in the *Cullavagga* and *Majjhima Nikāya*, prescribe in exceedingly careful detail the wearing of the robe, the walking amidst the houses, the comportment of the body as the renunciant meets the *gahapatānī* at the door, the holding of the bowl, and the careful focusing of the mind.[20]

In like manner, the *Ācārāṅga Sūtra* prescribes Jain practice of *bhikṣā* by focusing primarily on how the mendicant life can avoid injury to living creatures. As the renunciant monk or nun walks from door to door, the preeminent need for *ahiṃsā* is detailed in terms of where one goes, how one walks, whom one walks with, how one accepts food from the *dātṛ* ("giver") and most particularly what food one accepts into the bowl. Any food that is in any way suspected of containing live matter–in the form, for example, of seeds, sprouts, mildew or dust–is deemed unacceptable[21] and is to be rejected by the petitioner. Thus, the distinctions are clear: Vedic injunctions on the *bhikṣā* encounter are governed, as we will see, by concerns of ritual, caste, and *āśrama*; Buddhist injunctions are governed by the internal development of the mendicant and donor; and Jain injunctions are shaped throughout by the principle of noninjury.

The Obligations of the Relationship: Vedic, Buddhist, Jain

The encounter of the *brahmacārin* with the housemistress at the door is governed by two things: the identity of the donor and the identity of the petitioner. Because the *brahmacārin* goes to the household door under two different circumstances, once during the actual Upanayana and then again as part of his daily practice of studenthood, there are theoretically two different sets of donors to be identified. The Gṛhya Sūtras, for the most part, however, identify only the Upanayana donors. Thus, after the student is led around the fire by his teacher, with the right side facing in, he goes into the village to petition food. He is to petition, first, from his mother and then from a woman who will not refuse (*bhikṣeta apratyākhyāyinīṃ)* and, upon returning, to announce the alms to the teacher before getting permission to eat.[22] Straying slightly from the norm, the *Pāraskara Gṛhya Sūtra* enjoins the *brahmacārin* to petition from three women who will not refuse or from six or twelve or an indefinite number, [23] and the *Gobhila Gṛhya Sūtra* prescribes a total of three women or as many householder women as live in the neighborhood.[24] The only Gṛhya Sūtra to prescribe a male donor is the *Āśvalāyana*, which requires the student to petition from a man who will not refuse, or from a woman who will not refuse.[25] Manu then extends the range of possible female donors in the Upanayana from the student's mother to his sister and then to a maternal aunt, as well as to other local women who will not refuse.[26]

Although the Gṛhya Sūtras do not, as a matter of course, prescribe the donors for the student to seek out during his daily alms rounds, we are not to assume necessarily that they are the same as for the Upanayana; in fact, other texts list these donors in the reverse order of the initiation. The *Śatapatha Brāhmaṇa,* for example, enjoins the student to petition daily from women in whom he has confidence, and if no others are to be found, then (and only then) to petition from his teacher's wife and finally from his mother; this same standard is subsequently echoed in several of the Dharma Sūtras.[27] And Manu actually prohibits the student from petitioning on a day-to-day basis from relatives of his teacher or from his mother's family unless there are no strangers' houses available, in which case he may begin with his mother's blood relations.[28]

Social and familial structure also governs the identity, or identification, of the student petitioner. In the *Pāraskara Gṛhya Sūtra,* a brahmin student is asked to petition from a householder woman by putting *bhavati* "lady" at the beginning of his request, a *kṣatriya/rājanya* by putting "lady" in the middle, and a *vaiśya* by putting "lady" at the end. This injunction is then repeated in various Dharma Sūtras, as well as in Manu.[29]

Although a few other texts have formulas that could be applied to either a male or a female donor, we infer from the preponderance of the evidence that the norm for the formula of petition was for use in approaching the householder wife.[30] In the case of the *saṃnyāsin,* there are few examples of a similar verbal prescription; in most instances he is to eat food that has been given to him without his asking.[31]

The *bhikṣā* encounter between the *brahmacārin* and his donor thus serves to reaffirm the social placement of the participants in the external structures of brahminic society. Whereas the Upanayana petitioning brings the student into a newly distant and more formalized relationship with his own family, especially with his own mother, daily *bhikṣā* brings him into greater contact with other families in his wider social world. The formalized relationship of *bhikṣā,* then, heightens his awareness both of caste boundaries and of the need for a solemn, purity-maintaining etiquette. It also, importantly, underscores the role women have in representing the household within the framework of that etiquette.

The principle that governs the appearance of the *gṛhapatnī* [32] at the household door is ā*tithya*, being "hospitable." Although the celebration of Agni as the guest *(atithi)* of humans at the sacrifice is an important feature of Ṛgvedic religiosity, and although it is the brahmin officiant who is considered the "guest *par excellence*" at the ritual,[33] it is the guest reception (Ātithyā) of Soma, the king of the herbs, the food of the gods, the highest of oblations,[34] that provides ritual confirmation that the sacrificer's wife has a preeminent role when the household honors a guest. The guest reception or hospitality rite (Ātithyā) for Soma occurs after the ritual purchase of the plant and after Soma has been brought forward to "the house of the sacrificer" *(yajamānasya gṛha)*. At this point Agni "the fire" is kindled: "They kindle the fire when Soma the king has come" *(agniṃ manthanti some rājanyāgate)*.[35] A *Taittirīya Saṃhitā* passage that prescribes the reception of Soma is central here:

> ātithyaṃ gṛhṇāti yajñasya santatyai. patny anvārabhate, patnī hi pārīṇahyasya īśe; patniyā eva anumataṃ nirvapati. yad vai patnī yajñasya karoti mithunaṃ tad. atho patniyā eva (1) eṣa yajñasya anvārambho 'navacchityai.
>
> (The sacrificer/household) offers hospitality for the continuity of the sacrifice. The wife touches (the cart) from behind, for the wife is the mistress of the household goods; in this way (the household) offers what is approved by the wife. Verily that part of the sacrifice which is the wife makes a pairing. Now this touching (of the cart) from behind by the wife is for the uninterruptedness of the sacrifice. (6.2.1.1–2)

From this passage it is clear, first, that the success of the sacrifice depends on the hospitality of the sacrificer and, second, that the hospitality of the sacrificer is in fact the hospitality of his united household, that is, the pairing (*mithuna*) of the husband and the wife. It is only with the approval of the wife that the offering is made that results in the continuity of the sacrifice and, therefore, of the moral and material order within the cosmic schema.

A passage in the *Śatapatha Brāhmaṇa* describes this same event and the same centrality of the housemistress, the sacrificer's wife, in receiving Soma at the place of the ritual. What becomes even more evident here, however, is that whenever a worthy guest comes to the household, it is all household members who are involved in his honoring, and in this way it is the whole household unit that is implicated in the reception of the guest:

eva etan mithunena anvārabhete; yatra vā arhann āgacchati sarvagṛhyā iva vai tatra ceṣṭanti. tathā hāpacito bhavati.

Thus they enclose him (Soma) on two sides by a (husband and wife) couple; wherever in this way a worthy one comes, there indeed all the household members bestir themselves. Thus he is attended to. (3.4.1.6)

Another *Taittirīya Saṃhitā* passage reaffirms the importance of the pairing of the wife with the husband in ensuring the successful completion of the sacrifice, but it further develops what is understood by the hospitality offered by a household, that is, that it is done for friendship (*mitratva*) because the wife is the friend of everyone!

upānakti patnī hi sarvasya mitraṃ mitratvāya. yad vai patnī yajñasya karoti mithunaṃ tad. atho patniyā eva eṣa yajñyasya anvārambho 'navacchityai.

The wife (of the sacrificer) anoints (them) for friendship, for the wife is the friend of all. Verily that part of the sacrifice which is the wife makes a pairing. Now this touching (of the cart) from behind by the wife is for the uninterruptedness of the sacrifice. (6.2.9.2)

This passage, then, makes an important reference to the social cohesion and unbrokenness of household ties to the wider world, which would be effected by the *śrauta* ritual.

There is further development of the linkage between the housemistress and her household's hospitality obligations in the Gṛhya and Dharma Sūtras. First, the wife is identified with the house; it is her resting place and sanctuary, and she is the representative of the domestic fire.[36] The housemistress is then enjoined by the Dharma Sūtras not to refuse alms that are petitioned by students (for fear of violating those who are truly conscientious about their vows), to examine the qualities of those who petition her and to be favorable to those who are worthy, and to give to them according to her ability.[37] This open and gracious "friendliness" of *śrauta* hospitality, then, is reflected in the *gṛhya* injunctions above, which are given to the *brahmacārin*: that is, that he should go to women who will not refuse him (*bhikṣeta apratyākhyāyinīṃ*).[38]

The *ātithya* cordiality extended to Soma in the sacrificial setting is manifest as well in secular guest *(atithi)* etiquette, as another way of meeting the debt *(ṛṇa)* or moral obligation owed by the householder;[39] its prescriptions are detailed at length in both the Gṛhya and Dharma Sūtras. The guest is a "friend" *(priya)*, and it is to him and to the religious mendicant that offerings of food are most appropriately due, for he is to come only to the place where the wife or the domestic fire is.[40] By definition, the guest is someone who belongs to a different village and who is intending to stay only one night; if he comes in the evening he is not to be turned away, and whoever comes into the house is not to go without the offer of cooked food.[41] Although the *Pāraskara Gṛhya Sūtra* suggests that the householder might eat before the guest, thus keeping the best portion for himself, this is frowned on by most other schools, who clearly state that the guest eats first.[42] The host also offers the guest a seat, water to drink, water to wash his feet, and a room (with a bed, mattress, pillow, and cover) in which to sleep. The reward for honoring a guest is thought to be freedom from trouble and bliss in heaven.[43]

The obligations of the Vedic relationship, then, rest on a view of hospitality in which the agent of that *ātithya* behavior is the household, represented by the presence and hospitable functioning of the housemistress. There are only a few obligatory rules for the behavior of the guest (or *brahmacārin)* at the point of the encounter; most rest on the host, that is, on the hostess. The householder wife here does not act independently,[44] however, but instead stands in for the household itself, for not only does she complete the household but she is also the one whose graciousness in the donation of cooked food to others cements the bonds of a hierarchical and highly segmented society.

In the Buddhist *bhikṣā* relationship, there is a shift from household obligations toward the mendicant to individual patronage of him or her, that is, a shift from responsibilities that impinge on the donor to prescriptions given to the renunciant. Thus, instead of donor hospitality, the relationship is governed by mendicant dependence *(upanissaya)*. Shortly after his enlightenment, the *Vinaya* says, the Buddha rules that monks and nuns are to live only on the four *nissayas* "resources," things found in the surrounding environment that can be used for renunciant survival without causing harm, inconvenience, or anxiety to other people: meals taken from scraps of food, robes made from rags on a dustheap, lodgings taken at the foot of a tree, and medicine made out of the strong-smelling urine of cattle.[45] In time, as the relationship between renunciants and householders sympathetic to Buddhism settles into a comfortable reciprocity, these four resources become the four *parikkhāras*, or "requisites," of robes, alms food, lodgings, and medicine, things that are no longer "found" but routinely given by donors to the growing Saṅgha.[46]

This dependence on resources by the Buddhist renunciant is, in this way, curious: in spite of the fact that they are enjoined to live as islands unto themselves, as refuges unto themselves, with no one other for support, they do indeed need others; they need donors to give them, on a continual basis, the material means acceptable for maintaining a life on the middle way.[47] Though set now in the context of voluntary patronage instead of obligatory hospitality, the Buddhist encounter still remains primarily an encounter with the woman of the household. Thus it becomes, instead of pure patronage, partly a system of "matronage."[48]

Renunciants' dependence on the generosity of the villages and towns around them is the basis for the ritualized household encounter, which is provided for in the *Cullavagga* and in the *Brahmāyu Sutta* of the *Majjhima Nikāya*. Two elements are central as the *bhikkhu* or *bhikkhunī* walks silently amid the houses, properly clad in three robes, and waits at a threshold for the *gahapatānī* of the house to put food into his or her bowl: the anonymity of both the donor and the petitioner, and the need for the petitioner to consider and maintain the good will of the donor. In the Cullavagga the renunciant is enjoined to walk among the houses with his eyes cast down (*okkhittacakkhunā antaraghare gantabbaṃ*), looking a plough's length ahead (*yugamattañ ca pekkhati*), according to the *Majjhima Nikāya*, and to not look at the face of the donor of the alms (*na ca bhikkhādāyikāya mukhaṃ ulloketabbaṃ*).[49] In discussing the commentary on this passage, Horner notes that "the donor may be a woman or a man. One is not to look at his (or her) face at the time when the alms are being given."[50]

In this way, there is a striking contrast to the practice of the *brahmacārin*. Not only is the petitioner not to look at the face of the donor, and thereby not to notice the donor's gender (although, as we will see, the texts designate clearly that the donor is normally the mistress of the house), but also there are no prescriptions for announcing the status of the petitioner. Although certain unmistakable signs would signal to the donor that it is a Sakyaputtiya, a follower of the Sakyamuni, who has come to the door—the nature of the robes, the material of the bowl, the comportment of the body—there is no overt sign, and certainly no verbal formula, indicating the petitioner's status along the pathway. It is true that the donor accrues greater merit by giving to increasingly more potent "fields of merit" *(puññakkhetta)*,[51] but external markers for this are nowhere present in texts that prescribe the threshold encounter. However, in contrast to the Vedic paradigm, the Buddhist paradigm does not focus on the external qualities of the parties to the *bhikṣā* relationship (e.g., caste and gender), in which a woman's place as a woman vis-à-vis the household is heightened. The Buddhist paradigm turns a blind eye to the externals of gender, in the case of both the donor and the petitioner, and focuses instead on the internal qualities of those in the transaction.[52]

First, whereas the downcast eyes reaffirm the anonymity of the threshold relationship, they also express a virtue crucial to the dependence of the renunciant on the donor: humility. Because the merit to the donor increases with the spiritual advancement of the donee and because the inner spiritual advancement of the donee is thought to be visible in his or her external comportment, donors are more likely to give when the donee's behavior fits their notion of an exceptional "field of merit." As Gombrich notes: "The more a monk demonstrates his indifference to worldly comforts, the more he impresses the laity and comes to be regarded as worthy of their material support. Indifference to comforts thus causes them to be provided."[53] Thus, whereas in the Vedic instance the obligation is, to a great degree, one of hospitality that impinges on the donor, in the Pali instance it is an obligation on the renunciant to encourage and preserve the good will of the donor. Downcast eyes are, then, the first recognition of the monk's or nun's deferential dependence on the donor and of his or her need to keep the channels of generosity open.

Preserving the good will of the donor in the threshold transaction is effected, second, by a renunciant's ritualized "testing of the waters" in which he or she sees how willing the donor, here explicitly the housemistress,[54] might be to giving food. According to the *Cullavagga*, at each instance of petitioning food, a monk or nun is to do the following:

> ṭhitakena sallakkhetabbaṃ bhikkhaṃ dātukāmā vā adātukāmā vā 'ti. sace kammaṃ vā nikkhipati āsanā vā vuṭṭhāti kaṭacchuṃ vā parāmasati bhājanaṃ vā parāmasati ṭhapeti vā, dātukāmā viyā 'ti ṭhātabbaṃ.
>
> While standing, he or she should consider: "Is she willing to give alms food or is she not willing to give?" If she lays her work aside, or rises from her seat, or wipes a spoon, or wipes a dish, or sets it out, he or she should stand still thinking: "it is as though she is willing to give."[55]

The Buddhist renunciant's search for signs that the housemistress is willing to give food is similar to that of the Vedic *saṃnyāsin*. Here the ascetic is enjoined to go to a household late, after people have finished their meals. He must also wait to petition until after the smoke and the embers of the kitchen fire have gone out and after the pestle for grinding and all the dishes have been put aside.[56] These signs will indicate that he will not intrude. The difference here is that whereas the *saṃnyāsin* is looking for signs among the inanimate objects of the household that the family's meal is over, the *bhikkhu* or *bhikkhunī* is looking for signs that the donor herself is open to the encounter, is willing to give on the basis of the renunciant's integrity and of her own good will. Although the obligation of hospitality for the donor would still be operative in the *saṃnyāsin* case, the burden is shifted in the Buddhist case to the petitioner, who must demonstrate anew by his inner worthiness the appropriateness of the dependent relationship.

Thus, in the Vedic case, the obligation of the *bhikṣā* relationship highlights the role of the wife as the representative of the household in its hospitality obligations, whereas in the Buddhist case the downcast eyes negate the importance of gender in the donor, much as the shaved head of the renunciant has done in the case of the *bhikkhu/bhikkhunī*. Moreover, whereas the giver of food in the Vedic case is in fact the whole household, in the Buddhist case it is the actual individual who has come to the door and who by various signs can indicate whether or not giving food is something she wants or is prepared to do. The element of choice in the Buddhist case thus denotes the housemistress as an individual with attributes of personal judgment who acts primarily as an agent on her own behalf.[57]

In the case of the Jain renunciant, the *Ācārāṅga Sūtra* prescribes that the male or female renunciant, unlike his or her Buddhist counterpart, may petition only from households whose members are actively supportive of the Jain community; they may reject as donors those who have stolen what is not theirs or who have injured living creatures in order to give, those who have prepared food for the sake of a great many (non-Jain) *śramaṇas* and brahmins, or those who have in any way acted to make the given food *ahimsically* impure and unacceptable. The Jain renunciant may petition from a great number of families—for example, noble, royal, merchant, barber, or weaver—as long as the family is blameless,[58] and somewhat like the *saṃnyāsin*, he or she is to wait until family members have all received their share of food and are eating their meal before making the petition.

As in the Vedic (but not the Buddhist) case, the Jain renunciant approaches the donor with a verbal formula. To the householder's wife, sister, daughter-in-law, or nurse, or male or female slave or servant, the renunciant says: "O long-lived one! (or 0 sister!) will you give me something to eat?" (This formula parallels that spoken to the housemistress when petitioning for clothing.) If the woman, in agreement, should move to wipe or wash her hands or spoon or plate in water, the renunciant is to intervene by asking her not to, saying, "If you want to give me something, give it as it is," for such a washing might cause injury to the creatures in the water, thus making the food impure and unacceptable. This concern is so great that the Jain mendicant is to look carefully to see if any householder hands that give food are in any way wet or not. When the renunciant asks for water or something to drink, however, the proper procedure is for the donor to allow the renunciant[59] to draw or pour the drink by and for himself or herself.

The Jain *bhikṣā* contract thus places obligations on both the donor and the renunciant. The donor household, again represented by a woman (although other women besides the householder wife may serve in the Jain case), is obliged to give food for the sake of the mendicant,[60] although her giving is severely restricted or shaped by *ahiṃsā*. The petitioner here is not primarily concerned with preserving the good will of the donor but with maintaining *ahiṃsā* both in the process of giving and in the food that is given. The primary allegiance to a principle, as opposed to donor hospitality or renunciant dependence, is seen in the issue of bathing: Although both *brahmacārins* and *bhikkhus* and *bhikkhunīs* are to bathe regularly and wear clean clothes, the Jain mendicants normally do not, giving rise to a smell that is notably disagreeable to householders.[61] Whether for reasons of *ahiṃsā* or because of an indifference to the outside world,[62] the effect in Jain prescriptions is to disregard what Buddhists hold so central, that is, the maintenance of good will in the donor.

A Woman's Economic Life

Differences in the encounter at the threshold also reflect differences in the understanding of a woman's economic life. The Dharma Sūtras and Śāstras lay out in detail what *strīdhana*, or the property of a wife, constitutes, and Kane has suggested that from the Ṛgvedic period onward gradually "such kinds of property went on increasing in extent and value." Although the chronology of changes in women's use and disposal of property in Vedic India is not altogether clear from the texts, its development, Kane suggests, is set against a background of worsening textual strictures for women in other areas.[63] The Vedic and Buddhist paradigms for the mendicant encounter suggest two of the prevailing understandings of women's rights over property—what they control, and how they control it—seen as a function of understandings of the household aggregate. Vedic ritual assumes the properness and naturalness of the marital unit.[64] The *Atharva Veda* enjoins wife and husband to be mutually dear (*sampriya*);[65] the *Taittirīya Saṃhitā* has the sacrificer's wife say: "I go as wife united with my husband" (*sampatnī patyāhaṃ gacche*);[66] the *Gṛhya Sūtra* of Hiranyakeśin enjoins a formula on the husband at the time of intercourse in which souls, hearts, and body parts are made one;[67] and *Manu* notes that "the husband is declared to be one with his wife" (*etad ayo bhartā sā smṛtāṅganā*).[68] The unit that is marriage is both effected by the ritual and has a ritual function. *Śatapatha Brāhmaṇa* for example, in reference to the Vājapeya, says:

> tad yaj jāyā māmantrayate: 'rddho ha vā eṣa ātmano yaj jāyā; tasmād yāvaj jāyāṃ na vindate na eva tāvat prajāyate 'sarvo hi tāvad bhavaty. atha yadā eva jāyāṃ vindate 'tha prajāyate tarhi hi sarvo bhavati. sarva etāṃ gatiṃ gacchānīti, tasmāj jāyā māmantrayate.
>
> Now as to why he addresses his wife: the wife is indeed half of his own self; therefore as long as he is not with his wife, he is not regenerated, for that long he is incomplete. But, as soon as he is with his wife, then he is regenerated, for then he is complete. "Complete, may I go to that supreme goal," he thinks and then addresses his wife. (5.2.1.10)

Dharma literature makes clear that neither husband nor wife can perform the *śrauta* ritual alone,[69] and the *Taittirīya Saṃhitā*, for example, notes that a good sacrifice, beneficial to the patrons and the cosmos alike, results from husband and wife participating together: "that part of the sacrifice which is the wife makes a pairing; now this touching (of the cart) from behind by the wife is for the uninterruptedness of the sacrifice."[70] Thus, the presence of the wife not only completes the ritual unit but legitimizes the patronage of the sacrificer and empowers his (that is, their) agency in the ritual.

Why is this marital unit so important in ritual efficacy? In his discussion of the *dakṣiṇā*, Heesterman argues that although the sacrificial gift given by the patron to all who have participated in the ritual creates a "generative alliance" bound by "the procreativeness of the union between giver and donees," the real product of that generative cycle is the "reproduction of *dakṣiṇā* wealth."[71] What he is pointing out is that one aspect of the *śrauta* ritual is economic, the goal being material prosperity at home.[72] Although there are indeed many ways to characterize the household unit—sexually or procreatively being one—that it is an economic unit is certainly obvious; that it is an economic unit in the *śrauta* discussion of marital togetherness is perhaps less so. We take, by way of example, the *dakṣiṇā*. Beginning in the *Ṛgveda*, *dakṣiṇā* was associated with cows,[73] horses,[74] camels, [75] chariots,[76] young girls,[77] food,[78] gold,[79] and garments;[80] by the time of the *Śatapatha Brāhmaṇa*, the list and its order have been more practically established as gold, cows, garments, and horses.[81] Although, as a sacrificial fee, the *dakṣiṇā* comes from the husband and the wife as a pair out of their household goods, some of these goods, especially if they are gold, could be the specific property, as ornaments, of the wife.[82] Passages in the *Atharva Veda*, *Chāndogya Upaniṣad*, and *Baudhāyana Śrauta Sūtra* each make reference to women's gold ornaments,[83] and it could well be that the *dakṣiṇā* offered by the household as a whole contains specific elements that belong to the wife's *strīdhana*.

An economic understanding of the marital unit has its basis in the *Taittirīya Saṃhitā* passage (6.2.1.1–2) discussed previously.[84] Here, in the guest reception of Soma to "the house of the sacrificer," [85] the wife is deemed essential to hospitality precisely because she is the "mistress of the household goods" (*patnī hi pārīṇahyasyeśe*). Just as her full participation in the ready availability of property to be handed over as *dakṣiṇā* is required in other parts of the ritual system, "so her *permission* to give [household goods] . . . away to a guest is required" here as well.[86] Jamison has discussed this passage and the possible origin of *pā́rīṇahya* in "the moveable goods that the bride brought to her new home at marriage" as a way of focusing on the rights of use and disposal a wife may have had over a wider range of goods and property in the household:

> These she would have control of, and even when pārīṇahya came to refer to household goods in general, the old notion of the wife's ownership of what she literally brought to the marriage may have been preserved. This may in turn help explain why the wife's permission is needed to give away what she does not really own, hence part of the reason why she is so necessary to the exercise of hospitality.[87]

Thus, the sacrificer's wife is and needs to be present in this ritual. When hospitality obligations are called on in the *śrauta* setting, the wife is required to represent the household in service to the guest; this proper performance of hospitality obligations will then ensure, according to the *Taittirīya Saṃhitā* passage, the continuity and thus the effectiveness of the sacrifice. Because it is the unit or marital pairing (*mithuna*) that is the agent (representing the whole household),[88] this pairing takes on, in addition to its sexual implications, economic ones as well.

In the Vedic model, then, the wife is the manager or guardian of the household property. As McGee and Jamison point out in their chapters, this aspect of marital relationship is crucial for wives' participation in rituals. The inclusion of the wife in the *Ātithyā* ritual for Soma, then, is precisely because she is the supervisor of the domestic goods, and it is only with her agreement and active presence that they can be offered to the guest. Although it is not clear from the *Taittirīya Saṃhitā* passage, or from *Manu* 9.11, exactly how she is to manage or dispose of the goods, that she is going to do so is clearly established. In the *bhikṣā* ritual, then, when the wife comes to the door, the *pārīṇahya* model is at work: as disposer of the household goods and as representative of the household in an *ātithya* setting, it is the woman of the household to whom the *brahmacārin* and even the *saṃnyāsin* go to as dispenser of food on behalf of the household unit. In the threshold encounter, that a woman as the hospitality representative of the marital unit actually manages the property of the household is critical, and in this way, in terms of *dāna*, a woman's identity is given to her by the structure of her marriage.

The Buddhist setting for the *bhikṣā* encounter reflects a number of changes, two of which are important here. First, the household is no longer depicted in the texts as a religious unit, having agency for ritual effectiveness. Now, the household, clearly headed by a *gahapati* and a *gahapatānī* of broader background (no longer, for example, just the brahmin or *rājanya* of *Śatapatha Brāhmaṇa* 11.8.4.1 and 12.1.1.1), is more generally a social unit with important economic implications. Many passages in the early Pali Canon show the Buddha trying to redefine the household within a broader social network of resources and responsibilities and to encourage, within that network, a potential sympathy and support for the young religion, so that new wealth might be directed its way. Discussions with donors like King Pasenadi, who once prepared a great sacrifice with hundreds of animals,[89] and brahmin performers of the Aggihotta,[90] for example, show that for Buddhists the Vedic understanding of the household as the preeminent ritual agent is not fully operative. Rather, a new understanding of the household is refocused on issues of proper accumulation and disposition of property and set within a vigorously pluralistic religious environment.[91]

Second, there is a greater emphasis on the role and importance of the individual. Whereas Olivelle argues that the new value placed on the individual derives from the "emergence of kingship and urban culture," the king being "the supreme individual in society," and is "facilitated by a similar individualistic mentality . . . among merchants, whose success depended less on following an inherited and ritualized pattern of behavior than on initiative and enterprise,"[92] an older source needs to be noted. Heesterman has long discussed the individual nature of the *śrauta* ritual. Not only is it "man by himself and alone, not the gods or any other supernatural agency, who must realize the absolute static order by unquestioningly submitting to the exacting rule of ritual," but also it is the specialized use of the fire drill that emphasizing "the exclusive link with its owner . . . makes [the sacrificer] . . . independent, allowing him to make fire where there" is none.[93] As the *śrauta* ritual develops, moreover, a process evolves, called by Heesterman the "individualization of the ritual," whereby the sacrificer no longer relies on an array of ritual officiants to create the world but only on his own ritual work. Now an interior process, the individualizing of the ritual places a premium on individual effort in the maintenance of moral order and also leads, eventually, to greater hierarchy and fixity in social relations.[94]

In the period when this emergence of the individual is evolving, a number of developments important to our discussion are recorded in the Pali texts. This emergence, for example, seems to have allowed for more open discussions about, one, disposable property belonging specifically to the wife of the household and, two, the possibility that women themselves could be wage earners.[95] Illustrating the first possibility are two stories similar to each other in which well-meaning parents use three piles of wealth, one of them belonging specifically to the mother, to entice an ordained son back into the household life. In the case of the monk Sudinna, part of what he refuses is *mātumattikaṃ itthikāya itthidhanaṃ* "the mother's portion, the wife's property due her because she is a woman/wife,"[96] and in that of the monk Ratthapala it is *mattikaṃ dhanaṃ* "the mother's property."[97]

Not only is the property of the wife clearly differentiated in each story, but we might also propose that its appearance in each household's "enticement pile" is a matter of the wife's choice, unusual here because the normal devolution of a woman's *strīdhana* in Hindu law is on her daughters. Illustrating the second possibility is the Buddha's counsel to the daughters of the *gahapati* Uggaha: he advises them not only to guard and protect the material property of their future husbands and to manage deftly and sensitively the household staff but to learn their husbands' crafts as well:

> ye te bhattu abbhantarā kammantā uṇṇā ti vā kappāsā ti vā, tattha dakkhā bhavissāma analasā, tatrupāyāya vīmaṃsāya samannāgatā alaṃ kātuṃ alaṃ saṃvidhātun.
>
> We will be skilled and diligent at the domestic crafts of our husbands, whether they be of wool or of cotton, focusing on understanding the techniques therein, in order to do it and to get it done.[98]

In another passage, a wife tells a sick husband that, having learned his crafts well, she will be able to support herself and her family handsomely on its proceeds should he die.[99]

This movement toward the individual handling and disposal of wealth by women is seen nowhere better than in the great number of individual women donors to the Saṅgha, who on their own give not only monumental quantities of food, medicine, and robes but land and lodgings as well. The greatest woman donor is Visākhā, called Migāramātā because she is instrumental in the conversion to Buddhism of her father-in-law Migāra. She feeds hundreds of monks each day, and her construction and gift of the monastery, Migāramātupāsāda, often provides Buddhist renunciants with lodging and retreat.[100] The courtesan *(gaṇikā)* Ambapālī frequently gives large meals to groups of Buddhist monks and nuns and signs over a residence at her Mango Grove (Ambapālivana) to the Saṅgha for their use;[101] the daughter of the king of the Koliyans becomes the foremost woman[102] to give good alms food (*agga panītadāyikānaṃ*); and the Buddha's aunt who raises him, Mahāpajāpati, becomes a conspicuous donor of robes, though she is most known to the Pali Canon for trying to give them to individual monks, including the Buddha, rather than to the Saṅgha as a whole.[103]

The possibility for a woman to be a donor of any and all of the four requisites (*parikkhāra*) is certainly a factor in understanding the *bhikṣā* relation at the household door. Although the fact that households in the Pali Canon are normally designated by reference to both the householder and his wife (*gahapati* and *gahapatānī*)—indicating a continued influence of the Vedic "unit" model of marriage (*mithuna*), of the hospitable (*ātithya*) reception of guests, and of Vedic views on household wealth (*pārīṇahya*)—the threshold ritual tells more. That the petitioner does not look at the face of the donor and that the donor may be a man or a woman[104] indicate a new trend at work. If it is not important that the food giver at the door be a woman, then the understanding of the wife as manager and dispenser of household goods is of less importance; what seems to be more important is that whoever comes to the door, man or woman, is giving food out of individual sympathy and support for the movement, rather than as a function of a household unit that is operating under obligations of hospitality and understanding of the female management of joint household goods. The woman as a singular agent of the disposition of wealth separate from the men of the family (who may also be donors) thus allows an identity for her that is tied to individual actions rather than to accidents of her birth.

A Woman's Sexuality

One curious item remains. It has been suggested that "the Vinaya does not simply lay down the rules for the monastic community, but tells us how and on what occasion the Buddha gave the various precepts," and that this setting of rules within the context of a narrative of their origin goes "back to the Vedic model."[105] In the case of the instructions about *bhikṣā* etiquette in the *Cullavagga,* it is most likely that the rules and the narrative setting in which they are housed are contemporary, and that there is an historical link between the two as well. With this, we turn to the *Cullavagga* narrative, as follows. There was once a time when a certain monk, who was dressed improperly and who walked among houses improperly, happened to come upon a woman lying naked on her back in the inner chamber of her house. The husband seeing the monk there accused him of seducing her and thrashed him. The beating woke the woman who then came to the monk's defense. Hearing of this the Buddha lay down rules for proper alms touring,[106] which emphasized more stringent measures by the monk or nun to reign in his or her senses and to guarantee donor-suitable comportment. If the rules and their narrative setting do indeed belong together, why is this the setting for the rules and not some other, and why do we not find similar concern built into the rules for the *brahmacārin* and the *saṃynāsin?*

In the Vedic *bhikṣā* model, the institution of marriage is the defining structure for women. Although it is clear throughout Dharma literature that women are thought to be thoroughly bodily beings with sweeping sexual and amoral inclinations,[107] this sexuality can be controlled, primarily through the institution of marriage. When tamed by marriage, a woman's erotic tendencies are domesticated, stabilizing her as a threat to the social and moral order. Thus, marriage becomes a context in which *rati,* or sexual pleasure, can be expressed and where the goal of *prajā,* or offspring, can be pursued;[108] women and wives who then stay within the constraints of their marriages for these two pursuits become honored by the men of their families.[109] In the *bhikṣā* relationships, therefore, the threshold encounter is founded on and circumscribed by the properly functioning institution of marriage: the two woman specifically named in the defining and sustaining ritual of Upanayana *bhikṣā* are the wife of the father and the wife of the teacher. Although Vedic literature, and especially Dharma literature, is conspicuously mindful of the distracting and seductive powers of women,[110] these do not play into the threshold encounter with a mendicant, for here the controlling model of the household unit is so strong that the untamed sexuality of the woman at the door is not an issue.

In the Buddhist case, however, where the household unit is not the prevailing model, the *bhikṣācara* is instructed to be forever on his or her guard. Unlike Vedic prescriptions, defining the households not to beg from as those whose heads do not have Vedic expertise but saying nothing specific about certain women's households,[111] Buddhist prescriptions deride those who petition among prostitutes (*vesiyā*), among widows (*vidhavā*), among grown girls (*thullakumārikā*), among eunuchs (*paṇḍaka*), or among nuns (*bhikkhunī*),[112] in order to protect, we assume, the male mendicant from the untamed sexual powers of such people. More specifically, the *Cullavagga* text, in giving rules for the encounter at the household door, works within a newer context in which the woman who meets the *bhikkhu* and who indicates her willingness to give by certain subtle actions in the kitchen is doing so not necessarily as a representative of the household unit but as an individual sympathetic to the new religion.

Appearing, then, in a role that is, for all intents and purposes, unprotected by the Vedic ramparts of marriage, the woman becomes a source of a more loosely contained sexuality against which the poor renunciant must "now guard himself with all mindfulness." As in the more general Vedic understanding of women and as in the Jain vision in the *Ācārāṅga Sūtra*,[113] the Pali Canon's view of the individualized encounter is this: Whereas it is the woman who tempts, it is the male renunciant who must be on his guard.

Although the *piṇḍapāta* rules set within the story of the "naked encounter" seem to be exclusively about the sexual seductiveness of women, they are in fact as much, if not more, about maintaining the good will of the donor. Nath has observed that most "of the Buddhist . . . alms-seeking procedural rules . . . [are] ostensibly framed to suit the donor's convenience and to win over his regard and approbation, so that his continued patronage . . . [can] be ensured."[114] With the *Cullavagga* passage as the base for these procedural rules, this good will is certain to be preserved if the onus for the "safeness" of the threshold relationship rests on the renunciant. That it is the responsibility of the renunciant for maintaining the "sexual safeness" of the donor-renunciant relationship is reaffirmed when the genders are switched, for a number of times in the *Bhikkhunī Vibhaṅga* nuns are enjoined to keep their desires in strict control when around male donors,[115] indicating that bearing the burden of safeness in the threshold encounter is not, at its base, a gender-bound issue.

In these ways, then, there are two processes that seem to be at work in the Buddhist treatment of the renunciant encounter with the housemistress at the door that make it different from the Vedic, both of which favor an understanding of the woman as an increasingly independent agent in the donation of food. There is, first, a process of internalization whereby external, socially defining, features—such as specific family and caste—become less important in both the donor and the donee and internal features become more so. Thus, while the mental composure and mindfulness of the renunciant become preeminent, in like manner internal aspects of the figure at the door do also: no longer is she fully contained by her role as wife, for she is now also a woman with all the potentially unleashed powers that that entails. Second, there is a process of individualization that heightens the issues of freedom and selectivity, and concomitantly that of responsibility. In this way, the threshold contract becomes more complex. Whereas the housemistress may now choose to give or not—her willingness being signaled by several agreed-upon signs—she now takes responsibility for her, albeit loose, religious affiliation.

To be sure, that responsibility is differently configured than the responsibility of the woman in the colonial era, as discussed by Falk elsewhere in this volume, or the Hindu nationalist in the contemporary era, as discussed by Bacchetta. However, even in this early period we can see that each individual renunciant now bears greater responsibility for his and her own comportment. Unlike the Vedic housemistress, then, for whom marriage structures are all encompassing, the Buddhist housemistress is a donor for whom hospitality obligations have given way to all the complexities of choice exercised within a pluralistic arena.

Notes

1. Vin 4.2.213, 220-21, 233, 234.

2. Sukumar Dutt, *Buddhist Monks and Monasteries of India: Their History and Their Contribution to Indian Culture* (London: Allen & Unwin, 1962), p. 36.

3. Patrick Olivelle, "Introduction," in *Saṃnyāsa Upaniṣads* (New York: Oxford University Press, 1992), p. 103.

4. Manu 3.99–117; see ĀpDS 1.1.3.26.

5. Vijay Nath, *Dāna: Gift System in Ancient India (c. 600 B.C.–c. A.D. 300): A Socio-economic Perspective* (New Delhi: Munshiram Manoharlal Publishers, 1987), pp. 191–95.

6. Stephanie Jamison, *Sacrificed Wife/Sacrificer's Wife: Women, Ritual, and Hospitality in Ancient India* (New York and Oxford: Oxford University Press, 1996), p. 254. "Introduction," in *Karma and Rebirth in Classical Indian Traditions*, Wendy Doniger O'Flaherty, Ed. (Berkeley: University of California Press, 1980)

7. O'Flaherty, *Karma and Rebirth* pp. xvii–xviii.

8. Dutt, *Buddhist Monks and Monasteries*, (p. 73), for example, discusses the Buddhist Uposatha's ties to the Vedic new and full moon sacrifices, and Erich Frauwallner argues at length in *The Earliest Vinaya and the Beginnings of Buddhist Literature*, L. Petech, Trans. (Rome: Is. M.E.O. 1956), p. 62, for example, for the modeling of Vinaya teacher lists on similar Vedic ones, "in order to bestow on the own [Buddhist] tradition an authority similar to the Vedic one."

9. Olivelle, "Introduction," p. 12.

10. BĀU 3.5.1; KBU 2.1.

11. RV 10.109.5; AV 5.17.5; 6.133.3; CU 4.4.1–4; 6.1.1–7.

12. Olivelle, "Introduction," p. 54

13. ŚB 11.3.3.5–7; see Manu 2.48.

14. Most Gṛhya Sūtras give the initiatory ages as follows, eight for the brahmin, eleven for the *kṣatriya*, and twelve for the *vaiśya* (ŚGS 2.1.1–5; ĀśGS 1.19.1–4; PGS 2.2.1–3; KhādGŚ 2.4.1–5; GGS 2.10.1–3; KpGS 4.10.2–3). Only HGS (1.1.2–3) prescribes seven for the brahmin. The *upanayana* can be performed for brahmins until age sixteen, for *kṣatriyas* until age twenty-two, and for *vaiśyas* until age twenty-four (ŚGS 2.1.6–8; ĀśGS 1.19.5–7; PārGS 2.5.36–38; KhādGS 2.4.2–6; GGS 2.10.4). The CU (4.10.1; 6.1.2) suggests that the period for studenthood was twelve years, although the Gṛhya Sūtras suggest twelve years for each Veda or as long as it takes (PārGS 2.5.13–15).

15. ŚB 11.3.3.3–6; CU 4.3.5; 4.10.1–2

16. ŚGS 2.6.4, 7, 8; ĀṣGS 1.22.10; PārGS 2.5.11; ĀpDS 1.1.3.25, 31–34; GDS 2.35, 39–40; VāSDS 7.14; BDS 1.2.3.18; Manu 2.51, 182, 183, 188. *Brahmacārins* are not allowed to petition from *apapātras*, that is, those born from a high-caste mother and a low-caste father, or from *abhiṣastas*, those who have committed certain heinous crimes (see ĀpDS 1.9.24.6ff.).

17. ĀpŚS 6.28.11; ĀśSS 3.10.6. For a full discussion see Olivelle, "Introduction," pp. 86–94.

18. Manu 6.50, 43, 55, 57; GDS 3.11, 14, 16, 17; VāSDS 10.6, 24, 25; BDS 2.10.18.4, 12, 22.

19. Vin 3.6, 242–48; 4.243–45; 1.90–91; MN 1.31, 108, 109, 146, 160, 171, 206, 227, 237, 336, 359, 456–57; 2.61–63; 104, 112; 3.247.

20. Vin 2.212.215; MN 2.136–39.

21. Hermann Jacobi, *Jaina Sūtras*, Part 1. *Sacred Books of the East*, vol. 22 (Oxford: Oxford University Press, 1884; rpt. Delhi: Motilal Banasidass, 1964), p. 88.

22. ŚGS 2.6.5–7; ĀśGS 1.22.6–7; PārGS 2.5.5–8; KhādGS 2.4.27–30; GGS 2.10.42–44; HGS 1.2.7.15–19.

23. PārGS 2.5.5-6
24. GGS 2. 10. 43
25. ĀśGS 1.22.6-7.
26. Manu 2.50.
27. ŚB 11.3.3.7; GDS 2.37; BDS 1.2.4.7.
28. Manu 2.184. A. L. Basham, *History and Doctrine of the Ājīvikas: A Vanished Indian Religion* (London: Luzac, 1951), p. 122, discusses a practice among the Ājīvikas that is similar, although for different reasons: "The ascetic followers of Gosāla did not beg food of their female relations, because Gosāla himself was once disappointed at not receiving alms, presumably from his own kin."
29. PārGS 2.5.2-4; ĀpDS 1.1.3.28-30; BDS 1.2.3.17; Manu 2.49.
30. GDS 2.36; BDS 1.2.3.16; ĀśGS 1.22.8-9. See Jamison, *Sacrificed Wife*, p. 294 n. 61.
31. BDS 2.10.18.5, 12.
32. See AV 3.10.2; ŚB 11.8.4.1; 12.1.1.1. On *patni*, see Jamison, *Sacrificed Wife*, pp. 30, 263 n. 3.
33. J.C. Heesterman's argument in *Broken World of Sacrifice: An Essay in Ancient Indian Ritual* (Chicago: University of Chicago Press, 1993), pp. 155-56, 188-89, is that in eating the sacrificial food, the brahmin "takes over the burden of death. . . for in order to be prepared the food must first be killed."
34. AV 6.96.1; CU 5.10.4; AV 6.15.3.
35. AB 1.15, 25; TS 1.2.10; KB 8.1; ŚB 3.4.1.1-26. Jamison's (*Sacrificed Wife*) discussion of the wife's place in the *śrauta* ritual is indeed detailed (pp. 38ff.) and need not be recapitulated here. We do note, however, her discussion of the unusual aspects of the wife's participation in the Soma sacrifice (pp. 115ff.).
36. ŚB 3.3.1.10; KhādGS 1.5.17; GGS 1.3.15.
37. ĀpDS 1.1.3.26; 2.5.10.2; GDS 5.22; VāsDS 8, 13; 9, 18
38. The risks and dangers open to the petitioner in the mendicant encounter are substantial, and Jamison (*Sacrificed Wife*, pp. 157, 195-203) details the many ways, in the Vedic context, he can become vulnerable at the household door.
39. This debt *(ṛna)* is owed to the gods, seers, ancestors, and all living creatures *(bhūta)* and is carried out through *dāna*, that is, by making obligatory offerings to the four groups directly or through some representative. See Nath, *Dāna*, pp. 35-39.
40. GGS 4.10.24; PārGS 2.9.12; ŚGS2.16.3.
41. GDS 5.40; VāsDS 8.7; ŚGS2.16.3; ĀpDS 2.3.6.5.
42. VāsDS 8.4, 5; PārGS 2.195; ĀpDS 2.2.4.11; 2.3.73; 2.4.8.2; VāsDS 11.6-11.
43. GDS 4.10.1-26; ĀpDS 2.3.6.6-20; 2.3.7.1-17; 2.4.8.1-14.
44. GDS 18.1; VāsDS 5.1; BDS 2.2.3.44, 45.
45. *Piṇḍiyālopabhojana, paṃsukūlacīvara, rukkhamūlasenāsana, putimuttabhesajja.* Vin 1.58.
46. *Cīvara-piṇḍapāta-senāsana-gilānapaccayabhesajja-parikkhāra.* Vin 1.248; 3.89, 90, 132, 184, 211, 266; MN 1.104-108, 126, 271; 2.101; 3.254; SN 4.288; AN 1.247; 2.26-27; 54-55, 65; 3.124-126, 130, 135; 4.114, 134, 366; 5.15, 67, 131, 201, 350.
47. DN 3.58. The religious dynamics of this relationship are complicated. Often characterized as a kind of "exchange," the relationship promises the donor earned merit as a result of her or his gift, the amount of which depends on many factors (one being the worthiness of the recipient) and the proof of which is not normally realized until the next life. Although the ethic of wealth in Buddhism encourages donors of all types to give, in part, to provide for the comfort and well-being of their fellows, *dāna* in early Buddhism is not normally thought to be extended specifically to relieve the needy. Nath (*Dāna*, p. 149) discusses the problems raised for caste-based commensality rules when members of heterodox orders accept cooked food from brahmin households.

48. I am indebted to John Nelson for this term. On the role of female lay patronage in the rise and development of Buddhism, see Janice D.Willis, "Nuns and Benefactresses," in *Women, Religion and Social Change*, Yvonne Yazbeck Haddad and Ellison Banks Findly, Eds. (Albany: State University of New York Press, 1985), p. 73, and "Female Patronage in Indian Buddhism," in *The Power of Art: Patronage in Indian Culture*, B.S. Miller, Ed. (Delhi: Oxford University press, 1992), " pp. 46–53.

49. Vin 2.213, 216; MN 2.137.

50. I.B. Horner, Trans. *The Book of the Discipline*, Vol. 5. *Cullavagga* (Oxford: Pali Text Society, [1952] /1988), p. 303n.

51. MN 1.446; AN 1.244, 284, 284; 2.117, 171; 3.134, 161, 248, 278, 387; 4.113, 290–91; 5.67, 198.

52. The anonymity of the *saṃnyāsin's* alms round is echoed here, for not only is he to stop at houses chosen randomly and accidentally (VāsDS 10.7), but also, like the brahmin guest who is not to boast of his family background to get a meal (Manu 3.109), he is to make no humble salutations at all, so as not to fall into a hierarchically predefined relationship (Manu 6.58). Horner (*Women under Primitive Buddhism: Laywomen and Alsmwomen*, p. 324, Delhi: Motilal Banarsidass Publishers, [1930]/1989), however, renders the Buddhist household almost identical to the Vedic: "She performed this function, her duty and privilege, because the home was looked upon pre-eminently as her sphere, and not because she was in any way the owner of the house."

53. Richard Gombrich, *Theravāda Buddhism* (New York: Routledge, 1988), p. 95.

54. Nancy Auer Falk, in "Exemplary Donors of the Pāli Tradition," in *Ethics, Wealth, and Salvation: A Study in Buddhist Social Ethics*, Russell F. Sizemore and Donald K Swearer, Eds. (Columbia: University of South Carolina Press 1990), pp. 132–133, 265 n. 21) argues that female donors to early Buddhism could be distinguished from male by the size of their donations—women often giving "small but thoughtful items and services that will ease the monastic community's day-to-day burdens." But this pattern does not remain long, she argues, for even with the author (Visākhā) of these prototypical donations the nature of the donation soon changes to larger gifts of land and buildings.

55. Vin 2.216. See Frauwallner, *Earliest Vinaya*, p. 125.

56. GDS 3.17; VāsDS 10.8; Manu 6.56.

57. A striking example of a female donor who is acting on her own behalf is the story of Suppiyā, who, hearing of a sick monk in need of a meat broth, goes in search of meat in the markets with which to make it. Finding none (this being a nonslaughter day, *māghata ajjā*) and intent upon making a medicinal gift to the monk, Suppiyā cuts a piece of her own thigh with which to make the broth. When it is done, she has a servant bring it to the monk and she takes to her room in sickly confinement. Hearing of Suppiyā's illness, the Buddha visits her and, seeing her thigh, heals the wound with his powers *(iddhi)*. However, the Buddha then returns to the community and, berating the monk who accepted the broth for not inquiring into its origins, rules against the use of human flesh (Vin 1.216–220). Another, happier story that highlights the independence of a woman's giving is the long account of Visākhā's insistent request to the Buddha to be a permanent donor of eight items (rain cloths, food for the incoming, food for the outgoing, food for the sick, food for the sick-tenders, medicine for the sick, conjey, and bathing cloths for the nuns). It is only after a protracted time and much discussion that he is persuaded to grant her her wishes (Vin 1.290–94).

58. Jacobi, *Jaina Sutras*, pp. 64–66, 91–93.

59. Ibid., pp. 93, 159, 103, 117–19, 107–108.

60. Ibid., pp. 101–102, 121.

61. Ibid., pp. 124–25; but see p. 242.

62. Ibid., pp. 24, 27.

63. P.V. Kane, *History of Dharmaśāstra* 2nd ed. (Poona: Bhandarkar Oriental Research Institute, 1941, 1946), vol. 3: p.772; vol. 2.1: pp. 576–77.

64. AV 6.60.1–3; 6.78.1–3; 7.36.1; 7.37.1.

65. AV 2.36.4.

66. TS 1.1.10.

67. HGS 1.7.24.4.

68. Manu 9.45.

69. Manu 9.18, 96.

70. TS 3.2.8.4–5; 6.2.9.1–2.

71. J.C. Heesterman, "Reflections on the Significance of the *Dakṣiṇā*," *Indo-Iranian Journal* 4 (1959): 241–58; 245, 251. ŚB 4.3.4.2

72. See, for example, AV 6.79.1–3; Heesterman, *Broken World*, pp. 35, 39, 68, 69, 209. He notes as well that as a development of the role of the *dakṣiṇā* in the ritual, *dāna* replaces *yajña* as the primary duty of the fourth era, the Kali Yuga, pp. 141, 210.

73. RV 1.126.3; 5.30.12; 8.5.37; 8.46.22; 10.107.1–11.

74. RV 1.126.2; 5.18.5; 6.47.23; 7.16.10; 8.46.22; 10.107.2, 7, 10.

75. RV 8.5.37; 8.46.22.

76. RV 1.126.3.

77. RV 1.126.3; 6.27.8; 7.18.22; 8.19.36; 8.68.17.

78. RV 10.107.7; 10.117.6.

79. RV 1.126.2; 6.47.23; 8.5.38; 10.107.2, 7.

80. RV 10.107.2.

81. ŚB 4.3.4.24–27.

82. ĀśGS 1.6.1–2; PārGS 1.8.9.

83. AV 9.5.2426; CU 4.2.1–4; Kane, *History of Dharmaśāstra*, Vol. 2.2: p.871; Kala Acharya, *Purāṇic Concept of Dāna* (Delhi: Nag Publishers, 1993), pp. 116–77.

84. Parallel passages in KS 24.8 and MS 3.7.9 (88.5).

85. AB 1.15.

86. Jamison, *Sacrificed Wife*, p. 117.

87. Ibid., p. 118. Nath (*Dāna*, p. 74) interprets the household goods the wife is mistress over as her *strīdhana*, wealth and goods peculiarly hers as a wife. The passage, however, as Jamison suggests, might bear a wider interpretation.

88. See ŚB 3.4.1.6 and Manu 9.11.

89. SN 1.75–76.

90. DN 1.9.

91. E.B. Findly, "Forging a Balance: The Dynamics of Giving in Early Buddhism," *International Journal of Hindu Studies*, July 1996.

92. Olivelle, "Introduction," pp. 32–33.

93. Heesterman, *Broken World*, pp. 81, 101.

94. J.C. Heesterman, *The Inner Conflict of Tradition: Essays in Indian Ritual, Kinship, and Society* (Chicago: University of Chicago Press, 1985), pp. 32–44; and Heesterman, *Broken World*, pp. 216, 218.

95. See Nath, *Dāna*, pp. 41, 71–72.

96. Vin 3.17.

97. MN 2.63.

98. AM 3.37.

99. AN 3.295–98.

100. Vin 3.187–88, 191–92; 4.161–62; 1.290–91; 2.129–30, 169–70, 236; DN 3.80; MN 2.112; 3.1, 78, 104; SN 1.77, 190; 5.216, 222, 269; AN 1.26, 193, 205; 2.183; 4.204, 255, 269. See the discussions in Horner, *Women Under Primitive Buddhism*, pp. 325–61; Willis, "Nuns

and Benefactresses," pp. 73–74; Falk, "Exemplary Donors," pp. 131–33. The *Vimāna Vatthu* (see Nath, *Dāna*, p. 75) records the somewhat later tradition that Visākhā paid for the building with her own ornaments, that is, out of her *strīdhana/itthidhana*.

101. Vin 1.231–33; DN 2.95–98. Moti Chandra notes: "It is significant that though the *gaṇikas* were not free persons legally, they had full authority over the assets which consisted of jewellry, income from salary and the gifts received from their lovers." See Nath, *Dāna*, p. 75.

102. AN 1.26; 2.62–63.

103. MN 253–57; see Findly, "Ānanda's Case for Women," *International Journal of Indian Studies* 3.2 (July-December 1993), p. 1–31.

104. See Vin 2.213–16.

105. Frauwallner, *Earliest Vinaya*, pp. 63, 65, 153–54.

106. Vin 2.215–16.

107. Manu 2.213; 9.5, 7, 12.

108. AV 2.36.3; TS 3.2.8; BĀU 6.4.3, 28; HGS 1.6.19.7; Manu 3.45; 5.153; 9.26, 27, 45.

109. Manu 3.55.

110. See ŚGS. 4.11.1, 6, 10; 6.1.3; Manu 2.213.

111. Kane, *History*, 2.1.309–10.

112. Vin 1.70.

113. Jacobi, *Jaina Sūtras*, pp. 21–22, 48–49, 94–95, 124.

114. Nath, *Dāna*, p. 230.

115. Vin 4.2.213, 220–21, 233, 234.

2

Ritual Rights

The Gender Implications of *Adhikāra*

MARY MCGEE

Power and authority in Vedic times were very much connected with the ritual of sacrifice. The performance of a sacrifice conveyed power and prestige to the sacrificer, and great authority was attributed to the priests who knew about the proper performance of ritual. Access to power in every culture and at all times in history seems to be closely guarded, so it is not surprising that the *mīmāṃsā* school of India philosophy, which focused on the power and efficacy of Vedic rites, considered quite seriously the question of who was entitled to perform a sacrifice. The term *adhikāra*–variously translated as "entitlement," "qualification," "eligibility," "right," "and authority"–refers to this technical subject of entitlement. *Adhikārin* is the term used for one who is qualified or authorized for a particular privilege, duty, or possession–in this case, someone who is entitled to perform a particular ritual. As Francis X. Clooney (1990) explained, the point of the *mīmāṃsā* inquiry into *adhikāra* is to identify "legitimate performers of the sacrifice and conditions for their exercise of that eligibility" (p. 96).

Whereas the earliest *mīmāṃsakas'* inquiry into *adhikāra* focused specifically on Vedic ritual, interpreters of later brahminical and Hindu ritual traditions were also concerned with this question of entitlement and used mimansic hermeneutics to shape and inform their inquiries. This chapter focuses primarily on the *mīmāṃsā* texts, but it is situated within a much more encompassing inquiry in which I try to connect *mīmāṃsā* discussions of *adhikāra*, especially pertaining to women, with much later textual debates, found in the *dharma-nibandhas*–encyclopedic texts of *dharma* compiled between the twelfth and eighteenth centuries C.E.–about women's entitlement to perform such rituals as *homa* (sacrifice), *pūjā* (worship), *vrata* (vows and fasts), and *śrāddha* (memorial rites).[1] Whereas the specifics of women's images and roles in early Indian ritual and literature are discussed by other authors in this volume (Jamison, Findly, and Patton), this chapter is concerned primarily with a ritual concept or category, namely, *adhikāra*, and debates relevant to women's *adhikāra*. Katherine Young's chapter addresses the application of such a concept in her discussion on the eligibility of women in the Vaiṣṇava tradition to recite the sacred syllable *om*.

The questions I am concerned with in my investigation are as follows:

- Do women have *adhikāra*; that is, are they entitled or competent to perform sacrifice (and by extension, other rituals)?
- Are there any gender specifications for *adhikāra*?

- What are the qualifications and entitlements of an *adhikārin* and do they differ for men and women?
- What are the implications of these textual deliberations for the contemporary performance of rituals by Hindu women?

Although the process of this kind of investigation is somewhat technical, involving an understanding of both legal and grammatical points, my aim is to relate the technical treatment of *adhikāra* to a more general discussion of the gendered nature of dependence, interdependence, and independence within Hindu culture. My overall agenda, though, is to suggest ways in which the traditional discussion on *adhikāra* can be used as evidence and argument to support women's authoritative rights and status in Hindu culture, both historically and in contemporary times.

Do Women Have *Adhikāra*?

This question is not a new one; indeed the *mīmāṃsakas* themselves asked this very question. The sixth *adhyāya* of Jaimini's *Mīmāṃsā Sūtra* concerns itself with types of people and their capacity to sacrifice. In particular, it addresses the question of who is competent to sacrifice (6.1) and who is entitled to perform sacrifice (6.1, 6.6, 6.7). Jaimini specifically brings up the question of women's and *śūdras*' entitlement to sacrifice. There are other texts that treat this question as well, the earliest being the *Kātyāyana Śrauta Sūtra*, which begins its text on rules for Vedic sacrifices with a discussion of *adhikāra* (*athāto 'dhikāraḥ* KSS 1.1.1). For the purposes of this chapter, I have relied on the following texts:

Kātyāyana Śrauta Sūtra (KSS), a handbook of rules for Vedic sacrifices

Mīmāṃsā Sūtra of Jaimini[2] (JM)

Jaiminīya Mīmāṃsābhāṣya of Śabarasvāmī (SB)

Trikāṇḍamaṇḍana of Bhāskara Miśra[3] (TM)

Mīmāṃsānyāyaprakāśa of *Āpadeva* (MNP), an influential seventeeth-century treatise on *mīmāṃsā*[4]

Arthasaṅgraha of Laugākṣi Bhāskara (AS), a standard *mīmāṃsā* handbook from the seventeenth century[5]

Nirṇayasindhu of Kamalākarabhaṭṭa (NS), a seventeenth-century *dharma-nibandha* on rituals, especially *vratas*[6]

Clooney's discussion of *adhikāra* in *Thinking Ritually* has also contributed to my ideas about the *adhikāra* of women.

I have structured the presentation of my investigation on the *adhikāra* of women along the lines of mimansic hermeneutics, as I find this method particularly effective for articulating the different positions staked out by different schools and thinkers. However, I have taken certain liberties in introducing sidebar discussions relevant to the matters under discussion by the *mīmāṃsakas*. For example, the *mīmāṃsakas* bring up the subject matter of women's right to ownership; taking a cue from them, I introduce *strīdhana* (women's property), a topic not explicitly covered by the *mīmāṃsakas*, but which I think pertains to their discussion of *adhikāra* and will help us to better understand their argument; it is a technical topic that is also relevant to several other essays in this volume. The *mīmāṃsa* format for discussing a topic—investigating it and resolving disputes or doubts that arise in the process—is in the form of a discussion known as the *adhikaraṇa*. Each investigation or discussion (*adhikaraṇa*) has five parts, or steps. Jaimini's presentation, as explained by Śabara, is arranged in the following manner:[7]

1. *Viśaya*: the subject of investigation
2. *Saṃśaya*: doubts about the subject matter
3. *Pūrvapakṣa*: the prima facie view or standpoint of the opponent
4. *Uttarapakṣa*: arguments against or responses to the prima facie view
5. *Siddhānta* or *nirṇaya*: the conclusion or decision and its relevance

The Subject of Investigation: *Adhikāra* of Women

The *viśaya*, or subject of our investigation, is women's *adhikāra*; that is, are women entitled to perform sacrifices? To understand the discussion on women's *adhikāra*, or entitlement, we must first understand the criteria of *adhikāra*.

Criteria for Adhikāra

What are the criteria for *adhikāra*? What qualifies one to perform sacrifices? According to the *mīmāṃsā śāstras*, to be eligible to sacrifice one must be a married member of one of the three *varṇas* (*brāhmaṇa*, *kṣatriya*, or *vaiśya*); have the appropriate time, materials, and means for the sacrifice; be of sound mind and body; and have a desire for the fruits of the ritual action.[8] Of these criteria, the *phalotsāha*, or eagerness for the fruits, and *artha*, one's means or wealth, are critical qualifications. The former constitutes an internal qualification and refers to an individual who wants to attain the particular benefit that accrues to the specific ritual to be performed (JM 6.1.4); the latter is an external qualification and has to do with the wealth that is needed to perform sacrifices (JM 6.1.39–40). Jaimini explains that since wealth (*dravya*) is not necessarily a permanent condition, it cannot be a condition for eligibility; in other words, a person cannot be disqualified from performing a ritual on the basis of poverty. However, Jaimini does acknowledge that although secondary to the actions of the ritual, material wealth (*dravya*) is still necessary for the performance and efficacy of the ritual.[9]

This raises a question pertinent to women's eligibility, or *adhikāra*, to perform sacrifices: did women have the wealth or material goods that could be used for the sacrifice? One prima facie position argues that women, along with *śūdras*, are barred as potential performers of sacrifice on the basis of their lack of personal property (6.1.10–11). Two main arguments respond to this position. The first is based on evidence that women did have property (6.1.16–17). The second position, which is elucidated by Clooney (1990), argues that one cannot be barred from the performance of a sacrifice because of factors that pertain to secondary matters such as materials (*dravya*); exclusion from eligibility should be based on the primary factors of the ritual, namely, action. In this chapter, we are primarily concerned with the first argument, which is gender based. We will come back to this concern about women's ownership shortly, but first let us conclude our review of the qualifications of *adhikāra*.

In addition to these criteria, there are also certain prerequisites and competencies that the potential sacrificer must have. As a prerequisite, one must have the right to own the fruits of the sacrifice. For example, sovereignty can be possessed only by kings, and thus one who is not of the kingly class is ineligible to perform those rituals that accrue sovereignty (cf. MNP 225–26; AS 48). This prerequisite further qualifies our understanding of the *phalotsāha*, namely, that having the desire for a particular outcome is not enough to establish one's right to perform the ritual; rather, in addition, one must be eligible to own the fruit. In the case of sovereignty, ownership is determined by class (*kṣatriya*), which is hereditary. Yet desire and eligibility are still not enough to qualify one to sacrifice and be the beneficiary of its fruits; one must also be competent to complete the ritual. According to the *adhikāra* tradition, competence is gained through (1) knowledge, and specifically knowledge gained from studying the Vedas; (2) the kindling and possession of sacred fires; and (3) capacity, or *śakti*; that is, one must have the physical, intellectual and financial capacity to perform the required acts (cf. AS 49; JM 6.1.35; SB 1.4.30). Since the kindling and possession of the sacred fires are associated with the householder stage of life, those who are not married would be considered incompetent to perform the ritual sacrifice. So, to summarize, a potential sacrificer should be

- A married householder of one of the upper three classes who maintains the sacred fires
- In possession of wealth and good health
- Versed in the Vedas, especially those pertaining to the rites and mantras
- Desirous of the fruits of the sacrifice and eligible to possess them

Although these criteria exclude a priori certain individuals on the basis of class, they do not exclude on the basis of gender. Thus, based on this initial set of criteria, one could conclude that women do have *adhikāra*, although some doubts have been raised.

Doubts Raised about the *Adhikāra* of Women

The *saṃśaya* section of a *mīmāṃsā* investigation involves voicing doubts or problems related to the subject. The first challenge to the decision that women have *adhikāra* is an observation that the rules and discussion regarding eligibility are all formulated in the masculine gender. This observation suggests that women must therefore be excluded as potential sacrificers.

The second challenge is the question of whether or not women have the property that gives them the means (*artha*) to sacrifice. This question relates to a previous contention of whether it is necessary to have property (*dravya*) in order to sacrifice. This particular question is compounded by the cultural and religious issue of whether women are themselves property, that is, the property of men. (See Jamison's relevant discussion in this volume on the dilemma of women as property and as givers of property.) The prima facie position represented in Jaimini maintains that since women are sold as brides, they are a kind of property (JM 6.1.20).

The two reservations concerning the resolution that women do have *adhikāra* are of different kinds: one is a question of semantics, the other a legal issue. The *mīmāṃsakas* require an investigation into and representation of the different points of view on these matters before a final resolution is presented; this forms the *pūrvapakṣa* and *uttarapakṣa* sections of the discussion. Before I examine the preliminary and counter positions on these questions of semantics, I think it is important to point out that no doubts are raised by Jaimini or Śabara about (1) issues of purity and impurity; (2) the inherent nature of women (*strīsvabhāva*); or (3) (lack of) access to or knowledge of the Vedas. I cannot emphasize this point enough. All three of these concerns are the basis of later arguments used in the authoritative texts to exclude women from ritual activity. It is noteworthy that these issues do not even raise an eyebrow of doubt among the *mīmāṃsakas* in their discussions about women's eligibility to perform sacrifices. I will come back to this point in my conclusion. I now turn to the debates over gender semantics and women as property owners.

Contested Issues Concerning Women's *Adhikāra*

The Gender Issue Debated

> *Pūrvapakṣa*: The text is in the male gender, thus women are excluded.
>
> *Uttarapakṣa*: Gender is not relevant here since no distinction is made on the basis of gender. Furthermore, women desire heaven as much as men do so they have the right to sacrifice.

The opposing or prima facie position states that women are excluded from sacrificing because the masculine gender is used in reference to the agent of the sacrifice in the textual prescription that defines and confers *adhikāra* (JM 6.1.6). Jaimini raises an objection (*uttarapakṣa*) to this conclusion and argues that if an action is enjoined in the text (*śruti*), it should be performed (JM 6.1.9). This *sūtra* is further qualified by Śabara, who explains: "Where it is said that a person desirous of heaven should perform a sacrifice, it includes both male and female though the nominative is in the masculine gender."

An even earlier text, the *Kātyāyana Śrauta Sūtra*, also supports Jaimini's position. In its opening discussion on *adhikāra* for Vedic rituals, the *Kātyāyana Śrauta Sūtra* concludes that persons belonging to the upper three *varṇas* are eligible, whereas eunuchs, *śūdras*, the maimed, and those who do not study the Vedas (*aśrotriya*) are disqualified (KSS 1.2.5–6). The text indicates that since there is no specification (*viśeṣāt*) of who among the three classes is eligible, women are included in the general ruling that confers eligibility. In contrast, by specifying the three classes of *brāhmaṇa*, *kṣatriya*, and *vaiśya*, it is understood that *śūdras* are excluded from this privilege. Evidence to support women's eligibility is supplied in KSS 1.1.8, which attests that women are seen to be participating in the ritual (*darśanāc ca*). Yet the opposing point of view in the *Mīmāṃsā Sūtra* is concerned more with semantics than physical evidence, and the question asked is especially pertinent to historians who work with religious texts and scriptures, which are usually written in the masculine gender: are we to take the use of the masculine gender as including or excluding women? Jaimini specifically argues that in this case the masculine gender is inclusive of the feminine (JM 6.1.8). Commentators such as Śabara cite Bādarāyaṇa in support of Jaimini's position and share with him the opinion that since a class is referred to without any further distinctions (*jātyarthasyāviśeṣatvāt*), women are also included (*strīyāpi pratiyeta*).

Jaimini's position is further supported by significant rules of Sanskrit grammar. In his second-century B.C.E. *Mahābhāṣya*, Patañjali discusses the importance of learning grammar (*vyākaraṇa*) for the sake of preserving the Vedas (see *Mahābhāṣya* 1.1.1). He notes that among other things, from the study of grammar one learns the rules concerning the modification (*ūha*) of case and gender affixes; this was especially important for the recitation of Vedic mantras. Since mantras are not given in cases to suit every gender and context, one needs to know how and when to modify the mantra accordingly.[10] "[Mantras] have to be used in different genders and cases during the performance of sacrifices. A man who does not know grammar is not able to use their forms with changed gender and case-affixes where necessary. It is therefore essential to make a study of grammar."

Pāṇini, India's ancient and most influential grammarian, also provides guidelines for cases in which the masculine gender incorporates the feminine. In *Aṣṭādhyāyī* 1.2.67, Pāṇini provides this rule: "When a word in the masculine gender is used together with a word in the feminine gender, the word in the masculine gender is the sole remaining, provided that the difference between them consists only in that (i.e., only in their gender)."[11] In particular, this rule is invoked in cases of plurality. The *Kāśikā* commentary on Pāṇini gives an example of the plural form (in this case dual) for a dog (*kukkuṭaḥ*) and a bitch (*kukkuṭī*), namely, *kukkuṭau*. Another example from the *Siddhāntakaumudī* is that of *haṃsau*, or geese, used to speak of a goose (*haṃsī*), and a gander (*haṃsaḥ*). In these cases one gender is used to refer to groups of mixed gender within a single genus.

We must ask ourselves how representative and widely accepted was and is this interpretation of Jaimini, for it could have significant implications and relevance for our rereading of Vedic and Hindu texts and the implied inclusion of women. Julia Leslie discusses this question briefly in her treatment of Tryambaka's eighteenth-century *Strīdharmapaddhati*.[12] She notes that Tryambaka took the position that "general rules (*sāmanyadharmāḥ*) prescribed for men are equally applicable to women," partly out of necessity, because few rulings concerning such matters as daily duties and hygiene pertained specifically to women. More important is Leslie's observation that "Tryambaka feels free to invoke the *ūha* of gender when its suits him to do so without any fear of the logical consequences" (p. 43). Somewhere and somehow, between the time of Jaimini and that of Tryambaka, the rule of *ūha* ceased to be invoked as pertaining to gender, and the *adhikāra* of women as ritual practitioners became increasingly limited and denied. As Leslie observes, "In all kinds of ritual contexts, the male is invariably taken as the paradigm. . . . In theory, a woman can invoke the *ūha* of gender; in practice, it is assumed that ritual information is really intended for the male" (p. 43). So, theoretically, even legally, women shared certain rights and privileges with men; however, these rights and legal loopholes were eclipsed by customs, traditions, and practices that not only denied women autonomous agency as ritual performers but also denied them access to many of the component parts of rituals. Because practice and custom are defining authorities in interpreting Hindu law, the practice of denying women ritual rights or access to certain rites eventually took on the weight of law.

What we see is that later texts and commentaries increasingly take the position of the *pūrvapakṣa*, arguing against the *adhikāra* of women. However, their supporting arguments do not use as evidence the fact that the text conferring *adhikāra* is in the masculine form (perhaps they are afraid to do battle with the influential and time-proven rules of Pāṇinian grammar). Rather, the doubts that are raised in later texts have more to do with women's access to Vedic learning. For example, when Āpadeva, in his seventeenth-century *Mīmāṃsānyāyaprakāśa*, discusses the denial of *adhikāra* to *śūdras* on the basis that they lack knowledge of the Vedas, an objector counters, "Then a woman has no *adhikāra*, as she is [also] forbidden to study the Veda" (MNP 1.232). Clearly, this represents a significant change in the dominant, orthodox position concerning women's involvement in religious and ritual matters from that of the time of Jaimini. The disqualification of women on the basis of lack of knowledge of the Vedas is not argued by Jaimini, though he does use this argument to exclude *śūdras* from the performance of sacrifice. We may infer from this that women in Jaimini's time did study and have access to Vedic knowledge; a similar inference can be drawn from the Tamil commentator Tirukkōnēri Dāsyai, whose work is discussed by Vasudha Narayanan in this volume. On the other hand, Śabara, who provides a later commentary on Jaimini, does emphasize the disability of women because of their ignorance of the Vedas.

The Property Issue Debated

Pūrvapakṣa: Women as potential performers are barred on the basis of lack of personal property and materials. Since women are bought and sold as brides, they themselves are property and cannot own property. Therefore, they are not entitled to sacrifice.

Uttarapakṣa: Women do possess wealth and have the wherewithal to sacrifice. Furthermore, though a bride-price may be given, this is just a convention; it does not mean that the woman is a commodity.

The second argument made against women's *adhikāra* is based on the position that women have no independent property and thus are not entitled to sacrifice. Among the evidence in support of this position is the reference to the sale of women at the time of marriage (JM 6.1.10, 19). Jaimini opposes this conclusion and argues that women do have the wherewithal to sacrifice as they do possess *artha* or wealth (JM 6.1.14, 16). He further explains that the sale of women is only a religious formality (*dharmamātra*) and does not infer that women themselves are commodities. In commenting on this *sūtra* of Jaimini, Śabara cites a verse from *Taittirīya Saṃhitā*: "A wife is certainly the mistress of the household furniture; he makes an offering with the wife's permission" (6.2.1.1).

The *pūrvapakṣa* position wants to understand wealth as personal property and not as material owned or shared in common by a husband and wife; it is argued that women not only lack personal property but also are property themselves (*dravya*) since they are bought and sold as brides (JM 6.1.10, 19). The conclusion reached is that women are in the same position as other material properties (*dravya*) used in the sacrifice. An issue related to this is inheritance: if women themselves are property, they cannot own property, and thus they are not entitled to inherit.

Women's Property and Women's Inheritance

Property What does not enter early arguments (e.g., those in Kātyāyana, Jaimini, and Śabara) about women as owners is a discussion of *strīdhana*, the property and inheritance of women, a topic of more relevance to the Dharma Śāstras. It is possible that

Jaimini's claim that women do possess wealth was in reference to *strīdhana*, though he does not specifically refer to it. In one of its earliest usages (cf. Gautama 28, 24–26), as well as in a general context, *strīdhana* refers to a woman's estate, or any property belonging to a woman. Some authors of the Sūtras and Śāstras are often more specific in their definitions of *strīdhana*. Baudhāyana (2.2.3.43) understands *strīdhana* as the ornaments a woman inherits from her mother; Āpastamba (1.6.14.9) includes ornaments and wealth received or inherited from a woman's family; Kauṭilya equates *strīdhana* with *śulka*, a fee given to a bride at her marriage over which she had complete control.[13] Later texts separate the notion of *strīdhana*, the personal property of women, from *śulka*, the bride-price. In the Kātyāyana and Jīmūtavāhana texts, *strīdhana* is defined as any property that woman may sell, give away, or use, independent of her husband's control.[14] Viśveśvara, a commentator on the *Mitākṣara*, specifies that *strīdhana* includes not only wealth gained from inheritance but also earnings that come from things such as spinning or finding a treasure (*Mitākṣara* 11.11 2.3–4; *Vyavahāra Mayūkha* 4.10). Jagannātha concurs: "The trifle which is received by a woman as the price or reward of household labor, of using household utensils, of keeping beasts of burden, of watching milk cows, or preserving ornaments and dress, and of supervising servants is called her perquisite" (5.9.468).

This is quite different from Manu's view (8.416) that any wealth earned by a wife (or a son or a slave), accrues to the "owner," that is, the husband (father or master). Medhātithi (4.434–35) does not interpret this verse as prohibiting independent ownership by women but rather as meaning that wives, along with sons and slaves, could not dispose of their property independently. Manu provides a sixfold classification of *strīdhana*,[15] but most commentators take his list as illustrative rather than exhaustive. In general, the later the text, the more restricted is the interpretation of *strīdhana*. Several texts specify that women cannot be the sole owners of immovable property, inherited property, and objects exceeding 2000 annas; these items must be shared with the husband.[16] Some texts such as the *Mitākṣara* allow a husband to use his wife's *strīdhana* in certain circumstances. Kauṭilya advises that if a husband uses his wife's property for three years and she has not objected, the wife loses any claim to that property (3.2.17–18). Kauṭilya explains, "The purpose of giving women the right to own property is to afford protection [for them] in case of calamity" (3.2.34); this principle, it seems, would not support women who are using their property for ritual sacrifice. This interpretation is supported by another rule of Kauṭilya which specifically allows a husband to use his wife's property for the performance of religious rituals, whereas a previous verse restricts the woman's use of her *strīdhana* to maintenance of her family if a husband leaves without making provisions for that maintenance (3.1.16–18).

Yet even with the various restrictions and legal opinions applied by different schools of traditional Indian law,[17] there is no doubt that there was a general consensus that women did have rights of ownership to certain kinds of property (usually gifts from her natal family) independent of their husbands (cf. *Mitākṣara* 11.11.2–3). However, hers was a limited estate.[18] The definition of what constituted a woman's estate was belabored by the different legalists in relation to laws of inheritance, and the partition of *strīdhana* has traditionally been one of the stickier points of inheritance law. For example, special laws developed concerning the appropriation of *strīdhana* after a woman's death:[19] "Now, when the mother has died, all the uterine brothers and all the 'umbilical' sisters should share equally in the mother's estate. Something should even be given to the daughters of these daughters out of the estate of their maternal grandmother, through affection and according to their desserts" (Manu 9.192–93; Doniger and Smith, 1991, p. 219). Another text, the *Mitākṣara* (9.124), divides inheritance along gender lines: "Woman's property goes to her daughter because portions of her abound in her female children, and the father's estate goes to his sons because portions of him abound in his male children."

Although some *mīmāṃsakas* and *śāstrīs* may have voiced doubts about a woman's eligibility to sacrifice because of the lack of independent property with which to finance the ritual, there is overwhelming evidence that women did possess some form of property, and thus as a group they could not be disqualified on those grounds. Jaimini goes on to argue that not only do women have the financial means to sacrifice but also that *phalotsāha*, or desire for heaven, as well as for other fruits of the sacrifice, are equally present in men and women. And *phalotsāha* is one of the key criteria that entitles one to the performance of sacrifice (cf. JM 6.1.4).

Inheritance As with *strīdhana*, there is a range of positions on women's right to inherit. Traditional inheritance laws were not uniform, and they varied according to region and school of law.[20] Although there was a consensus among the different schools of law that everyone had a right to sustenance, attitudes toward the division of property, as well as its control, varied. Gautama (28.21) was of the opinion that women could inherit in certain circumstances, whereas Baudhāyana (2.23.46) was unambiguous in his opinion that women may not inherit. Kauṭilya (6.14.4) allows a widow to inherit from her husband's estate until such time as she remarries. Yājñavalkya (2.35), seeking equanimity, said that inheritance was to be divided among children, including married daughters. And Manu (9.187) allowed the same share of inheritance to the wife of the deceased as was allotted to the sons, and he expected the sons to share their portion with their unmarried sisters (9.118). The *Vīramitrodaya* cites several authorities (Nīlakaṇṭha, Vācaspati Miśra, Vidyāraṇya, and Aparārka) who provide arguments in favor of women's right to inherit. Bṛhaspati is quoted by both the *Mitākṣara* (2.2) and the *Dāyabhāga* (9.2.8) as having the following liberal-minded verdict: "The wife is pronounced successor to the wealth of her husband and in her default, the daughters. As a son, so the daughter of the man proceeds from his several limbs. How then when one's self is living in the form of one's daughter can anyone else take the wealth?" However, the *Dāyabhāga* qualifies its position by determining that only those women specifically named in the texts can inherit (and, by way of example, it cites an opinion that daughters, widows, mothers, and paternal grandmothers have a right to inherit the property of paternal grandfathers). Whereas the *Mitākṣara* cites an opinion in support of Manu's position that a widow gets the same shares as a son, it upholds a commonly made technical distinction between inheritance (an equal share) and maintenance (a subsistence allowance) and declares that widows, daughters, and mothers cannot inherit but have a right to maintenance.

The opposing view, that women are incompetent to inherit (as represented by Baudhāyana and Jīmūtavāhana), is interpreted by Vidyāraṇya in a very specific way, which has particular relevance to our discussion of *adhikāra*. Vidyāraṇya takes "incompetent to inherit" as meaning that a woman who retires to the forest once she has been widowed is not entitled to her share of inheritance. He continues: "The term 'Anindriyas' embodies the reason for the same—the Soma juice indeed is the 'Indriya', and 'anindriya' means not entitled to taste the 'Soma juice.'"[21] Here we see a direct connection between inheritance and ritual obligations. Many Smṛti texts link women's incapacity to inherit to their ineligibility to partake in the Soma sacrifices. Inheritance laws were traditionally deduced from opinions on the right to perform sacrifices. Related to this, inheritance had a direct correlation to the performance of *śrāddha* rites, the funeral oblations. Since widows were barred from performing these rites, according to the Smṛtis they were also barred from inheritance. As traditional law evolved, becoming more diversified and sophisticated, the dominant opinions supported a woman's right to inherit, though restrictions applied. To reach this opinion, the legalists had to separate opinions on women's inheritance rights from the contexts of discussions on women's ineligibility to sacrifice.

There were practical reasons why such a distinction had to be made; for example, if a husband was away on a journey, it was the wife's responsibility to continue the *śrauta* sacrifices. Or as the *Trikāṇḍamaṇḍana* observes (1.49): "Should either the husband or wife die while an *iṣṭi*, etc. remains unfinished, the one remaining should perform that sacrifice to completion as prescribed." In a similar vein, the rule commonly cited concerning *smarta* rituals, in this case *vratas*, states:[22]

> If a husband cannot do the *vrata*, his wife may do so, and if a wife cannot complete her *vrata*, the husband should do so for her. If both are unable to do this, the *vrata* is not broken by that. An elder sister who is properly instructed should do it, or a brother. If they are not there, then some other brahmin might do it.

One of the technical problems discussed by ritualists in the Sanskrit texts pertains to employing a substitute for the *śrāddha* (memorial) rites when there is no male heir. In these cases, a daughter or other significant female relative was designated as the *pratinidhi*. A daughter who is recognized as the heir to her father's property, in lieu of any male heirs, is called a *putrikā-putra* and is technically viewed as a son: she inherits his wealth, performs his funeral oblations, keeps his *gotra* and *piṇḍa*, and her son is deemed to be in the lineage of her father rather than of her husband.[23] This last tradition was often of great concern to the husband's family, who was not happy that a son born into its household would serve, ritually and legally, the maternal grandfather's lineage rather than the paternal lineage.

There are numerous citations of women sacrificing alone, either as proxies or in the absence of their husbands, which counter opinions, such as those expressed by Manu, that a woman cannot sacrifice or undertake vows or fasts (Manu 5.155). From these textual references, we can infer that women were (eligible to be) independent and sometimes even sole performers in ritual contexts. However, in most of these examples, the women are completing the rituals in their capacity as proxies (*pratinidhi*), partners (*dharmapatnī*), or designated sons (*putrikā-putra*). In each case, their capacity can be attributed to their relationship to a male relative, particularly a father or husband. To what extent, then, is their *adhikāra* to sacrifice dependent on a significant male relative? Is this a modification of the qualifications for *adhikāra* that is particular to women? We have already seen evidence that women have two of the four key criteria of *adhikāra*, namely, wealth and the desire to possess the fruits of the sacrifice. We have also examined the argument that the masculine agency of the rubric concerning *adhikāra* need not be interpreted as excluding women. What of the other two criteria for *adhikāra*: being versed in the Vedas, and being married and maintaining the sacred fires?

Women's Access to Vedic Knowledge

As previously mentioned, access to the Vedas is not a concern expressed in the *pūrvapakṣa* or the *uttarapakṣa* in Jaimini's *sūtras* on the *adhikāra* of women; however, doubts about the *adhikāra* of *śūdras* are raised by Jaimini concerning their access to the Vedas, and it is because of their exclusion from *upanayana* and Vedic learning that they are denied the eligibility to sacrifice.[24] Women's access to the Vedas, however, does become a contested issue in later texts and a basis for their exclusion from certain religious opportunities and privileges. In the *Mīmāṃsānyāyaprakāśa*, an opponent charges that if a *śūdra* is denied *adhikāra* because of lack of knowledge of the Vedas, then a woman also should be so barred, as she is forbidden to study the Veda (MNP 1.232). The objection is countered by an explanation that a woman, specifically a wife, shares a joint *adhikāra* with her husband (*ato dampatyoḥ sahādhikāraḥ*) since a married couple offer sacrifices jointly (see JM 6.1.17–21). A woman thus has access to the necessary Vedic knowledge to perform the rituals through this joint qualification (MNP 1.233–34). Āpadeva goes on to explain: "However, since the acts which the wife alone performs, such as the inspection of the butter, cannot be performed without (some) knowledge, it is admitted that so much is posited for her by the injunctions covering those (acts)."

We do have inferential evidence that women studied the Vedas and underwent the *upanayana*, although as *brahmavādinīs* they remained within their parental home rather than retreating to the *āśrama* of a teacher. According to Hārīta, the number of *brahmavādinīs* was greatly reduced by the sixth century B.C.E.; increasingly, less amount of time was devoted to Vedic learning as part of the education process of young girls. The *upanayana* ceremony for girls eventually is absorbed into and identified with the marriage *saṁskāra*. Manu explains: "The ritual of marriage [*vivāha*] is traditionally known as the Vedic transformative ritual [*upanayana*] for women; serving her husband is (the equivalent of) living with a guru, and household chores are the rites of the fire." (2.67). Since the *upanayana* is a prerequisite for Vedic learning and the *adhikāra* to sacrifice, the eclipse of this ceremony for girls leads to an exclusion of females from access to Vedic learning and performance of *śrauta* rituals. Since *śūdras* were denied *adhikāra* to sacrifice, even as early as Jaimini, by virtue of their not having an *upanayana*, the ritual status of women comes to be compared to that of *śūdras*. A justification then develops that attributes the exclusion of women from the Vedic learning to issues surrounding their impurity and (corrupt) inherent nature (*svabhāva*). These are not the usual criteria for exclusion from ritual and religious privileges, as detailed by the early scholars and exegetes.

Stephanie Jamison identifies another kind of *upanayana*, which she says "establishes [the wife's] ritual equality with her husband for the purposes at hand," namely, the performance of a *śrauta* sacrifice.[25] This *upanayana* consists of the rite of girding the wife (*patnīsaṃnahana*) prior to the sacrifice, and Jamison quotes this verse from *Taittirīya Brāhmaṇa* as evidence:

> This (yoking) is the initiation (*upanayana*) of the vow of the wife.
> With it he [the priest] initiates her into her vow. (3.3.3.2)

From her scrutiny of Vedic texts, Jamison also presents conclusive evidence that women did know, hear, and often recite the Vedic mantras appropriate to their roles in the *śrauta* rites (pp. 45–47); and although women were excluded from certain rites, they did have knowledge of those rites and mantras that pertained to the rituals they performed with their husbands. We must remind ourselves that neither the wife nor the husband was knowledgeable in all the details of the special-occasion rituals, for which they relied on the expertise of specially trained priests, but there is no reason to expect that women had any less knowledge of the rites and mantras of the daily sacrifices than did their husbands. If we were to use contemporary ethnographic evidence to provide some insight into the store of ritual knowledge in the past, it would not be hard to argue that women have long been primary sources of the technicalities of ritual, especially those that occur on a regular basis.

Maintenance of the Sacred Fires

> Women were created to be mothers and men to be fathers; religious rites therefore are ordained in the Veda to be performed by the husband together with his wife.

This verse, from Manu 9.96, supports the view that the performance of sacrifice, along with the maintenance of the sacred fires, was a joint responsibility of the husband and wife. Jaimini states succinctly that the husband and wife are the *svāmī* (owners and masters) of the sacrifice. As such, a husband and wife should sacrifice together.[26] At the time of marriage, the husband and wife become partners in *dharma* (cf. Śabara on JM 6.1.18). This verse from the *Bṛhaspati Saṃhitā* is similar to many found in authoritative texts, which expound on the marital relationship: "A wife is considered half the body of her husband, equally sharing the results of his good or wicked deeds" (24.11). Jamison quotes this passage from the *Mānava Śrauta Sūtra* which elaborates specifically on the newly married couple's ritual responsibilities and their impact on the wife:[27]

> This couple comes together mutually; together they establish the fires; together they produce offspring . . .
> Therefore she is half-sharer (in the ritual).
> Women are fit for ritual. The wife is half-sharer in the ritual of the Sacrificer. (8.23.10)

There is clear evidence in the Vedas that women had a role in the sacrificial rituals:[28] they chanted *sāma* songs, pounded the sacrificial rice, bathed the animals to be sacrificed, and laid the bricks for the sacrificial altar. Along with their husbands, wives prepared the sacrificial offerings, kindled the sacred fires, offered oblations, recited ritual formulas, and performed the concluding ceremonies. If a husband had to take leave before a sacrifice was concluded, a wife continued it. One of the most convincing pieces of evidence for a women's independent agency as a ritual actor is highlighted by Jamison, who persuasively argues that the daily and special-occasion oblations of a pious widow, as described in *Śrauta Sūtra* (8.23)—which are offered to a fire that is derived from those that she had first kindled with her husband—although construed as *gṛhya* rites (and therefore more appropriate to be accessed and performed by women) are indeed "śrauta analogues" and constitute for the widow a kind of "shadow śrauta ritual life."[29] The necessity of this shadow *śrauta* life is a result of the fact that as a widow she was not permitted to remarry, whereas widowers were allowed to remarry and could reestablish their *śrauta* fires and ritual lives anew with a new wife. And one of the key criteria that makes one eligible for the performance of Vedic sacrifice is the status of being a married householder. So, presumably a widower who does not remarry does not possess the *adhikāra* to sacrifice.

A Preliminary Conclusion: *Adhikāra* Modified for Women

In the *mīmāṃsā* texts, as we have seen, the discussion of women's entitlement to perform rituals is primarily concerned with the following two issues:

1. Whether masculine gendered statements included women
2. Whether women have a right to ownership

Arguments are offered to support negative and affirmative positions on these two issues, but the *nirṇaya,* or conclusion, is that women do indeed have the *adhikāra* to perform sacrifices. However, particular conditions qualify her eligibility and performance: she must have a husband and she must sacrifice with him. Although the general criteria for *adhikāra* implicitly includes being married, even for a man (who must be a maintainer of sacred fires, a responsibility that comes with marriage and householdership), the requirement of marriage is specifically stated only in reference to women in the *mīmāṃsā śāstras*. However, the *Taittirīya Brāhmaṇa* in several places underscores the expectation, if not the necessity, of marriage for the male sacrificer.[30] "He who has no wife is indeed without sacrifice" (TB 2.2.2.6). Both are needed to perform the ritual, and thus the fruits of the ritual accrue to both.

What becomes apparent in much of these exegetical discussions is that the *adhikāra* of a husband and wife is joint. This somewhat technical passage from the *Mīmāṃsānyāyaprakāśa* (233) elaborates on this.

> [A woman] is qualified, but not independently, since that is forbidden by such sentences as "A woman does not merit independence." Also because if she could act independently (in sacrificing), then certain subsidiary elements in both (her husband's, and her own independent) sacrificial performances would be lacking. For in the (male) sacrificer's performance the inspection of the butter and other things which are done by the wife would fail, and in the wife's rite the inspection of the butter, etc. (which would in that case have to be) done by the (male) sacrificer would fail. Therefore there is joint qualification for a married couple. Because of this joint qualification, through the sacrificer's knowledge simply his wife also can act, and it does not follow that she is disqualified for want of knowledge. And moreover the sentence "But from marriage there is common sharing in (sacrificial) actions and in the fruits of merit" assures qualification to a woman . . .

All of this posturing on the part of the ritual legalists demonstrates simultaneously the necessity of women in the performance and the continuation of the *śrauta* sacrifices, as well as the patriarchal tradition's discomfort with giving women absolute control or authority over such organs of power.[31] This brings me back to my opening remark that guarding power and authority in Vedic and brahminical times involved tight control over rituals and their access because rituals were viewed as sources of great power. This manipulation through the control of rituals and ritual knowledge has continued throughout Hindu religious history, even with the deemphasis on rituals found in the Upaniṣads and in some later *bhakti* traditions. The locus of this control has primarily rested with brahmin male priests, whose livelihood is certainly threatened these days (if not since medieval times or earlier) by the number of women who have asserted—not just within the domestic sphere, but publicly as well—their ritual knowledge and expertise and are performing rituals, both Vedic and *smarta*, for themselves and for other women and men.

What is particularly striking to me in this investigation and its focus on ancient texts is that the concerns about women's purity, inherent nature (*strīsvabhāva*), and knowledge of the Vedas are not issues of doubt (*saṃśaya*) for someone like Jaimini concerning women's qualifications to perform rituals. This, I think, is significant, for women's impurity and their lack of access to and knowledge of the Vedas are key arguments in later texts for denying women ritual access and ritual responsibilities. This suggests, along with much additional evidence about the wife's participation in *śrauta* rituals drawn from even older texts (as documented particularly by Jamison), that in different contexts and in different times women's access to and authority within the ritual were more publicly acknowledged, respected, and needed.

The Relevance of This Subject

Let us now concern ourselves with the implications of these textual debates and evidence for matters pertaining to rituals currently performed by many women in India, such as *vratas*, *pūjās*, *homas*, *yajñas*, and *śrāddhas*. Again, if we took ethnographic evidence alone to measure women's power within and contribution to the ritual realm, we could easily do so without turning to any Sanskrit texts. Yet too often such evidence is labeled folk practice, leading many to conclude that whereas women may perform folk rituals, they have no ritual authority within the elite and orthodox brahminical tradition. I argue that women did and do have ritual rights within Vedic and brahminical traditions, though these rights have often been contested. Furthermore, evidence is found to support this position in both ancient textual traditions and contemporary practice. Despite this evidence, we continue to hear the same old textual passages invoked against the ritual authority of women, and they are quoted by many Western scholars who lecture about Hinduism and its suppression of women, as well as by many Indian pandits who object to women's performance of *yajñas* and *pūjās*. As I have tried to show here, and as is evident in the many textual references in Jamison's *Sacrificed Wife/Sacrificer's Wife*, ample verses from these same authoritative texts provide different kinds of evidence and provoke different or perhaps more nuanced historical interpretations of the ritual rights, access, and authority of women in Vedic, brahminical and Hindu traditions.

The question of *adhikāra* posed and discussed by the *mīmāṃsakas* was specifically in reference to *śrauta* rituals, *yajña* in particular. These same mīmāṃsic principles were later applied by the *nibandhakāras* to *smārta* and Purāṇic rituals such as *vrata* and *pūjā*.

What can we learn from this that might help us in our efforts to construct a history of women Indian history, with particular relevance to their religious roles and ritual responsibilities? And how might someone make use of this kind of textual evidence? I offer some preliminary suggestions on further steps that might be taken by scholars, feminists, social activists, or ritual practitioners.

1. We have seen that feminist rereadings of Christian texts and traditions, along with increased historical attention to earlier Christian history and documents, have led some Christian communities to lift the ban on the ordination of women as priests and deacons. Textual studies have found evidence of the authority and sacerdotal roles of women in the early church, which has led to a reclaiming of the authority and ritual status of women. Although there is evidence that Hindu women have long participated in and performed many key Hindu rituals, the dominant brahminical authorities have long denied them legitimate and independent access to these rites. A reexamination of the discussion of women's *adhikāra* in earlier times and texts could be used in contemporary times to bolster their legitimate and authoritative involvement in Hindu rituals (not to mention their rights to equal property and inheritance).[32]
2. Jaimini's argument that the masculine includes the feminine—a perspective elucidated by his commentators and also other grammarians and exegetes—is another point that must be carefully reconsidered and studied in light of current debates about rereading texts to uncover and construct a history of women. This investigation is analogous to questions that have come up about the rereading, as well as translating, of Christian texts. When is the masculine gender used in a generic way and when does it specifically refer to the male gender? If "man" means man and woman, should our translations be gender neutral or gender inclusive? Similarly, how do we know when a Sanskrit masculine nominative includes women and when it refers only to the male? What clues do we look for in the text or in the context? How do we know when an author means to be inclusive or exclusive?
3. The *mīmāṃsā* discussion on the *adhikāra* of women provides evidence that there were increasing restrictions on women and that women's ritual roles began to be eclipsed. The public performance role of women moved into the private sphere of the home, where women continued to perform rituals, although often unseen and unacknowledged by the dominant tradition, which increasingly denied women ritual roles and responsibilities. In contemporary times, Hindu women are again moving into the public sphere as religious practitioners, and questions have arisen about their legitimacy and roles as *pūjārīs*, *brahmacāriṇīs*, *saṃnyāsinīs* and *purohitās*. In Pune in western Maharashtra, young girls are undergoing *upanayana* and married women are performing *yajñas*, and this has generated debates about women's ritual rights, as well as the efficaciousness of these rituals. Women's participation in these rituals is considered unconventional, and counters a long, weighty and authoritative tradition that has denied women these roles. These contemporary practices and the debates surrounding them need closer scrutiny.

There are different ways to read and interpret these authoritative texts, many of which themselves contain conflicting statements about the attitudes toward women. Though the information about women in these brahminical texts is limited and always filtered through male eyes and voices, contemporary scholars, both male and female, in India, Europe, Japan, and North America, are reading these texts with new questions and with additional historical information and comparative data. We are gaining new insights and drawing new inferences from the accumulated evidence we have gathered about women from ancient texts and their commentaries. The more public role of women in contemporary times in religious, social, economic, and political realms causes us to ask new questions, and we bring these questions with us to the texts, which in turn often leads to a rereading or reinterpretation of the texts, as well as of history.

My purpose here is not to argue that ritual authority for women should be claimed on the basis of some ancient textual evidence, though certainly such evidence could be used and manipulated to claim such power and respect, just as other evidence has been used to build the exclusive authority of male brahmin priests in certain contexts and histories. My point rather is to show that these issues have always been debated, and the construal, articulation and outcome of that debate is contextually sensitive to the politics of the time. Despite Jaimini's clear argument that women had *adhikāra* to perform Vedic rituals, we see women's *adhikāra* eclipsed in the texts and times that follow. To say that Jaimini was a feminist might be attributing to him a political position that he did not choose; rather it is possible that the debate on women's *adhikāra* as presented by Jaimini represents a historical reality about women's privileges during his time or in his region; if so, that evidence should be used to counter many contemporary arguments that women in the Vedic and Hindu traditions never had the rights or privileges that were conducive to sharing or asserting authority and power.

The arguments presented here are deliberately technical, limited, and theoretical, in that they respond to counterarguments that are similarly limited by their boundedness to orthodox texts and technical terminology pertaining to legal and ritual issues in the brahminical tradition. The point of this academic exercise is to demonstrate how a different argument can be made from these same "authoritative" texts, depending on the evidence that is compiled and presented. Although some may choose to dismiss altogether the authority and hegemony of these texts, particularly when it comes to asserting a subaltern perspective, others find that alternative perspectives are represented in the multiple voices and sources brought to bear on a particular argument. Drawing out these alternative positions—sometimes subtle, other times unpopular—is more than just an academic exercise; it has political implications as well. For although this chapter has focused on the *adhikāra* of women in the religious and ritual circles of brahminical Hinduism, it is relevant and consequential that *adhikāra* is the Indic term used in contemporary India for human rights, where gender justice is a significant concern in human rights discourse.

Notes

1. *Nibandhas* such as the seventeenth-century *Nirṇayasindhu* of Kamalākara and eighteenth-century *Dharmasindhu* of Kāśīnātha are the standing authorities for the contemporary performance of many traditional brahminical rituals, and I am concerned with how these textual authorities address the *adhikāra* of women and how they might be drawn on to support or contest the ritual agency of Hindu women. The compilers of these texts—*nibandhakāras*—were usually trained in *mīmāṃsā*, and they apply mīmāṇsic categories, questions, and logic to discussion on such subjects as *vrata-adhikāra*, that is, who is eligible to perform regimens of domestic asceticism (*vratas*).

2. The dates of Jaimini are unknown. Scholars have placed him anywhere between the fourth and second centuries B.C.E. Śabara's *Prapañcahṛdaya*, better known as the *Śabarabhāṣya*, is the

earliest extant commentary on Jaimini's *Mīmāṃsā Śūtra*, but Śabara's dates are also unverified (Ganganath Jha, *The Prābhākara School of Pūrva Mīmāṃsa*, Delhi: Motlal Banarsidass, 1978, places him in the middle of the first century B.C.E.). This extensive commentary has greatly elucidated subsequent interpretations of Jaimini. Kumārilabhaṭṭa is another well-known commentator on the *Mīmāṃsā Sūtra* (and *Śabarabhāṣya*) and it is really because of his discussion of metaphysical principles concerning the *mīmāṃsā* system that *mīmāṃsā* evolved from a school of hermeneutics and ritual exegesis to a philosophical school. Placed during the seventh century, his key works include the *Ślokavārttikaa*, *Tantravārttika*, and *Tupṭīkā*. Prabhākaramiśra, alleged to be a student of Kumārila, is the third of the most influential scholars of *mīmāṃsā*; he also wrote commentaries on the *Śabarabhāṣya*, one known as the *Laghvī*, the other *Bṛhatī*. Despite their teacher-student relationship, they differed on a substantial number of points so that two schools of *mīmāṃsā* developed, based on their differing interpretations. There are many subsequent commentaries on the works of all three of these *mīmāṃsākas*.

3. This text is a commentary on *Āpastamba Śrauta Sūtra* and is of interest to our discussion because of its concern with such topics as *adhikāra* and *pratinidhi* (substitutes). Bhāskara Miśra's dates overlap with those of Hemādri (thirteenth century) and Lakṣmīdhara (twelfth century), both prolific *nibandhakāras*, who wrote large compendia on *vratas*.

4. This text is often called by its informal name, *Āpadevī*.

5. The full name of this treatise is the *Pūrvamīmāṃsārthasaṃgraha* and it is remarkably similar in content and language to the *Mīmāṃsānyāyaprakāśa* of Āpadeva.

6. Kamalākarabhaṭṭa was from a family well known for its erudition in the *mīmāṃsā* system.

7. Some *mīmāṃsākas* call the fourth step *siddhānta* and the fifth or final step *saṃgati*, referring to the relevance of the topic to the particular context, or *nirṇaya*, meaning "decision" or "conclusion." The respondent to the prima facie position is often named the *siddhāntin* in pertinent discussions.

8. Cf. JM 6.1.25–38; SB on JM 1.4.30; AS 48; MNP 227–28, 231.

9 Jaimini infers that a poor person can be motivated by the promised fruits of a ritual to obtain the goods necessary for its performance (JM 6.1.40).

10. Patañjali, *Vyākaraṇa-Mahābhāsya*, K. V. Abhyankar and J. M. Shukla, trans. (Poona: Bhandakar Oriental Research Institute, 1974), 1.1.1, p. 8.

11. See *Aṣṭādhyāyī* 1.2.64–71 for a fuller discussion, with additional examples, of this grammatical rule.

12. *The Perfect Wife; The Orthodox Hindu Woman According to the Strīdhamapaddhati of Tryambakayajvan* (Delhi: Oxford University Press, 1989), pp. 39–43.

13. According to the *Madanaratna*, *Smṛticandrikā*, *Vīramitrodaya*, *Vyavahāra Mayūkha*, and other *dharma-nibandhas*, *śulka* refers to the price paid by the groom for the objects that a bride brings to the marriage and to their joint household, such as household utensils, cattle, and ornaments.

14. Jīmūtavāhana's *Dāyabhāga* 4.1.18 and Kātyāyana as cited in *Smṛticandrikā* 9.1.6–9.

15. "A woman's property is traditionally regarded as of six sorts: what was given in front of the (marriage) fire, on the bridal procession, or as a token of affection, and what she got from her brother, mother, or father. In addition, any subsequent gift and whatever her affectionate husband might give her should become the property of her children when she dies, (even) during her husband's lifetime" (Manu 9:194–95; *Laws of Manu*, Doniger and Brian K. Smith, Trans., London: Penguin, 1991, 219). Cf. *Yàjñavalkya* 11.143 and *Viṣṇu Smṛti* 17.18, which have a similar list but add *adhivedanikā*, or compensation to a superseded wife, to this list.

16. Cf. *Vyavahāra Mayūkha*, *Smṛticandrikā* 9.1.6–10. The *Vyavahāra Mayūkha* explains that *strīdhana* consists of *saudāyika*, the property of a woman that has been given to her by an affectionate relative and property other than *saudāyika*, largely immovable property. Although a wife has full control of *saudāyika*-type property, other property, such as land, is subject to her husband's

control. This distinction is especially important for the laws that govern inheritance. See *Vyavahāra Mayūkha* 4.10.18, 24–27.

17. Two of the most influential schools of traditional law are the Mitākṣara school, widely followed in the Deccan, and the Dāyabhāga school, followed in the Bengali region. The Mitākṣara school includes four divisions: Bombay, Banaras, Madras and Mithila.

18. The Hindu Succession Act of 1956, which is largely based on the *Mitākṣara* and greatly influenced by British law, abolished the concept of a woman's limited estate and stated that all property owned by a Hindu woman was her absolute property. Yet, as pointed out in a discussion of this act in the March–April 1990 issue of *Manushi*, the act, which was meant "to create a uniform codified law for all Hindus and to give women equal rights in inheritance in accordance with the constitutional guarantee of nondiscrimination between sexes before the law," neither gave women equal rights nor provided for adequate protection of the limited rights that were conferred on women. For example, one of the problems with favoring the Mitākṣara school led to a ruling that meant that women did not inherit ancestral property as men did, a significant change from the traditional laws that gave women "certain inalienable rights in ancestral property" (pp. 8–9).

19. See Yājñavalkya 2.115, Manu 9.118, and Vasiṣṭha 17.46.

20. For example, "Females are included as heir to this kind of property [inheritance by succession] by almost all schools of Mitākṣara law, but some schools recognize more categories of females than do others. Under the Bengal, Benaras and Mithila schools, only five females can succeed as heirs to a male, namely, his wife, his daughter, his mother, his father's mother, and his father's father's mother. The Madras school recognises, in addition, the son's daughter, daughter's daughter, and the sister as heirs. The Bombay school, which is, in many respects the most liberal to women, recognises a number of other female heirs, including a half-sister, father's sister, and women married in to the family, such as stepmother, son's widow, brother's widow, and also many other females classified as bandhus." See Madhu Kishwar and Ruth Vanita, "Inheritance Rights for Women: A Response to Some Commonly Expressed Fears," *Manushi* 57 (March–April 1990), 3.

21. Madhu Shastri, *Status of Hindu Women: A Study of Legislative Trends and Judicial Behaviour* (Jaipur: RBSA Publishers, 1990), p. 37; quoting from Gopal Sarka Shastri, *The Law of Inheritance in Vīramitrodaya*, Calcutta, 1879.

22. From the *Garuḍa Purāṇa*, cited by Raghunandana in the *vratatattva* section of his *Smṛtitattva*, 2.152.

23. Sometimes her name was changed to that of a male.

24. See MNP, 1.228–231.

25. *Sacrificed Wife/Sacrificer's Wife: Women, Ritual, and Hospitality in Ancient India* (New York: Oxford University Press, 1996), p. 46. In her discussion of this rite of girding, Jamison offers a very convincing counterargument to one put forth by Frederick Smith, "India's Curse, Varuṇa's Noose, and the Suppression of the Woman in the Vedic Srauta Ritual" in *Roles and Rituals for Hindu Women*, Julia Leslie, Ed. (Delhi: Motilal Banarsidass, 1992), pp. 42–48, in which he interprets this rite as one that decreases a woman's participation, responsibility, and independence.

26. See Śabara on JM 6.1.18–19.

27. Of particular relevance to our discussion here is Part III of Jamison's book *Sacrificed Wife*, which focuses on "The Wife in Ritual," with its numerous textual references.

28. Jamison's book provides a good bit of this evidence; however, she does not directly address the question of the *adhikāra* of women, though much of the evidence she brings to her other arguments can be used in support of arguments for the ritual rights (*adhikāra*) of women, as I have demonstrated here.

29. Jamison, *Sacrificed Wife*, pp. 36–37.

30. See *Taittirīya Brāhmaṇa* 2.2.2.6; 2.9.4.7, 6.3.10.5.

31. Jamison's comment after highlighting some of the ritual restraints pertaining to women in the contexts of certain Vedic rituals is that "the wife's scope of actual activity must be restricted, because she embodies danger and 'untruth.'" *Sacrificed Wife*, p. 55.

32. Women's property and inheritance rights have been one of the most debated (and written about) issues in modern Hindu law. The 1995 Supreme Court decision affirming that a widow and daughters of a deceased coparcener have equal rights to his property (along with male heirs) occasioned an editorial in the *Times of India* (November 29, 1995), which observed, "In the cases on which the Supreme Court has ruled in favour of women recently, it must be noted that in almost all instances the court has only insisted on the application of existing legislation." It goes on to point out that practice does not always conform to law; this chapter makes a similar observation about differences between ritual law and ritual practice as they pertain to women's entitlement.

3

Mantras and Miscarriage

Controlling Birth in the Late Vedic Period

LAURIE L. PATTON

A young woman is pregnant for the first time in fourth-century B.C.E. India. She is living in a brahmin family, of the Aśvalāyana lineage, who is faithful to all of the prescriptions outlined for them in the domestic family book, the *Aśvalāyana Gṛhya Sūtra*. Her husband has recently returned from his final period of Vedic studentship and has started householder life. She and her husband keep the family fires according to prescription. He not only knows the domestic rites but also occasionally participates in the public, or *śrauta* rites from the Aśvalāyana tradition of their lineage, according to his priestly role. Her husband is one of the caretakers of the tradition, an intelligent and able student who may be able to, in the course of further Vedic study, continue the illustrious line from which both of their families descend. Her most fervent wish is that she will be able to give birth to another boy like her husband, one who will learn the Vedas, bring prestige to her family, and symbolize the prosperity and auspiciousness of her way of life. About seven months into the pregnancy, she begins to experience pain and to bleed, and she is afraid that she may be undergoing *garbhaśrava*, the loss of the fetus she carries in her womb. What does she do?

Whereas other chapters in this volume focus on portrayals of women as givers and given (Jamison and Findly) or as topics of legal concern (McGee), this chapter focuses on the imaginative and ritual world available to those involved in the rituals for difficult childbirth—both the woman and the brahmin. Such a world is conjured by the mantras of the Ṛg Veda (RV) and the rites that accompany them. If a woman were from such a proper Vedic lineage, her husband would consult all of the specialists in the technological aspects of controlling birth, that is, the controllers of mantras. He would consult someone who knew the right Vedic mantras to counteract this most inauspicious of events—someone who knew the Vidhāna text of Śaunaka. Writing in the fourth century B.C.E., the ancient author Śaunaka, or someone of his school, advocated the recitation of a particular Vedic hymn, 10.162, and a burnt offering in the case of a woman who may miscarry. He did so in a text called the *Ṛg Vidhāna*, a fourth-century B.C.E. work focusing on the canonical *Ṛg Veda* (ca. 1500), the earliest group of religious compositions known to Indologists.

The *Ṛg Vidhāna* is not simply a text that focusus on difficulty in childbirth but also is one that contains for which Ṛgvedic mantra is appropriate in which situation. The Ṛgvedic mantra is usually a single verse dedicated to a particular deity, with a particular purpose in mind—agricultural prosperity, long life, material wealth, sons, and the like. So the *Ṛg Vidhāna* describes a difficult situation—getting lost in the woods, the sudden flight of an unwanted pigeon into one's kitchen, the theft of cows from a rival, the bickering of cowives—and tells us which mantra to recite from the ancient text to solve the problem. It would be the equivalent of a text that told us which verse from the Psalms or the New Testament to recite when in the same situation.

As the *Vidhāna* states, if the Ṛgvedic hymn 10.162 is properly recited and the rite performed correctly, a fetus will be born alive. What is the imagery of *Ṛg Veda* 10.162? The hymn consists of a rather plaintive appeal to a form of Agni that drives away demons—in this case, the flesh-eating demon called *ámīvā*. That the plaintive tone alone of this hymn might cause one to think that it would be powerful enough to prevent *garbhaśrava*—literally, the gushing forth of an embryo.

Yet the miscarrying young wife and her husband would not have stopped with only this Ṛgvedic hymn. The *Vidhāna* tells us that other Ṛgvedic hymns should be employed for the same purpose: RV 5.78, the hymn to the *ṛṣi* Saptavadhri, who was childless, and RV 1.101, the hymn to Indra to drive away the "outsider" people of Kṛṣnagarbhā. Her husband, who knows the language of the Ṛgvedic scriptures, is puzzled: these other prescriptions of hymns seem very strange indeed. Their content doesn't seem to have much to do with miscarriage at all. The first hymn, *Ṛg Veda* 5.78, although relevant to the subject of embryos, seems to be an obscure choice since it is not used in any of the rituals of either the śrauta (public) or the gṛhya (domestic) traditions that he performs on a regular basis in his worship. The second hymn, *Ṛg Veda* 1.101, seems to have a mistaken etymology, in which *garbha* is misunderstood as "embryo" and is not the name of a people.

But time is running out: the specialist priest says that the correct mantras must be recited to stop the bleeding. They are recited, the rite is successful, and at a later moment the husband engages the senior priest in a debate about these Vedic mantras. This might well be an earlier version of the debates about the role of women, mantras, and om, which Katherine Young describes in the context of Śrīvaiṣṇava debates elsewhere in this volume. In the Vedic world, how is he to understand this odd mobilization of textual resources?

When it comes to the study of ancient India, womb and embryo imagery has received a lot of attention. Historians of Indian culture take it as an overall image of the larger, sexual symbolism that makes up the imagery of the sacrifice, and it is later transposed onto the temple architecture in the inner chamber that houses the image. Feminist historians of religion (some rightly and some wrongly) have focused on it as a generally positive indication that something of the feminine survives in the imagery of the sacrifice and that some celebration of fertility is in fact part of the more public, solemn rites. (Most recently, among many examples, is Kartikeya Patel's article on using traditional Vedic categories as a form of feminist philosophy.[1]) All of this is well known. Yet very few studies have been done on the imagery of the loss of embryos—specifically the imagery of abortion and miscarriage. Indeed, if we follow the old dictum "You don't know what you've got till it's gone," a study of the imagery of the loss of an embryo can give us some notion of what was understood to be "there" in the first place.

In this chapter I will argue that in tracing some of the history of the symbolic construction of *garbhaśrava* and related imagery, we see a movement from the concrete, maternal meaning (wherein the embryo is referred to as part of the mother, and therefore something that the mother might lose) to a symbolic and paternal one (wherein the embryo is a kind of storehouse for sacrificial knowledge, and therefore something that the father might waste or even murder). I will show this first through the increasing language of control employed by the Ṛgvedic commentaries (ending with the *Ṛg Vidhāna*) involving *Ṛg Veda* 10.162 as a set of mantras against miscarriage. Second, I will reconstruct the imaginative universe of the *Ṛg Vidhāna* and analyze what images the brahmin who are offering on behalf of the miscarrying embryo was asked to hold in his mind. We will see that these are images that compare the embryo to the brahmin in quite explicit terms. Third, I will examine briefly the phrase *bhrūṇahan* "embryo killer"; in certain contexts, the term *bhrūṇa* ceases to become a female-identified possession and becomes a word meaning "male brahmin." In the discourse about the loss of a *garbha*, we see the anxiety of loss in a stark transfer of gender imagery.

I want to be very clear at the outset that I will be restricting my analysis in two important ways: first, I will keep, insofar as possible, to an analysis of *garbha* as an embryo and not as its other, more symbolic meanings. Second, I will be following a strictly Vedic commentarial perspective and not delving into the larger and fascinating question of embryology in the *Caraka* and *Suśruta* medical texts.[2]

Because there is not enough space for a long general discussion of *garbha* in Vedic India, it might be well to begin, with some basic points about the Ṛgvedic textual tradition from which *Ṛg Veda* 10.62 emerges. *Garbha* is a body part and, like other body parts, has a deep metaphoric meaning in ancient India. As the linguist and Vedist Tatyana Elizarenkova describes, a basic feature of the vocabulary of the *Ṛg Veda* is the symbolic use of words with a very concrete basic meaning, particularly a small group of wordsthat denote body parts. *Garbha*, along with *cākṣus* "eye," *tvac* "skin," *pṛṣṭhā*; "the back," and many others, is an important example. Some of these words are in fact more frequently used in their symbolic meanings (at the ritual and cosmic levels) than in their basic, literal meanings: "Obviously, no question of polysemy arises, since this is a clear metaphorical transfer of a single basic meaning onto different, but isomorphic levels."[3] *Garbha* is certainly one of these words. Its primary meaning is the concrete one of womb, or embryo, such as in RV 5.78.7: "Like the wind moves the lotus pond all around, so may your embryo (*garbha*) stir" (my translation). Its secondary meaning is that of "fruit," such as RV 3.31.7: "The rock made [its] fruit (*garbha*) ripe for its benefactor"; or "offspring," such as in RV 6.48.5: "He whom the waters, the stones, the trees/feed as offspring (*garbha*) of the cosmic law." Finally, the use of *garbha* in cosmogonic speculations, such as in RV 10.121.1, where it is referred to as the golden germ, is well known. Many Hindu textbooks refer to the creation hymn of the golden embryo and write about the embryo as the cradle of Hindu images in temples.

As Stephanie Jamison states, several Vedic myths and ritual texts identify places of narrowness and darkness as womb substitutes.[4] In many descriptions of the consecration of the sacrificer, skin (*carman*), usually of an antelope, is associated with the birth apparatus (*Aitareya Brāhmaṇa* 1.3). Moreover, in Vedic and epic tales, both the pot and the hollow of earth are also identified as a place of "second birth" after a failed birth, or miscarriage [*Śatapatha Brāhmaṇa* (SBM)1.81; the *Mahābhārata* is the story of Gāndhārī, in particular, 1.14.13; 3.104.118–20]. As we shall see, although the motif of "a second womb" will not be present in the case of a single, miscarrying woman, it is present in the mantras that are recited to *prevent* her miscarriage.

Jamison also provides a detailed discussion of the mythic imagery of failed birth, abortion, and miscarriage in early India. Although her main focus is the Svarbhanu myth, whereby the sun is wounded by Svarbhanu, she also discusses the ways in which the healing of the sun, and its brightening, is compared to a birth process, whereby the caul, or covering, of the embryo is progressively stripped away from the newborn. (*Jaiminīya Brāhmaṇa* (JB) 1.80; 3.3.34.5; 4.3.4.21; *Maitrāyaṇī Saṃhitā* 1.65; *Kāṭhaka Saṃhitā* (KS) 11.5–12.13; 8.5].

Moreover, Jamison connects anxiety about the birth of the sun with the motif of the failed birth of the sun. In one myth *Pañcaviṃśa Brāhmaṇa* (PB) 4.5.9–12; KS 12.6, 13.6; TB 1.2.4.2]. the gods feared the "falling down" of Aditya, or the sun, from the heavenly world, they and secure the sun with reins or fasteners of various kinds. Moreover, the same verbal root to describe the falling down of the sun, *ava pad*, is also used for the miscarriage of an embryo (TS) 5.1.6–7; JB 1.306]). In the case of the falling-down embryo, the umbilical cord is sometimes used as the fastener that keeps the embryo in place.

Further cosmological implications of miscarriage are contained in the well-known myth of Mārtāṇḍa Aditi's eighth child, who is aborted by his brothers and born as a shapeless egg (KS 11.6; MS 1.6.12). In certain version the Mārtāṇda becomes Vivasvant Āditya by name, the ancestor of humans, as the dead parts of the miscarried embryo are cut away and he is shaped into a living whole (SBM 3.1.3.4) As Jamison notes, several stories of miscarriage are about the birth of the sun, or a form of the sun, where he is a patched-up result of a failed birth. Moreover, his rebirth after injury must be accomplished in the prescribed manner.[5]

The Texts and Commentarial Trail on Human Miscarriage

Certainly, RV 10.162, the first hymn used by the *human* miscarrying couple and prescribed in the late Vedic text the *Ṛg Vidhāna*, is concerned with the most basic, literal meaning of the term.[6]

> Let Agni, the slayer of the *rákṣas*-demons, in accordance with the formula, drive him away from here who, as *ámīvā*, is established in your embryo [and as] the evil-named one, in [your] womb.
>
> Agni, together with the formula, has utterly destroyed that flesh-eater who, [as] *ámīvā*, is situated in your embryo [and, as] the evil-named one, in [your] womb.
>
> We make him, who slays [the embryo] leaping and settled [in the womb], who [slays it when it is] moving about [in the womb], who tries to kill your [new] born [child], perish from here.
>
> We make him, who separates your thighs, who is situated between husband and wife [and] who licks inside the womb, perish from here.
>
> We make him who, after having become a brother, a husband, or a lover, lies down with you [and] tries to kill your offspring, perish from here.
>
> We make him who, after having confounded [you] with a dream [and] with darkness, lie down with you [and] tries to kill your offspring, perish from here.[7]

As we can see, the hymn is concerned with protection against a demon, *ámīvā*, who is mentioned in other texts, particularly the *Atharva Veda* (8.6) as a flesh eater, consuming raw meat, human flesh, and embryos. This demons sleeps with women and attacks at night; remedies against it were the *bajā* and *piṅgā* plants were to be worn in the undergarments, which perhaps in the form of an amulet. In RV 10.162, however, this demon is to be characterized as female, and it could attack at either of two stages of the very simple Vedic embryology: the first when the sperm flies into the womb and results in the fertilization of the egg, and the second when the fetus begins to kick and move about, leading finally to the birth of the child.

Notice here that explicit language identifies the *garbha* as the mother's; the use of the second person, both in pronominal and possessive forms, is frequent throughout the progress of the hymn. In the Atharvavedic (AV) hymn mentioned above, which has several of these verses, AV 8.6 makes this relationship even more obvious: verse 4 of that hymn states, "Both the ill-named and the well-named—both seek access. We destroy the force of destruction (*arāya*); let the well-named seek what is a woman's (*straiṇa*)." Whereas the idea that a *garbha* is *straiṇa*, belonging to a woman, may seem obvious to twenty-first-century perspectives, such a relationship is not always the case. When the term *garbha* is used in its more metaphoric usages, as described above, it is not usually identified with the mother at all.

Notice, too, that in this hymn, as well as in other terms for the destruction of the embryo (*garbhaśrava*, *garbhaḥ pramīyeta*, and *bhrūṇahan*), there is a close semantic connection—in fact, one is tempted to say, no real distinction—among what we today might term "miscarriage," "abortion," and "still-birth." All of the terms have to do with the injury or death of the fetus, and the agent of death is seen as a demonic, outside force of some kind. Moreover, as the verses of RV 10.162 suggest, even the conduct of improper sexual relations, while a woman is already pregnant, is seen as part of this threat to the embryo; the husband, friends, lovers, or brothers who come to sleep with the woman at night are seen as the demon *ámīvā* in disguise. All of these meanings for and concerns about the loss of the embryo remain on the specific, concrete level.

So much, then, for the Ṛgvedic hymn. At first glance, the commentarial tradition that utilizes it for ritual purposes seems straightforward enough: the Anukramaṇī or indexical tradition, around the fifth century B.C.E., uses it for *garbhasaṃśrave prāyaścittam*—atonement for a miscarriage or abortion.[8] The *Bṛhaddevatā*, dated slightly later, says that the hymn is to be directed to the demon-slaying Agni, called Brahmāgni, and that it is used as an *anumantra* (accompanying mantra) for a miscarriage.[9] The *Ṛg Vidhāna*, also dated slightly later, regards it, as we have seen, as a rite to secure the successful birth of a child who may otherwise have been aborted.

Yet if we consider these texts more carefully, we see two important things: first, a natural progression toward the idea of brahminical control over the fetus and, second, an increase in the mobilization of mantras to control the demonic forces that may threaten it. This is parallel to the clear movement toward understanding the fetus, not as related to or the possession of the mother but that of the Brahmin, whose potential mantric legacy it holds.

How does this progressively more aggressive attitude toward the control of the *garbha* manifest itself? I think we can conceptualize the changing attitude in terms of time. The first text, the *Anukramaṇī*, seems to accept the fact that something will, in fact, inevitably go wrong in childbirth, which needs to be cleaned up and atoned for. It names RV 10.162 as a kind of expiation for that inevitability: it is a *prāyaścittam* for what has already occurred. The wrong has been done, and the purification needs to proceed accordingly. This notion of the expiatory function of the hymn is similar, in fact, to that which Paul Thieme has suggested is the import for the final verses of many Ṛgvedic hymns. they can act as a kind of expiatory charm addressing the possibility of a transgression.[10] (RV 1.179, for instance–the conversation between Agastya and Lopāmudrā–is a good example. The last two verses may very well be the sentences uttered for the expiation of the violation of one's vows of abstinence.[11]) In fact, RV 10.162's placement in book 10, a later book of the RV, also suggests that it might well be a kind of mythologization of a ritual innovation, which Stanley Insler has suggested recently may well be the motivation behind several of the hymns in the later book of the *Ṛg Veda*.[12]

The second commentarial text, the *Bṛhaddevatā*, suggests a different slant than that of the *Anukramaṇī*: the hymn is used as a kind of mantra while the miscarriage is occuring. The term used by the *Bṛhaddevatā*, *anumantra*, can mean either "to consecrate" or, more likely in this case, " to accompany," by the use of mantric formulas. Thus, the demonic *ámīvā* can be controlled in situ during the event itself, not after the disaster has occurred.

Finally, the *Ṛg Vidhāna* prescribes the use of RV 10.162 in a rite that is not involved in either cleaning up after the loss of the embryo, such as the *Anukramaṇī* suggests, or witnessing the loss of the embryo, such as the *Bṛhaddevatā* suggests. Instead it advocates the abolition, through the uttering of the mantra, of any possibility of the potentially aborting fetus:

> In the case of a woman whose fetus might be destroyed, there one should offer a burnt-offering with ghee into the fire, in accordance with the ritual rule, while reciting [RV 10.162, the hymn beginning] "Agni, joining Brahmā." Let the pregnant woman, after anointing herself with the remnant of the ghee and also drink the remnant of the ghee; then her child will be born alive. And if her children die after being born, one should, after consecrating the ghee, offer [it with RV 10.162, the hymn beginning] "Agni, joining Brahmā," pour the residue on an amulet and fumigate the amulet [which is fixed] on a threefold thread together with a cloth made out of the sheath of a young bud of the Nyagrodha tree, and which is wrapped up with white and red. The amulet is praised with [RV 10.162, the hymn beginning] "Agni, joining Brahmā," after having consecrating it 10,000 times with the Sāvitrī verse (RV 3.62.10) in accordance with the ritual rule." (Ṛvid 4.86-90; 92-94)[13]

Several things in this passage are worth noting. First, the *Ṛg Vidhāna* no longer deals solely with the occasion of the flowing forth of the fetus but also with prevention the miscarriage. Note the text's quasi-"magical"[14] overtones: with the uttering of this mantra, the "child will be born alive." Only after this preventative power is declared by the text does its author go on to consider the possibility of the child's death. In this case, the author then advocates the creation of a fumigated amulet and the mobilization of a massive recitation schema of other mantras: the Savitri verse 10,000 times and the offering of the oblation 10,000 times. Just after the passage cited, the author of the *Ṛg Vidhāna* advocates the use of this same amulet during pregnancy in order to bring forth a male child. This male child will then be endowed– with the continued proper recitation of the mantra, specifically, the *śraddhā* hymn, or the hymn to faith (RV 10.151), and the Medhā hymn (RV Kh 4.8), or the hymn to intelligence–with the appropriate mental capacities.

This phenomenal mantric mobilization is not, I believe, accidental. The *Ṛg Vidhāna* text as a whole shows two other hymns being used for the prevention of the flowing forth of the embryo, neither of which has been used in early texts for such a purpose. The first hymn, *Ṛg Veda* 5.78, is not used in any of the ritual texts for any purpose, and yet it is used here in a very specific manner. It concerns the *ṛṣi* Saptavadhri, and reads as follows:

1. Aśvins, come here; Nāsatyas, do not avert your gaze. Fly like two geese upon the Soma juice.
2. Like two deer, Aśvins, like two buffalos on the pasture, fly like two geese upon the Soma juice.
3. Aśvins, rich in food, find pleasure in my offering as you wish; fly like two geese upon the Soma juice.
4. Just as Atri, escaping from the fire, propitiates you like a solicitous wife, therefore come with the speed of a falcon, bringing happiness.
5. Open yourself up, o tree, like the womb of the woman in labor. Hear, you Aśvins my cry and free Saptavadhri.
6. For the anxious *ṛṣi* Saptavadhri, who is in misery, through magic you Aśvins climb the tree up and down.
7. Like the wind moves the lotus pond all around, so may your embryo stir; may it emerge ten months old.
8. Like the wind, the forest, the sea moves, like this may your ten-month child be released along with the afterbirth.
9. After the boy has lain in the mother for ten months, may he emerge from the living woman alive, unharmed, alive.[15]

The story of Saptavadhri is contained in several commentarial texts. The background given by commentators to this hymn is as follows:

> Having committed seven failures[16] in a childless marriage, the king Aśvamedha of the race of Bharata employed the *ṛṣi* Saptavadhri—presumably to beget a son upon his queen. On his eighth failure, the king, throwing him into the trough of a tree [and] into an abyss,[17] restrained the i, described as "the one who had shed his seed[18] at night." The *ṛṣi* praised the Lords of Light with the hymn RV 5.78. The Aśvins, having raised him from that [abyss], made him fruitful again.

The commentary states that the triplet in the hymn that refer to the embryo (RV 5.78.7–9) is for the purpose of an embryo for himself—as the commentary says, because the *ṛṣi* slept like an embryo in the tree. But commentators also say that the earlier two Vedic verses, 5 and 6, referring to the tree opening itself to free Saptavadhri, are to be known as belonging to the Aśvins. These verses are also seen as a mantra for embryos that miscarry[19] (BD 5.82–87).[20]

Hymn RV 5.78 and its related story of Saptavadhri explicitly address the anxiety provoked by the continuation of the male line, combined with the ways in which the birth can be invoked as proceeding smoothly. Thus, just as Saptavadhri himself escaped from the tree, so, too, must the embryo stir in an uncomplicated emergence from the mother. Moreover, the Ṛgvedic hymn explicitly compares the birth process, the bending of the tree together and apart, with the process of the composition of sacred formulas, which allow the stirring to occur. Finally, the commentarial tradition about the hymn compares Saptavadhri to an embryo—"he who slept like an embryo" in the tree where he had been thrown. Therefore, as others have also noted, the escape of the *ṛṣi* and the birth of the child are straightforwardly homologized in this hymn.[21]

In addition, some attention must be paid to the fact that Atri is mentioned as a paradigmatic figure in this Ṛgvedic hymn. Atri is in both the ritual and mythical texts the very symbol of a failed birth and second birth. As Jamison writes, in the story of the *Śatapatha Brāhmaṇa* (2.4.2.15) and the *Vādhula Sūtra*, Atri resulted from a miscarriage or abortion. The premature fetus is placed in a pot or a skin, mentioned earlier as a common "womb substitute" in Vedic mythology. In the *Śatapatha Brāhmaṇa*, the gods assemble, in a rather ad hoc way, the aborted material (similar to *martāṇḍa*, the eighth birth of the sun, mentioned above). The end product is the seer Atri. in a parallel story in the *Jaiminīya Brāhmaṇa* (1.151), a mother violently casts a child into a cleft, and the child, Sudīti ("very bright"), is then freed by an Aśvin-like pair.[22]

Jamison also discusses at length the role of the Ātreya, the descendant of Atri, in the Āṣvamedha ritual, the grand year-long horse sacrifice. In this ritual, the Ātreya is someone with mottled skin, brought into the sacrificial arena and then ritually banished from the territory. Mantras that invoke abortion, or *bhrūṇahatyam* (to be discussed below), are recited over him. In Jamison's interpretation, the Ātreya represents the mniscarried/aborted fetus, and his appearance reflects the nebulous shape of an embryo not brought to term. The man in his ugliness is the aborted Atri of the myth, who survived an abortion and lived to tell the tale. As she puts it, "By invoking abortion they acknowledge its power, but by invoking it while libating an Ātreya, they undercut its power."[23]

In sum, RV 5.78's use in the later Ṛgvidhānic rite for the prevention of miscarriage implies several different perspectives on a miscarrying woman. First, the birth of any child could potentially be a birth of a great brahmin sage, like Saptavadhri or Atri. Second, the way out of a potentially failing birth is to invoke a successful second birth, as is recounted in the various tales of Atri and is clearly the case in the story of Saptavadhri. The second birth may not be through a natural womb but rather through a womb substitute, such as that of a pot, or an earth cleft, or a tree trough. The Ṛgvedic mantras imaginatively "start the birth again" as the miscarriage is occurring.

The second hymn recited in the Ṛgvidhānic context for prevention of miscarriage is RV 1.101.1. It is a verse addressed to Indra, and in it Indra is invoked to drive away indigenous peoples, called *kṛṣṇagarbha*, and to remain on friendly terms with the worshipper.[24] *Ṛg Vidhāna* 1.23 employs it as a charm for safe delivery, which is a major departure from the explicit meaning of the text.[25] Scholars such as M. S. Bhat[26] speculate that the word *kṛṣṇa garbha* may have "misled" both the author of the *Ṛg Vidhāna* and the author of the *Sarvānukramaṇī*, but he makes an assumption that I am unwilling to accept: that scribes are easily misled. I would venture to argue that this hymn was consciously utilized for the prevention of *garbhaśrava*. I do so for two reasons: (1) the Ṛg *Vidhāna* frequently uses Ṛgvedic hymns for purposes other than those indicated by their explicit meaning, and (2) the *Ṛg Vidhāna*'s overall purpose is not to ascertain the "correct meaning" of the verses, as a twenty-first-century scholar's might be, but their application in everyday life. The imagery in that small verse of the hymn was felicitous for this purpose and not another, such as vengeance against enemies—a theme found far more frequently in the Vidhāna material than the prevention of miscarriage. The verse's explicit "insider vs. outsider" language was not missed by the author of the *Ṛg Vidhāna* because he argued for its inclusion as a spell, preventing the "flowing forth" of the embryo. Part of the overall understanding of the danger of "flowing forth," as mentioned above and as we shall see in further detail below, is its potential wasting of male brahmin seed.

If we place ourselves, insofar as we can, into the minds of those uttering the Ṛgvedic hymns that the Vidhāna enjoins, we get a very intriguing picture of what the brahmins were asked to imagine as they were chanting the verses from the *Ṛg Veda*. In addition to reciting hymn 10.162, which explicitly addresses the issue of miscarriage, the reciter is asked to recite, and thereforecall to mind, two more hymns: the first makes an explicit comparison between the safe birth of a child and the emergence of the *ṛṣi* Saptavadhri from bondage, and the second explicitly engages "insider vs. outsider" imagery. This fact, in addition to the clear growing sense of control over birth that the different wordings of the successive commentaries suggest, implies that the process of birth and the prospect of the loss of an embryo indicate the loss of a brahmin—more importantly, a brahmin who knows verses. I would add that the *Ṛg Vidhāna* and many other later texts[27] also use the term *vedagarbha*, the womb of the Vedas, to mean, precisely, a knowledgeable brahmin; what was once, then, the concrete reference to the body part of a woman has come to mean, if not its opposite, at least its converse: the sacred, traditional knowledge of a man.

Embryo Killer

This semantic movement is also reflected in another curious word related to abortion and miscarriage: *bhrūṇahan*, which is the final subjectin this chapter. *Bhrūṇahan*, in most lexicons, confuses the translator immediately because it can mean (not surprising to us now) either the killer of an embryo or the killer of a learned brahmin. Albrecht Wezler has brilliantly discussed the Dharmśāstric and other early usages of *bhrūṇahan*. He argues that Śabara and many other early Indian thinkers believed that, if one kills an embryo before the sex is known, it may well be a male. That male could grow up to learn the Vedas, perform sacrifices, and benefit both worlds.[28] If we trace the word's usage, briefly in the earliest texts, we see a similar semantic linkage between the fetus and the learned brahmin, and a key passage—*Taittirīya Āraṇyaka* 2.8—sheds further light on the topic.

We first encounter the term *bhrūṇahan* in *Ṛg Veda* 10.155, where it means the killer of an embryo. Here the *ṛṣi* Śirimbiha, son of Bharadvaja, desperately wishes to scare a female *deva* of destruction, Arāyi, away from the world. if we are to follow Sāyaṇa's more elaborate formulation, Arāyi is *alakṣmi*, or the goddess of misfortune; or perhaps even *durbhikṣādidevatā*, the goddess of famine. In a later verse she is called *bhrūṇahan*, the destroyer of all embryos. As the poet implores, "Let sharp-horned Bṛhaspati come near, the one who drives away all distress" (RV 10.155.2).

Her next incarnation is in *Atharva Veda* 3.112, where she is male, as well as the expiation of the wrongdoing of a younger son who has married before the elder. The sin of this kind of inappropriate marriage is "wiped off" on the *bhrūṇahan*, or embryo slayer. Here, it is unclear who or what exactly the embryo slayer is, but it is more likely than not to be a nonhuman force that absorbs sin for others. The implication in the hymn is that an inappropriate marriage will create a seed inappropriately, and it is thus considered to be a kind of social slaying of an embryo, an abdication of the responsibility to reproduce in the appropriate manner.

Bhrūṇahatyā is also, not surprisingly, related to the person and name of Atri. In the *Maitrāyaṇi Saṃhitā*, there is a legal provision about the killing of an embryo (*bhrūṇahā*) of unknown sex. In both the *Jaiminīya Brāhmaṇa* (2.219) and the *Śatapatha Brāhmaṇa.* (2.4.2.15), there is an explicit injunction against the killing of an *ātreyī*, which could be interpreted as a female relative of Atri (either mother or daughter) but is more accurately read as a "woman fit to conceive." This injunction is also echoed in the later Dharmaśāstric texts.[29] In one (*Manava Dharma Śāstra* 11.87), the killing of the unknown embryo is equated, more specifically as equal in nature to the killing of an *ātreyī*, or "woman fit to conceive." As Jamison conjectures,

> Originally *ātreyī* was a term applied to women particularly fit for conception an childbearing whose fertility was violently interfered with—just like Atri's mother. The term became particularly associated with a legal provision, a provision that condemns the violence against such a woman.[30]

Jamison joins with Hans-Peter Schmidt in arguing that women merit special treatment precisely because of their fitness for conception; therefore killing her is tantamount to killing an embryo as well. As Schmidt has also noticed,[31] a father who does not marry off his daughter as soon as she begins to menstruate is guilty of *bhruṇahatyā*. As Jamison notes, "Preventing potential pregnancy is legally as serious as aborting real ones; . . . it is not for herself that an *ātreyī* woman is valued but as a potential vessel for a fetus."[32]

Building on this initial insight of Jamison's, we can go further into the mechanics of how the *garbha* as "vessel" became the lynchpin for the semantic shift from womb to brahmin. The linkage between *bhrūṇahan* and the person of the brahmin is further reinforced when we see its next usage. Here, it is participating in the expected analogy of the body part of the womb that is being mapped onto that of the proceedings of the sacrifice; in particular the *āhavanīya* fire of the sacrificial arena is frequently referred to as a *garbha*, or womb. Yet before we go celebrating this fact as the inclusion of women's imagery in the Vedic world, let us look more carefully at the dynamics of the symbolism. in the *Maitrāyaṇī Saṃhitā*, the *āhavanīya* fire is likened to a *garbha*. Even more important for our purposes, he who allows it to become extinct is likened to a *bhrūṇahan*, or embryo killer. And as *Śatapatha Brāhmaṇa* 12.9.3.10–16 echoes, the *āhavanīya* fire is the *garbha* of the gods, and when they perform the sacrifice on it, they perform the sacrifice for the gods in the *garbha* of the gods. The text goes on to admonish that just as the slayer of an embryo is despised, so, too, is the one who allows his sacred fire to go out.

This set of associations among the *garbha*, the sacrificial fire and the sacrificing brahmin is solidified in two key passages of later texts—the *Taittirīya Āraṇyaka* and the *Vaikhana Gṛhya Sūtra*. In *Vaikhana Gṛhya Sūtra* 1.1, we see one of the rare usages of the term *bhrūṇa* on its own. One who maintains the fires for the Soma ritual is called a *bhrūṇa*; this status is attained after he has mastered the Veda, all the sacrifices involving cooked food, the sacrifices of *havis*, and finally those of Soma. Here, then, the term *bhrūṇa* is designating not just the one tending the "embryo" of the fire but also the fact that he has become identified with the fire. And again, in a later passage (6.16), the one who lets the fire go out is seen as a *bhrūṇahan*, or embryo killer, and therefore by implication the killer of his status as a tender of the fires.

Taittirīya Āraṇyaka 2.8 is even more helpfully explicit. The passage is contained within a larger discussion of the ways in which one can maintain the status of a *dikṣita*, or consecrated sacrificer, in the midst of various kinds of wrongdoing. As the passage postulates: "The one who pours semen outside of the yoni is like a thief (*stena*), like a *bhrūṇahan*, one killing an embryo." Here, the simile is clear: any wasted semen is akin to a theft, or murder, because it is wasting the potential of the sacrificer's, and therefore the brahmin's, line. With these two texts, we see a semantic transfer taking place: the sacrificial fire is likened to an embryo and is further identified with the brahmin who takes care of it. Its destruction is the destruction of the embryo, and by implication, then, the destruction of the line of potential sacrificers. This implication for the family line is made clear in the "wasted seed" imagery of the *Taittirīya* text, which equates the killed embryo and the wasted seed as one and the same.

Thus the symbolic imagery is complete: the embryo that was once to be protected from a quasi-demonic force in the early Vedic imagery becomes a responsibility, or even better—the controlled substance—of the brahmin. What arāyi or *ámīvā* threatens to do to the embryo becomes, by the late Vedic period, what the brahmin himself might do if he is not careful: kill the embryo, and therefore kill his heritage.

Conclusion

The imagery of miscarriage in the late Vedic period shows an increased anxiety over the potential loss of lineage, and in doing so wrests the embryo further and further away from the body of the mother. The commentarial tradition of *Ṛg Veda* 10.62 does so by implying increased mantric control over the process of birth itself. We see its conclusion in the *Ṛg Vidhāna*, where the text enjoins the brahmin to engage in a massive mobilization of mantras against the possibility of the destruction of the embryo. Moreover, these additional mantras, which control the process of birth, compare any birth to the emergence of the *ṛṣi* from capture and the victory over outsider (and, therefore, possibly seed-mixing) elements. Later texts, that use the term *bhrūṇahan*, engage in comparisons that link the embryo to the tender of sacrificial fires. Anxiety over its loss is also anxiety over the loss of the Brahmin, who has, in effect, become the sole signification of the *garbha*.[33]

What can we learn, then, from this mass of trivia about the loss of an embryo, other than adding a grain of sand onto the mountain of Vedic scholarship gone before? I would ask historians of religion, particularly feminist ones, to think twice before they celebrate the metaphorical transfer of a female body part into a larger, public, and predominantly male activity, and call it inclusion. It is more likely to be a form of symbolic exclusion, whereby the person from whom the image is taken becomes less and less visible in the production of new meaning for the image. As we see in this case, if the symbol is manipulated successfully enough, what is once identified with the female turns into the exclusively male; the meaning of the female is reduced to what the female is expected to produce. Tatyana Elizarenkova also speaks of the need to study the ways in which a Vedic word can come to mean its converse and the sacrificial and devotional environments that produce such a change in meaning.[34] Certainly the converse imageries of miscarriage throughout the Vedic period can contribute to such a study. Finally, and most importantly, the implications of such semantic histories can be far-reaching for students of gender studies and historians of religion. Before they rush to celebrate the fertility imagery of Vedic texts, they might reconsider. When it comes to keeping and losing embryos, at any rate, Elizarenkova's notion of metaphoric transfer is not simply poetic conceit; it can also be a very serious and far-reaching process indeed.

My small case study of ancient India raises other, larger questions—ones that would be worth exploring in a more general way. Mary McGee, in her chapter in this volume, also raises these normative questions in relationship to ancient texts. The first issue in this case is what kind of imagery informs moral, legal, and medical thinking about embryos and their losses. (I am struck, for instance, by Judith Jarvis Thompson's use of the imagery of screens, windows, and living rooms to speak about birth control as a natural, matter-of-fact process that occurs in other forms of living, such as going in and out of a house.)[35] It was, I think, the use of this imagery that made the work influential. In the case of early India, reproduction of all forms is good, and if you forgive the redundancy, reproduction is also reproductive of cosmology. Those who obstruct reproduction are likened to the Asuras and Rakṣasas, cosmological competitors for the goods that are usually gained by sacrifice. Thus, the Vedic categories of barrenness, miscarriage, stillbirth, and abortion are also linked (some might even say, not clearly distinguished at all). They are bound together by the same cause and, therefore, objects of the same kinds of ritual and philosophical thought.

Also, the Indian data might inspire us to ask of other commentarial traditions; what is the function, or cosmological frame, of reproductive success and reproductive catastrophe? How are such successes and catastrophes linked to other processes in the universe, thereby generating certain categories of thought? The idea that the embryo is competed for by Asuras and Devas, as a particularly rich sacrificial offering would be, suggests an intriguing avenue for theoretical thinking: how might we explore these linkages among embryology, imagination, and moral thought?

This is a particularly relevant exercise for two particular reasons—one theoretical and one practical and pressing. The first is that there is a growing literature on the comparative study of abortion practices, as well as the need to embed our thinking about abortion and laws about abortions, in the cultural worldviews in which those laws are written. The work of Harold Coward, Julius Lipner, and Katherine Young in India,[36] Marie Therese Fontanille in Greece,[37] and William Lafleur[38] in Japan are just some recent examples of the relevance of traditional thinking about abortion in the formation of contemporary laws and practices.

So my challenge is the following: having just demonstrated the necessity of going beyond what I call a careless feminist reading of the early Indian history of embryos and having advocated a more sophisticated reading of early Indian history, which reveals a growing control over women's bodies through the manipulation of the imagery of *garbha*, I am now faced with the challenge of what I might do with feminist principles and Sanskrit knowledge to reinterpret the tradition. This task is, if I do it well, neither an attempt to legitimize ancient myths in order to valorize the current situation for women in India nor an attempt to raid ancient myths for equally problematic feminist purposes. We might instead be feminist Mīmāṃsakas, or traditional interpreters of Vedic ritual. Mary McGee has, elsewhere in this volume, discussed the ways in which particular arguments of Jaimini might be useful for contemporary women. Here, I argue that certain formal perspectives on knowledge from the Mīmāṃsā and other Indian philosophical traditions could also be of great use.

Our method might be to focus on the power of metaphor in the very kinds of Vedic texts that I have laid before you. Our modus operandi might be threefold: first, following Mark Johnson's work *Moral Imagination*,[39] we assume that ancient texts can provide us with both metaphors and narratives, which Johnson argues are the stuff of more informed and complex ethical thinking. Second, we assume that this idea of ethical thought is the Sanskrit equivalent of *pramāṇa*, or logical reasoning, of traditional Vedic interpretive philosophy, called Mīmāṃsā. Third, an inquiry into *strīdharma*, or the codes of conduct by and about the lives of women, is a legitimate and necessary form of inquiry that should be the appropriate topic of Mīmāṃsā. Fourth and finally, because *pramāṇa* can and does outrank *sadācāra*, or traditional practice, as a form of reasoning about Vedic texts, reinterpretation of Vedic texts can and should provide a critique of *sadācāra*, or contemporary traditional practices, such as female infanticide in present-day India. In other words, basing our arguments on these four principles, we might use Vedic texts to provide a sophisticated, traditional argument against religious practices concerning abortion that harm women.

In this chapter I retold a commentarial history and made an interpretive suggestion. The retelling of the historical story was an argument for closer textual reading than both religionists and feminists have done in the past and against the romanticism of raiding ancient texts for utopian images of the female body. I introduced instead the idea that we could retell a history whereby, in early India, textual authority was mobilized in the service of greater control over the female body. Through a series of metaphoric linkages, the womb was no longer viewed as part of the woman's body, and therefore, as a kind of detached item, it was able to be controlled by the technology available at the time—that of the Vedic mantra. That was the more careful commentarial history.

But I also suggest that textualists should be ethically accountable and thus take up the challenge of being a Vedic interpreter with women's lives in mind. One might use traditional interpretive categories that involve the hierarchical authority of different Vedic texts and the authority of story and poetry for moral thinking in ancient India. In certain, very carefully chosen cases, actual Vedic hymns that involve abortion and miscarriage could be used in the service of the lives of women today. They would be of service not because they themselves represented some kind of actual feminist utopia or golden age (both questionable history and questionable ethics); rather, they would be of service because, by the strict rule of traditional Vedic interpretation, they could be read with a view toward protecting the welfare of women.

So, I end this chapter with a kind of overall challenge for those of us who are textual scholars interested in mythology and commentary and yet who retain ethical principles of our own. We have mastered the languages and the forms of reasoning in the commentaries. Perhaps, as we continue to perform our primary task of writing good and careful history, it is also occasionally incumbent upon us to write in the tradition of those religious commentaries as ethically committed interpreters: in the best of all worlds, we would write our late twentieth-century commentaries in Hebrew, Latin, and Sanskrit, according to the forms of reasoning set down for us by the traditions we are interpreting. This is different from arguing that we find feminism in Calvin or the Church fathers or rabbinic Judaism, a process that again I would claim is questionable history and questionable ethics. Instead, we might take the very principles of reasoning which are set out for us in these traditional forms and respond by writing an ethics from our own intellectual environments.

Perhaps feminist Indological colleagues take up the discussion with these questions in mind and return to the image of the miscarrying woman in the late fourth century B.C.E. Certainly there are no records in which she spoke for herself, and certainly it is a kind of interpretive violence to impose false historical interpretations on her world. In my view, the utmost respect we can give her is to imagine what forms of reasoning might have been most likely to keep her, and her descendants, alive as they gave birth to the next generations.

Notes

1. "Women, Earth, and the Goddess: A Shākta-Hindu Interpretation of Embodied Religion," in *Hypatia* 9. no.4 (Fall 1994), 69–87.

2. For recent work in this area, please see Martha Selby, "*The Color of Gender: On Embryology and Sex Determination in the Caraka and Suśruta Saṃhitas*," unpublished manuscript.

3. Tatyana Elizarenkova, *The Language and Style of the Vedic Ṛṣis* (Albany: State University of New York Press, 1994), p. 34.

4. Stephanie Jamison, *The Ravenous Hyenas and the Wounded Sun* (Ithaca, N.Y.: Cornell University Press, 1991), pp. 235–39.

5. Ibid., pp. 202–11.

6. In addition to this new translation, see Ken Zysk's excellent discussion of early embryology in *Religious Medicine* (New Brunswick, N.J.: Transaction Publishers, 1993).

7. bráhmaṇāgníḥ saṃvidānó rakṣohā́ bādhatām itáḥ/
ámīvā yás te gárbhaṃ durṇā́mā yónim āśáye//1
yás te gárbham ámīvā durṇā́mā yónim āśáye/
agníṣ ṭám bráhmaṇā sahá níṣ kravyā́dam anīnaśat//2
yás te hánti patáyantaṃ niṣatsnúṃ yáḥ sarīsṛpám/
jātáṃ yás te jíghāṃsati tám itó nāśayāmasi//3
yás ta ūrū́ vihárati antarā́ dámpatī śáye/
yóniṃ yó antár āréḻhi tám itó nāśayāmasi//4
yás tvā bhrā́tā pātir bhūtvā́ jāró bhūtvā́ nipádyate/
prajā́ṃ yás te jíghāṃsati tám itó nāśayāmasi//5
yás tvā svápnena támasā mohayitvā́ nipádyate/
prajā́ṃ yás te jíghāṃsati tám itó nāśayāmasi//6 (RV 10.162)

8. *Sarvānukramaṇī* on RV 10.162:
brahmaṇā ṣaḍ brāhmo rakṣohā garbhasaṃsrāve prāyṣcittam ānuṣṭubhaṃ hi/

9. *Bṛhaddevatā* 8.65cd–66ab on RV 10.62:
rākṣoghnāgneyaṃ ity uktaṃ yat tv etad brahmaṇeti tu/
svatatām api garbhāl̄ṇāṃ dṛṣṭaṃ tad anumantraṇam//

10. Paul Thieme, "Agastya und Lopāmudrā," in *Kleine Schriften* Teil 1 (Wisebaden: Franz Steinder Verlag GMBH, 1971).

11. See my "The Fate of the Female Ṛṣi," in *Myths and Mythmaking in India*, Julia Leslie, Ed. (London: Curzon Press, 1996).

12. Stanley Insler, "On the Soma Rital," an address to the Columbia University Seminar on the Veda and Its Interpretation, November 9, 1995.

13. yasyāḥ garbhaḥ pramīyeta tatrāgnau juhuyād dhaviḥ/brahmaṇāgniḥ saṃ vidāna ity ājyena yathāvidhi//
ājyaśeṣeṇa cābhyajya garbhiṇī prasavet tataḥ/pibed evājyaśeṣaṃ tu jīvaṃs tasyāḥ prajāyate//
jātāni cet pramīyerran ājyaṃ kṛtvānumantritaṃ/juhuyād brahmaṇāgnir iti saṃpātān ninayen maṇau//
maṇiṃ tu triyṛti sūtre vāsayed vāsasā saha/nyagrodhaśuṅgayā tatra śukhalohitaveṣṭitam//
taṃ sāvitry ayutenaiva anumantrya yathāvidhi. . ./

śirasā dhārayen nārī prayatā garbhiṇī satī/tṛtīye garbhamāsa tu maṇim etaṃ samāsajet// puṣpavatī śaradaṃ nārī gauḥ savatsā vased yathā/bahupānīyayavasā vatsena pibatā saha// jātasya tu kumārasya kaṇṭhe taṃ maṇim āsajet/ājyaśeṣaṃ puraskṛtya tan abhyajya kumārakam (R Vidh. 4.86–90, 92–94)

14. I have dealt with the problematic issue of terming the Vidhāna material "magical" elsewhere; see "Making the Canon Commonplace," in *The Journal of Religion*, January 1997, pp. 1–19.

15. áśvināv éhá gacchataṃ nā́satyā mā́ ví venatam/
haṃsā́v iva patatam ā́ sutā́m̐ úpa//1
áśvinā hariṇāv iva gaurā́v ivā́nu yávasam/
haṃsā́v iva patatam ā́ sutā́m̐ upa//2
áśvinā vājinīvasū juṣéthāṃ yajñám iṣṭáye/
haṃsā́v iva patatam ā́ sutā́m̐ úpa//3
átrir yád vām avaróhann ṛbī́sam ájohavīn nā́dhamāneva yóṣā/
śyenásya cij jávasā nū́tanena ágacchatam aśvinā śáṃtamena//4
ví jihīṣva vanaspate yóniḥ sū́ṣyantiyā iva/
śrutám me aśvinā hávaṃ saptávadhriṃ ca muñcatam//5
bhītā́ya nā́dhamānāya ṛ́ṣaye saptávadhraye/
māyā́bhir aśvinā yuvā́ṃ vṛkṣā́ṃ sáṃ ca ví cācathaḥ//6
yáthā vā́taḥ puṣkaríṇīṃ samiṅgáyati sarvátaḥ/
evā́ te gárbha ejatu niraítu dáśamāsiyaḥ//7
yáthā vā́to yáthā vánaṃ yáthā sumudrá éjati/
evā́ tvā́ṃ daśamāsiya sahā́vehi jarā́yuṇā//8
dáśa mā́sāñ chaśayānáḥ kumāró ádhi mātári/
niraítu jīvó ákṣato jīvó jīvantiyā ádhi//9

16. That is, *sapta kṛtva aparadhan*; cf. the name of Saptavadhri in ṚV 5.78.

17. That is ṛbīse—perhaps fire, here.

18. Here I part from A.A. Macdonell in his translation of Bṛhaddevatā; he renders rather prudishly "leapt up at night" for "*skannaṃ ratrau nyadhārayat*"; it seems more appropriate to the story to render "shed his seed at night."

19. The word *śravatām* has the meaning of miscarriage, as well as the more neutral "issue from the womb."

20. For a larger discussion, see my *Myth as Argument: The Bṛhaddevatā as Canonical Commentary* in Religionsgeschichtliche Vorsuche und Vorarbeiten, vol. 41 (Berlin: Degruyter, 1996), pp. 333–36.

21. See Jamison, *Ravenous Hyenas*, pp. 234–35; Wendy O'Flaherty, *The Rig Veda* (New York: Penguin Books, 1981), p. 186; T. Baunack, "Uber einige Wunderthaten der Aśvin," *Zeitschrift Der Deutschen Morgenlandischen Gesellschaft* 50, 263–87.

22. Jamison, *Ravenous Hyenas*, pp. 231–35.

23. Ibid., p. 228.

24. prá mandíne pitumád arcatā váco yáḥ kṛṣṇágarbhā niráhann ṛjíśvanā/
avasyávo vṛ́ṣaṇaṃ vájradakṣiṇaṃ marútvantaṃ sakhiyāya havāmahe// *Ṛg Veda* 1.101

25. pra madine 'ti sūyantyām japed garbhapramocinīm/
indraṃ ca manasā dhyāyen nārī garbhaṃ pramuñcati// *Ṛg Vidhāna* 1.123

26. See M. S. Bhat, *Vedic Tantrism: A Study of the Ṛg-Vidhāna of Śaunaka* (Delhi: Motilal Banarsidass, 1987)

27. See, for instance, *Bhāgavata Purāṇa* 2.9.19, 3.9.29, 3.32.12, 8.17.26; *Skanda Purāṇa* 1.1.3.73, 1.1.17.107,5.3.85.11, among many others.

28. Albrecht Wezler, "A Note on Sanskrit *Bhrūṇa*, and *Bhrūṇahatyā*," in *Festschrift Klaus Bruhn*. Nalini Balbir and Joachim K. Bautze, Eds. (Reinbek: Verlag für Orientalistische Fachpublikationen, 1994), pp. 623–48.

29. *Vāsiṭḥha Dharma Sūtra* 20.34–36; *Baudhāyana Dharma Sūtra* 1.10.19.3, 2.1.1.10–12 among many others discussed by Wezler.

30. Jamison, *Ravenous Hyenas*, pp. 216–23.

31. Hans-Peter Schmidt, *Some Women's Rites and Rights in the Veda* (Poona: Bhandarkar Oriental Institute, 1987), pp. 78ff.

32. Ibid., p. 216.

33. Again, but more speculatively this time, it is also at this late Vedic period that we see the emergence of stories about *ṛṣi* in wombs, "learning the Vedas in the womb," such as that of the *ṛṣi* Dṛḍhasyu, son of Agastya, who learned the Vedas in his mother Lopāmudrā's womb, or the seer Dīrghatamas, whose sight was spoiled in the womb by the curse of Bṛhaspati, whose seed was not allowed to enter the womb.

34. Tatyana Elizarenkova, *The Language and Style of the Vedic Ṛṣis* (Albany: State University of New York Press, 1994).

35. Judith Jarvis Thompson, *Rights, Restitution and Risk: Essays in Moral Theory* (Cambridge, MA: Harvard University Press, 1986).

36. Harold Coward, Julius Lipner, and Katherine Young, Eds. *Hindu Ethics: Purity, Abortion, and Euthanasia, McGill Studies in the History of Religions* (Albany: State University of New York Press, 1989).

37. Marie-Therese Fontanille, *Avortement et Contraception dans la Medecine Greco-Romaine* (Paris: Laboratiore Searle, 1977).

38. William LaFleur, *Liquid Life: Abortion and Buddhism in Japan* (Princeton, N.J: Princeton University Press, 1992).

39. Mark Johnson, *Moral Imagination: Implications of Cognitive Science for Ethics* (Chicago: University of Chicago Press, 1993).

Part II

CLASSICAL ARGUMENTS

4

Giver or Given?

Some Marriages in Kālidāsa

STEPHANIE W. JAMISON

Questions about women and questions about property intersect in a number of significant ways in ancient India and raise a number of vexed questions. We can, too simply, divide the questions into two types: (1) to what extent can a woman *be "owned"* as property; in particular is the wife the property of her husband in the same way a cow or a pot is? Such is in part the issue in the aftermath of the dicing match in the *Sabhā Parvan* of the *Mahābhārata* (MBh): did Draupadī remain the "property" of her husband after he had lost himself? I will not pursue this matter further here, instead concentrating on some aspects of the second question: (2) what can a woman herself "own" as property. I will approach this question through a single facet of the issue: the giving of gifts.[1] The institution of gift giving seems a useful one to examine in this connection, for ownership is most clearly visible when it is transferred. "Giving" something *might* seem to require "owning" it first—though this perhaps is one of the issues that needs clarification. To approach the connection of women and property, I will examine some instances of women giving gifts, as well as the more conventional "gift" of women in marriage. Indeed, this chapter primarily deals with a potentially explosive combination of the two, as exemplified by two unusual marriages found in classical "court" literature. Elsewhere in this volume, Ellison Findly discusses the issue of women's gift giving in an earlier context, particularly the transition from woman as a symbol of the wealth of the Vedic household to woman as giver in her own right in the Buddhist context. My own chapter continues this focus, only I emphasize not the historical development but the simultaneous juxtaposition of woman as both giver and gift.

Two of the plays of Kālidāsa contain depictions of marriages or quasi marriages that share some striking traits—traits that seem to run directly counter to proper, dharmic marriage rites. In this chapter, I will first describe the scenes and characterize their deviations from orthodoxy, then explore the reasons for and possible justifications of the remarkable features of these incidents.

In Act 3 of the *Vikramorvaśī* (Vik.) the Mahiṣī or chief wife of King Purūravas, Ausīnarī, *gives her husband* to the Apsaras Urvaśī, for the satisfaction of their mutual infatuation. Although an actual wedding ceremony is not performed, the vocabulary of marital transfer is employed, as we shall see. Similarly, at the end of *Mālavikāgnimitra* (Māl.), the Mahiṣī of King Agnimitra, Dhāriṇī, *gives her ex-servant* Mālavikā to her husband Agnimitra, again for a union of mutual desire. Here there is actual ceremonial action; indeed, the queen dresses the bride in her wedding clothes, and the vocabulary of marriage is even more fully deployed.

What little comment these scenes seem to have elicited concentrates on the "false" nature (Gitomer,1984, Vik. 3.14) of the sentiments expressed by the principal participants or the "reproachful" nature (Kale, 1898,p. 3) of the queen's consent to the marriage.[2] But the remarkable aspect of these scenes to me is the power ascribed to the Queen, the power to *give*, to convey one person to another in marriage. This is a direct role reversal: marriage is constantly defined in the dharma texts as *kanyā-dāna* 'gift of a maiden', and the giver is generally her father or, in default of him, another close male relative. But here a woman serves as giver, and in the Urvaśī she actually gives away a man. Before examining the dharmic material more thoroughly, let me first demonstrate exactly how explicit the "gift" theme is in Kālidāsa's scenes.

In Act 3 of the *Urvaśī*, Purūravas meets his previously jealous queen at her request: she is performing a *vrata* that requires his participation—or so she claims. At this point she makes a ceremonial promise to him, to treat any woman he fancies kindly:

> ajjappahudi jaṃ itthiaṃ ajjautto patthedi jā ajjauttassa samāamappaṇaiṇī tāe mae pīdibandheṇa vattidavvaṃ ti [adyaprabhṛti yāṃ striyam āryaputraḥ prārthayate yā āryaputrasya samāgamapraṇayinī tayā mayā prītibandhena vartitavyam iti]
>
> From now on whatever woman his worship "seeks"[3] whatever (woman) is desirous of union with his worship, with her a bond of favor is to be formed by me. (Vik. 3.13+)
>
> The king responds to this avowal with a strong assertion of *her power* to give him away:
>
> *dātum* vā prabhavasi mām anyasmai[4] kartum eva vā dāsam
> nāhaṃ punas tathā tvaṃ yathā hi māṃ śaṅkase bhīru
>
> You have the power to *give* me to another or to make me slave. For still I am not such as you suppose, O timid one. (Vik. 3.14)

Note in passing that the metrical and rhetorical structure of this Āryā verse nicely underlines its theme: with the phonologically similar, semantically critically words *dātum* 'to give' and *dāsam* 'slave' polarized at the two ends of the first line (and rhyming *nāham* 'not I', opening the next line), and with *mām/anyasmai* ('me to another') over the caesura and *tvam* 'you' also just before caesura so that it is in vertical relation to *mām*. All the principal roles and actions are thus strategically positioned metrically.

> // dātuṃ mām/ anyasmai dāsam//
> // nāhaṃ tvaṃ/

We will return to the somewhat puzzling second line of this verse below.

Although the queen does not, strictly speaking, say *dadāmi tvām* ["I give you"], the other participants interpret her words and actions as if she had. Citralekhā, Urvaśī's companion, tells that tremulous nymph that her union with Purūravas has been "permitted" *abbhaṇuṇṇādo (abhyanujñātaḥ*; 3. 13+) by the queen, a term in technical marriage vocabulary. And Urvaśī soon makes an even stronger assertion—and proposition—to the king:

> *devīe dinno* mahārāo/tado se paṇaavadī via sarīrasaṃpakkaṃ gada mhi [*devyā datto* mahārājaḥ/tato 'sya praṇayavatīva śarīrasaṃparkaṃ gatāsmi]
>
> The king *has been given by the queen*. So I have come, like a lover, to mix with his body. (Vik. 3.16+)

The king takes up these words in his next verse:

> *devyā datta* iti yadi vyāpāraṃ vrajasi me śarīre 'smin
> prathamaṃ kasyā*numate* coritam etat tvayā hṛdayam
>
> If you have employment for this body of mine (only) because (I was) "*given by the queen,*"
> By whose *permission* was my heart stolen by you in the first place? (Vik. 3.17)

Here the king uses two technical terms from wedding arrangements (*anu*√*man* 'permit', a variation on *abhy-anu*√*jñā* above and √*dā* 'give') for his own sly purpose.

Let us now turn to the second play. In *Mālavikāgnimitra* the queen has also been jealous of her young rival and servant *Mālavikā*. Like her counterpart in the Urvaśī, she puts aside this jealousy and, as it were, blesses her union with the king Agnimitra. But here the queen's role is even more clearly ceremonial than in the Urvaśī: she almost officiates at the wedding in the final act of the play.

The first we hear of this is the Vidūṣaka's report to the king that his queen has had Mālavikā dressed in bridal garments:

> ajja kila devīe dhāriṇīe paṇḍidakosiī bhaṇidā / . . . taṃ daṃsehi mālaviāe sarīre vedabbhaṃ *vivāha*ṇevatthaṃ ti [adya khalu devyā dhāriṇyā paṇḍitakauśikī bhaṇitā/. . . tad darśaya mālavikāyāḥ śarīre vaidarbhaṃ *vivāha*nepathyam iti
>
> Today the queen Dhāriṇī told the learned Kauśikī [a nun in her household], "Display the Vaidarbhan *wedding* costume on the body of Mālavikā."[5] (Māl. 5.3+)

Much later in the act, indeed, after the royal birth of the supposed servant Mālavikā has been revealed, the queen announces her intention to *give* Mālavikā to the king. She seeks approval for this act from two people, both *women*: her co-wife Irāvatī and the supposed nun Kauśikī (whose own high position has likewise been revealed). Her request of the latter is phrased thus:

> bhaavadi tue *anunnādā* icchāmi ajjasumadiṇā puḍhamasaṃbhāvidaṃ ajjauttassa mālaviaṃ *padivādedum* [bhagavati tvayā*nujñātā* icchāmi . . . āryaputrasya mālavikāṃ *pratipādayitum]*
>
> Reverend lady, *permitted* by you, I wish to *bestow* Mālavikā on his worship. (Māl. 5.17+)

Notice the technical term *anu*√*jñā* 'permit' again.

Kauśikī's reply ascribes to the queen full *power* over Mālavikā—even though it is now clear that Mālavikā is a princess, not a servant—by using the same lexeme (*pra*√*bhū*) with which Purūravas acknowledged the queen's power above:

> idānīm api tvam evāsyāḥ *prabhavasi*
>
> Even now it is you who *have power* over her. (Māl. 5.17+)

The queen then *takes Mālavikā by the hand* (*mālavikāṃ haste gṛhītvā*), a clear ceremonial gesture, and announces her desire to convey ownership to Agnimitra:

> ajjautto imaṃ piaṇivedaṇāṇurūvaṃ pāritosiaṃ *padicchadu* [āryaputra idam priyaniveda-nānurūpaṃ pāritoṣikaṃ *pratīcchatu*]
>
> Let your worship *accept* this gratuity as a fit counterpart to the good news [that he had just announced about her son]. (Māl. 5.17+)

The king seems to hang back; after some consideration the queen has further festive garments brought to adorn Mālavikā—in fact, the *avaguṇṭhana*, a veil that seems elsewhere to be to be a symbol of wifehood.[6] The queen herself drapes Mālavikā with this wedding veil and tries again, saying, "Now let his worship accept (her)."

> [mālavikām *avagunthya]* dāṇiṃ ajjautto paḍicchadu [idānīm āryaputraḥ pratīcchatu]
>
> [*Having veiled* Mālavikā:] Now let his worship accept (her). (Māl. 5.18+)

And he finally does.

Before discussing the possible legal and ritual sources of these two scenes, let us note in passing two other examples in classical Sanskrit literature of a woman giving another woman in marriage. In Śūdraka's *Mṛcchakaṭika* (Mṛcch.), the courtesan Vasantasenā gives her maidservant to the brahmin-thief, as was already mentioned in note 6. In Bhavabhūti's *Mālatīmādhava* (Mālatīm) the nun Kāmandakī gives her young friend Mālatī to Mādhava with the quite explicit *iyam . . . mālatī ca tubhyam dīyate* "here is Mālatī; she is given to you by me also" (Māl 6.15+).

The extraordinary peculiarity of these scenes can only be appreciated with reference to the dharmic provisions for marriage, on the one hand, and women's property, on the other hand. As was already mentioned, marriage ordinarily is explicitly identified as the "gift of a maiden." In *Manu* (MDŚ) the first five types of marriage (the most clearly legal of them) are defined with variants of this phrase: *dānaṃ kanyāyāḥ* (Brāhma), *sutādānām* (Daiva), *kanyāpradānam* (Ārṣa, Prājāpatya, Āsura*)*.[7] The father (or other male relative) is the giver, the husband the receiver; and according to *Manu,* it is this transferral of property, this gift, that creates the husband's lordship over the wife: *pradānaṃ svāmyakāraṇam* (MDŚ 5.152).

Women pass their lives under perpetual ownership of one male figure or another, as a famous provision in *Manu* makes clear:[8]

> pitā rakṣati kaumāre bhartā rakṣati yauvane
> rakṣanti sthavire putrā na strī svātantryam arhati
>
> Her father guards her in girlhood; her husband guards her in youth; Her sons guard her in old-age. A woman does not deserve independence. (MDŚ 9.3)

Marriage is an occasion at which the previous guardian consigns control to the next. It is therefore quite striking that Kālidāsa depicts two marriages at which a *woman* asserts her control over the person of one of the parties to the wedding and, as does the father at an ordinary wedding, voluntarily passes this control to the partner in marriage. The ability to "give away" in marriage implies that the giver has dominion over the given in the first place.

These scenes are also striking because women ordinarily have almost no property rights to inanimate objects, much less to persons. According to one provision in *Manu,* women, or at least wives, have no property rights at all:

> bhāryā putraś ca dāsaś ca traya evādahnāḥ smṛtāḥ
> yat te samadhigacchanti yasya te tasya tad dhanam
>
> The wife, the son, and the slave are three (categories of persons) considered to be without property.
> What they acquire, that is the property of him whose (possession) they are.[9] (MDŚ 8.416)

However, the situation is, of course, much more complicated. Another famous passage in *Manu* implicitly grants women some property rights by cataloguing the six types of women's property:

adhyagnyadhyāvāhanikaṃ dattaṃ ca prītikarmaṇi
bhrātṛmātṛpitṛprāptaṃ ṣaḍvidhaṃ strīdhanaṃ smṛtam

What is given at the (wedding) fire, on the wedding (journey), in token of (her husband's) affection, what was acquired from brother, mother, father: such are traditionally the six types of women's property. (MDŚ 9.194)

The subject of *strīdhana* is, in fact, frequently (and contradictorily) treated not only in dharma texts proper, but also, notably, in considerable detail in Kauṭilya's *Artha Sāstra* (especially, 3.2.124, 34–36).[10] I will not pursue the subject further beyond pointing out the obvious fact that neither husband nor maidservant falls into any of the usual categories of women's property. That is a woman should not "own" either one of them. Moreover, even those things she indisputably "owns," her *strīdhana*, she cannot usually give away. According to most authorities, she has *use* of the property during her lifetime, but she cannot *alienate* it. The disposition of a woman's property after her death is stipulated in the law books and the *Artha Sāstra* [cf. MDŚ 9.192–93, 195–200; *Gautama Dharma Sūtra* (GDS) 28.24; KA 3.2.35–36; Kane, 1941: 788ff.], and the uses she may put it to while alive are also strictly controlled (cf. especially KA 3.2.16, 31–33). Thus, though she has limited rights of *ownership*, she seems to have little latitude to *give it away*.[11]

What, then, are we to make of these Kālidāsan Mahiṣīs, boldly giving away people in marriage—a particularly dramatic form of gift? We can, of course, pay little attention to these scenes, interpreting them as polite contrivances to salvage the dignity of the spurned and aging queen who sees the handwriting on the wall and "makes a gift" of what she never possessed—a pathetic show that the spectators pretend to believe in. This seems to be the opinion, overtly expressed or not, of many modern commentators. It also seems to be the opinion of the Vidūṣaka in the *Urvaśī*, who likens the queen to an unsuccessful fisherman who suddenly and conveniently practices *ahiṃsā*:

chinnahattho macche palāide ṇivviṇṇo dhīvaro bhaṇādi dhammo me havissadi tti [chinnahasto matsye palāyite nirviṇṇo dhīvaro bhaṇati dharmo me bhaviṣyatīti]

When a fish saves itself, the fisherman from whom it broke loose, though downcast, says "This will be a piece of meritorious conduct for me." (Vik. 3.13+)

Citralekhā, Urvaśī's friend, also remarks that sophisticated men become exceedingly polite to their wives when they fall for other women:

aṇṇasaṃkantappemmāṇo ṇāari ahiaṃ dakkhiṇā honti [anyasaṃkrāntapremāṇo nāgarikā adhikaṃ dakṣiṇā bhavanti]

Men-about-town whose fancy has wandered to another become very proper (to their wives). (Vik. 3.13+)

She thus seems to be suggesting that Purūravas is humoring the queen by pretending to give her power over him.

But I think it would be a mistake to dismiss these scenes so easily. The ceremonial forms and technical vocabulary of that central cultural institution, marriage, are unlikely to be used so lightly, as a mere screen for the feeling of a wounded woman. It must have been in a sense shocking to hear the words "I want to give" (a bride/a groom) coming from female lips. There are other ways, less disturbing to social convention, for a woman to remove herself graciously from the scene.

We can approach a solution to this conundrum from several directions: first, we can find structurally similar, though less dramatic, gifts by women portrayed elsewhere in Sanskrit literature; second, we can find some traces of a more prominent role for women in wedding arrangements than most texts allow; finally, we can trace the roots of women's giving in rites appropriated from or developing out of early *śrauta* and *gṛhya* rituals. Let us begin with another famous incident in Sanskrit dramatic literature in which a wife makes a gift.

This episode is less shocking because the item exchanged is inanimate and does indeed belong to her, but the effect is no less poignant or powerful. In the *Mṛcchakaṭika* and in the exactly corresponding scene in the *Cārudatta* (Cār) ascribed to Bhāsa, when the jewels of Vasantasenā, the courtesan, are stolen from Cārudatta's house, his wife seeks to give him her own necklace, to rescue his honor. She knows he will be too proud to accept it, but she ultimately succeeds in giving it by way of the Vidūṣaka. The source of this necklace is important. She says:

> iaṃ ca me ekkā *mādugharaladdhā* raaṇāvalī ciṭṭhadi [iyaṃ ca ma ekā *mātṛgṛhalabdhā* ratnāvalī tiṣṭhati]
>
> "This single jewel-necklace remains to me, *received from my mother's family.*" (Mṛcch. 3.26+) [Sim. Bhāsa (Cār 3.15+) mama ññādikuḷādo *ḷaddhā* (mama jñātikulād labdhā).]

The necklace is thus classified as one of the types of *strīdhana* 'women's property', as defined in MDŚ 9.194 above (*bhrātṛmātṛpitṛprāptam*). If she has the right to give anything away, it is surely this. But, even so, she must arrange an elaborate ruse and a go-between to effect this simple transfer. When the Vidūṣaka finally presents the necklace to Cārudatta, he is distressed to be pitied and wounded in his vanity, an issue to which we will return.

The point here is that Cārudatta's wife's gift fits the same pattern of action as those of the two queens in Kālidāsa: she *gives* to her husband something that enables him to fulfill his desire for another woman. Since her necklace is a substitute for the courtesan's stolen one, it is almost as if she is giving the courtesan, or a token of her to the husband—just as Dhāriṇī literally both adorns Mālavikā for her wedding and then gives her away. The existence of episodes like this one in the *Cārudatta and Mṛcchakaṭika*, involving a gift by the wife but a gift of her own property, may have provided precedent to the more dramatic scenes of Kālidāsa.

Now let us turn to the evidence for a larger female role in marriage arrangements. We can cull this evidence from dharma texts, from the *Artha Sāstra* and the *Kāma Sūtra,* and from epic narrative. Let us begin with the wedding ceremony itself, whose form I must admit to having oversimplified. Though most of the dharma texts allow only male relatives of the girl to give her away, a few permit the *mother* of the bride to officiate if all the others in line are incapable:[12]

> pitā pitāmaho bhrātā sakulyo *jananī* tathā
> kanyāpradaḥ pūrvanāśe prakṛtisthaḥ paraḥ paraḥ
>
> The father, paternal grandfather, a brother, a kinsman, *the mother*—such is
> (the roster of) the "giver of the maiden": on the failure of the previous one (in the list),
> each next one (performs it), if healthy.[13] [*Yājñaavalkya Smṛti* (Yāj Smṛ) 1.63]

The mother is also allotted some role in the arranging, or at least the approving, of marriage in the *Artha Sāstra*. Following a brief conspectus of the eight forms of marriage comes this statement:

pitṛpramāṇāś catvāraḥ pūrve dharmyāḥ/*mātā*pitṛpramāṇāḥ śeṣāḥ

The first four are legal with the authority of the father, the rest with the authority of the *mother* and father. (KA 3.2.10)

These last four are what we might call the "problematic" ones, in most of which the parents *seem* to play a minimal role: the Gāndharva (satisfaction of mutual lust), Āsura (purchase), Rākṣasa (abduction), and Paiśāca (rape of an incapacitated girl). I assume here that the parents' authorization does not in general precede the event but must be sought after the fact.[14] The irregularity of the original "marriage" may require the official approval of both parents to legitimize it or perhaps the bride's mother was considered likely to be more forgiving to a penitent young couple.

We may see some trace of the mother's role alluded to in this passage in narrative texts as well. Consider Bhīṣma's abduction of Ambā and her two sisters in the MBh—an act specifically identified as a Rākṣasa marriage. This abduction is treated at length twice in the text, and in both places Bhīṣma seeks and receives the permission of his (step-)mother Satyavatī. In the treatment in book 1(1.96.4), he does so before he even embarks on the act (*anumate mātuḥ*); in book 5 (170.2– 171.4), after the abduction he approaches her ceremonially, officially informs her of his undertaking, and asks for her permission to arrange the marriage between the girls and his stepbrother. Satyavatī grants it with the same level of formality:

tato mūrdhany upaghrāya paryaśrunayanā nṛpa
āha satyavatī hṛṣṭā diṣṭyā putra jitaṃ tvayā (MBh 5.171.3)
satyavatyās tv *anumate vivāhe* samupasthite

Then having kissed [lit. "sniffed"] his head, with eyes full of tears, excited,
Satyavatī said, "Congratulations, child; you've won!"
With the permission of Satyavatī, the wedding ceremony was undertaken. (171.4)

Note that this is a Rākṣasa marriage, one of the types for which the mother's[15] consent is required, according to the *Artha Sāstra*.

But even in the most respectable of marriages, the consent of the wife may be sought. In the Sixth Sarga of *Kumārasaṃbhava* (Kum.), the formal "wooing"[16] of Pārvatī by Śiva's representatives, Pārvatī's father, Himālaya, turns to his wife, Menā, to receive formal approval before accepting the offer of Śiva's hand. Note that both the request and its approval are justified by appeals to general, dharmic procedure:

śailaḥ saṃpūrṇakāmo 'pi *menāmukham udaikṣata*
prāyeṇa gṛhiṇīnetrāḥ kanyārtheṣu kuṭumbinaḥ(Kum. 6.85)
mene menāpi tat sarvaṃ patyuḥ kāryam abhīpsitam
bhavanty avyabhicāriṇyo bhartur iṣṭe pativratāḥ(6.86[17])

The mountain, though his desire [to marry Pārvatī to Śiva] was fulfilled, *looked to Menā*'s face.
In general, householders have their wives as guides[18] in matters regarding girls. (6.85.)
Menā approved everything her husband wanted to do.
Loyal wives do not go contrary to their husband's wishes. (6.86)

So far we have been discussing the ceremonial role of the *mother* of the bride.[19] This figure may seem a far cry from the "giving" *wives* of Kālidāsa, but there are several ways in which we can bring them closer together. First, consider that the eldest of the cowives enacts a somewhat maternal role with the younger ones. In fact, the *Kāma Sūtra* (KāmSū) prescribes that the younger wife should look upon her "like a mother":

> kaniṣṭhā tu mātṛvat sapatnīṃ paśyet
> The youngest should look upon her co-wife as a mother. [KāmSū 4.2, p. 245 (16)][20]

We can also marshall some evidence for the wife's participation in an additional marriage of her husband. *Manu* (9.81) allows a wife with childbearing problems to be superseded after a certain number of years: eight if she's barren, ten if her children all die, eleven if she has only daughters. The next verse requires a "sick" wife to *consent* to the second marriage;

> yā rogiṇī syāt tu hitā saṃpannā caiva śīlataḥ
> *sānujñāpyā*dhivettavyā nāvamānyā ca karhi cit
> One who is "sick," but agreeable and accomplished in conduct–she is (only) to be superseded [lit., "to be married over"] with her permission,[21] and she is never to be scorned. (MDŚ 9.82)

It is not clear to me if "sick" here refers to the childbearing problems in the previous law,[22] or if the wife is seriously afflicted with some other illness. The important point is that some wives "give permission" (with the *anu√jñā* we saw in both plays) to a second marriage. In the *Kāma Sūtra* it is also suggested that a barren wife will "urge" her husband to take another wife:

> prajānutpattau ca svayam eva sāpatnake codayet
> Or else (she) herself, in the absence of offspring, might urge (him) on to another wife [lit., a state of co-wifehood]. [KāmSū 4.2, p.242 (2)]

It is thus tempting to assume that the Kālidāsan heroines exactly fit this legal provision, that is, are "sick" with childlessness, but this neat solution won't entirely work. Dhāriṇī of the *Mālavikāgnimitra* has a grown son, whose brave exploits we hear about in the last act.[23] She should not be vulnerable to this necessity.

On the other hand, Auśīnarī in the *Urvaśī* does appear to be childless,[24] and her giving away may in part be motivated by this state. In fact, I am inclined to interpret the enigmatic second half of the king's declaration, quoted earlier, in this light:

> nāhaṃ punas tathā tvaṃ yathā hi māṃ śaṅkase bhīru
> For still I am not such as you suppose, o timid one. (Vik. 3.14)

This is usually[25] taken as a patently false denial by the king of his infatuation with Urvaśī. Since this passion will be joyously indulged before many minutes elapse, a denial by him would be remarkably stupid. I suggest instead that Purūravas is merely stating that he is not such a cad that he would pursue this infatuation, would not "marry over" his childless wife without her permission, as required by law. Such is her "power" over him: he recognizes his legal responsibility to obtain a formal release from her.

There is one other place in the marital system where a woman has considerable latitude in the disposition of the marriage, and in some ways this may be the most important for our purposes because it confers on a female the right not merely to "consent" or to "urge" but also actually to *give*. This is the Gāndharva marriage, or marriage by mutual consent. Here the bride makes a "gift of herself" (*ātmadāna*), rather than relying on some other donor. The clearest statement of this that I have found is in Duḥṣanta's smooth and sophistic enticement of Śakuntalā in the MBh version of that story and her straightforward response:

ātmano bandhur ātmaiva gatir ātmaiva cātmanaḥ
ātmanaivā*tmano dānam* kartum arhasi dharmataḥ

[Duḥśanta:] You yourself are your own relative. You yourself are your own means. You ought to make *a gift of yourself* by yourself according to law. (MBh 1.67.7)

yadi dharmapathas tv eṣa yadi cātmā prabhur mama
pradāne pauravaśreṣṭha śṛṇu me samayaṃ prabho

[Śakuntalā:] If this is a legal course and if I myself am my own master, O best of the Pauravas, hear my terms of agreement in my *giving* (of myself in marriage), O lord. (67.15)

Although, as we discussed above, women cannot usually give away even the trinkets they supposedly own, the form of the Gāndharva marriage accords them a remarkable—if dangerous—autonomy, the latitude to give away their own persons.[26] It is perhaps not such a great step from giving oneself away in marriage to giving someone else away, as in the plays, and it is perhaps also significant that the two Kālidāsan marriages in which women "officiate" are of the Gāndharva type, for the satisfaction of mutual infatuation.[27]

Let us now seek the roots of the gifts we have observed in the religious roles allotted to women in ancient India. I suggest this as a potential source because of a feature common to all three scenes we are considering, namely, that *the wife's gift always forms part of a ritual observance,* or the pretext of one. In the Urvaśi, Auśīnarī summons her husband to help her in the performance of a *vrata*, indeed the *piāṇuppasādaṇa* (Vik. 3.12+) [*priyānuprasādana*] 'propitiation of the beloved' vow. The *vrata* is not simply mentioned but also much is made of it—the time and location (cf. 3.4+), the queen's appropriate attire (3.11+, 12), the fetching and presentation of the oblation (3.13+), and even the distribution of goods to the Vidūṣaka afterward (3.13+). The queen's solemn declaration to the king of her favor toward his new beloved (quoted earlier) is prefaced by an invocation of deities and a ceremonial announcement of her ritual intention—almost a speech act—while doing pūjā to the king:

(rājñaḥ pūjām abhinīya prāñjaliḥ praṇipatya) esā ahaṃ devadāmihuṇaṃ rohiṇīmialañchanaṃ sakkhīkaria ajjauttaṃ aṇuppasādemi
[eṣāhaṃ devatāmithunaṃ rohiṇīmṛgalañchanaṃ sākṣīkṛtya āryaputram anuprasādayāmi]

[Acting out *pūjā* to the king, bowing down with reverent gesture.] Calling as witness the divine pair Rohiṇī and the moon, I hereby propitiate your worship. (Vik. 3.13+)

In *Mṛcchakaṭika* and again in the corresponding scene in Bhāsa's *Cārudatta*, Cārudatta's wife also claims to be fulfilling a religious duty, in her case the necessity of finding a brahmin to accept a gift from her in connection with a fast (Mṛcch. 3.26+, Cār. 3.16+). Since she has so far found no brahmin to do so, she urges the Vidūṣaka to oblige her by accepting her necklace.

In the *Mālavikāgnimitra*, the gift of Mālavikā is bound up in two different ritual complexes. On the one hand, in 3.5+, in connection with the *aśoka*-tree ceremony, the queen promised to grant a favor to Mālavikā. The phrase used is *pasādaṃ dāissaṃ* [*prasādaṃ dāsyāmi*], with the same lexeme as Auśīnarī used in the Urvaśī at her "propitiation" ceremony: *ajjauttaṃ aṇuppasādemi [āryaputram anuprasādayāmi]*. As is well known, the word *prasāda* often has a ritualistic sense in Sanskrit, "a propitiatory offering," in addition to the more general "graciousness, auspiciousness." In these two plays the lexeme *pra√sad* is especially the property of the Mahiṣīs and seems to mark their ceremonial role.[28] Note especially the last verse of the *Mālavikāgnimitra*, in which the king asks for the continued *prasāda* of the queen:

tvaṃ me *prasāda*sumukhī bhava caṇḍi nityam

O fierce one, be always to me one with a *gracious* countenance. (Māl. 5.20)

In addition, the *prasāda* promised to Mālavikā in Act 3, there is a more specific ritual context in the climatic Act 5. Here a horse sacrifice is at issue. A message arrives from Agnimitra's father, announcing the successful conclusion to the Wanderjahr of the horse destined for an Aśvamedha ritual[29] (5.14+–5+)–to the queen's great joy, as her son was the chief guardian of the horse (and thus in danger). And the king and queen(s) are commanded to come and join in the actual celebration of the ritual, which will be performed for his father, Puṣpamitra:

. . . bhavatā *vadhūjanena saha* yajñasevanāyāgantavyam

You must come, *along with your women-folk*, to attend upon the ritual. (Māl. 5.15+)

Nothing further is made of the precise role they are to play in the ceremony, but one wonders—especially with the explicit mention of the *vadhūjana* 'womenfolk' in this command invitation. As I have discussed elsewhere,[30] one of the interesting features of the *Mālavikāgnimitra* is the presence of a third woman, in addition to the chief wife and the young object of desire. This is a subordinate wife named Irāvatī, quarrelsome and sometimes drunken, who displays jealous rage at the end of Act 3 and only grudgingly (and from offstage) accepts the king's new wife in Act 5. This trio of Dhāriṇī, Irāvatī, and Mālavikā exactly replicates, in function and character, the triad of royal wives necessary for the performance of an Aśvamedha: the Mahiṣī or chief wife; the Parivṛktī, or "avoided wife," and the Vāvātā, or "favorite." It is hard (or at least hard for one steeped in *śrauta* ritual) not to see a covert and stylized reference to this ritual complex.[31] The queen, by officiating at the marriage of her husband and Mālavikā, would thus supply the necessary third wife, the Vāvātā, for the proper performance of the Aśvamedha, to which they have been summoned.

In any case, as we saw above, the queen calls her presentation of Mālavikā a token of her gratitude for the good news (about the safety of her son). It therefore counts also as a countergift in the system of reciprocity that structures the entire Old Indic ritual complex–a thanksgiving offering to the king, who has given her good news.

Why are all these "gifts" made by the women in these plays embedded in a ritual context? I suggest that it is only in the fulfillment of religious observance that women are ordinarily given the right to dispose of property, especially of property not strictly part of *strīdhana*. In particular, women are the usual *givers* of food to *begging* brahmins, an important religious duty of the householder, as I need scarcely demonstrate. Although the food may not strictly "belong" to her, as housewife and inhabitant of the pantry and kitchen, she dispenses it. The *right to give* thus comes to women in their position as wife of the householder and in fulfillment of one of the five daily *yajñas*. A single quotation, from a Gṛhya Sūtra prescription of begging formulas, should suffice here to show the wife's role as "giver":

bhavatpūrvayā brāhmaṇo bhikṣeta bhavati bhikṣāṃ dehīti bhavanmadhyamayā rājanyo bhikṣāṃ bhavati dehīti bhavadantyayā vaiśyo dehi bhikṣāṃ bhavatīti

A Brahman should beg with (the word) 'Lady' at the beginning (of the utterance): "Lady, give alms." A Rājanya [= Kṣatriya] with 'Lady' in the middle: "Give, Lady, alms." A Vaiśya with 'Lady' at the end: "Give alms, Lady."[32] (JGS 1.12)

This ascription to wives of control over household property and the right to give it in ritual context can be traced back to early Vedic times. In the prose Saṃhitās of the *Black Yajur Veda,* the wife's participation in the Guest Reception of Soma (the Ātithya ceremony) is explained as follows:

patnī vai pārīṇahyasyeśe patnyaiva rātam anumataṃ kriyate

The wife is master of the household goods. Thus the gift (of them) is made with the approval of the wife.[33] [*Maitrāyaṇī Saṃhitā* 3.7.9 (88:5)]

But only in religious context do we actually see the "mastery" proclaimed here: the wife has the power to give only as long as she is doing so for the fulfillment of religious duties[34]—hence, I suggest, the elaborately set-up vows and rituals in the episodes from the dramas under discussion.

The last question I want to address here about the episodes with which we began is how *giving* affects the *giver,* that is, the wife. There is a tendency, on the part of both Indian and Western critics, to see the wife's action as purely self-sacrifice, a poignant and noble submerging of her own needs and desires to further her husband's.[35] And certainly this aspect of the episodes cannot be denied. For example, after Dhāriṇī's giving away of Mālavikā, the (pseudo-)nun praises her with the almost nauseating

pratipakṣeṇāpi patiṃ sevyante bhartṛvatsalāḥ sādhvyaḥ

Virtuous women, devoted to their husbands, attend upon the husband even by (supplying) a rival. (Māl.5.19)

We should also keep in mind certain dimensions of giving in ancient India. "Giving" confers power on the giver; "receiving" is a sometimes shameful act that can put the receiver in the power of the giver. I have discussed this at length elsewhere, as have many others.[36] The giving performed by these women is no exception. Perhaps the most striking statement of this in the three episodes under discussion is that made by Cārudatta when he accepts his wife's necklace from the Vidūṣaka in the Mṛcchakaṭika—a verse that is found almost identically in Bhāsa'a *Cārudatta* (3.17):[37]

ātmabhāgyakṣatadravyaḥ strīdravyenānukampitaḥ
arthataḥ puruṣo nārī yā nārī sārthataḥ pūmān

(One), with his substance destroyed by his own (mis)fortune, pitied by the substance of a woman (/his wife)—Because of money (this) man (becomes) a woman, and the one who was a woman, because of money, she (becomes) male. (Mṛcch.3.27)

He thus suggests that his wife's power to give and his need to take has literally *switched their sexes.*

Interestingly enough, in the Mṛcch this bitter statement is softened by an immediately following verse (Mṛcch. 3.28) in which Cārudatta declares himself a spiritually rich man because of his faithful wife (and his friend the Vidūṣaka), a much more conventional and comforting sentiment. Bhāsa's *Cārudatta* makes no such concessions;

rather, *his* next verse (3.18) continues the complaint about being rescued by women's property (*strīṇām dhaneṣu*).

The struggle to give and not to be given to is manifested later in the *Mṛcchakaṭika* as well, between the two women and rivals. In Act 6 in the scene that gives the play its name, the courtesan Vasantasenā attempts to return the necklace to its owner, Cārudatta's wife, and is haughtily rebuffed: Cārudatta's wife wishes to retain the status of giver, and Vasantasenā is reduced to sneaking the goods to the child in the famous clay cart.

The manifestations of power that accrue to givers in the Kālidāsa episodes are somewhat more muted but nevertheless discernible. First recall that the king was reluctant to receive Mālavikā from Dhāriṇī and required some persuasion. His reluctance to accept her may have stemmed in part from his reluctance to grant such power to his chief wife—just as Cārudatta resisted receiving the necklace from his wife. Moreover both Auśīnarī and Dhāriṇī are hailed at the time of their gift in extravagant terms; their power and commanding presence are celebrated. As we saw, the last verse (5.20) of the Mālavikāgnimitra is a plea for continued favor addressed by the king to Dhāriṇī, whose power has previously been acknowledged by all. In the Urvaśī Auśīnarī is compared to Indra's wife by Urvaśī herself:

> halā iaṃ ṭhāṇe devīsaddeṇa uvaarīadi/ṇa kiṃ pi parihīadi *sacīe* ojassidāe
> [halā iyaṃ sthāne devīśabdenopacaryate/na kim api parihīyate *śacyā* ojasvitayā]
>
> Friend, she is properly served with the title "Goddess." She is hardly
> outstripped by Śacī [= Indra's wife] in possession of power. (Vik. 3.12+)

The same comparison to Indra's wife may also be made in the *Mālavikgnimitra of Auśīnarī*. A verse recited in praise of her is uncannily reminiscent of the praise of Indrāṇī[38] in RV 10.86.

> bhartrāsi vīrapatnīnīṃ ślāghyāyāṃ sthāpitā dhūri
> vīrasūr iti śabdo 'yam tanayāt tvām upasthitaḥ
>
> By your husband you were established at the celebrated forefront of wives. This title "mother of heroes" has been bestowed on you from your progeny. (Māl. 5.16)
>
> . . . vedhá ṛtásya vīríṇīndrapatnī mahīyate
> indrāṇīm āsú nāriṣu subhágām ahám aśravam . . .
>
> She is magnified as the Ordainer of Truth, as one having a man/hero, having Indra as husband. (RV 10.86.10)
> I have heard of Indrāṇī as (most) fortunate among these women. (86.11)

It is tempting, though perhaps somewhat farfetched, to imagine some such litany of praise to Indrāṇī as the model for the similarly ceremonial verse celebrating Dhāriṇī. Thus, surrendering their husbands to their rivals in some ways seems to enhance rather than diminish their positions.[39]

I do not by the preceding discussion wish to distort any of these plays into a "feminist" fantasy of empowered ladies, central and successful figures in dramas that really concern sexual politics, not the courtly love that actually dominates the action. I readily admit that none of the episodes discussed is a major part of the play in which it is found; none of the giving wives is a major character. Nonetheless, I suggest that certain thematic complexes found in the earlier Indian tradition surface here and that paying attention to the potential legal and ritual connections of episodes in court literature may complicate our views of this genre. The curious role of "giver in marriage," assumed by two chief queens in two of

Kālidāsa's plays, loses some of its bizarreness when we place it in the context of some *ceremonial* aspects of ordinary marriage, of some *legal* provisions concerning superseded wives, and of some *ritual* roles allotted to women in earlier texts.

Notes

1. The general and very complex issue of *strī-dhana* lies outside the scope of this chapter. Many of the aspects of this topic were recently treated, with the author's usual clarity and deftness, in an unpublished lecture by Ludo Rocher, a copy of which he was kind enough to give me. It has informed my thinking in many ways, though I will not quote from his oral text directly.

2. "False": see D. Gitomer, "Urvaśī Won by Valor," in *Theater of Memory: The Plays of Kālidāsa,* Barbara Stoler Miller, ed. (New York: Columbia University Press, 1984), notes to 3.14, 3.14+; "reproachful": see M. R. Kale, *The Vikramorvaśīya of Kālidāsa* (1898), p.121 (English commentary).

3. On *prārthaya* as a possible technical term, see Stephanie W. Jamison, *Sacrificed Wife/ Sacrificer's Wife: Women, Ritual, and Hospitality in Ancient India* (New York: Oxford University Press, 1996), p. 301 n. 53.

4. For *anyasmai* we might prefer *anyasyai,* with Kale (*Vikramorvaśīya*), though it is not clear on what authority. No other edition I consulted has *anyasyai,* and A. Scharpe, *Kālidāsa Lexicon* (Brugge: De Tempel, 1956) Vol. 1.2, does not report this variant.

5. That her costume is specifically nuptial is mentioned several times (5.6+) by Mālavikā herself (*koduālaṇkāra-* [*kautukālaṅkāra-*]) and by the Vidūṣaka when he first sees her (vevāhiaṇevattha- [*vaivāhikanepathya-*]).

6. Consider Mṛcch. 4. 24, where the courtesan Vasantasenā gives her servant Madanikā in marriage to Śarvilaka, the thief. Her new husband says to her that she has achieved what is difficult to acquire: "the title and veil of a bride" (*vadhūśabdāvaguṇṭhanam*). At the end of the play (10.54+) Vasantasenā also receives this "title of bride" (*vadhūśabda*) simultaneously with the veil (*vasantasenām avaguṇṭhya*). A.W. Ryder calls the veil in his translation *The Little Clay Cart* (Cambridge, Mass: Harvard University Press, 1905), p. 174 "a token of honorable marriage." Similarly in the *Śakuntalā,* when our heroine arrives at Duḥśanta's palace, seeking to take up her wifely status, the king first remarks (5.13) *kā svid avaguṇṭhanavatī* "who is this veiled one?" and immediately forbears to look at her, with the words *anirvarṇanīyaṃ parakalatram* "The wife of another is not to be inspected." This sequence might indicate that the *avaguṇṭhana* was a sign of a respectable married woman. Soon after in this scene Gautamī, Śakuntalā's chaperone, says;

avaṇaissaṃ dāva de ouṇṭhaṇaṃ/tado tumaṃ bhaṭṭā ahijāṇissadi [apaneṣyāmi tāvat te 'vaguṇṭhanam /tatas tvāṃ bhartābhijñāsyati]

I will now remove your veil. Then your husband will recognize you. (5.18+)

Again this suggests that the *avaguṇṭhana* was a married woman's raiment, only to be removed in front of her husband. It must be admitted, however, that in other passages (e.g., Mṛcch. 6.10) *ava√guṇṭh* and its derivatives simply refer to some variety of covering of the face and head, also assumable by a male.

7. Cf. MDŚ 3.27–34 and the discussion in Jamison, *Sacrificed Wife,* pp. 210–18.

8. Cf. the almost identical provision in MDŚ 5.148:

bālye pitur vaśe tiṣṭhet pāṇigrāhasya yauvane/putrāṇām bhartari prete na bhujet strī svatantratām.

This provision is also echoed elsewhere, for example *Baudhāyana Dharma Sūtra* (BDS) 2.3.45, *Vāsiṣṭha Dharma Sūtra* (VāsDS) 5.3, and *Viṣṇu Smṛti* (ViṣSmṛ) 25.13.

9. Karṇa refers to this provision in the debate about Draupadī's status in the aftermath of

the dicing match. His point seems to be that Draupadī is doubly without rights, both as a woman and as the wife of a slave.

trayaḥ kileme adhanā bhavanti dāsaḥ śiṣyaś cāsvatantrā ca
narī dāsasya patnī tvaṃ dhanam asya bhadre hīneśvarā dāsadhanaṃ ca dāsī

These three are without property; the slave, the pupil, and the woman without independence. (As) the wife of a slave, you are his property, lovely one, and with your master/husband brought low, (as) property of a slave, you (also) are a slave. (MBh. 2.63.1)

Notice that Karṇa's definition is somewhat broader than Manu's: only the wife is explicitly mentioned in *Manu* (though it is certainly possible that all women were meant), whereas Karṇa's clause specifies *asvatantrā narā* 'nonindependent women'. By MDŚ 9.3 (already quoted) females are by definition *asvatantrā* throughout their lives.

10. But these make global reference to Kane's treatment of this subject in *History of Dharmaśāstra: Ancient and Mediaeval Religious and Civil Law* (Poona: Bhandarkar Oriental Research Institute, 1946) especially pp. 3.707ff. and 770–802, as well as to the work of Rocher mentioned in note 1.

11. Although, as Rocher points out, in some systems she may have much greater control over *strīdhana* proper than over goods that may come to her in some other way.

The same texts that explicitly circumscribe her power over her goods can also imply a greater control over disbursement than they state: for a number of offenses a woman is fined a certain sum of money, from which we might surmise that she had something to pay with. Cf., for example, MDŚ 8.369 (where a *kanyā* 'unmarried maiden' is the subject, one who is even less likely to have a source of cash than a wife) and KA 3.3.20–30. Of course, the monetary economy assumed by these laws marks them as rather late formulations.

12. And even in the standard wedding ceremony, where the father performs the official "giving," the mother sometimes has a minor role. According to some of the Gṛhya Sūtras, the mother takes part in the Lājahoma, which involves pouring roasted grain into the hands of the bride (and groom). The usual performer of this action is the bride's brother. [Or even the bridegroom himself. Cf. *Hiranyakeśin Gṛhya Sūtra* (HGS) 1.20.3; *Āpastamba Gṛhya Sūtra* (AGS) 5.4–5 (which also allows a relative of the bride).] But some texts allow the mother as an alternate [(*Gobhila Gṛhya Sūtra* 2.2.3; *Jaiminīya Gṛhya Sūtra* (JGS) 1.21], and in others she carries the basket containing the grain [*Mānava Gṛhya Sūtra* (MGS) 1.11.2–3, 10–11; JGS 1.20; *Vārāha Gṛhya Sūtra* (VGS) 14.8; *Khādira Gṛhya Sūtra* (KhādGS) 1.3.18]. Since the Lājahoma occurs in the heart of the ritual events that are the climax of the wedding ceremony proper—the treading on the stone, the circumambulation of the fire, and the seven steps—the participation of the bride's mother, even as a basket carrier, seems significant.

13. Cf. *Viṣṇu Smṛti* 24.38–39, which interposes the maternal grandfather (*mātāmaha*) before the mother; *Nārāyaṇa Smṛti* 20–22 (sim.). See also Kane, *History of Dharmaśāstra*, vol.2, pp.501-2.

14. Except for Āsura "purchase."

15. Though presumably the mother of the bride, not of the groom as here.

16. On the institution of "wooing," see Jamison, *Sacrificed Wife*, pp. 221–223.

17. This verse does not occur in all version, and may be an interpolation.

18. Or "keep their eyes on their wives."

19. Note also that in the *Mālatīmādhava* episode alluded to above, the nun who gives Mālatī away considers herself worthy of "more than a mother's love" (*sneho mātuḥ samadhikataraḥ*) for this deed (Māl. 10.5). This suggests in effect that she stood in loco matris in this deed.

We might note in passing a nonmaternal female figure operating in the marital realm. In Kālidāsa'a *Raghuvaṃśa* (Ragh.), in the description of the *svayaṃvara* (Ragh. 6), the princess who is making the choice is led from eligible man to eligible man by the "portress" (*pratihārarakṣā*) Sunandā, who introduces each prince with name, lineage, and accomplishments. In other *svayaṃvara* depicted in Sanskrit literature, the announcement of the roster of suitors is made by the bride's brother. Cf. the proclamation at Draupadī's *svayaṃvara* by her brother Dhṛṣṭadyumna (MBh 1.176.36ff.).

20. In citations of the *Kāma Sūtra* I give the page numbers of the 1891 edition, in addition to chapter and section numbers. I also give (in parentheses), for convenience, the *sūtra* number in the recent and widely available translation of A. Daniélou (*The Complete Kāma Sūtra*, 1994), without at all endorsing the often inaccurate renderings found therein.

21. The Sanskrit is phrased in a more sinister fashion: "she is to be made to agree," with the gerundive [or so I interpret it: given the *sandhi*, it could also be the gerund "having caused to agree," which makes little syntactic sense] of the causative of *anu√jñā*. The lexeme and the morphology both recall *saṃjñāpayati* 'makes to agree', the euphemism for killing a sacrificial victim in *śrauta* ritual. Another example in connection with co-wives is found in the *Kāma Sūtra* 4.2, p. 245 (19): where "permitted (by the oldest wife) (the youngest one) should sleep with (their) husband" (*anujñātā patim adhiśayīta*).

22. Which would, I think, be a peculiar usage of *rogin-*.

23. As well as a younger daughter, mentioned in Māl.1.3+.

24. See the Vidūṣaka's declaration in 5.0, and Gitomer, "Urvaśi Won by Valor," note to 3.0.

25. See, for example, Gitomer (ibid.).

26. For further discussion, see Jamison, *Sacrificed Wife*, pp. 247–50

27. This occurs also in the *Mālatīmādhava* example discussed above, where without the ritual intervention of the nun, a Gāndharva marriage would clearly have gone forward anyway.

28. For example, Vik. 2.20, 3.12, 3.14+.

29. Itself following a Rājasūya, a remarkable cluster of *śrauta* rituals to be named in a literary work of this nature.

30. "*Vṛtra et Vṛθragna* and *Sur la Structure du kāvya*—Some Intersections: Vedic Motifs in *Kumārasaṃbhava* III," *Langue, style et structure dans le monde indien: Centenaire de Louis Penou*, N. Balbir and G. Pinault, eds. Paris: Honoré Champion, 1996, pp. 123–42.

31. Kālidāsa would not have needed a specialist's knowledge of arcane ritual detail.

32. For the utterances, cf. *Pāraskara Gṛhya Sūtra* (PārGS) 2.5.2–4, MDŚ 2.49; *Āpastambha Dharma Sūtra* (ĀDS) 1.3.28–30; *Gautama Dharma Sūtra* (GDS) 2.36; *Vāsiṣṭha Dharma Sūtra* (VāsDS) 11.68–70; *Baudhāyana Dharma Sūtra* (BDS) 1.3.16–17; ViSmṛ 27.25. *Āśvalāyaṇa Gṛhya Sūtra* (ĀGS)1.22.6–8 is unusual in also allowing men to be approached, with the formula *bhavān bhikṣāṃ dadātu* "Let your honor give alms" (with the masculine honorific *bhavān* that corresponds to the femine *bhavati* "Lady" in the normal formula).

33. Cf. *Kāṭhaka Saṃhitā* 24.8 (98: 13); *Taittirīya Saṃhitā* 6.2.1.1.

34. In this connection we might remember something alluded to briefly above: in the Urvaśī one of Auśīnarī's activities connected with her vow is the distribution of sweetmeats to the Vidūṣaka after the ritual proper. Thus she enacts the role of *ritual* giver at the same time as she "gives" her husband away.

35. For example, J. A. B. van Buitenen, "The Classical Drama," in *The Literatures of India* (Chicago: University of Chicago Press, 1974), pp. 104f., calls this episode involving Cārudatta's wife "a quiet tragedy."

36. See Jamison, *Sacrificed Wife*, pp. 195–203.

37. The only difference is the first *pāda*: the semantically equivalent *mayi dravyakṣayakṣīṇe*.

38. However, it is ironically meant in the RV. See Jamison, *Sacrificed Wife*, p. 80.

39. One might also note that according to the Kām.Sū. the oldest wife exercises considerably authority over the behavior of the younger ones (4.2 p. 245), even to the extent of controlling the younger wives' property [4.2 (18): *jñātidāyam api tasyā aviditaṃ nopayuñjīta* "Even gifts from her relatives should not be used unknown to this (oldest wife)." Thus, the surrendering of the husband may lead to the acquisition of a subordinate in the household.

5

Om, *the Vedas, and the Status of Women with Special Reference to Śrīvaiṣṇavism*

KATHERINE K. YOUNG

The Meaning of *Om* in the Vedas

Much of women's status in classical and medieval Hinduism hangs precariously on the sacred syllable *om* (which combines *a-u-m*, according to Sanskrit rules of phonetic combination, or *sandhi*). To date, there have been few attempts to trace the history of *om*.[1] Despite its sacrality, it does not appear in the Vedas. The main synonym of *om* is *praṇava*, from the verbal root *praṇu* (to roar, bellow, sound, reverberate, or make a humming or droning sound). This root does appear in the *Ṛg Veda* (although the noun appears only in the *Vājasaneyi Saṃhitā*, *Taittirīya Saṃhitā*, and *Śatapatha Brāhmaṇa*). According to Hans Henrich Hock,[2] *om* originated in the *Yajurveda Saṁhitā* and the *Jaiminīya Brāhmaṇa* as an exclamatory particle; a filler particle; or a recitational substitute for part of an utterance, especially *ō* for *a* or *ā*. Regarding the last, he accounts for variants with the nasal (i.e., *om*) by *sandhi* in the final or prepausal position, by a type of vowel pronunciation (*pluta* or *trimoric*), or by avoiding a hiatus between some vowels.

Hock argues that the mystical significance of *om* is a secondary development from its exclamatory, filler, and recitational uses; all of these overlap in the context of Vedic rituals. He agrees with A. B. Keith's (1917) view that the idea of a *sacred* syllable is first found in the *Aitareya Brāhmaṇa* and belongs to the *Ṛg Veda* (not in the *Chāndogya Upaniṣad* of the *Sāma Veda* tradition, as argued by J. A. B. van Buitenen, 1959). The relevant passage of the *Aitareya Brāhmaṇa*[3] says that Prajāpati created the three worlds of earth, ether, and sky. From them emerged Agni and the *Ṛg Veda*; Vāyu and the *Yajur Veda*; and Aditya and the *Sāma Veda*, respectively. From these, in turn, he created the syllables *bhūr*, *bhuvas*, and *svar*, respectively. And from these, he created the three phonemes *a*, *u*, and *m*, which were then combined as *om*. Hock cites van Buitenen's suggestion that sacred significance developed from esoteric speculations. He observes that this was true also of other particles. *Vā* was identified with *Vāc*, for example, which was then identified with speech, syllable (*akṣara*), and Brahman.[4] From these passages and their elaboration in related Āraṇyakas, he attributes the religious meanings of *om* to peculiarities of the grammatical, phonetic, and recitational aspects of Vedic ritual,[5] whose overlap and repetition by various groups of priests gave rise to the idea of essence, and from essence to the idea of Brahman.

The placement of *om* as an exclamatory particle (at the beginning or end of texts and rituals or sections of them) has semantic implications. *Taittirīya Brāhmaṇa* 2:11, for example, *begins* with *om*. It says that he who knows Brahman as reality (*satya*), as knowledge (*jñāna*), and as infinity (*ananta*) in the secret place of the heart and in the highest heaven (*parame vyoman*) obtains all desires.[6] This alludes to *parame vyoman* in the *Ṛg Veda*:[7] '*ṛco akṣare parame* [*vyomni*]: worship in the supreme imperishable (*akṣara*) realm. One hermeneutical principle of Vedic exegesis is order (*krama*). The first, final, and middle positions usually define preeminence. Additional criteria are introduced in particular texts to define the relative importance of these three. In short, there is a hermeneutical reason for *om* at the beginning of a Brāhmaṇa passage.

In the Upaniṣads, four major motifs—creation, salvation, the essence of speech, and the idea of beginning—are linked with *om*. In the *Bṛhadāraṇyaka Upaniṣad*, *om* has also come to connote "yes," with the addition of a Dravidian particle of assent (*ām* which means "yes" in Tamil is assimilated into *om*).[8] According to the *Chāndogya*:[9]

> Oṁ! One should adore this syllable. Beginning with *om* one certainly sings the *udgītha*. The elucidation about that is as follows.
>
> The gods, when they were afraid of death, fled away for refuge in the threefold lore (of the) Vedas. They covered themselves in the metre. Because they covered themselves (*ācchādayan*), that is why the metre is called *chandas*. But death espied them in the same place, in the Ṛc, in the *Sāman*, in the *Yajus*, as one espies fish in water. The gods observed it; they rose above the Ṛc, the *Sāman* and the *Yajus* and fled for refuge in the sound. When one employs a Ṛc, *he sounds out in the sound om*; so also in the case of *Sāman* and *Yajus*. Therefore, the sound, it is that syllable; it is the immortal, fearless one. Because the gods fled for refuge in it, they became immortal and fearless. He who, having this knowledge, makes this syllable resound as *praṇava*, flies for safety to this syllable which sound [and] . . . is the immortal and the fearless one. And he, who flies for refuge in it, becomes also immortal, just as the gods are immoral.[10]

Chāndogya Upaniṣad[11] states:

> He brooded over these; out of them, as he brooded over them, flowed forth the sound *om*. That is why, just as by means of a nail (*śaṅku*), all leaves are perforated together (*saṃtṛṇṇa*), so also by means of *om*, all speech is perforated together. The sound *om* is this whole-world the sound *om* is this whole world.[12]

The identification of *om* with the whole world and with Brahman, is found in the *Taittirīya Upaniṣad*.[13] "The syllable *oṁ* is the Brahman, the syllable *om* is this whole world."[14] This text also uses *om* as a confirmatory particle. In the ritual context of the *agnihotra*, it is the affirmative reply of one priest to the command given by another:

> When one says "*oṁ*," it implies a compliant act and when also the Adhvaryu says: "O, let us hear the call or invocation," the Agnīdhra lets him hear it. With *om*, they sing the *Samans*, with *om*, Śom they recite the *śāstras* (the prayers), with *om* the Adhvaryu responds in reply to the invocation, with *om* the Brahman requests, the *yajamāna* (the sacrificer) gives his assent during the Agnihotram.[15]

In other words, *om* begins particular oral aspects of the ritual and is also used to express assent. According to this text, moreover, *om* is uttered by a brahmin about to begin studying the Veda in order to reach Brahman: "'May I attain the (Vedic word) Brahman,' and he attains the Brahman."[16] This suggests *upanayana* (the ritual that marks the beginning of the brahmin's study of the Vedas), in short, and links study of the Vedas with the realization of Brahman.

The *Chāndogya Upaniṣad*[17] refers to the three Vedas and their transcendence. This is reminiscent of the Puruṣasūkta of *Ṛg Veda* 10:90, which says that Puruṣa is three-quarters immanent and one-quarter transcendent. The *Māṇḍūkya Upaniṣad* describes all three of the sounds that constitute *om* as well as their combination: *a* represents the waking state, *u*, the dream state, and *m* deep sleep. The entire syllable represents the transcendent state (*turīya*). It represents past, present, and future, moreover, as well as transcendent time. It is both the universe and the soul (*ātman*).

From these passages,[18] it should be clear that *om* has a cosmogonic connection. It is eternal time or imperishable source. Alternatively, it is the first manifestation, as primal sound, of Brahman. It also has a soteriological function because it symbolizes the supreme refuge: where the gods flee to avoid death and where humans attain liberation.

My own reconstruction of the early history of *om* differs somewhat from that of Hock and other scholars I have mentioned. Because in Vedic rituals *om* is placed at the beginning or end of the ritual, it symbolizes the boundary between the sacred and the profane. Because it also marks the transition between sections of the ritual, it connects them internally. Already in the ritual of the Brāhmaṇas, therefore, *om* has the incipient meaning of sacred sound: beginning, end, and connection. It is just a small step to connect these with cosmogony (via the idea of the beginning, or first manifestation), soteriology (via the idea of the end), and the essence of Brahman (via the idea of internal connection)—as occurred in some of the Brāhmaṇas and Upaniṣads. The transference of *om* from the context of sacred ritual to sacred text can also be seen in the fact that the orthographic equivalent of the sound *om* was used visually to mark the *beginning* of the text (and thereby to set it off from profane words). The use of *om* to symbolize beginning was used in a more general sense to symbolize the beginning of Veda study itself (the *upanayana* ritual), and even the beginning of that (the *gāyatrī* or *sāvitrī* mantra), and even the beginning of the latter (*om* itself). It is significant that the *gāyatrī* mantra begins the daily *sandhyā* rituals at the transition points (or boundaries) of dawn, dusk, and noon.

The first reference to the mantra *om namo nārāyaṇāya*, which would become central to the Śrīvaiṣṇava tradition, is in the *Nārāyaṇa Upaniṣad* (which I date ca. 500–300 B.C.E.).[19] This one belongs to that collection of the Upaniṣads, beginning with the *Māṇḍūkya* and the *Praśna*, that is loosely associated with the *Atharva Veda*. It begins with a cosmogonic myth;[20] then, it describes how one goes, with Rudra as charioteer and the mind as reins, to the supreme hereafter, the eternal abode of Viṣṇu. Those who study this text eliminate fears, obtain all desires, and gain immortality. The passage continues with a comment on *om*:

> One should first utter *om*, then *namo*, and afterwards Nārāyaṇāya. *Om* is one syllable, *namo* are two syllables, Nārāyaṇāya are five syllables. This is the octo-syllabic metrical line of Nārāyaṇa. He who studies this octo-syllabic metrical line of Nārāyaṇa reaches the full span of life without a mishap, he enjoys happiness in offspring, growth of prosperity, possession of cattle, and he further participates in immortality. . . . He (Nārāyaṇa) merged into one with the inner bliss, the Brahman, the Puruṣa, the holy syllable consisting of *a*, *u* and *m*, it became the sound *Om*. The Yogin who has seen this, is free from birth and *saṃsāra*. And he who worships the formula: *om namo nārāyaṇāya*, he goes to Vaikuṇṭha's (Viṣṇu's) heaven. That city is here, this lotus-flower . . . who dwells in all beings, one, Nārāyaṇa, the cause, the *a*, the highest Brahman in the *Om* sound. He who studies this Atharvaśiras—if he studies it in the morning, then he annihilates the sins committed at night, if he studies it in the evening, then he annihilates the sins committed in the day:

> if he studies it at midday, facing the sun, then he is freed of the five major sins and the five minor sins, participates in the merit which is the goal of all Vedas, and attains communion with Nārāyaṇa—attains communion with Nārāyaṇa.[21]

The god Nārāyaṇa is identified with Brahman and Puruṣa. He is understood as the inner bliss and *om*, as well as the "highest Brahman" because he is the cause, the *a* in *aum* (*om*). Here, we see that one mantra is connected not only with a supramundane result (*phala*)—that is, Vaikuṇṭha, the celestial city, also present as the *ātman*, the self within each person—but with a mundane result as well. (The same motif is found in the *Atharva Veda*,[22] which says that *om* is the mother of the Veda and confers longevity, glory, offspring, and cattle.) The *Nārāyaṇa Upaniṣad* is called *atharvaśiras*. It is linked with the three times of the *sandhyā* ritual, in particular, and the Vedic tradition, in general. But even more significant is that worship of this mantra makes it possible to bypass the Vedas and directly attain immortality. In other words, the path to salvation has been universalized in this text dedicated to a deity not found in the *Ṛg Veda.*

Other texts link chanting the mantra with the creation of powers that can be projected to achieve any kind of result—victory, happiness, placating the planets, and so on.[23] Connecting the utterance of *om* to particular actions in Vedic ritual developed subsequently into the notion of mantra as a formula uttered by priests to identify objects with sacred forces and to direct them in acts of homage. This involved offering something *to* deities, expressed by the use of the dative case.[24] Given these developments, *om* was quickly becoming the all-inclusive, oral symbol par excellence.

According to the Dharmasūtras and the Gṛhyasūtras, *om* is closely associated with the *upanayana* ritual and salvation. The *Āpastamba Dharmasūtra*[25] (ca. 600–300 B.C.E[26]) remarks that *oṃkāra* "is the door to heaven; therefore one who is about to study the Veda should start his study by first repeating *om*."[27] The *Āpastamba Dharmasūtra*[28] refers to imparting the *gāyatrī mantra*.[29] The *gāyatrī*, in turn, is linked with the daily ritual of *sandhyā*, performed at sunrise and sunset:[30] "We contemplate that esteemed (longed for) refulgence (glory) of the divine *Savitṛ* who may inspire our intellects (or actions)."[31] There is considerable debate over the meter of this *mantra* when chanted by men of the three twice-born castes. Many sources say that the *gāyatrī* meter is for brahmins, the *triṣṭubh* for *kṣatriyas*, and the *jagati* for *vaiśyas*. The *Āpastamba Dharmasūtra*[32] observes that the recitation of *om* is equal to that of all the Vedas.

Later sectarian texts exploit the numerical symbolisms of "three" and "four." In the *Mārkaṇḍeya Purāṇa*,[33] for instance, the three letters of *om* are identified with Viṣṇu, Lakṣmi, and the soul, as well as with the three Vedas. The *Śiva Purāṇa* offers numerous expansions, aligning the three sounds with the three lines of the forehead emblem (*tripuṇḍra*), three types of utterance—mental, low voice, and verbal—and so forth. Śiva is the *praṇava*, in the final analysis, and the *praṇava* is Śiva.[34] Sometimes, symbolisms are arranged according to four items, inspired by the association of the four states of consciousness with *om*, according to the *Māṇḍūkya Upaniṣad*.

The Marginalization of Women in Vedic Ritual and Learning

Before describing the relation between women and the syllable *om* in medieval Śrivaiṣṇavism, I will examine women's education when *om* was becoming a sacred syllable. It is not my purpose here to trace in detail the history of women in Vedic education and Vedic ritual. I note merely that at least some women once knew some Vedic hymns, including some Vedic mantras, and once performed some Vedic rituals,[35] but the women were gradually marginalized. Hārīta, an author of an early *sūtra*,[36] mentions two kinds of woman: the *brahmavādinīs* and the *sadyovadhūs*. *Brahmavādinīs* undergo *upanayana*, feed the fire (i.e., keep it burning), study the Veda, and beg for alms in their own homes. As for *sadyovadhūs*, they should marry after having undergone the *upanayana* (just as a ritual, though, and not followed by study).[37] Male students (*brahmacārīs*) were formally required to live with their teachers and beg for their food (as did Buddhist and Jain monastics, both male and female). Clearly, an adjustment was made for female students (*brahmacāriṇīs*) in the brahminical tradition. The idea of begging for food in their own homes makes no practical or even religious sense, though, because food was readily available and women probably contributed their own labor to its preparation. Morever, begging for food at home could hardly teach them about dependency or humility—which is what it was intended to teach men. It must have been a concession to the letter of the law, therefore, rather than a genuine religious observance.

Equally important but seldom acknowledged by scholars, confining women to the home bolstered the identity of urban men—when it could no longer be based on survival functions related to male bodies (size, strength, and mobility)—by making public space exclusively male space. One result was that women were denied education, special expertise, or mobility.[38] Confining them to the home also ensured chastity. The *upanayana* became a perfunctory ritual for the second class of woman, the *sadyovadhūs*, and a symbol of their general twice-born (most likely brahminical) status rather than a real rite of passage into sacred learning. (For a more complete discussion of the role of women in both Vedic and Buddhist mendicancy, see Ellison Findly's chapter elsewhere in this volume.)

Hārīta alludes to a decline in women's Vedic education by referring to the two types of woman (one a Vedic student, the other uneducated and therefore ineligible to perform rituals). Yama, who is quoted by Manu and must have lived even earlier,[39] alludes not to the decline of Vedic education for women but to its disappearance. It belonged to an earlier age:

> In an earlier *kalpa* the tying of the *muñja* grass around women is prescribed; likewise, there is to be the teaching of the Vedas and [recitation] of the Sāvitrī [i.e. the *gāyatrī mantra*]. Their father, father's brother, or brother is to teach them but not another [a stranger]. Obtaining alms is prescribed for a maiden only in her own house. She is to avoid wearing deerskin, bark [garment] and *jaṭā* locks [matted hair].[40]

Thus, Yama assumes a direct link between initiation (*upanayana*) and Vedic education (which had become customary for male students). His reference to the *gāyatrī* is particularly significant, because recitation of this mantra has been at the core of subsequent orthodoxy. Yama stipulates, moreover, that a father must perform his daughter's wedding before she reaches puberty; otherwise, he drinks her menstrual blood, month after month and he, along with her mother and eldest brother, will go to hell (*Yama Saṃhitā*).[41] Finally, Yama opposes the involvement of women in asceticism. Their heads should not to be shaved. They should not follow cows or spend nights in cowpens—that is, wander about and sleep in the open. And they should not pronounce the *vaidika* (Vedic) *mantra*.[42]

In a discussion of the *vaidika* mantra, Manu[43] makes a direct link between *om* and women. I will begin by examining his general view of *om:* (1) it marks the beginning and end of Vedic recitation; (2) it is the essence of the three Vedas and the three exclamations of *bhūr, bhuvas, and svar;* (3) it is connected with the *sāvitrī (gāyatrī) mantra;* (4) it is performed at the time of *sandhyā* (rituals at the beginning and end of the day); (5) its repetition at *sandhyā* creates merit equal to that of reciting the entire Veda; and (6) its repetition frees one from great error. In addition, Manu says[44] that repeating *om* together with the three exclamations and the *gāyatrī* for three years allows one to "become wind" and reach ultimate liberation. It is not only the means (ten times as effective as a sacrifice) but also the supreme goal, the ultimate reality, the imperishable beyond the perishable rituals (the *uttara-mīmāṃsā* beyond *pūrva-mīmāṃsā*). Earlier in the text Manu addresses women's participation in ritual. *Upanayana* rituals for women should be performed at the right time *but without recitation of the vaidika mantras.*[45] (This verse equates the ritual of marriage with that of the *upanayana* for women, a woman's service to her husband with that of a male student's life with his guru, and household tasks with the rites of fire.)

Manu opposes the performance of public Vedic rituals by various people—these include those who do not know the Vedas, say, or those who are not discriminating about their ritual clients—and he explicitly mentions women in this context.[46] But some authors of the Gṛhyasūtras recognize that *married* women perform the household rituals, and Manu follows suit.[47] He forbids only virgins and young girls from these rituals, along with ignorant, naive, distressed, or uninitiated men. After describing the importance of guarding women and the bad things that befall a family when women are not guarded or are naturally inclined to bad conduct, he declares:

> There is no ritual with Vedic verses for women; this is a firmly established point of law. For women who have no virile strength and no Vedic verses, are falsehood; this is well established. There are many revealed canonical texts to this effect that are sung even in treatises on the meaning of the Vedas, so that women's distinctive traits may be carefully inspected.[48]

This is followed by a description of the ways in which women can overcome their bad conduct. In other words, married women cannot do any Vedic rituals with *om*.

In the *Kātyāyana Saṃhitā*,[49] Kātyāyana (who lived between the third century and the fourth) states that if one wife cannot perform the ritual by herself, then several should do it according to seniority or ability, serially or jointly, according to their own understanding and knowledge of the scriptures. They should "serve" the fire, in other words, even if lack of training makes it difficult for them.

The marginalization of women from Vedic knowledge and ritual, therefore, was probably due to several elements. First, it was the result of the specialization of Vedic knowledge (which led to a long period of study in the home of a male teacher—worrisome for parents increasingly concerned about protecting the virginity of their daughters and ensuring their marriage at an increasingly young age). Second, it was the result of a priestly desire to control more and more rituals (some of which were once located in the home and performed by women). And third, it was the result of women's real loss of Vedic knowledge. When commenting on the *Jaimini*,[50] for instance, Śabara (ca. 200–500 C.E.) writes that the sacrificer is a learned man, whereas the wife is without knowledge (*avidyā*).

The Link between Women and *Śūdras*

One other context must be addressed in this discussion of women: the role of *śūdras*. By the medieval period, the status of women became linked ritually and philosophically with that of *śūdras*. There are two possible, albeit related, reasons: women's lack of Vedic knowledge and therefore their inability to perform Vedic rituals (symbolized by their ineligibility to utter *vaidika* mantras); and, by contrast, the fact that their inclusion came to symbolize a universal, devotional religion. The former is a negative link, of course, and the latter a positive one.[51]

These reasons must be placed in a larger context: the changing fortunes of *śūdras*. The word *sūdra* is a general one for groups such as the Dāsa (Dasyu), considered by some scholars to have developed a mixed "Aryan" and Indus culture in the late Indus or post-Indus periods.[52] In the *Atharva Veda*, the Dāsa (Dasyu)—pastoralists, craftsmen, and warriors—are sometimes portrayed positively, as equals of the "Aryas" (5:11:3). This indicates an attitude of inclusiveness not always apparent in the *Ṛg Veda* and other texts. *Atharva Veda* 9:15, moreover, states that *śūdras* may undergo *upanayana*. This status was gradually lost, though, during a time of growing conflict[53] when *śūdras* were taken as prisoners of war. After expansion of the Vedic culture into the mid-Gangetic plain, war captives continued to be taken from the *śūdras*' ranks and were used as corvée labor to clear the land. The Mauryan emperors (ca. 320–186 B.C.E.) promoted the notion of service to make this status palatable. When the Mauryan state disintegrated, the elite in Mathurā, Kuru, and Pañcāla felt particularly threatened by political turmoil (ca. 200–100 B.C.E.). From the west came invading foreigners such as the Greeks and Śakas. From the east came political pressure by other kings.[54] The Sūtras and Śāstras of the period campaigned virulently against indentured laborers and slaves, no doubt because the latter were associated with these foreign or renegade kings. In this period, *śūdras* were often linked with women, and both were viewed negatively. According to Āpastamba, for instance, neither women nor *śūdras* may be taught the Vedas. The latter may neither undergo *upanayana* nor perform *yajña* (fire rituals). Manu represents this brahminical low point. So, both women and *śūdras* came to be considered *avaidika* (ignorant of the Vedas), though for somewhat different reasons.

After 100 C.E., the Gangetic plain became more prosperous, thanks partly to trade with Rome and China. Because the *śūdras* became more prosperous, they became more difficult to control, which led to greater concessions and rewards for their service. According to the *Yājñavalkya* (ca. 100–200), Vedic rituals may be done with the *namaskāra mantra*.[55] In fact, it mentions teachers of *śūdras*.[56] To adjust ritual life to these new circumstances, new texts were composed. The *Vaijavāpa Gṛhyasūtra* stipulates that *śūdras* may perform the rituals for conceiving, obtaining a son, parting the hair, birth, naming, first food, and tonsure. The *Vajrasūci*, a Buddhist text, refers to *śūdras* who know the Vedas, grammar, *mīmāṃsā*, *sāṃkhya*, *vaiśeṣika*, and *lagna*. By the fourth century, the position of *śūdras* had improved even more, especially in the Gupta empire. Some had better wages or sharecropping status. Others were rulers and priests, who performed Vedic rituals. According to the *Mahābhārata*, all four *varṇas* may hear the Veda.[57] The upper *varṇas*, moreover, may acquire knowledge even from *śūdras*.[58] Similarly, the three Vedas permit those *śūdras* who are initiated and have faith to perform the *pākayajñas* accompanied by the *svāhākāra-namaskāra* and mantra (*Mahābhārata*).[59] These themes are found in later texts, too. According to the *Mārkaṇḍeya Purāṇa*,[60] for example, *śūdras* may perform sacrifices (*yajña*) and offer gifts (*dāna*). According to the *Brahmāṇḍa Purāṇa*,[61] they may perform the five great sacrifices (*pañcamahāyajñas*). These passages suggest a more inclusive religion but also allude to discrimination based on lack of eligibility to utter specific mantras, presumably those with *om*.

Given their link, the improved status of *śūdras* might have contributed to the improved status of women. In the *Mahābhārata*,[62] a *brāhmaṇa* is said to have taught several mantras from Atharvaśiras to the mother of the Pāṇḍava heroes. According to the *Bhagavadgītā*,[63] moreover, "even *vaiśyas*, women, and *śūdras*, though born of evil womb, will attain the supreme goal." According to the *Viṣṇu Purāṇa*, even though woman's nature is evil, she will attain heaven if she serves her husband. The epics are called the "fifth Veda" (as is the *Nāṭyaśāstra*).[64] Therefore, these texts were accessible to women and *śūdras*. This improvement in the status of both, represented by a greater willingness for brahmins to offer them privileges, developed at a time of reduced societal stress; the tradition was not being threatened. I suspect that greater respect was given to *śūdras* in areas beyond the Gangetic plain, moreover, because rulers of northern origin had to include the local elite in Vedic rituals even though they would have been classified as *śūdras* in the northern texts. This, in turn, could have affected the status of women in those areas.

There were at least three basic opinions on the status of women and *śūdras*: conservative, liberal, and in between.These were based on whether or not *śūdras* were incorporated into religious communities with brahminical leadership. Within these communities, however, their status was based on whether or not women and *śūdras* were allowed to utter the sacred syllable *om* and study the Vedas. Communities with conservative brahminical leadership, those who valued the tradition of Manu, said no. Others offered a qualified yes, in the sense that women and *śūdras* were allowed the first type of initiation or even subsequent ones with mantras that excluded *om*. Still others allowed both women and *śūdras* to utter *om*. Some communities saw them even as exemplary figures in the quest for liberation. For them, the notions of surrender and service were exploited for their positive spiritual rather than their negative social dimensions.

Om and the Śrīvaiṣṇava Tradition

How did these three opinions influence medieval Śrīvaiṣṇavism? The Śrīvaiṣṇavas are a sectarian community in Tamilnadu. According to the etymology of their name, they worship Viṣṇu and his consort Śrī (hence the compound Śrīvaiṣṇava). But close examination of their tradition reveals a special attraction to the dark god Māl, or Māyōṉ, identified variously with Kṛṣṇa or Nāraṇa/Nārāyaṇa. Both of the latter are considered alternatives of Viṣṇu. In this tradition, three streams of literature converge. One includes the Tamil hymns of the āḻvārs. These were written between the seventh century and the ninth. Motifs are drawn heavily from earlier Tamil poetry called *caṅkam*. A second stream includes the Sanskrit *śruti* and *smṛti* texts. A third stream includes the Āgamas, especially the Pāñcarātra Āgamas. These three streams were integrated by a series of *ācāryas* writing in Tamil, Sanskrit, and Maṇipravāḷa, mainly between the eleventh century and the fifteenth.

Three basic mantras are recognized by the Śrīvaiṣṇava tradition: the *tirumantra*, also identified as the *mūlamantra* or the *aṣṭākṣara* (*om namo nārāyaṇāya*); the *dvaya*;[65] and the *caramaśloka*.[66] Because the *tirumantra* contains the word *om*, it will be the topic of this discussion. As I mentioned earlier, its first mention was in the *Nārāyaṇa Upaniṣad*.

The Āḻvārs

The *āḻvārs*, poet-saints of Śrīvaiṣṇavism, refer to the following mantras:[67]

1. *namo nāraṇa*:
   Poykaiyāḻvār: *Mutal Tiruvantāti* 57
   Periyāḻvār: *Periyāḻvār Tirumoḻi* 4.5.2; 5.1.3; 5.1.6
2. *namo nārāyaṇa*:
   Periyāḻvār: *Tiruppallāṇṭu* 11
   Poykaiyāḻvār: *Mutal Tiruvantāti* 91
3. *namo nārāyaṇāya*:
   Periyāḻvār: *Tiruppallāṇṭu* 4; 12
   Āṇṭāḷ: *Nācciyār Tirumoḻi* 5.11
4. *tiruveṭṭu eḻuttu*:
   Tirumaḻicai: *Tiruccanta Viruttam* 77
   Tirumaṅkaiyāḻvār: *Periya Tirumoḻi* 1.8.9; 6:10:1
   Periyāḻvār: *Periyāḻvār Tirumoḻi*[68]

Should we consider these distinct mantras? Vasudha Narayanan assumes that they are not. She explains the absence of *om* in mantras mentioned by the *āḻvārs* by arguing that the word *namo* (*namaḥ*) suffices, but she offers no other reason.[69] She suggests also that the versions *namo nārāyaṇa* and *namo nārāyaṇāya* are the "Tamil forms."[70] This is hard to understand, though, because the words are ostensibly Sanskrit and not Tamil. The first two phrases are obviously variants of one. In each, *namo*, or *namaḥ* (salutations), are offered to the deity whose name is given by two variants: *nāraṇa* and *nārāyaṇa*. The third phrase, too, is a variant because *namaḥ* might or might not take the dative case. The fourth phrase, though, signifies something quite different. *Tiruveṭṭu Eḻuttu* (the eight syllables) alludes to a mantra consisting of eight syllables—already identified in the *Nārāyaṇa Upaniṣad* as *om namo nārāyaṇāya*.

Because this fourth phrase alludes to *om*, and women and *śūdras* in some non-Śrīvaiṣṇava circles have been prohibited from uttering it, two questions arise. Are women and *śūdras* grouped together elsewhere in the hymns of the *āḻvārs*? And is it ever stated explicitly that women and *śūdras* may not say *om*? The answer is no. On the contrary, it is implied throughout the Tamil hymns that the means to salvation are available to all. By chanting the names of God, for instance, one can attain salvation.[71] Another way to salvation is chanting a *mantra*. In the *Tiruccanta Viruttam*,[72] Tirumaḻicaiyāḻvār connects uttering the eight-syllable mantra (om *namo nārāyaṇāya*) with ruling the skies—that is, with salvation. The theme of humility is underscored, moreover, in these hymns.

In the *Periya Tirumoḻi*,[73] for instance, Tirumaṅkaiyāḻvār says that "since he has learned the sacred eight syllables he has become the servant of the servants of God."[74] This might involve a reversal for hyperbolic effect.[75]

The brahminical tradition in circles influenced by Manu was exclusive and restricted the use of mantras with *om* to the elite: brahmins or twice-born men. Does this mean that in Śrīvaiṣṇavism, by contrast, *om* may be recited by anyone? But if the sacred syllable *om* were available to anyone, why do we have only indirect references to it? In Sanskrit sources written after the fourth century B.C.E., code words—*bīja* ("seed"), *mūla* ("root"), *tryakṣara* ("three syllables")—are often substitutes for *om*. Maybe *aṣṭākṣara* and (for the *ācāryas*) *tirumantra* were code words for the eight syllable mantra containing *om*. Maybe these were adopted to avoid saying the sacred word in public.

Whatever the exact context of *om*, it is obvious that the *āḻvārs* focused on four key phrases. All involve the name of the god Nāraṇa/Nārāyaṇa, assuming that my identification of the eight-syllable mantra is correct. Assuming also that these phrases have some special status, even that of a mantra, I suggest that the underlying identity of the *āḻvār* god is Nārāyaṇa, not Kṛṣṇa (the shared feature of dark color and the overlapping histories of these two gods notwithstanding).

Two other observations based on the *āḻvār* hymns deserve comment before proceeding. First, the word *namaḥ*, too, is common to all four phrases. This Sanskrit word is derived from *nam* ("to bend or bow" or "to submit to"). Not surprisingly, it refers to a bow, obeisance, referential salutation, or adoration by word or gesture.[76] Tamil *bhakti* hymns refer often to bowing. This semiritualized gesture consists of folding the palms in a gesture known as *añjali* (to "honor"), a word with other associations of non-Vedic worship such as decorating and anointing images with pigment. These words suggest *pūjā*. So does the act of offering flowers, widely acknowledged to be of Dravidian origin. Bowing while holding the palms together and offering flowers could indicate that one source of the *āḻvār* tradition is Dravidian. The word *namaḥ* has been featured in many Vedic mantras, which suggests that it has been integrated into the ever-evolving Vedic tradition but shorn in texts of its specific associations (bowing, with palms folded, to the feet of God and offering flowers). This integration first appeared in the *Taittirīya Śāka* and *Nārāyaṇa Upaniṣad*.

The second observation is that chanting the names of Gods such as Nārāyaṇa and Rudra while bowing points to a non-Vedic tradition. The fact that the *āḻvārs* refer to chanting *namo nāraṇa* and so forth suggests that this non-Vedic tradition was central to the *āḻvār* religion and had not been displaced by the vedicized version found in the *Nārāyaṇa Upaniṣad*. This tradition of chanting the names of God goes back to the *Śatarudrīya* (a litany consisting of the 100 names of Rudra) found in the *Yajur Veda* and the *Viṣṇusahasranāma* (a litany consisting of the 1000 names of Viṣṇu) in the *Mahābhārata*.

The Pāñcarātra Āgamas, Initiation Rituals, and the Utterance of Om *by Women and Śūdras*

The Pāñcarātra Āgamas are relevant texts for understanding how women and *śūdras* became linked negatively in some orthodox brahmin circles. The word *pāñcarātra*, according to the *Nārāyaṇīya* section of the *Mahābhārata*, refers to a sacred text. By extension, it refers to doctrines, rituals, and mantras.[77] It became a sectarian name (Pāñcarātra) of a group that worshipped Nārāyaṇa—especially when contrasted to the Bhāgavatas, whose key god was Vāsudeva-Kṛṣṇa.[78] The former was inspired by the *Nārāyaṇīya*, the latter by the *Bhagavadgītā*.[79] This development could have remained localized for some time, and there might have been other Nārāyaṇa traditions in other regions. A better working hypothesis to account for sectarian and regional diversity, therefore, is to presume many strands of development and interaction. The large corpus of Pāñcarātra texts (most of which have yet to be translated and analyzed) were written over several centuries. The first Āgamas[80] were *Pauṣkara*, *Jayākhya*, and *Sātvata* (ca. C.E 500.). These were followed by *Ahirbudhnya* (ca. 600); *Parama* (ca. 700); and *Sanatkumāra*, *Nāradīya*, *Pārameśvara*, *Lakṣmī Tantra*, *Viśvākṣena*, *Viṣṇu*, *Pādma*, and *Śeṣa* (ca. 800–1300). The final ones were *Īśvara*, *Śrīpraśna*, *Viśvāmitra*, *Brahmā*, *Sāṇḍilya*, *Aniruddha*, *Bṛhadbrahmā*, and *Nārada* (ca. 1300–1600).[81]

These Āgamas present doctrines of monotheism (*ekāntya*) and secrecy (*rahasya*). Their secret teachings must not be revealed to those who have no faith in the one true God.[82] The texts are particularly concerned with liturgy and mantras. In fact, the name *mantraśāstra* has been applied to this literature as a whole. "*Mantras*," says Sanjukta Gupta, "are the pure creation, and at the same time they are the means and the path to salvation. This salvation is the same as release from the influence of *māyā* and of the desire which is its consequence."[83] A mantra, moreover, is the oral form of a deity—as distinguished from its geometric (*yantra*) and personified (*para, avatāra, arcā*) forms. In some cases, mantras are linked to the cosmic stages of creation. They are linked also to *nyāsa*, placing the power of the mantra on the physical human body by marking it with sacred substances and designs (first taught at the time of initiation by a guru and henceforth practiced as a daily ritual, culminating in meditation on the mantra).[84] In fact, about one-third of the *Sātvata* and the *Jayākhya* are specifically about mantras.[85]

Most of the Pāñcarātra texts include sections on the types of initiation (*dīkṣā*) for various groups. When it comes to eligibility for a particular type of *dīkṣā*, these texts often comment on women and *śūdras* (sometimes whole sections being devoted to this topic): what level of *dīkṣā* they may perform, what kind of mantras they may chant, what time of year they may perform *dīkṣā*; and what type of special dispensations they have (such as whether the sacred thread may be worn at the time of *dīkṣā*).[86]

Several Saṃhitās say that the *pañcasaṃskāra* ceremony consisted of five rites: *tāpa*, *puṇḍra*, *nāma*, *mantra*, and *yajana* (branding, wearing sectarians marks, taking a new name, chanting a mantra, and worshiping God). This initiation into Vaiṣṇavism was available to everyone. It distinguished those who had faith in the one true God (*ekāntins*) from those who did not. The *Jayākhya Saṃhitā*[87] might be inclusive in its acceptance of everyone into the Vaiṣṇava community. Although women and *śūdras* were not barred explicitly from subsequent initiations, the lack of integration of the category of women makes [their inclusiveness] questionable; the silence on the *śūdras*' eligibility underscores this point. One must question the nature of this text for women at the higher stages of the path.[88] One text of the middle period (800–1300), the *Nāradīya Saṃhitā*, says little about initiation but does observe, in a liberal way, that initiates are born in the family of Bhagavān and are eligible to study the Vedas and the Āgamas.[89]

The Āgamas are, in any case, a generally conservative genre: "The Pāñcarātra literature as a whole reveals a pronounced leaning to Vedic orthodoxy,"[90] associating the texts with the Vedic corpus and the maintenance of duties of caste and stage of life (*varṇāśramadharma*). "These scriptures can be taught effectively only to an initiated Pāñcarātrin. Just as one has to undergo Vedic initiation to perform Vedic rituals, so also one must undergo Pāñcarātra initiation to perform Pāñcarātra upāsana"[91] (said to be equivalent to the Vedic sacrifice). Only brahmins, though, may worship the highest manifestation of the deity, the *vyūhas*.[92]

The *Pādma Saṃhitā*,[93] supposedly composed between the ninth century and the fourteenth, describes the *dīkṣā* with intriguing classification for women and *śūdras*. Here, too, everyone is eligible for the initial type, although there are distinctions based on caste and different names are given for each caste:[94] *bhaṭṭāraka* for brahmins, *deva* for *kṣatriyas*, *pāla* for *vaiśyas*, and *dāsa* for *śūdras*. The mantra consisting of the name of God without the dative case and without the words *namaḥ*, *svāhā*, *hum*, *phaṭ*, *vaṣat*, or *praṇava* (*om*), may be given to women and *śūdras*. The words—*svāhā*, *hum*, and so on—are sacred syllables found in solemn Vedic ritual. The exclusion of women and *śūdras*, therefore, is understandable. The only reason for the exclusion of *namo nārāyaṇāya* would be the fact that *nārāyaṇāya* is in the dative case, and that was associated with Vedic ritual.[95] This led to the avoidance of the dative case in the mantras of those texts that place restrictions on what women and *śūdras* may utter. But the avoidance of *namo*, as in *namo nārāyaṇa*, is difficult to explain. (This was particularly restrictive because even the *āḻvārs* mentioned *namo nārāyaṇāya* in public.) According to other verses,[96] although initiation is available to all four *varṇas*, it should be done only with the *dvādaśākṣaramantra* (the *mantra* consisting of twelve syllables), not those belonging to the three Vedas or the *sāvitrī* (*gāyatrī*). Moreover, the mantra should be uttered without Vedic elements (*bīja*, *śakti*, *aṅga*, *ṛṣis*, and *chandas* in the *svādhyāya* and *japa*). Despite the strict avoidance of any Vedic element by women and *śūdras* ironically, no caste should feel superior or inferior to the others.

In the *Viṣṇu Saṃhitā*,[97] similarly, the first three castes are initiated with mantras that have the Vedic element, such as *praṇava* (*om*).[98] If a disciple is deemed capable by the guru, all three mantras may be given; women and *śūdras*, on the other hand, may not be given these mantras. And *śūdras* may not be taught the procedures of sacrifice (*yāga*).[99] A *śūdra* should receive instruction in *karmābhigamana*, *upādāna*, *ijyā*, *svādhyāya*, and *yoga*.[100] The guru should establish the degree of purity of all aspirants, but especially that of women and *śudras*. Women and *śūdras* should be devoted to God and serve him steadily. God, in turn, will help them acquire perfections in this world and cross the ocean of *saṃsāra*.

The even more conservative *Śrīpraśna Saṃhitā*[101] was written after the fourteenth century. It divides initiates into four categories: *samayī*, *putraka*, *sādhaka*, and *ācārya*. Brahmins are named *bhaṭṭāraka* or *bhāgavata*; *kṣatriyas deva*; *vaiśyas vardhana*; and *śūdras dāsa* (similar to the *Pādma Saṃhitā*). *Śūdras* must have special instructions.[102] Only the first three *varṇas* are initiated with mantras that include the *bīja* and end with *praṇavaḥ* (om) or *namaḥ*. The guru may give to his initiates all the mantras, if they are capable, but not to *śūdras*. Sections of this text, probably addressed to ascetics, warn against eating with women and uninitiated people.[103] Otherwise, there is no reference at all to women.

What is the larger context of women in the Āgamas? In most of the Āgamas, according to Leslie Orr, women may have the initial form of initiation and perform ritual activities such as singing and dancing; participating in festival processions; lighting, placing, or removing auspicious lamps; and preparing purifying threads (*pavitras)* and other ritual ingredients like tumeric. However, they may not participate in higher forms of initiation and therefore are not eligible for spiritual practices, teaching, or temple priesthood. Nor are they eligible for salvation. This might have been a way of making the Āgamas attractive to the orthodox: incorporating conservative notions of *strīdharma* from the Dharmaśāstras. This conservative genre itself gradually became even more conservative. A supposedly early Āgama, *Pauṣkara Saṃhitā*, is comparatively inclusive and tolerant of the ritual roles of family women. The later *Śrīpraśna Saṃhitā*, at least some of which was composed in Tamilnadu during the Cōḻa period, consigns most women's rituals to a special class of courtesan. Women are not eligible to receive the higher teachings of the Āgamas. The temples sponsored by them are not considered sāttvika, (pure), and, other forms of religious giving by women are unacknowledged. In additon, there are more warnings to avoid menstruating, pregnant, or immoral women.[104]

To conclude, the Pāñcarātra Āgamas are generally conservative and entail restrictions for *śūdras* and women. At the heart of the restrictions of mantras is their association with Vedic rituals. The *praṇava* or *om* is a celebrated case in point, but this observation holds true for other so-called Vedic mantras as well, even for use of the dative case, which was understood not merely as a grammatical requirement but also as something integral to the ritual act itself (oblations to the deity). The *pañcasaṃskāra* ritual, as the general initiation of a Vaiṣṇava, includes mantras without *om* for women and *śūdras*, though sometimes for all classes as well. But the Pāñcarātra Āgamas have expanded the concept of *dīkṣā* to include more types and do not allow women and *śūdras* into the higher initiations (the *Lakṣmī Tantra*[105] and possibly the *Jayākhya* and the *Viśvāmitra Saṃhitā*[106] notwithstanding).

Pāñcarātra Āgamas and the Āḻvārs

From the above chronology, I would say that a few early Pāñcarātra texts might have been written just before the time of the *āḻvārs* (but probably outside of Tamilnadu, as were most of the Saṃhitās, and possibly in Kashmir).[107] Even though both the *āḻvār* and the Pāñcarātra traditions were devoted to Nārāyaṇa worship, the theology of the *āḻvārs* was considerably different from that of the Pāñcarātra texts. This suggests two separate, albeit related, traditions. Indeed, the *Śrīviṣṇusahasranāma* (in the *Mahābhārata*), *Harivaṃśa*, *Viṣṇudharma*, and *Viṣṇutattva* mention branding with conch and discus, which indicates that the ritual of initiation (the *pañcasaṃskāra*) was not confined to the Pāñcarātra tradition but belonged to a somewhat more common and probably more archaic Vaiṣṇava tradition.[108] It is difficult to know exactly when the *pañcasaṃskāra* ritual was introduced into the Śrīvaiṣṇava tradition. It could have been common even at the time of the early *āḻvārs* (given its appearance in the *Śrīviṣṇusahasranāma* of the *Mahābhārata*). The first explicit reference was made by Periyāḻvār (ca. 800–900) in *Periyāḻvār Tirumoḻi*.[109] He mentions wearing the discus on his shoulders; this is probably a reference to branding (*tāpa*),which is among the five aspects of the *pañcasaṃskāra* ritual. He mentions it also in the *Tiruppallāṇṭu*,[110] which says that "his family has been branded with the sacred discus and has served the Lord for generations."[111] He refers to himself as Bhaṭṭar (a variant of the name Bhaṭṭāraka, given to Āgamic brahmins according to the *Pādma Saṃhitā* and the *Śrīpraśna Saṃhitā*).[112] It is worth noting that Periyāḻvār is associated with the earliest Śrīvaiṣṇava temple that has as its main image the reclining Nārāyaṇa, built according to the specifications of the Pāñcarātra Āgamas.[113] Periyāḻvār refers directly to three mantras: *namo nāraṇa, namo nārāyaṇa* and *namo nārāyaṇāya.* So, unlike some Pañcarātra texts, his does not restrict the use of the dative. And his choice of mantra could have been for metrical rather than doctrinal considerations. He alludes to the fourth mantra only by the words *tiruveṭṭu eḻuttu*, however, which indicates his recognition of restrictions on the use of om—at least that it should not be uttered or read in public (so that it would not be available to the uninitiated). Like the other *āḻvārs*, in any case, he does not exclude women and *śūdras*. More importantly, his own daughter Āṇṭāḷ assumed liberation for herself and promised it in her poems to other girls who surrendered to the Lord. Whatever the Pāñcarātra influences on him, therefore, he exemplified the *āḻvār* tradition of inclusiveness.

Does any of this help us sort out the murky history of *om* in the Śrīvaiṣṇava tradition? There certainly are some striking differences between it and the Pāñcarātra tradition. Most of the early Āgamas mention several types of *dīkṣā*, or initiation as a set of steps along the path to salvation, but the *āḻvār* texts (like those of the subsequent *ācāryas*) do not. This suggests that the *āḻvār* tradition does not derive directly from an early Pāñcarātra one, and it might go back to a common, pre-Āgamic (yet brahminized and/or vedicized) source. But Periyāḻvār, a late *āḻvār*, might have bridged the *āḻvār* and Pāñcarātra traditions. I say this because of other evidence that links both him and his temple explicitly with the Pāñcarātra Āgama tradition.[114] Unlike some Pāñcarātra Āgamas, as I have already noted, *āḻvār* texts do not group women and *śūdras* together. They refer in general to devotees or the family (*kula*) of devotees. (Perhaps this is because the *varṇa* system of the northern texts had not taken root in Tamilnadu during the *bhakti* period, and any attempt to superimpose it on Tamil society—especially its corollary, the superiority of brahmins—could have generated considerable conflict, given the more open system of Tamil status acquisition.[115] As a result, the word *sūdra* was avoided by the *āḻvārs*.)

Two related possibilities could explain these observations. First, the Vaiṣṇava initiation ritual (*pañcasaṃskāra*) included the revelation of *om*. The syllable was universally available, therefore, to anyone who wanted to become a Vaiṣṇava. But it was revealed only during the ritual and was, therefore, secret (*rahaysa*). This interpretation does justice not only to the proselytizing inclusiveness of *āḻvār* hymns but also to the code words "eight syllables" (*tiruveṭṭu eḻuttu*), which were used when referring to the mantra with *om*. The secrecy surrounding *om* suggests a brahminical mindset, to be sure, but not the one found in orthodox circles influenced by Manu or the Pāñcarātra. It does not exclude women and *śūdras* from uttering the sacred syllable, but it does hide that fact from public view. One scholar has claimed that "for at least seven centuries, these mantras have been given to every Śrīvaiṣṇava at the time of the initiating ritual of *pañcasaṃskāra*. Bestowing of these mantras, along with the guruparamparā showing the line of instruction through which they came, is one of the five aspects of this rite, without which no one can call himself [or herself] a Śrīvaiṣṇava."[116] But I have not been able to find any proof in texts that identify explicitly the *tirumantra*, the *dvaya*, and the *caramaśloka* with the *pañcasaṃskāra ritual*. Tirumaṅkaiyāḻvār's statement that he has become the servant of the servants of God after learning the sacred eight syllables[117] could, however, allude to learning *om* at the time of initiation into the Śrīvaiṣṇava community (which sounds, therefore, like the time of *pañcasaṃskāra*). Another possible interpretation is that the *pañcasaṃskāra* ritual included mantras without *om*, whereas a subsequent initiation revealed it. But that, too, goes beyond the *āḻvār* hymns.

Discussions of Mantra in the Writings of the Śrīvaiṣṇava Ācāryas

By the twelfth or thirteenth century, the Śrīvaiṣṇava *ācāryas* began to write treatises on the *tirumantra*, the *dvaya mantra*, and the *caramaśloka*. It could be significant that these treatises are classified as secrets (*rahasyas*), but no passages bar women and *śūdras* from knowing them (except one significant passage by Vedāntadeśika). In fact, as I will show, there is evidence to the contrary. Because of the increasing popularity of the concept of *ubhayavedānta* (the two vedāntas, Sanskrit and Tamil) and the increasing presence of Pāñcarātra priests in the Vaiṣṇava temples of Tamilnadu (promoting an upgraded form of liturgy), the *ācāryas* integrated passages from the Āgamas despite their conceptual differences. This occurred partly because Yāmuna had legitimized the Āgama corpus in his *Āgama-prāmāṇya*;[118] Yāmuna and Rāmānuja had quoted the *Parama Saṃhitā*; Vedāntadeśika had referred to it by name; Yāmuna had quoted thirteen lines from the *Īśvara* (now considered a much earlier version of the extant text); Vedāntadeśika had quoted from the *Pārameśvara*, *Nāradīya Kalpa*, *Lakṣmī Tantra*, and so forth.

Rāmānuja (1017–1137?) The first reference to the *tirumantra* appears in the *Nitya-grantha*, a guidebook on daily ritual attributed to Rāmānuja. It refers on several occasions to recitation of the *mūlamantra* (i.e., *tirumantra*) while bathing or performing *pūjā*. Rāmānuja's authorship has been disputed, and I am inclined to agree with the critics.[119] The first reference to the word *dvayam*, no doubt alluding to the *dvayaṃ mantra*, occurs in the *Śaraṇāgati Gadya*, also attributed to Rāmānuja.

Bhaṭṭar (1223–1174 C.E.)[120] In the *Śrīviṣṇusahasaranāma Bhāṣya*,[121] the *ācārya* Bhaṭṭar (a disciple of Rāmānuja) refers to devotees marked with the conch and discus when he is commenting on the name Kṛtalakṣaṇa (a mark that is made). He cites several passages. According to the *Śrī Harivaṃśa*, those marked (*lakṣaṇa*) with the discus and conch may come to God; those umnarked may not. According to the *Viṣṇudharma*, those who wear the signs of having taken refuge in God—that is, the discus and conch—and obey his commands do not harm other devotees. And according to the *Viṣṇutattva*, just as women wear ornaments to indicate their marital chastity, devotees wear the discus and conch as ornaments to indicate their marital faithfulness to God. In other words, wearing the emblems makes one eligible to approach God; provides a visible way of being recognized as a *Śrīvaiṣṇava*; and because of this visible identity, creates public accountability for fidelity to Nārāyaṇa. These references allude to the *pañcasaṃskāra* ritual of branding, which originated in the *Mahābhārata*, or even earlier, and was first mentioned in Śrīvaiṣṇavism by Periyāḻvār in the ninth century.

In the *Śrīviṣṇusahasranāma Bhāṣya*, Bhaṭṭar comments on the word *namaḥ*.

> By this [word] we know that every person is qualified. . . . Worship does not entail the assistance of men and material, which sacrifices do. . . . [The Lord] can be worshiped even by men with bad qualities, as well as by those who have the great quality of having only a taste for bhakti. . . . It is said in the chapter [of the *Brahmasūtras*] which discusses

> the qualification of *śūdras* that those not of the upper three castes cannot light the [sacred] fire and perform ceremonies that involve the use of the fire; nor can they obtain the supreme knowledge (*para-vidyā*), for that involves a study of the Upaniṣads; nor can they undergo the sacrament that would enable them to approach a guru and learn the Vedānta. There is no contradiction when people other than those of the three castes take refuge (*āśraya*) in the Lord, if they long for liberation. . . . The books on *dharma* also permit all, including outcastes (*caṇḍālas*), to practice non-violence, truth, purity, and service to others. . . . In the Viṣṇudharma it is said, "O Narada, even if one who eats the flesh of a dog says namaḥ to me with *bhakti* and *śraddhā*, he will reach the eternal world."[122]

This passage comments on the nature of competency (*adhikāra*) for lower and higher Vedic knowledge (*apara* and *para vidyā*) and ritual, which was of great concern to the brahminical tradition. The *Brahmasūtras* said that *śūdras* are ineligible for these activities because they lack competence. Here, though, the utterance of *namaḥ* with devotion and faith is an alternative path for those who are not twice-born. In other orthodox brahminical contexts, of course, women, too, were excluded from Vedic knowledge and ritual; they might well be excluded here as well.

Another important text for this discussion is Bhaṭṭar's *Aṣṭaśloki*, a work so named because it has eight *ślokas*. These verses refer to the three traditional mantras—the first four referring to the *tirumantra* (*oṃ namo nārāyaṇāya*), the next two to the *dvaya mantra*, and the last two to the *caramaśloka* of *Gītā* 18:66. I find it striking that Bhaṭṭar refers to the *tirumantra* as superior. Although he comments on the components of *om* and calls them the *praṇava*, he nowhere mentions explicitly the sacred syllable itself. There is absolutely no confusion about this referent, though, given his elaboration of meaning for the individual sounds *a*, *u*, and *m*. His reference to this mantra as superior could mean that he considers it superior to *namo nāraṇa* or *namo nārāyaṇa* or *namo nārāyaṇāya* because it contains *om*. Alternatively, it could mean that he considers it superior to the *dvayam* and the *caramaśloka*, also because it contains *om* (and the other two do not). Moreover, the presence of *om* in the mantra could have given rise to the term *tirumantra* (the auspicious mantra). In any case, these verses interpret the sacred syllable *om* in light of Śrīvaiṣṇava doctrines elaborated by Yāmuna and Rāmānuja. The *mantra* is called the essence of the Vedas; it embodies the idea of God, the soul, and their relationship. Significantly, Bhaṭṭar explains the use of the dative case as denoting spontaneous service at all times, in all places, and under all conditions. This foreshadows Piḷḷailokācārya's understanding of surrender and service by everyone (a position rebutted subsequently by Vedāntadeśika, who said that the dative in the mantra could not be used by women and *śūdras*). The tradition of three key mantras must have been already established in the Śrīvaiṣṇava tradition for Bhaṭṭar to have devoted a text to their exposition. Is there a connection between the fact that Bhaṭṭar alludes in one work to the *pañcasaṃskāra* ritual (which involves the utterance of mantras) and in another to the three mantras (including one that uses *om*)? Perhaps, but the texts themselves do not make this connection explicit. Nevertheless, it is important to remember that the *Nārāyaṇa Upaniṣad* had already suggested that uttering *om namo nārāyaṇa* was an independent path to salvation that was available to all (exactly the concept of *prapatti* for Śrīvaiṣṇavas). Even Manu considered the utterance of *om* a way to attain salvation, although he restricted this means to the twice-born.

Piḷḷāṉ (d. 1161) Commenting on Nammāḻvār's *Tiruvāymoḻi*, [123] Piḷḷāṉ often explains the name of the Lord in connection with the word *tirumantra*. In one verse, which instructs devotees to "obtain the feet" of Kaṇṇaṉ (Kṛṣṇa) by thinking of his name and observing that Nāraṇa is the mighty refuge, Piḷḷāṉ comments that this can be accomplished by reciting the *tirumantra*. In another verse,[124] he links the reference to Nāraṇa by the *āḻvār* with the variant name of Nārāyaṇa and notes, when raising a question about the identity of this god, that he is "obtained" by the *tirumantra*. Commenting on *Tiruvāymoḻi*,[125] Piḷḷāṉ explains "sing his name" with the idea of repeating his name, offering flowers that never wilt, and bowing; all should be done daily at his sacred flowerlike feet as the way to "gain" these feet (i.e., to be saved). Commenting on a verse[126] that refers to placing flowers at his feet daily, Piḷḷāṉ observes that devotees should say the *tirumantra* at his "sacred flower-like feet." And commenting on yet another verse,[127] which contains a general reference to the Lord, Piḷḷāṉ states that this should be done by saying the *tirumantra*, offering beautiful flowers to his sacred feet, and thinking of him with affection.

Piḷḷāṉ's commentary on Nammāḻvār highlights differences between the *āḻvārs* and *ācāryas*. Nammāḻvār associates thinking of or singing the sacred name Nāraṇa with refuge. For Nammāḻvār, uttering the name is extremely powerful—the way to salvation. Chanting his name, therefore, is connected with semiritualized acts of worship such as bowing before and offering flowers to the Lord's feet. Piḷḷāṉ links chanting the name of God with chanting a mantra—more specifically, with the *tirumantra*. Because Bhaṭṭar understood this mantra as one that included *om*, Piḷḷāṉ might well have understood it in the same way. Thus, Nammāḻvār linked the name with taking refuge, worship, and salvation—but not with the specific context of initiation (*pañcasaṃskāra*)—and Piḷḷāṉ insisted that the reference to the name was really to the *tirumantra*, the chanting of which in the semiritualized context of worship was the means to salvation.

Nañjīyar (1182–1287) Nañjīyar wrote the now lost text *Rahasya Vivaraṇam Nuṟṟiyeṭṭu* (108 stanzas, explaining the secrets). In a commentary on *Tiruvāymoḻi*,[128] he relates Nammāḻvār's reference to the name Nāraṇa to a mantra. And in his commentary on another verse in *Tiruvāymoḻi*,[129] he asks why "Nammāḻvār referred to the name of the god (*tirunāmam*) rather than to his mantra, omitted the 'namas' and fourth case ending (dative), and said '*nāraṇame*' rather than 'Nārāyaṇa'. The reason he provides is that unlike other mantras, this one gives results even if said improperly."[130] It is well-known that *namaḥ* can take the fourth (dative) case. *Vaidika* mantras are especially associated with the dative case, as I have noted, because they accompany offerings to a deity. Therefore, it is understandable why an author who recited Vedic mantras would notice the absence of certain features such as the dative case. The fact that Nañjīyar himself refers to the *tirumantra* but does not refer explicitly to a mantra with *om* no doubt means that he is using that as a code word for the latter (to avoid having to say it in his commentary). Whatever the case, his comment points to the fact that the *ācāryas* were not so familiar with the name Nāraṇa. Although apparently linked to the name Nārāyaṇa, it was unfamiliar to them. They understood the mantra not just as a name, moreover, but as a phrase.

Āṇṭāḷ (ca. twelfth century) *and Koṉēridāsī* (ca. fifteenth century) Āṇṭāḷ (here Kūrattāḻvāṉ's wife, not Āṇṭāḷ, the *bhakti* poet), was a female intellectual.[131] According to the *Guruparampară Prabhāvam*, she was very scholarly; men consulted her to clarify their doubts. But she did not write anything. Besides the *bhakti* poetess Āṇṭāḷ, there was only one other woman in Śrīvaiṣṇavism who contributed to the tradition through her writings. This was Koṉēridāsī, a disciple of Nampiḷḷai. (Because Vasudha Narayanan discusses Koṉēridāsī's commentary at length elsewhere in this volume, I can be brief here.) Koṉēridāsī might have recorded both his and Vaṭakkuttiruvīti-piḷḷai's discourses on *Tiruvāymoḻi*. She herself wrote a commentary on Nammāḻvār's *Tiruvāymoḻi*, which is called the *Tiruvāymoḻi Vācakamālai* or *Vivaraṇa Caṭakam*.[132] The uniqueness of her commentary lies in the fact that it explains the entire *Tiruvāymoḻi* by commenting on the very first verse, which she defines as the essence of the whole. Koṉēridāsī did not originate the theology, which she had learned as a scribe for two great scholars of the day, although she became a skilled interpreter in her own right.

Although some women–Āṇṭāḷ, say, Koṉēridāsī –might have known of the Tamil hymns of the *āḻvārs* and the *Maṇipravāḷa* works of the Śrīvaiṣṇava *ācāryas*, we do not know whether they had any extensive knowledge of Vedic texts (in other words, whether they were *vaidika* in the traditional understanding of that word). Koṉēridāsī quotes from the *Taittirīya Upaniṣad* and is familiar with the Sanskrit Vedas. According to Narayanan,[133] this constitutes at least scholarly knowledge. Whether she officially chanted the Vedas or performed Vedic rituals cannot be determined. (I suspect this was not the case because it would have cast her in the formal role of priest.) Sanskrit texts had to be related to Tamil scriptures and interpreted for the community without knowledge of Sanskrit. The question is whether only brahmin men had this prerogative and, furthermore, whether that was by default or by design. If the former, it could indicate merely that women no longer had any Vedic knowledge. If the latter, it did not matter; chanting the word *namaḥ* provided an alternative path to salvation. The notion of an alternative path could have been the result of a very clever sleight of hand by Śrīvaiṣṇava brahmin men. They did not explicitly forbid women from pursuing knowledge of Sanskrit and the Vedas, nor did they ridicule women for being *avaidika* (in the sense of a lack of knowledge and therefore ignorant) or for being innately incapable as women of serious learning. Instead, they quietly bypassed the problem altogether by focusing on the Tamil Veda, which was accessible to everyone, male and female. Śrīvaiṣṇava brahmin men managed to have it both ways, so to speak. They were orthodox, in other words, but also liberal. This surely testifies to their hermeneutical sophistication.

Before leaving this topic, one final comment is in order. Seventy-four brahmin families were appointed, supposedly by Rāmānuja himself, to produce *ācāryas*. This institutionalized the role of brahminical men as teachers, thereby ensuring that only the men of specific brahmin families could be *ācāryas*. This also controlled the interpretation of the secret teachings (*rahasyas*), because it was the perogative of these *ācāryas* to teach only those initiates whom they chose and who demonstrated loyalty to them.

Periyavāccāṉpiḷḷai (*1167–1262*) In *Paranta Rahasya* and its abridged version, *Nigamanappati*,[134] Periyavāccāṉpiḷḷai discusses the three mantras. His discussions are similar in content to Bhaṭṭar's *śloka*. He elaborates on the mantras in terms of Śrīvaiṣṇava theological concepts such as the nature of the Lord, Śrī, the soul, and the means to salvation—that is subservience and exclusive worship of the Lord.

Piḷḷailokācārya (1250–1311)   This *ācārya* is known as the author of eighteen *rahasyas*, some of them about the three mantras.[135] In the *Tani Praṇavam*, he comments only on *om* in the *tirumantra*. In the *Navavidha Saṃbandham*, he explains the nine kinds of relationship between the soul and Lord that are found in the *tirumantra*. And in the *Parantapaṭi*, he says that *om* comes spontaneously to someone in need,[136] just as the word mother (*ammā*) comes to someone in trouble. This idea is made more explicit in his *Śrīvacana Bhūṣaṇam*,[137] according to which there are no restrictions by time and place for *prapatti*. Anyone can see that there is no need for strict regulation (*prakāraniyati*). He says that Draupadī performed *prapatti* without taking her bath. And as for *tirumantra*,[138] he says in the *Mumukṣup-paṭi* that Śrī will never leave the Lord's chest; like a mother who refuses to leave either her husband's bed or her child's crib, her nature is to remain without leaving either the first or last letters (*a* or *m*). In other words, she is like the letter *u* symbolizing the relationship. Just as mothers connect husbands and children, the *tirumantra* connects God and devotees.

Piḷḷailokācārya does not state explicitly that women may utter *om*, but he does say that it can be uttered spontaneously, just like the word "mother" (*ammā*). And he explains the role of the *tirumantra* by comparing it to the mediating role of a woman. If women had been forbidden to utter *om*, he would surely have avoided that simile. Morever, his assertion that anyone can perform *prapatti* at any time and the fact that he uses a woman in her menses as his example underscore the universalism of Śrīvaiṣṇavism regarding access to *om* and salvation in this life. That is exactly the opposite of most Pañcarātra Āgamas, which virtually always place women and *śūdras* in separate and lower categories; they are ineligible even to utter *om*, let alone to attain salvation in this life. But I am curious about the link between *om* and spontaneity because it indicates that this utterance was not regulated by initiation rituals.

Aḷakiyamaṇavāḷa-perumāḷnāyanār (1207–1309)   In the *Ācārya Hṛdayam*,[139] Aḷakiyamaṇavāḷa-perumāḷnāyanār (probably following a work by Nañjīyar called *Ātmavivāha*) creates an extended metaphor of marriage between the soul and God, one that refers to the *tirumantra*. Like Piḷḷailokācārya, Aḷakiyamaṇavāḷa-perumāḷnāyanār uses a simile involving a woman: the sacred thread (*maṅgalasūtra*) worn by a woman as a symbol of her marriage is, like the *tirumantra*, a symbol of the soul's marriage to God. (This might have been prefigured by a similar comment in the *Viṣṇutattva*, which was quoted by Bhaṭṭar.) In other words, just as women wear ornaments to indicate their marital chastity, devotees wear the discus and conch as ornaments to indicate their marital faithfulness to God. This idea of initiation into the *tirumantra* by an *ācārya* is significant. Because the soul is said to be reborn at initiation, a comparison with the *upanayana*—and therefore a ritualistic context rather than a spontaneous one—is suggested. And because the *gāyatrī* with *om* is the key mantra for the *upanayana*, it seems as though the *tirumantra* has replaced the *gāyatrī*. The implication is that initiation into the mantra may involve not just the mantra itself but also its explication. This passage draws on the concept of *upanayana* and also on Manu's opinion that marriage is the *upanayana* for women; marriage of the soul (considered feminine) to God is the ultimate initiation. By implication, once again, salvation is universal. And if salvation is universal, we can surely assume that saying *om* is not restricted (as in Manu and the Āgamas). Ineligibility to utter *om* is related to ineligibility for salvation in this life according to the Pāñcarātra Āgamas, to be sure, but the reverse might well have been true in other texts—including that of the Śrīvaiṣṇava *ācāryas*.

Vedāntadeśika (1269–1370) Vedāntadeśika wrote many *rahasyas*, including the *Rahasya Traya Sāra*, which includes a chapter for each of the three mantras. This author was more conservative than Piḷḷailokācārya and Aḻakiyamaṇavāḷa-perumāḷnāyaṉār. He was the first *ācārya* to state explicitly that women and *śūdras* may not pronounce the Vedic mantras. In the *Rahasya Traya Sāra*, for instance, he offers several texts in support of his position. According to the *Mahābhārata*, he says, a *śūdra* may not utter names of the Lord with the sacred syllable (*praṇava*). He quotes from the *Nāradīya Kalpa* to argue that chanting (*japa*) the *aṣṭākṣara* (i.e., the eight-syllable mantra) must be performed by women and *śūdra* without the dative suffix, without the *svara*—that is, without the *praṇava* (*om*)—and without being touched on the limbs (*aṅganyāsa*). He quotes several passages from the *Varāha Purāṇa*, moreover, to show the following: those of low caste sing the praise of Bhagavān and utter the mantra *namo nārāyaṇa*; those who go to Vaikunṭha uttering the *mūlamantra* (*namo nārāyaṇa*) will never return; those who utter the name of Bhagavān should say *namo nārāyaṇa*; and the middle of the *aṣṭākṣara* is appropriate for everyone if the first and the last syllables (*om* and the dative suffix) are removed, just as the sugarcane with eight joints becomes suitable for all if the root and the top are cut off. (Here again, I think we can assume that the dative has a special association with Vedic ritual.) Vedāntadeśika concludes that surrender (*prapatti*) is a perfect though momentary event (eliminating the need to do anything else for salvation). Nevertheless, it is delightful to chant the mantra as a result of surrender to the Lord (*prapatti*). For those who practice *bhaktiyoga*, it is an accessory of the path. Vedāntadeśika notes that the *āḻvārs*, too, referred to the mantra as *namo nārāyaṇa*, and he cites the *Periya Tirumoḻi*[140] and *Mutal Tiruvantāti*[141] to this effect. He classifies the mantras without *om* or *praṇava* as *tāntrika*, those with *om* as *vaidika*.[142]

Vedāntadeśika's declaration that women and nonbrahmins may not recite *om* indicates a major change in the Śrīvaiṣṇava tradition. I can think of several reasons for this.

- Vedāntadeśika's conservatism could be explained by his orientation to Sanskrit learning, which might have made him more interested in the Dharmaśāstras, the Āgamas, and the Purāṇas—many of which were more conservative about the issue of women and *śūdras* saying *om*—than the *āḻvār* hymns.
- Or it could be explained by the integration of late and conservative Āgamic material into his works, especially the *Nāradīya Kalpa* (ca. 800–1300), which is often cited in his *Rahasya Traya Sāra* and is among the most important Pāñcarātra Āgamas on the topic of *om*. One section, called the *aṣṭākṣara-brahmavidyā*, is exclusively about *om namo nārāyaṇāya*: the twice-born should meditate on that, but women and *śūdras* should meditate on *namo nārāyaṇa*. Once this position on women and mantras was accepted, Vedāntadeśika exploited the fact that the *āḻvārs* did not refer directly to *om* when he was consolidating his conservative position.
- During Vedāntadeśika's lifetime, the Muslims sacked Śrīraṅgam one or more times (variously dated 1311, 1323, and 1327),[143] and some members of the community were killed. The community's leaders were exiled for sixty years, along with their

statue of God, in Karnataka (Melkote). Vedāntadeśika himself had a narrow escape, according to traditional accounts. All of these events might well have made him feel protective toward the tradition, and thus conservative. After a pilgrimage to North India, he worried that Hinduism had begun to decline as a result of conquests by the Muslims. He found that it was necessary to reinforce the rules of caste and stage of life (*varṇāśramadharma*). Insistence on *varṇāśramadharma*, according to *śāstric* norms, could have led to greater distinction between brahminical roles (Vedic knowledge and ritual) and *śūdra* roles (service). It could also have led to an emphasis on the proper behavior of women (*strīdharma*) along the lines of Manu.

- Fear of conquest by the Muslims could have contributed to more generally conservative trends that affected the social climate of Tamilnadu and, in turn, Śrīvaiṣṇava sociology. Orr's (1994) study of inscriptions from the eighth century to the thirteenth points out that toward the end of this period, women who had once been active as donors and involved in land transactions–queens, palace women, consorts of minor chiefs, and Jain women–no longer performed these activities; their status had declined. Brahmin women, following the consolidation of land holdings by brahmin men, had gained more access to land. Nevertheless, even their status might have been declining. At first, they were referred to by the Tamil words for "wife." Later, the Tamilized form (*pāryai*) of the Sanskrit *bhāryā* ("wife") became common, possibly indicating Sanskritization (and a concomitant decline in their status). At first, women were commonly identified by their hometowns. Later, this became less common, possibly indicating less willingness by those who produced the inscriptions to recognize their independent status. At first, they made their property transactions independently. Later, this was done by male officials (*mutukaṉ*). At first, temple women were central figures in transactions or had the inscriptional records made in their own names (as did the women of other classes). Later, this was far less common. At first, many temple women owned property (because of inheritance or marriage gifts). Later, this was less common.
- The dramatic decline of Jainism and especially of Buddhism–religions that had encouraged women to become nuns or at least donors–took pressure off the Śrīvaiṣṇava *ācāryas* to proselytize among women and integrate their interests into those of the community.
- Finally, Vedāntadeśika worried that *ācāryas* such as Aḻakiyamaṇavāḷa-perumāḷnāyaṉār, who preceded him at Śrīraṅgam, had developed too radical an approach. For Vedāntadeśika, this was not in keeping with the tradition of Rāmānuja. In the *Ācārya Hṛdayam*, for example, Aḻakiyamaṇavāḷa had claimed that *varṇāśramadharma* was unnecessary because the Lord, out of his grace, saves everyone. Rāmānuja had insisted in his commentary on *Gītā* 18:66 and elsewhere, by contrast, on the maintenance of *varṇāśramadharma*.

Maṇavāḷamāmuni (1370–1443) Maṇavāḷamāmuni noticed these changes introduced by Vedāntadeśika. In the *Rahasya Traya Sāra*,[144] Maṇavāḷamāmuni takes up the problem of women reciting *om* and dismisses any possible support for Vedāntadeśika's view. He quotes the *Nārāyaṇa Upaniṣad*[145] to establish that the eight-syllable mantra includes *om*. He states flatly that any other way of construing this mantra is "not Vedic and ought to be rejected."[146] This is the tradition's strongest statement on the universal use of *om*.

Having done this, Maṇavāḷamāmuni reaffirms Piḷḷailokācāya's position: women are not inferior in any way. In fact, despite his mild manner and his utmost care not to be partisan, he makes this point even more boldly than Piḷḷailokācārya had. Commenting on Piḷḷailokācārya's[147] *Śrī Vacana Bhūṣaṇam*, he notes that in the *Mahābhārata* Draupadī performs her surrender to the Lord (*prapatti*) without taking a sacred bath (*snāna*). Dragged by Duḥśāsana into the great assembly, she says that she should not be taken by others into the presence of her teachers. She explains that she has her menses (*rajasvala*), a condition making baths ritualistically inappropriate for three days. According to Maṇavāḷamāmuni, this establishes that those who are impure (such as menstruating women, according to the Dharmaśāstras) may perform *prapatti* without any special effort; God accepts their surrender and rescues them. Thus, *prapatti* is for anyone at any time and any place.[148] Exploiting the freedom allowed by the concept of spontaneity, this author goes far beyond the idea that *om* should be taught in a secret ritual, an idea alluded to on several occasions in the Śrīvaiṣṇava texts. Maṇavāḷamāmuni has thrown down the gauntlet, as it were, to conservatives.

Maṇavāḷamāmuni alludes to the importance of the *tirumantra* on several other occasions. First, he associates taking the name of God with surrendering to God. Piḷḷailokācārya's *Mumukṣup-pati*[149] had stated that Draupadī's utterance of the sacred name Govinda inspired God to provide additional cloth as Duḥśāsana stripped off her sari in public (thereby exemplifying the words of Śrī Vasiṣṭha, who had advised people in danger to remember the Lord). If this is the result of uttering a sacred name of God (here Govinda), which is only part of the meaning signified by the name Nārāyaṇa, even greater results can be expected if the *tirumantra* itself is uttered. The holy name (*tirunāma*) Govinda stands for Nārāyaṇa. The name Nārāyaṇa is part of the superior expression (the *tirumantra* with *om*), and that provides protection against danger and even death. Therefore, "how much more" effective is the holy name of Nārāyaṇa.

But Maṇavāḷamāmuni takes his argument one step further. To illustrate the goddess Śrī as mediator between God and devotees, Maṇavāḷamāmuni comments on Piḷḷailokācāya's *Mumukṣup-pati.*[150] The Goddess (Śrī)—and by extension every married woman—is the paradigm for devotees because her nature is to serve, just as the nature of devotees is to serve. The author implies not only that a married woman has an advantage because she does these things in everyday life but also that she is an embodiment of the goddess. Like Śrī, she serves her husband, protects her children, and resolves conflicts between them. Commenting on Piḷḷailokācārya's *Mumukṣup-pati*[151] (which is about rendering service to God whatever the time, place, or situation), another commertator, Aḻakiyamaṇavāḷa-perumāḷnāyan*ār*, develops a simile (like Nañjiyar). He links the *maṅgalasūtra*, an auspicious thread (*sūtra*) worn by married women in Tamilnadu to symbolize their marital state, and the *tirumantra*, an auspicious short sentence (*sūtra*). Just as wearing the *maṅgalasūtra* means that a woman is married and belongs only to her husband, hearing the *tirumantra* means that the soul is married to God and belongs only to him.[152] In return, the divine husband protects her soul. (Here, once again, is an allusion to ritual—despite the *ācārya's* rhetoric of spontaneity on other occasions.)

Considering all of this evidence, I think that the tradition became dialectical. Piḷḷailokācārya and Aḻakiyamaṇavāḷa-perumāḷnāyaṉār argued for the inclusion of women, exploiting the idea of spontaneity to do so. Vedāntadeśika countered by introducing some conservative Pāñcarātra passages and exegetical skill to make the texts say what he wanted (the exclusion of women and *śūdras*). Maṇavāḷamāmuni reasserted the inclusive argument in no uncertain terms. He no longer restricted *om* to the ritualistic context, with its implication that only initiation could provide access to the mantra. The remaining task of the liberal *ācāryas* was to legitimize this inclusive approach, once and for all, by associating it with the life of Rāmānuja.

Piṉpaḻakiya-perumāḻjīyar (1400–1500?[153]) Piṉpaḻakiya-perumāḻjīyar attributed an incident to Rāmānuja, I suggest, to legitimate inclusivity. In the *Guruparamparā Prabhāvam 6000* (which contains hagiographies of the *āḻvārs* and *ācāryas*), Tirukoṭṭiyūr Nampi reveals the secret meaning of the eight-syllable *tirumantra* (*om namo nārāyaṇāya*) to Rāmānuja. And Rāmānuja, breaking the vow of secrecy, shouts it out from the temple tower at Tirukoṭṭiyūr. But why would he do so, assuming that the mantra contains *om*, in the tradition of Piḷḷailokācārya or Maṇavāḷamāmuni? Shouting *om* itself from the temple tower would have meant departing from the *āḻvār* tradition, which referred to *om* indirectly— a tradition presumably followed by the Śrīvaiṣṇava *ācāryas* in public. Moreover, the incident as a whole would have been out of character for Rāmānuja. Piṉpaḻakiya-perumāḻjīyar often added details to the lives of the *āḻvārs*, to be sure, and he might have done so for the chief *ācārya* Rāmānuja. But why? The influence of the Pāñcarātra Āgamas (which had generally not allowed the use of *om* by women and *śūdras*) was growing—witness the restrictions suggested by Vedāntadeśika. Thus Piṉpaḻakiya-perumāḻjīyar might have been concerned that this influence was eroding the Śrīvaisnava tradition that had included women and *śūdras*. In this context he might have wanted to reaffirm the Śrīvaiṣṇava tradition against growing Āgamic influence. Indeed, the polarization might have been so great that he was willing to use hyperbole. This episode is a return to the motif of spontaneity, which undercuts the need for the *pañcasaṃskāra* ritual (and/or *om* only for the initiated).

Nammāḻvār, Tiruppaṇṇāḻvār, and Āṇṭāḷ: Reversals of Status Śrīvaiṣṇava Style

This technical debate over eligibility to utter *om*—for the initiated, for the twice-born, or for anyone—can be glimpsed in comments by the *ācāryas* on the status of three particular people in the tradition. Stories about the status of Nammāḻvār, supposedly a *śūdra*; Tiruppaṇṇāḻvār, supposedly an outcaste; and Āṇṭāḷ, a young brahmin woman (presumably the daughter of Periyāḻvār) are very effective ways to explore this problem.

Internal references in works by Nammāḻvār indicate that he might have been a chieftain, political leader, or village headman of some sort. He is called *turaivaṉ, kōṉ, nakaraṉ,* and so on, which are titles found also in the works of other *āḻvārs*. On some occasions, though, he uses reversal motifs that suggest low status, one of the most famous being *Tiruvāymoḻi* (3.7.9), in which he defines a master as someone who is a slave of the Lord and serves the servants of enlightened ones, someone who is like a *caṇḍāla* (outcaste), even in the eyes of *caṇḍālas*, and below any of the four castes. Hardy observes that all the hagiographies of Nammāḻvār's life have agreed that he was a *śūdra*, but he can find no source for this in Nammāḻvār's works themselves.[154]

The first explicit identification of Nammāḻvār as a *śūdra*, according to Hardy, is by Nañjīyar (late twelfth century and early thirteenth) in the introduction to his commentary on the *Tiruvāymoḻi*. Nañjīyar says that the *āḻvār* hymns

are studied also by women, *śūdras*, etc. [and] the *āḻvār* rendered the meaning of the Vedas in Tamil out of his extraordinary compassion, so that even women, *śūdras*, etc. who are

> not entitled to study the Vedas can find salvation. They are composed by a person who was born in the fourth *varṇa* which in the present kali age is excluded from *jñāna* (knowledge). The *āḻvār* had accumulated so much merit (in his former lives) that it was appropriate for Viṣṇu in a whole series of births to make him His subject; he was the recipient of His uninterrupted grace; he was proficient in the *tattvas* and *hitas* and had the talent to teach them; and he was superior to Vidura, etc. . . . [The Tamil hymns] are accepted by people who do not follow a Vedic life-style (*avaidika*). It only contributes to their fame that even *avaidikas*[155] accept them when they see their excellence.[156]

This passage is important because it acknowledges that women and *śūdras* are excluded from Vedic knowledge, and it does so in connection with their lack of a formal entitlement rather than merely their lack of knowledge. This is reminiscent of Manu's position on women and *śūdras* as ineligible to know the Vedas *(avaidika)*, except that it offers an option. It was necessary to create an apologetic (presumably for other brahmins), in short, for the idea of a Tamil Veda being composed by a *śūdra*.

In the *Divya Sūri Caritam* (late twelfth century or early thirteenth, according to Hardy; fifteenth century, according to Carman[157]), the hagiographer identifies Nammāḻvār as a *śūdra* because "there was born among the foremost of *śūdras* a certain excellent *bhāgavata* [called] Śrīmad Vaḻutirājendra," the ancestor of Nammāḻvār.[158] The birth story of Nammāḻvār alludes to an extraordinary birth and early childhood, as does many hagiographies. After his birth in the village of Kurukūr, he does not drink from the breast, wet his bed, or cry. On the contrary, he immediately receives knowledge (*jñāna*) from the Lord and sits in silence at the foot of a sacred tamarind tree. Then he experiences a theophany in which Viṣṇu wants to transmit the four Vedas in Tamil through the mouth of Māraṉ (i.e., Nammāḻvār). This occurs during the following sixteen years, as the *āḻvār* remains seated in silence under the sacred tree. By the grace of God, according to the *Divya Sūri Caritam*,[159] the *āḻvār* knows the *tattvas*, *śāstras*, and Vedas. This yogic motif continues in a subsequent tale about Madhurakavi. This son of a brahmin of a nearby town, belonging to the *Sāma Veda* tradition, practices the eightfold path of yoga; travels around India; and then, following a great light, goes to the village of Kurukūr. There, he finds the great yogi Nammāḻvār, becomes his disciple, and learns the Tamil Veda (the thousand hymns of Nammāḻvār: the *Tiruvāymoḻi*). Whereas Nañcīyar is apologetic, *Divya Sūri Caritam* is hyperbolic in its discussion of Nammāḻvār's extraordinary birth, his yogic discipline from birth, and the fact that the *śūdra āḻvār* is a vehicle for God's grace.

In his *Ācārya Hṛdayam*, Aḻakiyamaṇavāḷa-perumāḷnāyaṉār goes even further, saying that God "descended low in order to raise those who were in a lowly position (viz. *śūdras*, women, etc.)."[160] In fact, he goes beyond this idea of the worthiness of a *śūdra* as a vehicle of the divine Tamil revelation and the fact that the Tamil hymns do not contradict the Sanskrit Veda; instead he praises the *śūdra* himself by saying that a *śūdra* naturally serves, and therefore this essence of his nature supercedes his other nonessential actions and is on a par with Brahmins; "Like the study of the Vedas turns an Ārya into a true brahmin, to learn the TVM [*Tiruvāymoḻi*] is the prerequisite for becoming a true bhakta and Vaiṣṇava."[161]

We would expect Vedāntadeśika to be troubled by the idea of a *śūdra* who knows the Veda. In the *Guru Paramparā Sāram*, he avoids this problem by referring to Nammālvār as an incarnation (*avatāra*) of the Lord. The *śūdra* is merely an appearance of the Lord, a vehicle used to convey the Tamil Vedas. The Vaṭakalai version of the hagiography, *Guru Paramparā Prabhāvam* 12,000, elaborates on Nammāḻvār's initiation (*dīkṣā*). Lakṣmī and Viṣṇu send Viśvaksena, of whom Nammāḻvār is an *aṃśa*, or partial incarnation, down to earth to teach him all the secrets (*rahasyas*). The heavenly general does so and performs the Śrīvaiṣṇava initiation.[162]

Because statues of the *āḻvārs* had been worshiped since the thirteenth century, the idea of incarnation enabled this tradition to talk about the extraordinary nature of a *śūdra* by distinguishing him from human status (with its social and political ramifications). Nevertheless, in these various sources, I find a tradition that presages the Teṉkalai sect—that the *śūdra* as a yogi, seer, and devotee is equal to the brahmin in social as well as theological terms—being opposed by a different understanding: because the *śūdra* is an incarnation, he is in a different category altogether from human *śūdras*. This latter theology has no social implications whatsoever.

On the same topic, consider Tiruppāṇṇāḻvār. Although bards (*pāṇars*) once had considerable status, they lost it gradually, beginning in the *caṅkam* period. Many bards became indigent because of changing values. In any case, they were displaced by another group of poets. Centuries later, by the time of the *ācāryas*, a work of ten stanzas entitled *Amalanātip-pirāṉ* has been attributed to the bard Tiruppāṇṇāḻvār. Unlike other *āḻvār* works, it has no formal verse that identifies the author; nor does it offer internal evidence about the author. It is possible, therefore, that this work was written by someone else but attributed to Tiruppāṇṇāḻvār. The first explicit reference to him occurs in a thirteenth-century inscription. It mentions a provision for ghee to be burned before an image. (All the *āḻvārs* were worshiped in statue form by this time, so we can assume that Tiruppāṇṇāḻvār had come to be considered an *āḻvār* and associated with the *Amalanātip-pirāṉ*.) According to the *Irāmanuca Nuṟṟantāti*,[163] Rāmānuja (the tradition's chief *ācārya*) wears the feet of this *āḻvār* on his head. This statement, in my estimation, was intended as a political message, linking the chief *ācārya*, someone who had orthodox brahminical credentials, with an outcaste. (This suggests either that the social implications of Tiruppāṇṇāḻvār's status had begun long before Piḷḷailokācārya and Vedāntadeśika took up the case or that this text belongs to the period of Piḷḷailokācārya or later.)

In Periyavāccānpiḷḷai's commentary on the *Amalanātip-pirāṉ*, this *ālvār* is said to be similar to the eternal divine beings (*nityasūris*) who were never born into one of the four castes (*varṇas*—a simile that eliminates the negative status of the fifth, or outcaste, category. From birth, moreover, this *ālvār* has the capacity to praise, and other *āḻvārs* must develop this art. In a commentary on the *Amalanātip-pirāṉ*, Aḻakīyamaṇavāḷaperumāḷnāyaṉar says that

> any man from a lower varṇa who through knowledge and devotion rises about the limitations of his birth should be honoured . . . at the time of inseparable service to God the general *karmas* will disappear, because at the time of service to the Lord, the individual will act as a slave (*śeṣa*) to Him, and this is different from other actions which are performed according to *varṇāśrama* and *dīkṣa* [presumably here *upanayana* is the brahminical initiation into Vedic learning]. . . . Therefore, we can conclude that the *dharma* of service (*kaiṅkarya*) is different from and supersedes other *dharmas*.[164]

In his commentary on the *Amalanātip-pirāṉ* (called *Muni Vāhana Pokam*), by contrast, Vedāntadeśika says that this work is the seed that "produces everything for the elaborate treatment of topics . . . by the Vetiyar (brahmins)." He goes on to say that these ten verses are for those who do not know the other disciplines of knowledge (referring to Veda and *vedāṅga*, as implied by the *Brahmasūtra*'s use of the word *bhakti*). (Later in the Vaṭakalai tradition, *Amalanātip-pirāṉ* was called *prapanna gāyatrī* and was recited by those who were ineligible for the Sanskrit *gāyatrī*.) Once again, Vedāntadeśika was cautious in his approach to the problem of status. He preferred to circumvent Tiruppāṇṇāḻvār's low status, along with that of other *āḻvārs*, by saying that they were really (partial) incarnations of God.[165]

In *Upadeśa Ratna Mālā*,[166] by contrast, Maṇavāḷamāmuni states (in his characteristic way) that those who consider the *āḻvārs* low will go to hell. And *Guru Paramparā Prabhāvam* 6000 says that Tiruppāṇṇāḻvār is like a *bhāgavata*, performing sacrifices (i.e., a brahmin), even though he belongs to the fifth caste. He is the victim of discrimination. He is stoned, in fact, by an ascetic. The Lord decries this sin against his devotee and instructs the ascetic to carry him into the temple on his shoulders (which implies that this was a time when outcastes were not allowed to enter temples). In other words, discussions of Tiruppāṇṇāḻvār's status have included the following motifs: that his work provided the foundation for that of the brahmins and that he was the equal of brahmins.

As for the symbol of woman, consider the case of Āṇṭāḷ (ninth century). She identifies herself in the signature lines of her poems as Kotai. She often refers to Viṭṭucittaṉ (Periyāḻvār) in her two poetic works, *Tiruppāvai*[167] and *Nācciyārtirumoḻi*.[168] Her name follows his name or title, and the genitive case (which would indicate kinship) is replaced by the nominative (a common practice in Tamilnadu to indicate kinship today).[169] Therefore, people have assumed that she was Viṭṭucittaṉ's daughter. Āṇṭaḷ might have been a posthumous epithet, meaning "she who rules." Because she composed poems, she could be considered an *āḻvār* like the others. But in *Guru Paramparā Prabhāvam* 6000, Piṉpaḻakiya-perumāljīyar identifies her with Sītā, divine heroine of the epic *Rāmāyaṇa*. He says that she was a (full) manifestation of Goddess Earth (Bhūdevī) and Goddess *Śrī* (both consorts of the supreme Lord). The notion of divine incarnation puts Āṇṭāḷ in a category distinct from that of other women. The author suggests in addition that her love was greater than that of the male *āḻvārs* because it was more natural (a woman naturally loves a man, and by extension a male deity). Her love was unique, moreover, because it was fully divine. Why was Āṇṭāḷ made into a goddess when other *āḻvārs* were made into nothing more than partial incarnations? The reason, I think, is that Āṇṭāḷ's refusal to marry any (human) man posed a danger to the marital norm for women and had to be circumvented by putting her in a divine category.

These examples—Nammāḻvār, Tiruppāṇṇāḻvār, and Āṇṭāḷ—show how how difficult it has been for the Śrīvaiṣṇava tradition to promote a universal theology and deal with its social ramifications. The latter caused deep tensions in the Śrīvaiṣṇava community, exemplified here by the debate over eligibility to utter the mantra *om*. It took several centuries for these tensions to result in a split into two sects: the Teṉkalai branch, which emphasized the teachings of Piḷḷailokācārya; and the Vaṭakalai branch, those of Vedāntadeśika.

The Mantras and Women's Access to Knowledge and Ritual in the Twentieth Century

What is the effect of all of these debates on contemporary India? *Śrīvaiṣṇava-tīpikai* (Dīpikā), by Alakiyamaṇavāḷa-rāmānuja-ekāṅki-svāmikaḷ, was written in the early twentieth century. It describes the role of the mantras for women. The author was probably a Teṉkalai because he mentions several works by Piḷḷailokācārya (that sect's main *ācārya*). According to the author, women should participate with men in the Śrīvaiṣṇava realm of sectarian learning. They should know the *guruparamparā* (the lineage of teachers), the mantras, the *ācārya taṉiyaṉ*, the 4000 *āḻvār* hymns (including Āṇṭāḷ's *Tiruppāvai*), and various philosophical or theological works of *ācāryas* (such as Piḷḷailokācāya's *Artha Pañcakam*, *Rahasya Trayam*, *Tattva Trayam*, and *Śrīvacana Bhūṣanam*). Like men, moreover, they should maintain their Vaiṣṇava identity by wearing the sectarian emblem, the *ūrdhvapuṇḍra*, and by avoiding Śaiva influence. And, like men, they should cultivate qualities such as the following: knowledge; devotion; indifference to worldly objects; control; compassion; forebearance; and being without ego, wealth, and desire. This will make them real Bhāgavatas. But the secrecy of *om* continues; it is only indirectly mentioned.

Patricia Mumme[170] describes Śrīvaiṣṇava initiation today as follows. Teṉkalais include, "as part of *pañcasaṃskāra*, surrender to the Lord through the *ācārya*, who introduces the initiate to the Lord and requests that he be saved by virtue of the *prapatti* that Rāmānuja performed in the *Saraṇā Gati Gadya*."[171] There are now three key elements: surrender (*prapatti*) is ritualized, the ritual is controlled by the *ācārya* (belonging to one of the seventy-four families), and it is justified by its association with the chief *ācārya's* (Rāmānuja's) own surrender. That was expressed in his *Śaraṇā Gati Gadya* and developed in the doctrine of his special status, which made him the intercessor between devotees and God (called *puruṣakāra*). Does this mean that Teṉkalais have come to ignore other understandings of *prapatti*—spontaneous surrender (on the model of the *āḻvārs* or Draupadī), for instance, or acts of devotion such as offering flowers and chanting the names of God? Spontaneous surrender is now either safely relegated to the past (the epic or *āḻvār* periods) or dismissed as poetic rhetoric. For contemporary Teṉkalais, then, *prapatti* is a ritual connected with the *pañcasaṃskāra* ritual. Nevertheless, it takes precedence over *bhaktiyoga* (which, in line with the *Brahmasūtras* and Rāmānuja's writings, came gradually to be associated with it even by brahmin men with knowledge of Vedic texts and yogic meditation). Ultimately God's grace takes precedence over prapatti, and *bhaktiyoga* is not mandatory. They admit, though, that some twice-born men might want to perform the rituals and duties of their caste and stage of life anyway.

But for Vaṭakalais today, *pañcasaṃskāra* may be followed by the voluntary ritual of *prapatti*, which must be preceded by much effort (an antidote to the rhetoric of ease and spontaneity promoted by Teṉkalais) and is usually postponed until late in life.[172] Vaṭakalais think that twice-born men must pursue *bhaktiyoga* in addition to the rituals of *pañcasaṃskāra* and *prapatti*. Those not eligible for *bhaktiyoga*, such as women and *śūdras*, may perform only the ceremonies of *pañcasaṃskāra* and *prapatti*. *Śūdras* and women are grouped together in a way that corresponds to that found in many Pāñcarātra Āgamas.

Of greater importance still is the fact that today *om* is chanted by Teṉkalai women and nonbrahmins, although not by Vaṭakalai women and nonbrahmin men. In light of the previous discussions, this reflects the liberal nature of Piḷḷailokācārya, Aḻakiyamaṇavāḷaperumāḷnāyaṉār, and Maṇavālamāmuni and the conservative nature of Vedāntadeśika, which plays out in the subsequent sectarian sociology.

All Śrīvaiṣṇavas claim that eligibility for salvation is universal, however, because everyone surrenders to the Lord, and the paths of *prapatti* and *bhaktiyoga* ensure that everyone has a way to attain the supreme goal (even though what is mandatory differs according to sect). The difference is nominal rather than substantial (unlike the Pañcarātra texts). And whatever the finer points of the doctrine:

> every Śrīvaiṣṇava subsequently is to recite the *paramparā* daily (after bathing), with gratitude toward the *ācārya*. This is to be immediately followed by recitation of the three *mantras*, while reflecting on their meaning. He [or she] should then worship the domestic image [when the *Tirumantra* is also recited for the purpose of ritual purification]. In addition, the three mantras—and particularly the *Dvaya* mantra—should be recited silently and reflected on throughout the day by the Śrīvaiṣṇava *adhikāri*."[173]

In both sects, a few especially devout Śrīvaiṣṇavas, after their *pañcasaṃskāra*, seek further instruction in the meaning of the three mantras to understand them more fully. These profound meanings of the mantras should not be taught to just anyone who has had pañcasaṃskāra but only to those who are particularly eager to learn their truths and who demonstrate deep respect for the *ācārya* and his tradition. Under no circumstances should the mantras or their meanings be given to, or discussed without, the proper qualification. This traditional use and treatment of the mantras has remained fairly constant up to recent times.[174]

Śrīvaiṣṇavas today, especially in the Teṉkalai tradition, have a traditional sociology that can stand the test of modern universalism because of its inclusiveness on the issue of *om* and salvation. With pressure from the contemporary women's movement, they might want to explore women's accessibility to Sanskrit and Vedic knowledge. This time, however, history might be on their side. More and more women are studying Sanskrit and the Vedas in universities, thus eliminating the issue of male brahmin status altogether. Furthermore, it might bode well that there is a general interest throughout Hinduism in universal access to Vedic knowledge and *om*. This is best captured by the Viśva Hindu Pariṣad's promotion and popularization of the sacred syllable as the very symbol of Hinduism in the most universal sense possible. One cannot help but think, however, that its journey toward universality has involved shedding its secrecy and mystique, the result being a greater focus on the visual emblem of the sacred sound than on the sound itself, an emblem adorning T-shirts and students' notebooks, and thus increasingly profane. This radical promotion of the visual symbol of *om* signifies "a leaning towards mundane matters, an inclusive definition of Hinduism and an insistence on the necessity of adapting Hinduism to modem times."[175]

Conclusions

In sum, there has been a basic difference between the conservative brahmanical view of women (*strīdharma*)—in the tradition of Manu—and the Śrīvaiṣṇava perspective. Conservative brahminism has considered women ineligible for Vedic learning. The Śrīvaiṣṇava tradition does not comment on this point per se (bypassing it by promoting the Tamil Veda). Whereas the conservative brahmanical tradition has often restricted the means to and goal of liberation to twice-born (*dvija*) men, Śrīvaiṣṇavism has opened the path to liberation (with no rebirth necessary) to everyone because of the *Nārāyaṇa Upaniṣad's* concepts of *prapatti* and Tamil Veda. Women have not been able to pursue asceticism in conservative circles. In Śrīvaiṣṇavism, though, this has posed no problem because women (indeed all people) have been able to attain salvation as householders. Woman have often been considered inferior in conservative brahmanical circles. In Śrīvaiṣṇavism, they have been considered equal or even preferred by God (hence the male imaginative adoption of female psychology to explore the relation with a male deity and the image of Āṇṭāḷ as goddess).

There are many differences between the Śrīvaiṣṇava approach to salvation and that of the Pāñcarātra Āgamas, too, even though some passages of the latter have been incorporated into the Śrīvaiṣṇava tradition. The differences became particularly sharp by the fourteenth century. The Pāñcarātra tradition itself had become even more conservative, and this influenced Vedāntadeśika (and the subsequent split into Teṉkalai and Vaṭakalai subsects).

These historical vicissitudes are highlighted when tracing the question of women's and *śūdras*' accessibility to the syllable *om*. Surely there have been long-standing connections of mantras and Vedic ritual, on the one hand, and mantras and *rahasyas* (such as the secret teachings of the Upaniṣads taught by gurus), on the other hand. The question of accessibility to *om* because of these connections with Vedic ritual, knowledge, and wisdom has been the product of a brahminical mindset and has resulted in some circles in privileges for twice-bom (especially brahmin) men. Alongside this brahmanized tradition has been another that considers mantras accessible. I have mentioned this in the context of bowing to the feet of God (*namaḥ*) and offering flowers, the universalism of the *Nārāyaṇa Upaniṣad*, and the symbol *om* as accessible to women and *śūdras* in these circles. Associating the sacred syllable *om*, which had developed out of the context of Vedic rituals, with these features might have been related to the gradual surfacing of a suppressed tradition (which had been caused by the collapse of the Indus civilization and nonacknowledgement or selective syncretism by the heirs of the Ṛgvedic tradition); a way to accommodate brahmanism to the tribal, folk, and temple traditions; or a way to compete with the universalism of Buddhism and Jainism.

From this overview, it should be clear that the *āḻvār* tradition is derived from a Nārāyaṇa-Viṣṇu tradition with a liberal brahminical orientation. There is no overt exclusion of women and *śūdras* from the utterance of *om*, and references to the eight-syllable mantra allude to the fact that all who are initiated have access to it. It has been difficult to know whether accessibility to *om* occurred during the basic initiation as a Vaiṣṇava (*pañcasaṃskāra*) or in another ritual. This is made especially confusing in the *āḻvār* hymns because chanting the name of God is associated with a rhetoric of spontaneity and allusions to semi-ritual bowing at the feet of God.

Whatever the exact practice, it is important to underscore the point that women's spontaneous surrender and utterance of the sacred syllable constituted the exemplary type of *prapatti* (at least as a rhetorical device to promote universalism) for Piḷḷailokācārya and Aḻakiyamaṇavāḷa-perumāḷnāyaṉār. Only with the development of more restrictive Pāñcarātra Āgamas and a period of great stress, perhaps because of the Muslim domination of north India and Muslim forays into Tamilnadu, affecting even Śrīraṅgam, did one Śrīvaiṣṇava (Vedāntadeśika) become more conservative. Vedāntadeśika's incorporation of Āgamic passages that forbid *śūdras* and women from uttering *om* became a way to prop up *varṇāśramadharma* and inspire brahmin men to preserve the tradition by reasserting a special status, the corollary of their special duty of years of memorization. It is important to remember that he does not deny women and *śūdras* salvation in this life, as do the authors of many Āgamas. Nor does he deny them knowledge of the secret teachings of the tradition. Thus, his removal of *om* and the dative case from the mantras for women and *śūdras* has only a nominal effect on a tradition that has long supported women, though it has carefully institutionalized the roles of preceptor and priest in male brahmin hands and possibly avoided women's Vedic education by making it irrelevant. Even so, the challenge to the liberal Śrīvaiṣṇava tradition by Vedāntadeśika is serious enough to inspire countersteps to shore up its position. The story of Rāmānuja's, shouting the meaning of *om* from the temple tower, is one case in point. Others include eulogies of Nammāḻvār's, Tiruppāṇṇāḻvār's, and Āṇṭāḷ's "low" status as exemplary. Closely related to their status is their symbolic link, analogous to the old negative link between women and *śūdras*, but more dramatic (in that an outcaste is included) and for precisely the opposite effect: to make them symbols of an inclusive tradition.

Taking an even longer view of the history of *om* and women, we can see that the two low points were the time of Manu for the general Hindu tradition and the time of Vedāntadeśika for the Śrīvaiṣṇava tradition. It might not be incidental that both of these periods were times of great stress, the earlier period experiencing the invasions of Greeks, Śakas, Kuṣāṇas, and so forth, and the latter invasions of the Muslims. In these times of high stress, men looked for security in tradition, one that was embodied by women, who, by their maintenance of it, were called the "pillars of the universe." This led to the projection of conservative norms by men onto women, the one "realm" they hoped to control. It led also to the projection of their fears of the outer world onto women in the inner (domestic) world. (Paola Bacchetta discusses this tendency in this volume in connection with the gender identities of the Hindu nation's ideal citizens. Her analysis focuses not only on women's domestic roles but also on their public uses of violence.) Those were tough times for women. And because misogynistic views became embedded in myths such as that of the Kali Yuga, in scripture, and in general attitudes, women's destinies were altered until reformers in the nineteenth and twentieth centuries were inspired to universalize the tradition again. Even though Śrīvaiṣṇavism was influenced by a period of stress, which had an effect on the status of women and *śūdras* (by denying them the utterance of *om* in the thought of Vedāntadeśika and then the Vaṭakalai sect), this was largely symbolic. As a result, the history of Śrīvaiṣṇavism should be remembered when the topic is liberal and universal Hinduism.

Notes

1. See M. Bloomfield, "On the Etymology of the Particle *Om*," *Journal of the American Oriental Society* 14 (1890), cl–clii; A. B. Keith, "*Om*," in *Encyclopedia of Religion and Ethics*, J. Hastings, Ed. (1917) 11.490–92; J. A. B. van Buitenen, "*Akṣara*," *Journal of the American Oriental Society* 79 (1959), 176–87; Klaus K. Klostermaier, A *Survey of Hinduism* (Albany: State University of New York Press, 1994), p. 78. See also T. S. Rukmani "A Critique of OM Based on Early Upaniṣadic Sources," *Journal of the Institue of Asian Studies* (March 1998): 101–12.

2. Hans Henrick Hock, "On the Origin and Early Development of the Sacred Sanskrit Syllable Om. Perspectives on Indo-European Language, Culture, and Religion," *Studies in Honor of Edgar C. Polomi* (*Journal of Indo-European Studies Monographs* 7 (1991), 89–110.

3. *Aitareya Brāhmaṇa* 37, admittedly a somewhat late one.

4. As in *Aitareya Brāhmaṇa* 38.

5. Hock says that *o(m)* is a "common bond that exists between different priests, their functions and performances in the ritual, and their respective branches of the Veda. For it is indeed true that *o(m)*, in one form or another, is the linguistic element in ritual recitation that is most prominently employed by all of the participants in the ritual. . . . The syllable *om*, therefore, lends itself most readily as the ONE *akṣara* that embodies all that is shared by the three Vedas—and that which transcends them. The fact that it can be analysed into *three* component parts, *a*, *u*, and *m*. . .no doubt further supported this 'triune' character of *om*, as did perhaps the fact, noted by van Buitenen. . .that *om* frequently has TRImoric, pluta pronunciation" (Hock, "On the Origin," p. 109).

6. Robert Ernest Hume, *The Thirteen Principal Upanishads* (Oxford: Oxford University Press, (1921/1968), p. 283.

7. *Ṛg Veda* 1.164.39.

8. The fact that *om* also came to mean compliance or yes, too might indicate that it is related to the Dravidian particle *am*, an expletive that expresses permission; *Tamil Lexicon* 6 vols. (rpt. Madras: University of Madras, 1982), See vol.1, p. 232. Asko Parpola, "On the Primary Meaning and Etymology of the Sacred Syllable *Om*," *Studia Orientalia* 50 (1981) 195–213, argues that this Dravidian confirmatory particle was, in fact, the very origin of om. Hock, "On the Origin," advances several arguments to show that *am* was not the origin per se but a later development.

9. *Chāndogya Upaniṣad* 1.4.1–5.

10. Paul Deussen, *Sixty Upaniṣads of the Veda*, V. M. Bedekar and G. B. Palsule, Trans., 2 vols. (Delhi: Motilal Banarsidass, [1987] 1980) vol. 1, p. 74.

11. *Chāndogya Upaniṣad* 2.23.3.

12. Deussen, *Sixty Upaniṣads*, vol. 1, pp. 98–99.

13. *Taittirīya Upaniṣad 1.8.*

14. Deussen, *Sixty Upaniṣads*, vol.1, p. 227.

15. Ibid.

16. Ibid.

17. *Chāndogya Upaniṣad* 1.4.1–5.

18. For other Upaniṣadic references to *om*, see *Maitri* 4.4; 6.2–4; *Praśna* 5, 5:2. *Katha* 2.15–17; *Chāndogya* 8.6.5; and *Sveteśvatara* 1. 13–4, 4.18, in which *om* or *praṇava* is variously described as Viṣṇu, *paraṃ brahman* is an arrow to hit the mark of *brahman;* the greatness of brahman is the *ātman*, a basis for meditation; and so forth.

19. Others have assigned this text to 100 B.C.E.– C.E 100, but no specific reasons have been provided. Because this period was generally very hostile toward the idea of women and *Śūdras* having accessibility to *om*, I think this text was composed earlier.

20. In this cosmogonic myth, breath, mind, and so forth are born from Nārāyaṇa. He consists of Brahman, Śiva, Śakra, and so forth. He is the entire universe; he is eternal. He is spotless, inexpressible, changeless, artless, pure, and one.

21. Deussen, *Sixty Upaniṣads*, vol.2, pp. 803–805. The *Maha Upaniṣad*, though not using the formula, does begin with *om*. From Nārāyaṇa came sweat, then the primordial waters, a golden egg, and Brahmā with his four faces. Associated with the southern face is the exclamation *om janad*, the *anuṣṭubh* meter, and the *Atharva Veda*. This is particularly interesting given the fact that the *anuṣṭubh* meter has been connected with *śūdras*, and the *Atharvavedins* had an early presence in Tamilnadu (if the caṅkam references to the four Vedas is any indication). The results of studying this Upaniṣad are initiation; purification; and becoming one who is an authority on scripture, has bathed in all the holy places, has performed all the sacrifices, and has uttered 60,000 stanzas of the Itihāsa-Purāṇas, the Rudra hymns, and 1,000 *praṇavas*. This is the way to attain immortality (Deussen, *Sixty Upaniṣads*, vol.2, pp: 799–801).

22. *Atharva Veda* 19.71.

23. Kailash Vajpeyi, *The Science of Mantras: A Manual for Happiness and Prosperity* (New Delhi: Arnold-Heinemann, 1979).

24. Wade T. Wheelock, "The Mantra in Vedic and Tantric Ritual," In *Understanding Mantras*, Harvey P. Alper, Ed. (Albany: State University of New York Press, 1989), pp. 114–15.

25. *Āpastamba Dharmasūtra* 1.4.13.6.

26. P.V. Kane, *History of Dharmasāstra: Ancient and Mediaeval Religious and Civil Law*, 5 vols., 2nd ed. (Poona: Bhandarkar Oriental Research Institute, 1968–1977) vol.1, p. 74.

27. Ibid., vol. 2, p. 302.

28. *Āpastamba Dharma Sūtra* 1.1.1.19.

29. *Ṛg Veda* 3.62, which invokes the Sun (Savitṛ) as the source and inspiration of everything, another suggestion of the beginning.

30. During the *upanayana* (as described in the *Aśvalāyana Gṛhyasūtra*), the teacher utters Ṛg Veda 82.1 as he releases the water in his hands into those of the boy. After several other ritual gestures, the boy, embracing his guru's feet, asks him to recite the *sāvitrī*, the *gāyatrī mantra*. See Kane, *History*, vol.2, 281.

31. Ibid., p. 302.

32. *Āpastamba Dharmasūtra* 1.1.1.10.

33. *Mārkaṇḍeya Purāṇa* (chap. 42).

34. Ludo Rocher, "Mantras in the *Śivapurāṇa*," in *Understanding Mantras*, Harvey P. Alper, Ed. (Albany: State University of New York Press, 1989), p. 182.

35. See the references to Gārgī and Maitreyī in *Bṛhadāranyaka Upaniṣad* 2.4. 1, 4.5.15. As is well known, the *Kāśika* on Pāniṇi (who lived in the fifth century to the fourth century B.C.E.) mentions female teachers and preceptors, noting the difference between *ācaryā* (a female teacher), and *ācāryaṇī* (a teacher's wife) and between *upadhyāyā* (a female preceptor), and *upadhyāyinī* (a preceptor's wife) (*Pāniṇi* 4.1.59 and 3.3.21). For women performing Vedic rituals, see *Jaimini* 6.1.17–24 and the chapter by Mary McGee in this volume.

36. Kane, *History*, vol.1, p. 127.

37. yattu hāritenoktam'dvividhāstriyo brahmavādinyassadyovadhvaśca: tatra brahmavādinīnām-upanayanamagnīndhaṇ vedādhyayanaṃ svagṛhe ca bhikṣācaryeti: sadyovadhūnāṃ copasthite vivāhe kathaṃcidupanayanamātraṃ kṛtvā vivāhaḥ kāryaḥ iti (*Hārīta Dharma Sūtra*, quoted in Devannabhaṭṭa's *Smṛticandrikā*, (Kane, *History*, vol. 1, p. 132, for the Sanskrit).

38. Paul Nathanson and Katherine K. Young, *Transcending Misandry: From Feminist Ideology to Intersexual Dialogue* (forthcoming).

39. Kane, *History*, vol. 1, pp. 522ff.

40. tatkalpāntaṛābhiprāyam: tathā ca yamaḥ purā kalpe tu nārīṇām mauñjībhandhanamiṣyate: adhyāpanaṃ ca vedānāṃ sāvitrīvacanaṃ tathā: pitā pitṛvyo bhrātā vā naināmadhyāpayetparaḥ:: svagṛhe caiva kanyāyāḥ bhaikṣacaryā vidhīyate:: varjayetajinaṃ cīraṃ jaṭādhāraṇam eva ca: (cited in Devanabhaṭṭa's *Smṛticandrikā*).

41. *Yama Saṃhitā* 22–23.

42. *Yama Saṃhitā* 73.

43. *Manu* 2:74–79.

44. *Manu* 2:81–85.

45. *Manu* 2:66.

46. *Manu* 4:205–206.

47. *Manu* 11:36.

48. *Manu* 9:18–19. Wendy Doniger, Trans. *The Laws of Manu* (London: Penguin Books, 1991), p. 198.

49. *Kātyāyana Saṃhitā* 3ff.

50. *Jaimini* 6.1.17–24.

51. See Jan Gonda, "The Indian Mantra," *Oriens* 16, (1963)244–97. Reprinted in Gonda, *Selected Studies, Presented to the Author by the Staff of the Oriental Institute, Utrecht University, on the Occasion of his 70th Birthday*, 4 vols. (Leiden: Brill, 1975), vol. 4, p. 264.

52. Asko Parpola, *Deciphering the Indus Script* (Cambridge: Cambridge University Press, 1994), pp. 149–52.

53. George Erdosy, Ed. *The Indo-Aryans of Ancient South Asia: Language, Material Culture and Ethnicity* (Berlin: Walter de Gruyter, 1995).

54. Norvin Hein, "Kālayavana, A Key to Mathurā's Cultural Self-Perception," in *Mathurā: The Cultural Heritage*, Doris Meth Srinivasan, Ed. (New Delhi: American Institute of Indian Studies, 1989), pp. 223–26.

55. *Yājñavalkya* 1.21.

56. *Yājñavalkya* 1.223.

57. *Mahābhārata* 12.328.49

58. *Mahābhārata* 12.319.87ff.

59. *Mahābhārata* 12.60.36.

60. *Mārkaṇḍeya Purāṇa* 28.7–8.

61. *Brahmāṇḍa Purāṇa* 3.12.19.

62. *Mahābhārata* (Vanaparvan) 3.305.20.

63. *Bhagavad Gītā* 9.32.

64. Still, *śūdras* and women are instructed in Sanskrit dramas to speak Prakrit, whereas higher caste men speak Sanskrit. Some exceptions are allowed by the *Nāṭyaśāstra* for queens, courtesans, and female artists, who are allowed to speak Sanskrit (Nāṭyaśāstra 17.37 and 17.39).

65. śrīman nārāyaṇa caranau śaraṇam prapadye, śrīmate nārāyaṇāya namaḥ

Patricia Y. Mumme, *The Mumukṣuppati of Piḷḷai Lokācārya with Maṇavāḷamāmuni's Commentary* (Bombay: Ananthacharya Indological Research Institute, 1987), translates the *dvayam* as "I take refuge with the feet of Nārāyaṇa joined with Śrī; Homage to Nārāyaṇa joined with Śrī" (p. 31). But I think this is a translation in line with the late theology of Śrī, the consort of Nārāyaṇa. Instead, Śrī might have signified an honorific for the sacred name Nārāyaṇa.

66. *Bhagavad Gītā* 18:66: sarvadharmānparityajya māmekam śaraṇam vraja: aham tvā sarvapāpebhyo mokṣayiṣyāmi mā śucaḥ. Mumme (*Mumukṣuppati*, p. 3) observes that "for at least seven centuries, these *mantras* have been given to every Śrīvaiṣṇava at the time of the initiating ritual of *pañcasaṃskāra*," but she offers no documentation for this claim.

67. K. Venkatacami Reddiar, Ed. *Nālāyirativyappirapantam* (Tiruvenkatattan: Tirumantram, 1973).

68. This is mentioned by Narayanan but no verse number is given.

69. Vasudha Narayanan, *The Way and the Goal: Expressions of Devotion in the Early Śrī Vaiṣṇava Tradition* (Cambridge, Mass: Center for the Study of World Religions, Harvard University, 1987), p. 120.

70. Ibid., p. 204 note 88): "This entire phrase, *om namo Nārāyaṇa*, has eight syllables, but the ālvārs tend to use the Tamil form *namo nāraṇa* in their poems."

71. See Nammālvār's *Tiruvāymoḻi* 10:5.8.

72. *Tiruccanta Viruttam* 77.

73. *Periya Tirumoḻi* 1.8.9.

74. Narayanan, *Way and the Goal*, p. 49.

75. In fact, they sometimes refer to themselves as the servants or the devotees of even the servants of the servants of the servants . . . of the devotees of the Lord, a hyperbolic reversal motif (using the sacred number seven) (Nammāḻvār, *Tiruvāymoḻi* 3.7.10).

76. Rocher ("Mantras") mentions the recitation of mantras and *stotras* as "verbal rituals" *(vācikam yajanam)* according to *Śiva Purāṇa* 1.15.57. The word *namaḥ* is related, in turn, to the word *namaskāra*, suggesting a semiritualized context of expressing devotion or honor—that is, by making a bow.

77. Mitsunori Matsubara, *Pañcarātra Saṃhitās and Early Vaiṣṇava Theology* (Delhi: Motilal Banarsidass, 1994), p. 7.

78. Ibid.,11.

79. Although, by the first century B.C.E. the two were identified, according to the Ghosundi inscription, and with this merger developed the characteristic *vyūha* theory.

80. The chronology here follows that established by Matsubara, *Pañcarātra*.

81. Ibid., p. 34. By the time of the *Parama*, the terms *bhāgavata* and *Vaiṣṇava* were synonyms.

82. *Pauṣkara* 30.210–19, perhaps following *Mahābhārata* 12.326.113.

83. Sanjaktu Gupta, "The Pāñcarātra Attitude to Mantra," In *Understanding Mantra*, Harvey P. Alper, Ed. (Albany: State University of New York Press, 1989), p. 227.

84. Ibid., pp. 238–39.

85. Matsubara, *Pāñcarātra*, p. 36.

86. I would like to thank Dr. J. Brzezinski for assistance in researching the Pāñcarātra Saṃhitās on this topic and Dr. L. Orr for drawing my attention to some key passages.

87. *Jayākhya Saṃhitā of Pāñcarātra Āgama*, Embar Krishnamacharya, Ed. (Baroda: Oriental Institute, 1967).

88. *Jayākhya Saṃhitā* (ca. 500 C.E.) states in 1.53–54 that anyone who comes with devotion and faith is eligible to be instructed in this Śāstra. According to 4.34–38, one must have a good understanding of Bhagavān as the supreme form of Brahman in order to use the mantras for the purpose of liberation. (Many mantras are given in this text, the basic being *om kṣiṃ kṣiḥ namaḥ nārāyanāya viśvātmane śrīm svāhā: Jayākhya Saṃhitā* 31.) The sixteenth chapter describes a preparatory ceremony for initiates that involves bathing, sacrifice, purifying the ground with *pañcagavya*, and installing the mantra in the water pot to become the deity. Verse 16.2 refers to initiation for women and children, and verse 16.53 notes that disciples must belong to one of the four *varṇas*. In 16.59ff, various types of initiation are discussed. The first type mentions boys (*bālāḥ*) and devoted young girls (*kanyakāḥ*). (Verses 16.68–71 say that the type of mantra for this initiation is a *Nārāyaṇa-mantra*.) Chapter 17.3–11 says that these boys are Viṣṇu conscious and astute but says nothing more about girls. The second type refers only to sons (*putraka*). (In chapter 17.12–16, the *putraka* is described as he who has great devotion to his mantra; is a *brahmacārin*; has conquered his senses; is truthful, clever, patient, faithful, intelligent, listens to scriptures, engages in *pūjā* and *tarpitam*, follows the proper times for *sandhyā*–and still remembers his *mantra*! The third type refers to *sādhakas* on the path to liberation (which is elaborated in 17.17–45). The fourth type refers to teachers: *deśikas* or *ācāryas* (elaborated on in 17.46–62). The fifth type refers to women (*aṅganā*). Because of an increase in status for the people in these categories, I am surprised that women are mentioned in the final position–which, unlike the others, is not elaborated on in the seventeenth chapter. Were women included here simply as an afterthought or as some later interpolation? There is another reference in this chapter to women. A description of the purification rituals (the *bhūtaśuddhis*) in 16.82–88 indicates that women are required to take more steps for their purification. There is a reference to the *tryakṣara-mantra*–the mantra that is the syllable (*akṣara*) consisting of the three (*a-u-m*)-*om*, the *praṇava*–in the context of this ritual purification for women (see 16.82). Even so, this mantra should be offered by the guru rather than the woman; he is supposed to chant mantras associated with the various *tattvas*, including the final one, the *tryakṣara*, by which he meditates on Nārāyaṇa (see 16.88: *krama eṣa hi dīkṣāyā, ācāryāṇāmudāhṛtaḥ strīṇaṃ tu bogasiddhiyortaṃśṛṇu dīkṣākramam mama*).

89. *Nāradīya Saṃhitā*, Raghava Prasada Chaudhary, Ed. (Tirupati: Kentriya Vidyapeetha, 1971). (9.:346b–347a).

90. Gupta, "*Attitude to Mantra*," p. 240.

91. Ibid.

92. Ibid., p. 242.

93. *Pādma Saṃhitā*, 2 vols., Seetha Padmanabhan and R. N. Sampath, Eds. (Madras: Pancaratra Parisodhana Parisad, 1974).

94. *Pādma Saṃhitā* 4.2.59–63.

95. *Svāhā*, with the dative, is the exclamation "hail," which is to accompany Vedic offerings (e.g., Ṛg *Veda*) but it also means the wife of Rudra or Agni. See Monier Monier-Williams, *A Sanskrit-English Dictionary* (Oxford: Clarendon Press [1899/1970), p. 1284. *Hum* is an exclamation used in the Vedic ritual before the prelude and in magical charms and spells (p. 1300). *Phaṭ* is a mystical syllable, according to several Vedic texts (*Vajasaneyi Saṃhitā, Atharva Veda, and Taittirīya Āraṇyaka*) (Monier-Williams, *Sanskrit-English Dictionary*, p. 716). *Vaṣat*, which also takes the dative in the Vedic ritual, is the Hotṛ priest's signal at the end of a sacrificial verse to the Adhvaryu priest to cast the oblation offered to the deity into the fire (RV, VS, Br, etc.) (p. 930). These syllables are found in Vedic rituals, although some are found in charms and spells, which may indicate an original non-Vedic tradition of magical sounds.

96. *Pādma Saṃhitā* 4.21.37–41.

97. *Viṣṇu Saṃhitā*, M. M. T. Ganapaati Sastri, Ed. (Delhi: Sri Satguru Publications, 1990).

98. According to 17.58ff, the eight-, twelve-, and six-syllable mantras.

99. *Viṣṇu Saṃhitā* 141a.

100. *Viṣṇu Saṃhitā* 10.4–6, 138.

101. *Śrīpraśna Saṃhitā* 16.24–25

102. *Śrīpraśna Saṃhitā* 16.138.

103. *Śrīpraśna Saṃhitā* 17.52b.

104. Leslie C. Orr, "Women of Medieval South India in Hindu Temple Ritual: Text and Practice," in *The Annual Review of Women in World Religions*, Arvind Sharma and Katherine K. Young, Eds. (Albany: State University of New York Press, 1994), vol. 3, p. 122.

105. The *Lakṣmī Tantra* 21:39–41 promotes universal accessibility. The disciple could "be a brahmin, kṣatriya, vaiśya or śūdra devoted to Lord (Viṣṇu). After regarding himself as [the disciple's] preceptor [and ascertaining] that he [the pupil] possesses all the necessary qualifications, the preceptor who is God Himself should teach him all the mantras [and he should accord the same treatment even] to a woman who respects her husband, never neglects her religious and social duties, has a clear notion of truth and has obtained her husband's permission [to become an adept]" (Gupta, "*Attitude to Mantra*," p. 273). Although the *śūdra* is marked by some distinctions, he, like the others, will first learn *om*, after which his own seed mantra, and so on. Although this text includes women, it nevertheless portrays them in a conservative way: they are married and subservient to their husbands.

106. *Viśvāmitra Saṃhitā*, Undemane Shankara Bhatta, Ed. (Tirupati: Kentriya Sanskrit Vidyapeetha, 1970). This late text states in 3.27 that the guru should not refuse women, *anuloma* (those men who legitimately marry women of lower status), or *śūdras* if they have auspicious qualities (*strīyaḥ śūdraścānulomaḥ kalyaṇaguṇa-samyutaḥ: yadi tan api śiṣyatve gṛhniyat kṛpaya guruḥ*). Chapter nine describes the giving of the eight-syllable mantra with *praṇava* and so on in the right ear, then the twelve-syllable mantra, and then the *mūrti mantra*. Verse 9.72 is particularly interesting:

śūdrānāṃ ca tathā strīnāṃ anuloma-bhuvāś/
namaḥ-svāhā-phaḍ-ādi-rahitaṃ praṇavena ca//
varjitam viṣṇu-nāmaiva caturhy-antaṃ ca pāṭhayet/
gāyatrīṃ japa-homaṃ ca ādadyād brāhmaṇo manum//

Here again, three categories are mentioned: women, *anulomas*, and śūdras. They may be initiated without (*rahitam*) *namaḥ-svaḥ-phaṭ* and *praṇava*. Brahmins, by contrast, may take the mantra used in the recitation of *gāyatrī* and *japahomam* (presumably *om*).

107. Matsubara 17–18.

108. These references are mentioned by Parāśara-bhaṭṭar in his commentary on the

Śrīviṣṇusahasranāma Bhagavadguṇadarpaṇākhyām Śrīviṣṇusahasra-nāmabhāṣyam; P. B. Annagara-calyayam, Ed. (Kancipuram: 1964).

109. *Periyāḻvār Tirumoḻi* 5.4.1.

110. *Tiruppallāṇṭu* 7.

111. Narayanan, *Way and the Goal*, p. 197 n. 25.

112. Leslie C. Orr, "The Vaiṣṇava Community at Śrīraṅgam in the Early Medieval Period," *Journal of Vaiṣṇava Studies* 3, no.3 (1995).

113. K.V. Soundara Rajan, "The Typology of the Anantaśāyi Icon," *Artibus Asiae* 29 (1967), 67–72.

114. In this context, it might be relevant that the term *prapatti* appears in the Pāñcarātra Āgamas after 800—not in the *Pauṣkara, Sātvata, Jayākhya, Ahirbudhnya*, and *Parama*—although the term *śaraṇāgati* related to *śaraṇam* of Gītā 18.66, appears in the *Ahirbudhnya* and other Saṃhitās (Matsubara 32).

115. Iravatham Mahadevan, "From Orality to Literacy: The Case of the Tamil Society," *Journal of the Centre for Historical Studies* (New Delhi: Sage, 1995), pp. 173–88.

116. Mumme, *Mumukṣuppati*, p. 3; she does not provide any references, however, for this explicit identification of the mantras used in the *pañcasaṃskāra* ritual.

117. *Periya Tirumoḻi* 1.8.9.

118. The first text to quote the *Pauṣakara, Jayākhya*, and *Sātvata* is the tenth-century Kashmiri work *Spaṇḍapradīpikā* by Utpala Vaiṣṇava (Matsubara 17).

119. 1 doubt that Rāmānuja wrote the *Nityagrantha* because this text mentions the five forms of God as *para, vyūha, avatāra, arcā*, and *antaryāmin*, but nowhere else in Rāmānuja's works are the forms of God described in this way (although this is common in the works of his successors).

120. These dates are suggested by some scholars.

121. *Annagarācārya* 135. The Nārāyaṇa tradition, including the Pāñcarātrins, stresses fidelity to the one supreme God; from this probably developed the comparison between fidelity to God and the chastity of a wife.

122. A translation of Bhaṭṭar's *Viṣṇusahasranāma-bhāṣya* by Narayanan, *Way and the Goal*, p. 135.

123. *Tiruvāymoḻi* 10.5.1–10. See Narayanan *Way and the Goal*, p. 116. She concludes that Piḷḷāṉ introduces the idea of the *tirumantra*, even though the āḻvār mentions only the name of God. See also John Carman and Vasudha Narayanan, *The Tamil Veda: Piḷḷāṉ's Interpretation of the Tiruvāymoḻi* (Chicago: University of Chicago Press, 1989).

124. *Tiruvāymoḻi* 10:5.2.

125. *Tiruvāymoḻi* 10.5.5.

126. *Tiruvāymoḻi* 10.5.4.

127. *Tiruvāymoḻi* 10.5.10. 1.2.10.

128. Nañjīyar 9000, in *Bhagavadviśayam: (Commentaries on Nammāḻvār's Tiruvāymoḻi.* Kṛṣṇamācāryar, Ed. (Madras: Nobel Prcss, 1925–1930).

129. *Tiruvāymoḻi* 10.5.1.

130. Mumme, *Mumukṣuppati*, p. 13.

131. See Nancy Ann Nayar, "The 'Other' Āṇṭāḷ: Portrait of a 12th Century Śrīvaiṣṇava Woman," *Journal of Vaiṣṇava Studies* 3 (1995), 149–72, and the chapter by Vasudha Narayanan in this volume.

132. In the manuscript of this text, the first thirteenth leaves and the fifteenth and sixteenth leaves are missing. The colophon says that it was written in the Aṅkirasa year in the month of Mārkaḻi. It is an explanatory commentary (*vivaraṇa-cataka*) of the first stanza and is a garland of words offered to the feet of the Lord of Kumpakoṉam temple by Koṉēridāsī, who does service (*aṭimat*) to him. The text has been edited by Navalpakam Sri Devanathachariar and published by S. Gopalan. This information was furnished by Dr. K. K. A. Venkatachari, director of the Ananthacharya Indological Research Institute, Bombay.

133. Vasudha Narayanan, "Brimming with *Bhakti*, Embodiments of *Shakti*: Devotees, Deities, Performers, Reformers, and Other Women of Power in the Hindu Tradition," in *Feminism and World Religions*, Arvind Sharma and Katherine K. Young, Eds. (Albany: State University of New York, 1999), p. 62.

134. See *Periyavāccāṉpiḷḷai Śrīsuktimālā*, Ayankar R. Srinivas, Ed. (Tirucci: n.d.).

135. Śrīraṅganārāyaṇa Jiyar, Ed., *Aṣṭadasarahasyam of Piḷḷailokācārya* (Madras: Ananta Press, 1911).

136. See *Parantapaṭi*, Ibid., p. 52.

137. *Śrī Vacana Bhūṣanam* 26–29.

138. *Mumukṣuppaṭi* 42.

139. Gurusamy Damodaran, *Ācārya Hṛdayam: A Critical Study* (Tirupati: Tirumalai Tirupati Devastanams, 1976), pp. 61–63.

140. *Periya Tirumoḻi* 6.10.1.

141. *Mutal Tiruvantāti* 57, 95.

142. Rajagopala Ayyangar, Trans. *Śrīmad Rahasyatrayasāra* (Kumbakonan: Agnihothram Ramanuja Thathachariar 1956), pp.296–97.

143. Mumme, *Mumukṣuppaṭi*, p. 11.

144. *Rahasya Traya Sāra Cūrṇa* 28.

145. Also known as the *Nārāyaṇa Atharvaśiras Upaniṣad*.

146. Mumme, *Mumukṣuppaṭi*, p. 19.

147. *Śrī Vacana Bhūṣanam* 26–29.

148. The incident of Draupadī is often used by the *ācāryas* to suggest that *prapatti* may be performed at any time and in any place. Today, this is not the case, because the *ācāryas* refuse to perform it during the three days of menstrual impurity.

149. *Mumukṣup-paṭi* 16.

150. *Mumukṣup-paṭi* 42.

151. *Mumukṣup-paṭi* 112.

152. See also *Ācarya Hṛdayam*, in which the *ācāryas* are said to be like Sītā. Just as Sītā exists only for the Lord and serves as the intermediary between God and his devotees, so do the *ācāryas* (Damodaran *Ācarya Hṛdayam* , p. 76).

153 I date the *Guru Paramparā Prabhāvam* in the fourteenth or fifteenth century. For my reasons and a critique of other positions, see Katherine K. Young, "Theology Does Help Women's Liberation: Śrīvaiṣṇavism, a Hindu Case Study;" *Journal of Vaiṣṇava Studies* 3, no. 4 (1995), 173–233.

154. F. Hardy, "The Tamil Veda of a *Śūdra* Saint: The Śrīvaiṣṇava Interpretation of Nammāḻvār," in *Contributions to South Asian Studies*, G. Krishna, Ed. (Delhi: Oxford University Press, 1979), vol. 1, pp. 38–59.

155. From the context, this should read *vaidikas*.

156. Hardy, "Tamil Veda," p. 49.

157. John Carman, *The Theology of Rāmānuja* (New Haven, Conn.: Yale University Press, 1974), p. 49. I find it curious that if the *Divya Sūri Caritam* is early (twelfth to thirteenth century, as Hardy claims), it contains a reference to Maṇavāḷamāmuni (a fourteenth-century figure) in its discussion of the *aṃśas* (see Hardy, "The Tamil Veda," p. 43), even though the hagiography ostensibly stops with Rāmānuja.

158. Hardy, "Tamil Veda," pp. 35–36.

159. *Divya Sūri Caritam* 4.43.

160. Hardy, "Tamil Veda," p. 53.

161. Ibid., p. 51.

162. Ibid., p. 38.

163. *Irāmanuca-nuṟṟantāti* 10.

164. K. K. A. Venkatachari, *The Maṇipravāḷa Literature of the Śrīvaiṣṇava Ācāryas: 12th–15th Century, A.D.* (Bombay: Anantacharya Research Institute, 1980), p. 157.

165. Ayyangar, *Śrīmad Rahasyatrayasāra*, p. 4.

166. *Upadeśa Ratna Māla* 35.

167. *Tiruppāvai* 30.

168. *Nācciyārtirumoḻi* 1.10, 2,10, 3.10, 6.11, and so on.

169. Hardy, *Viraha Bhakti* (Delhi: Oxford University Press, 1983), p. 353 n. 24.

170. Mumme, *Mumukṣuppaṭi*, p. 3.

171. Ibid., p. 9 n.2.

172. Ibid.

173. Ibid., p. 3.

174. Ibid.

175. Eva Hellman, "Political Hinduism: The Challenge of the Viśva Hindu Pariṣad," Doctoral dissertation, Department of the History of Religions,Uppsala University, Uppsala, Sweden: 1993, p. 80.

6

Casting Light on the Sounds of the Tamil Veda

Tirukkōnēri Dāsyai's "Garland of Words"

VASUDHA NARAYANAN

The right of a woman to recite and study the Veda has been disputed in many Hindu communities. In August 1994, Jagatguru Shankaracharya Kapileswaranand Saraswati is reported to have said that the recitation of Vedas by women will adversely affect their health and prevent them from having healthy babies.[1] Although restrictions to study the Sanskrit Veda may have existed in some measure in many parts of India, around the thirteenth century we find a woman who seems to be very familiar with the Vedas. Tirukkōnēri Dāsyai, from south India, includes quotations from the Samhita and Upaniṣad sections of the Vedas in her commentary on the *Tiruvāymoḻi* ("Sacred word of Mouth" or "Sacred Utterance") of Nammāḻvār. Elsewhere in this volume, Katherine Young compares Tirukkōnēri Dāsyai with other commentators of the Śrīvaiṣṇava tradition, particularly on the issue of women reciting mantras. The *Tiruvāymoḻi* was probably composed around the ninth century and was in the Tamil language. The Śrīvaiṣṇava community of South India acknowledged the *Tiruvāymoḻi* (TVM), a Tamil poem of 1102 verses, as being equivalent to the *Sāma Veda*. Tirukkōnēri Dāsyai, in her commentary on the *Tiruvāymoḻi*, shows considerable familiarity with parts of the Sanskrit Veda and quotes the *Taittirīya Upaniṣad* and other works as proof texts for the Tamil work, proving that at least this woman had more than a cursory knowledge of what was considered to be revelation in Sanskrit and in Tamil.

Whereas the Śrīvaiṣṇava community considers about five commentaries on the *Tiruvāymoḻi* to be extremely important, and in fact only studies the poem through the prism of the commentaries, Tirukkōnēri Dāsyai's work is *not* one of them and seems to have been unknown until the manuscript was found in this century. This is the only commentary on the *Tiruvāymoḻi* by a woman that is still extant; the commentaries revered by the tradition were all written by men. The Śrīvaiṣṇava community has honored Āṇṭāḷ, a woman, as a saint and recites her poems daily in temple rituals, but this philosophical commentary by a woman has not even been known. Even after the manuscript was found in the library, edited, and published, it has been marginalized and delegated to footnotes in other scholarly works on the *āḻvārs*.

Why has there been relatively benign neglect of the only commentary by a woman? Is it because she was a woman? Are there substantial differences between her works and that of the male commentators in style and in content, and were these responsible for the neglect of her work? To what extent did geography, regional and sectarian community politics, and class and caste prevent the dissemination of her commentary? It would be necessary to explore these questions to understand the relationship of women and the Veda and women's access to salvific knowledge in the Śrīvaiṣṇava community.

One may also observe that there are not too many women philosophers in the many Hindu *sampradāyas*. Although Gargī and Maitreyī of the Upaniṣads are well known, there is a significant dearth of information on women philosophers. Ellison Findly has treated the Upaniṣadic sages in her 1985 article, and here, in this volume, addresses the larger philosophical issue of women's intentionality in both Vedic and Buddhist contexts. This is particularly striking when compared to the comparatively large numbers of women poets. Why is it that the various Hindu *sampradāyas* have recognized and venerated women poets but have not remembered the philosophers? Before trying to address some of these questions here, let us briefly look at the text that Tirukkōnēri Dāsyai commented on, and the tradition that reveres it.

The *Tiruvāymoḻi* and the Commentarial Tradition

The Śrīvaiṣṇava tradition of South India became organized around the time of its fifth, and most important, teacher (*ācārya*), Rāmānuja (ca. 1017–-1137 C.E.). The Śrīvaiṣṇava community emphasizes exclusive devotion to Lord Viṣṇu and the goddess *Śrī*. As do many of the other Hindu traditions, it accepts the Sanskrit Vedas, the epics *Rāmāyaṇa* and *Mahābhārata*, and the Purāṇas as scripture, but in addition it claims that the compositions of Tamil poet-saints (*āḻvārs*) who lived between the eighth and tenth centuries to be "revealed." The twenty-four works of the *āḻvārs* are about 4000 verses long, and they came to be known as the *Nālāvira Divya Prabandham*, the *Sacred Collection of Four Thousand Verses*. The Śrīvaiṣṇavas refer to the poems simply as the Divya Prabandham. Specifically, the community considers one of the *āḻvārs*, Sāthakōpan (ninth century), known affectionately as Nammāḻvār or "Our *Āḻvār*,"[2] to be a paradigmatic devotee, and his *Tiruvāymoḻi* to be the equivalent of the *Sāma Veda*.

Canonized as "scripture," the *Tiruvāymoḻi* has been of seminal importance in the piety and liturgy of the Śrīvaiṣṇava community of South India, and extraordinarily significant in the history of Hindu literature. It was the first "vernacular"[3] work within the Hindu consciousness to be considered as "revealed"; it was also the first work in a mother tongue to be introduced as part of the domestic and temple liturgy. Unlike the Sanskrit Vedas, which could be recited only by male members of the upper castes, the *Tiruvāymoḻi* has been recited by men and women of all castes of Śrīvaiṣṇava society. It is historically significant as a key part of the Tamil devotional literature that influenced the religious patterns in medieval northern India. The devotion voiced in the *Tiruvāymoḻi* was transmitted through the Sanskrit text known as the *Bhāgavata Purāna*,[4] through the teacher Ramananda (ca. 1360–1470), and through Sanskrit hymns and oral tradition, and it appeared in different forms in the teachings of Caitanya, Vallabha, Surdas, Kabir, and Guru Nanak.

The *Tiruvāymoḻi* was interpreted either by long commentaries or by short summaries. Chronologically, the long commentaries came first, beginning with the recording of the oral commentaries in the late eleventh and early twelfth centuries. The earliest commentary was written by Tirukkurukai Pirān Piḷḷān (late eleventh to early twelfth century). This commentary was called the *Āṟāyirappaṭi*, or *Six Thousand paṭi*.[5] Later commentaries that are considered to be classical by the community are called the *Nine Thousand paṭi*, *Twelve Thousand paṭi*, *Twenty-four Thousand paṭi*, and the *Thirty-six Thousand paṭi*. A *paṭi* was a literary unit of 32 syllables. Thus, the earliest commentary, that of Piḷḷān's, has 32-×-6000 syllables and is numerically modeled on a Sanskrit work of the same length, the *Viṣṇu Purāṇa*. This self-conscious modeling is, of course, significant in the two-fold Sanskrit-Tamil tradition.[6]

Starting in the thirteenth century, several short summaries were written, usually in the form of a poem. These poems were either independent pieces or part of a longer narrative. Independent pieces include Vedānta Deśika's Sanskrit poem *The Gem-Necklace of Reality in the Tamil Upaniṣad* (*Dramidopaniṣad Tātparya Ratnāvali*; thirteenth century) and Maṇavāḷa Māmuni's Tamil poem *The Hundred Verses on the Tiruvāymoḻi* (*Tiruvāymoḻi* Nūṟṟantāti; ca. fourteenth to fifteenth century). Both of these works have a similar format: each set of "ten" verses in the *Tiruvāymoḻi* is summarized by one verse in the poem. Each set of ten verses in the *Tiruvāymoḻi* is presented as containing a coherent theme, and the main philosophical idea of those ten verses (as perceived by the interpreting poet) is condensed into a single verse. Other summaries of the *Tiruvaymoḻi* are contained in the Tamil poem Nammāḻvār Tiruttāllāṭṭu (*A Lullaby for Nammāḻvār*; ca. fourteenth to fifteenth century) and the biographical poem on the *āḻvārs* called *Āḻvārkaḷ Vaipavam* (*The Glory of the Āḻvārs*; ca. fifteenth century). Thus, in these summaries, there was a "translation" either from Tamil into Sanskrit or from "older" Tamil into a more current Tamil of that age.

The longer commentaries, on the other hand, were detailed prose interpretations of the original *Tiruvāymoḻi* verses, containing several quotations from Sanskrit scripture. Piḷḷān, the first commentator on the *Tiruvāymoḻi*, elucidated each verse and frequently wrote a short introduction to each set of ten verses. The comment is not a word-by-word elucidation of the poem (as later commentaries tended to be) but an interpretation of the verse as a whole, with the commentator supplying a context or framework to the verse.

All of the early commentaries on the *Tiruvāymoḻi*, including the one by Tirukkōnēri Dāsyai, were in Maṇipravāla, a new hybrid language of communication used in Śrīvaiṣṇava circles. The Tamil of Nammāḻvār was "translated" and explained in a new "situational language." *Maṇipravāla* means "gems and corals" or "pearls and corals" and refers to a combination of Sanskrit and Tamil. Unlike other forms of Maṇipravāla[7] the Śrīvaiṣṇava variety always retained Tamil grammar and endings, though the sentences were heavily interspersed with Sanskrit words. The language of the commentary itself gave the message effectively, proclaiming the equivalency of the Sanskrit and Tamil languages and literatures. This style of communicating—in speech and writing—flourishes even today in the Śrīvaiṣṇava community.

Casting Light on the Sounds of Tamil Revelation

Tirukkōnēri Dāsyai: Placing Her in Time

The commentary by Tirukkōnēri Dāsyai is called *The Garland of Words on the Sacred Utterance* (*Tiruvāymoḻi Vācakamālai*), as well as "The Exposition of a Hundred Verses" (*vivarṇa sathakam*). The commentary by Tirukkōnēri Dāsyai remained in manuscript form until 1950, when it was painstakingly edited by a scholar in the Sarasvati Mahal library, Tanjore. The commentary for the first five sets of ten verses (1.1 to 1.5) is missing and it begins with 1.6. We know very little about the author, and what little we do know comes in the colophon at the end of the commentary:

> I bow to my teacher (guru). I surrender to the sacred feet of the *āḻvār*. I surrender to the sacred feet of Emperumānār [Rāmānuja]. I surrender to the sacred feet of Chandragiri Ayyan (chief). I surrender to the sacred feet of Sriman Narayana Ayyar. I surrender to the sacred feet of Tirukkōṭṭiyur Jīyar. I surrender to the sacred feet of Vaṭakku Tiruvīti Piḷḷai.
>
> This garland of words which has the name of "The Explanatory Hundred" and which is on the first song "Who is he who has . . ." is an appropriate garland which is [placed] at the sacred feet of He who needs nothing. Tirukkōnēri Dāsyai did this service (*ceyta aṭimai*) on the twenty sixth day of the month of Mārkaḻi, in the Ankiraca year.
>
> If there is any mistake made by my hand [which wrote this], let the elders forgive me!

Tirukkōnēri begins with an intriguing lineage of teachers. She makes a salutation to the guru and then salutations to the *āḻvār* (Nammāḻvār) and Rāmānuja (ca. 1019–1039). This is followed by three other teachers and, finally, Vaṭakku Tiruvīti Piḷḷai (1167–1263). I have not been able to trace the three names that appear in between. If we assume that the lineage is arranged chronologically, with the one furthest in time being the first (after the initial perfunctory salutation to her own guru), Tirukkōnēri ends with Vaṭakku Tiruvīti Piḷḷai, who may have been her immediate teacher. This will place her around the late thirteenth century, and she may well have lived into the early fourteenth century.

The convention of starting with the earliest *ācārya* is one used by some Śrīvaiṣṇavas. Almost all Śrīvaiṣṇava recitations and rituals begin with a verse that states the initial set of teachers. This verse, composed probably in the early twelfth century, starts with Viṣṇu and Śrī and then mentions Nāthamuni, Yamunā, and so on. Tirukkōnēri Dāsyai's colophon reflects this convention, although she does not use that particular verse itself.

If Tirukkōnēri Dāsyai is mid-thirteenth century, we may assume that soon after her lifetime or even very late in her lifetime, there was relative confusion in the Śrīvaiṣṇava world. Between 1311 and 1362, the Srirangam temple was in a state of dilapidation after the raids of Malik Kafur, the military general of Allaudin Khalji. No one worshiped in the Srirangam temple, and the Muslim military expedition from the north went as far south as Madurai. During this time, the processional, "festival" image of the deities at Srirangam were sent elsewhere for safekeeping. The restoration of the Srirangam temple took place with the advent of the Vijayanagara kings, but their main patronage was then extended to Tiruvenkatam. It is possible that during this period of confusion, her commentary was moved around and eventually forgotten.

The manuscript as we have it now, however, is not more than three hundred years old. We have to assume either that (1) Tirukkōnēri Dāsyai lived and wrote her commentary around the end of the thirteenth century and the beginning of the fourteenth, and then someone copied from the original manuscript around three hundred years later, or (2) Tirukkōnēri Dāsyai lived in the seventeenth century (the approximate date of the manuscript). If she lived in the thirteenth century, and her manuscript was tossed around in the time of historical confusion, it is significant that someone in the seventeenth cenutury thought it was worthy of being preserved, mistakes and all. Furthermore, it is interesting that the hypothetical copyist also copied the illustrations that are on the front of the manuscript and preserved the same style of thirteenth-century line drawings.

On the other hand, if we assume that Tirukkōnēri Dāsyai lived in the seventeenth century and wrote the manuscript herself, there would be some major problems. She would have been going against all tradition if she had saluted teachers only several centuries removed from her and not the immediate ones. In other words, the teacher who is last on her list is Vaṭakku Tiruvīti Piḷḷai, who lived in the early thirteenth century. It is rather unlikely that she would skip several generations of teachers in her salutation. And since the Śrīvaiṣṇava tradition carefully preserves protocol in the ordering and recitation of teachers, we can only assume that the other teachers after Rāmānuja were her immediate teachers or teacher's teachers–which would still place her as the student of Vaṭakku Tiruvīti Piḷḷai.

Going on the basis of the manuscript in hand, one cannot prove whether she lived in the thirteenth century and the manuscript was copied later or she actually lived in the seventeenth century. One way in which we can get a fairly good idea of what time she lived in is through internal evidence, that is, her commentary. We can look at the teachers Tirukkōnēri Dāsyai mentions. It is also significant that she does not mention Vedānta Deśika, Piḷḷai Lōkācārya, and Maṇavāla Māmuni, all important teachers of the late thirteenth and fourteenth centuries. Furthermore, in the Śrīvaiṣṇava tradition, clear theological positions were being enunciated after the thirteenth century. Vedānta Deśika and Piḷḷai Lōkācārya (also cited as Piḷḷailōkācārya) articulated very specific positions in their discussions on the relationship between the human being's surrender to Viṣṇu and Śrī and divine grace. Precise, theologically loaded terms became characteristic of the two schools, and all later writers aligned themselves with one or the other. Vaṭakku Tiruvīti Piḷḷai, on the other hand, coming a generation before this theological divergence, is more fluid in his terminology. If Tirukkōnēri Dāsyai was his disciple, this fluid terminology for one's theological position would be maintained. If, on the other hand, she came later, her position would be more crystalized, with clear demarcation of which theological position she favored.

The Author's Native Place

Tirukkōnēri Dāsyai's name simply means "she who is the servant (*dāsyai*) of [the Lord of] the Sacred (*tiru*) lake (*eri*) of the King (*kon*)." The lotus pond (*puṣkariṇi*) in Tiruvenkatam (modern Tirumala/Tirupati) is called Swami Pushkarini, which is the Sanskrit translation of Tirukkōnēri. There is also a Tirukkōnēri in Tamilnadu, but from the mention of Chandragiri Ayyan (The chief of Chandragiri), we can surmise that Tirukkōnēri is in fact from Tiruvenkatam in present-day Andhra Pradesh. Chandragiri is a small town, about ten miles from Tirupati. It is possible that some of the teachers were contemporary, and thus she could have had two or three teachers, like Vaṭakku Tiruvīti Piḷḷai and Chandragiri Ayyan, sequentially. We hear that Rāmānuja learned from five different teachers, although in later years it did become the convention to have just one primary teacher. It is possible that the Dāsyai family moved from Tiruvenkatam to the Tamil hinterland, and she acquired learning from two or three teachers. Vaṭakku

Tiruvīti Piḷḷai lived most of his life in Srirangam, and it is possible that this is where Tirukkōnēri Dāsyai also lived.

The only other place she may have lived is Kumbakonam, in the modern state of Tamilnadu. She seems to have a special affection for the Viṣṇu enshrined in the temple there and has commented extensively on the verse that deals with this town. The lord is called there "He who does not sate," and a line drawing of the icon appears in front of her manuscript.

The editor says that the Tamil orthography in the manuscript is lamentable. This may well be the fault of the copyist. Her Tamil spelling leaves much to be desired also, although her Sanskrit, written in grantha characters, is impeccable. This gives us reason to believe that Tamil was not her native language. If she was indeed from the Tiruvenkatam area, her mother tongue would have been Telugu and Tamil would have been an acquired language.

Tirukkōnēri Dāsyai's *Garland of Words* Commentary

The commentary focuses on about hundred verses of the *Tiruvāymoḻi* (TVM); these are considered to be the "fragrant blossoms" and are woven into a verbal commentary. Tirukkōnēri Dāsyai sees the entire poem as elucidating the meaning of the very first verse of the *Tiruvāymoḻi*, and so she weaves phrases from the first verse into the comments on the later ones, and whenever she explains a later verse, she explicitly says that it elucidates the first one. Like a flower garland in South India, which is held together with twinings of fragrant herbs and silver threads, she weaves the first verse around the poem, holding it together. She calls her work a "garland of words" in the colophon; she also uses this phrase in her commentary. The poet Nammāḻvār says:

> Catakopan, generous
> has composed a thousand songs:
> with these ten, we can place
> lovely garlands at his feet. (TVM 2.4.11)

Tirukkonēri Dāsyai, comments on this verse:

> "A beautiful garland to be placed at the feet [of the Lord]." This Garland of Words (*vācakamālai*) is a beautiful garland that can be placed at his feet. Just as the son is sure to get the father's wealth, we too will get the [inheritance of service to the lord]. . . .[8]

She is also the only commentator to illustrate her work with drawings, which depict important themes of the poem. Three pictures are drawn on the manuscript after TVM 5.8.1. The first is a representation of Viṣṇu, who is reclining on a snake, a form that is seen in many temples of South India; the second is Nammāḻvār, who is pining like a woman for "her" beloved; and the third is the baby Krishna, tied to a mortar and going in between two trees. The picture of Viṣṇu on a snake is identified by the author as the manifestation in Kumbakonam (TVM 5.8.1). As noted earlier, this place seems to be especially important for Tirukkōnēri Dāsyai because her longest comment is on the first poem addressed to Viṣṇu in Kumbakonam.

Tirukkōnēri Dāsyai's Emphasis on the First Verse of the Tiruvāymoḻi

Tirukkōnēri Dāsyai apparently considers the very first verse of the *Tiruvāymoḻi* to be the most significant one in the whole poem—the parent verse that spawns all other verses. She is the only commentator to do so, and this itself makes her style different from that of others. Let us look at *Tiruvāymoḻi* 1.1.1 and then discuss how she highlights this verse:

> Who is he
>   that has the highest good
>   cutting down all other heights
> who is he,
>   who bestows wisdom and love
>   slashing ignorance?
> who is he,
>   who commands the tireless[9] immortals?
> worship his radiant feet
> that quell all sorrow,
> and rise O mind.

Each time she uses the words of the first verse to interpret the meanings of the later verses, she teases out a new meaning and a different nuance, giving the reader a breathtaking kaleidoscope of linked images and pictures. For example, the word "radiant" is used as an adjective for Viṣṇu's feet in the first verse; in subsequent verses, she uses this word to indicate the lord's glory, which is like the "brilliance" of a million suns; to refer to the "radiance" of luminous knowledge; or to describe Viṣṇu as "an eternal flame." Tirukkōnēri Dāsyai highlights illumination and radiance. She refers to Lord Viṣṇu thus: "He is a form of overwhelming splendor (*tejorupa*), he is eternal . . . a spectacular flame. [As the *Mahābhārata* says] Viṣṇu resides in a place more thousands of times brighter than the fire and the sun; [heaven] is brighter than the brilliance of a thousand crore (10 000 000 000) suns."[10]

Elsewhere, she says: "He is a flood of luminous knowledge, shining a fiery lamp, an eternal flame."[11] Viṣṇu is the sun worshipped by "those who know no sorrow" (TVM 1.1.1), the Āditya (solar lord) who illumines the two areas of glory (*ubhaya vibhuti*). The two areas of glory in Śrīvaiṣṇava parlance generally refer to the created universe and the celestial realm of heaven.[12]

In commenting on another verse, she glosses a phrase from TVM 1.1.1 thus: "'Who is he,/ who bestows wisdom and love,/ slashing ignorance?' He terminates the darkness of ignorance by giving rise to the moon and sun of wisdom and love, that is bhakti and *jñāna*. He makes these rise through his grace which has no cause (*nirhetuka kṛpa*)."[13] In this comment, wisdom and love are compared to the moon and sun; their light expels the darkness of knowledge. The Lord also glows through his wisdom and bliss (comment on 3.4.10). The radiance and flame is also translated as "purity" in some places by Tirukkōnēri Dāsyai. Thus, in interpreting the phrase "radiant feet" in 1.1.1 in the context of commenting on TVM 3.9.9, she says: "The radiant feet that destroy all sorrow—it means, without any blemish. By making [the *āḻvār*] exceedingly pure, the Lord too becomes pure."[14]

Although her delight in this word play makes her commentary unique, it is important to note that the technique of using a word or phrase and interpreting it in dozens of ways is an integral part of singing and dancing in the Indian tradition. A singer may repeat a phrase from the *Tiruvāymoḻi* several times, exploring the nuances of a raga, a dancer may interpret a phrase in many ways, each time bringing new associations to the original meaning.

Tirukkōnēri Dāsyai seems to have applied a performing art technique to a verbal commentary. The colophon at the end of her text says clearly that she finished writing it in the Tamil month of Mārkaḻi (December–January). It is in this month that the Festival of Recitation, which includes the performance of the "Sacred Utterance" takes place, and it seems clear that the verbal commentary was being written as the author was witnessing the performative one.[15] During this month, the *Tiruvāymoḻi* is recited in all Śrīvaiṣṇava temples in India and abroad. In Srirangam and a few other places, it is also sung and danced by some traditional families who have the exclusive right to perform in the temple, rendering "loving service" to the deities.[16]

The Commentator's Emphasis on Music and the Sāma Veda

Tirukkōnēri Dāsyai also emphasizes the importance of singing the *Tiruvāymoḻi*. It is not just a poem that is to be recited or meditated on; it is to be joyously sung. Since many of the philosophical Hindu traditions consider the singing of the *Sāma Veda* to be the ultimate musical experience, it is not surprising to hear Tirukkōnēri Dāsyai emphasize that *Veda* as well. Let us first look at Nammāḻvār's *Tiruvāymoḻi* 2.4.11:

> Unwithering is the praise
> for the Dwarf. Setting it to music,
> Caṭakōpan, generous
> has composed a thousand songs:
> with these ten, we can place lovely garlands at his feet.

Tirukkōnēri Dāsyai highlights the musical component of the work thus:

> He, "who bestows wisdom and love" (TVM 1.1.1) proclaimed [the *Tiruvāymoḻi*] so it can be famous in all the worlds. [The *Tiruvāymoḻi*] is the essence of the Sāma Veda fused with music; the sacred words of Sáṭhakōpa are the equivalent of the Upaniṣad [Sāma Veda] of a thousand branches. These ten verses are the "words of Sāṭhakōpan which have music." The Lord is that one "who commands the tireless immortals" (TVM 1.1.1). The eternal ones [the celestial beings who are eternally emancipated] sing the Sāma. Taking the music of the Sāma, and the thousand branched Veda, Nammāḻvār, not content with just a mental experience [of the Lord] transforms "the ten verses of the thousand" [a reference to a set of ten verses from the *Tiruvāymoḻi*] into words and makes the country live and prosper. This is [the Lord's and Nammāḻvār's] generosity.[17]

Notice her frequent reference to TVM 1.1.1. We will come back to this stylistic characteristic soon. Elsewhere, Tirukkōnēri Dāsyai draws an analogy between the music of the Sāma Veda, the music of lyrical *Tiruvāymoḻi*, and the delightful sounds of the waterfalls in Tiruvenkatam/Tirupati. Commenting on a set of verses that glorifies the sacred place of Tiruvenkatam/Tirupati, she says that "it is as if the waterfalls with great love invite us, saying: 'come and sing songs with beautiful lyrics; this will be like the music of Sāma. [The singing] will be loving service in the form of words.' Thus say the clear water falls as they pour down."[18]

As noted earlier, Tirukkōnēri Dāsyai shows in every comment how a particular verse in a set of eleven verses elucidates the first verse. For example, after a brief introduction to verse 5.8.1, she says: "The song 'Who is he that has the highest good/cutting down all other heights' (1.1.1) is explained by the verse 'O nectar that does not sate . . .' (5.8.1). If you were to ask 'How?' we will explain it thus. . . ."

It is not just words from the first verse of *Tiruvāymoḻi* that Tirukkōnēri Dāsyai uses often. In explaining almost every verse, she uses the Sanskrit phrase "beginning with the bliss of human being all the way to the bliss of Brahman." The line is from the *Taittirīya Upaniṣad*, and she sees it as the interpretive concept for the first line of the TVM: "Who is he/that has the highest good/cutting down all other heights?" Tirukkōnēri Dāsyai starts many sentences with the words "beginning with the bliss of human being all the way to the bliss of Brahman" but ends the sentence with different concepts and phrases. Her point generally is that Viṣṇu cuts down the chasm that exists between human notions of bliss and the true bliss that one gets through the experience of Brahman. In other comments, this formulaic line may stand for something like the modern expression "from A to Z." Thus in one verse she comments: "Beginning with the bliss of human being all the way to the bliss of Brahman, paradise (*svarga*), and all other worlds, highly priced gems . . . the Vedas, the Śāstras, [gods like] Brahma, Rudra, and other divine beings . . . all these I created."[19]

In another verse Tirukkōnēri Dāsyai uses the same beginning words but ends the sentence differently: "Beginning with the bliss of human being all the way to the bliss of Brahman each being has a measure of happiness. But even those [forms of happiness] are paltry. So it is said that only the bliss of the Supreme Brahman is the highest good."[20] This comment is for a verse that seems to be her favorite: *Tiruvāymoḻi* 5.8.1, which also has the longest commentary. The verse itself does not talk about happiness, but Tirukkōnēri Dāsyai weaves that concept in her commentary. Let us look at Nammāḻvār's verse:

> O ambrosia that never sates,
> you make this servant's body,
> so much in love with you,
> sway
> wander like waters
> of the sea,
> melt, and dissolve.
> O Tall One
> in sacred Kutantai
> where lush fields of paddy
> move like yak-tails over the rich waters,
> I saw you, my Lord,
> radiant and reclining
> in a lovely posture.

Although the verse does not talk about bliss or happiness, Tirukkōnēri Dāsyai's point is that it is the vision of the Lord that is the most gratifying and that is equivalent to experiencing the supreme one. Thus she uses the *Taittirīya Upaniṣad*'s words in the beginning of a sentence in almost every comment, and then she concludes the sentence with different words. This repetition is almost like a refrain, the rhythm in the composition.

Whereas almost all commentators interpret every song of the *Tiruvāymoḻi*, Tirukkōnēri Dāsyai picks and chooses one or two verses from each set of ten. Usually she chooses the first verse, but in some sets she selects two, saying that they interpret the first song. Thus, in 7.5 she interprets both 1 and 10; in 7.9 she comments on both 1 and 7, and in 8.3 she elucidates 1 and 6. Only in the last set of poems does she comment on as many as three songs. Many of the commentaries on the *Tiruvāymoḻi* contain stories of previous teachers. Thus, in commenting on 10.2.5, she quotes Parāśara Bhaṭṭar, a twelfth-century teacher and a direct disciple of Rāmānuja, the well-known philosopher. At issue is the question of authority and qualification to recite the holy name of Viṣṇu. Tirukkōnēri Dāsyai quotes Bhaṭṭar as saying that a desire and taste to do so is qualification enough to say the name:

> Namjiyar asked Bhaṭṭar: should one purify oneself before reciting the sacred Names [of the Lord]? Bhaṭṭar graciously replied: When one goes to bathe in the Ganga, is it necessary to take a dip in a little puddle first? That [recitation of names] which will give us the highest good, will also give us the fortune of having the qualification to do so.
>
> To say the sacred name, having the desire, the taste to do so is enough. Those who have the desire are all qualified to say it.[21]

The Theology of Tirukkōnēri Dāsyai

Reading *Garland of Verses*, one has a sense of the clarity of Tirukkōnēri Dāsyai's theological ideas and the ambiguity of others. Let us consider a few of her ideas briefly. She clearly thinks of the *Tiruvāymoḻi* as revelation, though different in texture from the *Bhagavad Gītā*. In commenting on 10.7.5, she says: "Like a father who gifts a cow to a son and then stands next to the son and gets the gift, he teaches the words to the son and hears the words, delighting in it. If he sang the song, it would become equal to the Gītā."[22]

Thus, whereas the *Tiruvāymoḻi* is revelation, it is different from the *Gītā* in one important way. Viṣṇu does not preach; rather, he teaches Nammāḻvār the words and makes his devotee sing the song. Using Nammāḻvār's utterance of the sacred words as a pretext, he gives salvation to him. This, she says, is analogous to a father who gives his son a cow. When the son wants to give a gift to the father, he gives him the cow, only vaguely cognizant of the fact that he had, in fact, received it from him.

Tirukkōnēri Dāsyai also highlights the use of formulaic mantras in her commentary. These became textually important after the twelfth century, and the Śrīvaiṣṇava tradition recognizes three mantras as significant to salvation: the "primary" (*mula*) or the "sacred mantra" (*tirumantra*), "two lines" (*dvaya*), and the "last verse" (*carama śloka*, i.e., *Bhagavad Gītā* 18:66). She explicitly refers to these mantras and further adds that the first song of the *Tiruvāymoḻi* explains the primary mantra: "The goal spoken of in the last part of the *tirumantra* which ends in the fourth case (grammatically) is explained by the first song of this *Tiruvāymoḻi*."[23] There are frequent references to the mantras and connected rituals throughout the work.[24] In her explicit references to these mantras, she is closer in spirit to Periyavāccān Piḷḷai and Vaṭakku Tiruvīti Piḷḷai, the thirteenth-century commentators, than she is to the first commentator, Piḷḷān.

However, like Piḷḷān, the first commentator, Tirukkōnēri Dāsyai talks about the two forms of Viṣṇu: his all pervasive form, by which he is immanent in all of the universe and by which he is recognized as the soul (*ātma*) of the universe (*divyātma svarūpa*), and his handsome, auspicious body, which is seen in incarnations (*divya maṅgala vigraha*). She says that "'he is the embodiment of consciousness' by his wisdom and bliss he glows and has both *divya maṅgala vigraha* and *divyātma svarūpa*."[25]

Tirukkōnēri Dāsyai also paints vivid word pictures in her commentaries. In describing the glowing form of Viṣṇu, she says: "As the husband of Śrī, his body glows like a blue sapphire with a brilliant radiance. His sacred eyes are filled with maternal compassion. They shower the rain of nectar-like compassion."[26] Elsewhere, she says that the Lord's brilliant feet will banish all ignorance, just as the rising suns in the time of cosmic destructions banish the darkness of chaos. Quotations from the *Tiruvāymoḻi* are in italics:

> My father's house is good:
> O Lord who swiftly destroyed
> the elephant's distress
> by bringing your lotus feet
> to his head!
> My father! I long for the same (fate). (2.9.1)

> "*Long for the same fate*" *The radiant feet that quell all sorrow,* [TVM 1.1.1] will appear in my heart, rising like the sun in the time of *pralaya* (chaos), banishing the dark night of sorrow and the ignorance, the lack of discriminating knowledge (*aviveka*) that makes me lose direction. *Worship* [TVM 1.1.1] these sacred feet *and rise* [TVM 1.1.1]. Thus he says, advising all.

In this comment, as elsewhere, she sticks to the traditional interpretations but adds her own word picture to illustrate the concept and also, as usual, introduces words and phrases from TVM 1.1.1.

One of the issues that may help date Tirukkōnēri Dāsyai is her theological leanings concerning divine grace. The Śrīvaiṣṇava community theologically split into two groups after the thirteenth century on the issue of divine grace and the practice of human surrender to the Lord. In reading Tirukkōnēri Dāsyai's commentary, I am convinced that she precedes these theological differences. The details of this argument are beyond the scope of this chapter, but I base my impressions on her use of terms that are employed both by later Vaṭakalai and Teṅkalai writers. In general, although there are some exceptions, the phrase "grace without cause" (*nirhetuka kṛpa*) is used by Teṅkalai writers, and *bharanyāsa* ("the transfer of burden" of protecting oneself) is used by Vaṭakalai theologians. Tirukkōnēri Dāsyai uses both terms freely. She says that by the Lord's "*nirhetuka kṛpa* he graciously gives wisdom (*jñāna*) filled with devotion (bhakti)."[27]

However, like the later Vaṭakalais, Tirukkōnēri Dāsyai also speaks of the sacrament of *bharanyāsa*, by which one formally places the burden of saving oneself on the Lord and the earthly *ācārya* (teacher):

> Saṃsara (i.e. the cycle of life and death) is a vast ocean that no one can cross. You Great Lord should make sure we cross it. [The Lord} stands as a surety for those who have done *bharanyāsa*: he is the raft, the ferryman who takes them across [the sea of life and death]. He will alleviate the burden of all. O *my mind, worship and rise* [TVM 1.1.1]."[28]

As does the later Vaṭakalai theologian Vedānta Deśika, she also avers that Viṣṇu does not pervade the universe alone; he and the Goddess Śrī/Lakṣmī pervade it together.[29] This is a position that later Teṅkalais reject.

This straddling of both theological frameworks probably puts her at a time before the split became obvious. Furthermore, she repeats the words of the commentator Vaṭakku Tiruvīti Piḷḷai almost exactly in a few verses. For example, the two comments on TVM 9.10.5 are almost verbatim, and it seems probable that she heard it directly from him.

However, although her commentary is strikingly similar to the male commentators in some cases, she is not shy about explaining the erotic attitudes that the poet displays in talking to Viṣṇu. In some of these verses (as in 10.3.5), she elucidates them in considerable detail.

How, then, are we to assess her contribution? We have seen that at times she is strikingly similar to male commentators, and yet stylistically she is very distinctive. There is no one either before her or after her who has used her style of writing, interweaving the first verse as a thread through the verse flowers that she picks. In theology she is orthodox and displays a worldview consistent with the presplit period in Śrīvaiṣṇava history. Why, then, was her commentary ignored and marginalized? Was it disregarded simply because it was not good enough, did not meet a "standard," or was "unauthorized," or because she was a woman?

Historical and Geographical Issues

The gender issue prompts us to turn to the context. Tirukkōnēri Dāsyai's Tamil is apparently not the best; the printed version of her manuscript has been edited throughly to make her Tamil readable. The editor of this work has also published a sample of her Tamil followed by his edited version of the same passage. The difference is striking. Spelling and grammatical mistakes have been corrected. Although, on the one hand, it is convenient to have an edited version that makes the language comprehensible, on the other hand, we are left without her "original," which may provide clues to her native language or dialect. As of now, from the initial verses in which she pays homage to teachers of the Chandragiri area and from her name, we may presume that she is from the Tirupati area. This is reinforced by her lack of command over the Tamil language; if Telugu was her native language, Tamil may have been acquired at a later stage. She is very familiar with Sanskrit vocabulary and shows a striking knowledge of Sanskrit texts. Even if we assume that most of the texts that she quotes are familiar to a Śrīvaiṣṇava audience because of hearing oral commentary regularly, she has retained them in her memory and has used them in appropriate ways. Her command of the Sanskrit Vedic, Puranic, and epic quotations and her usage of them at relevant places are impressive.

Why, then, was this commentary not known or quoted by others? Here, we face several possibilities that pertain to language, tradition, and protocol in the writing of commentaries. Whereas Tirukkōnēri Dāsyai is extraordinarily successful in her painting of word pictures, is innovative in her style of comment (by showing how the entire *Tiruvāymoḻi* elucidates the first verse), is fluent in her command of Sanskrit vocabulary and quotations all the way from the Vedas to the Smṛtis, is familiar with earlier interpretations of the *Tiruvāymoḻi* by the various Śrīvaiṣṇava commentators, and is solidly grounded in the intricacies of Śrīvaiṣṇava theology and interpretation, she has written a commentary with grammatical and spelling errors that would be considered intolerable by purists. This alone, at a time when there were no spell-checks or diligent copy editors may well have caused the marginalization of her work.

And then there is the problem of style and creativity. The style of assuming that one verse from each set of eleven verses elucidates the first song of the *Tiruvāymoḻi* is innovative, never having been used before. It obviously involves a deep contemplation of the poem. The author does pay homage to many gurus, and it is certain that she heard their commentaries over several months in semipublic forums, as was the custom in those days. It is also possible that having heard the commentary for the day, she may have reflected on the verses and come up with her own ideas. The primary idea—that she could find one verse in every set to elucidate the first song—makes her commentary unique. This theory may not have found favor if her teacher was a stickler for the rules and wanted to follow the traditional pattern of commentary, which was done by males.

It may also be possible that the writing of the commentary was initiated without prior and express permission from her teacher. The writing or recording of commentaries was considered to be a serious task and one that could only be done by the command of the teacher. There is a recorded story in Śrīvaiṣṇava hagiography about Vaṭakku Tiruvīti Piḷḷai. Apparently he would listen to the commentary on the *Tiruvāymoḻi* given by his teacher Naṁpiḷḷai every evening and then go home and record it. At the same time, his contemporary Periya Vaccan Piḷḷai was also writing a commentary on the TVM, based on the same teacher's exposition. However, the latter was writing his commentary with the express permission and authorization of this teacher. When Vaṭakku Tiruvīti Piḷḷai presented his unauthorized recording to Naṁpiḷḷai, he was admonished for recording it without permission, and the only copy of the commentary was confiscated. Several months or even years later, the teacher had a dream in which Lord Viṣṇu appeared and told him to make Vaṭakku Tiruvīti Piḷḷai's commentary available to others in the community. This commentary then became the most famous one on the *Tiruvāymoḻi*; it is called the *Īṭu* ("Equal") and is considered to be equal to the *Tiruvāymoḻi* itself.[30] It is significant that Tirukkōnēri Dāsyai mentions the main person in this incident as the last guru in her colophon. If Vaṭakku Tiruvīti Piḷḷai had been one of her gurus, she must have known about this incident and known what would happen to her manuscript if it had been unauthorized.

In all these discussions, we have only lightly touched on the gender issue. A close reading of her commentary does not reveal any "woman's" position or any explicit discussions that would make us see an "essentialist" woman's perspective. Some chapters in this volume (by McGee, Patton, and Young) focus on the complexity of men's textual debates about women or on the subtleties of classical literary portrayals of particular gender roles, such as in gift giving (Findly) and marriage (Jamison). This chapter adds another kind of complex dimension to the picture: the participation of women in the creation of traditional textual commentary. In Tirukkōnēri Dāsyai's case, we see that distinction of literary form is, in fact, not explicitly related to gender. Despite the commentary's unique structure, it does not reveal anything that we can ascribe only to gender differences. She quotes the Vedas as much as does a male commentator. Although a lot of these quotations may have been learned through ritual usage and commentarial exposition, the juxtaposition of vernacular and Sanskrit revelation with ritual and commentary provides a milieu in which men and women of the community have extensive access at least to those parts of the Vedas that have theological and salvific import. Tirukkōnēri Dāsyai had access to this vast learning and was able to express herself creatively; this alone makes her a felicitous example of a learned and articulate woman from one prominent Hindu tradition.

Notes

The author would like to thank the John Simon Guggenheim Foundation for a fellowship that supported the research for this chapter.

1. *India Today*, August 15 1994, p. 26.

2. The name Nammāḻvār, "Our Āḻvār," is supposed to have given by the Lord at Srirgangam. V. N. Rao Hari, V.N., Ed. and Trans., *Koil Olugu: The Chronicle of the Srirangam Temple with Historical Notes* (Madras: Rochouse and Sons, 1961), p. 10.

3. Tamil is "vernacular" only because it is an indigenous language and is a "mother tongue," but it is *not* vernacular in the sense of being "nonclassical." Tamil literature dates back to (approximately) the first century C.E., and the earliest extant poems are sophisticated pieces. In this connection, see A. K. Ramanujan, *The Interior Landscape: Love Poems from a Classical Tamil Anthology* (Bloomington: Indiana University Press, 1967).

4. For further details, see Friedhelm Hardy, "Mādhavendra Pūri: A Link Between Bengal Vaiṣṇavism and South Indian Bhakti," *Journal of the Royal Asiatic Society* 1 (1974), 23–41.

5. I have discussed Piḷḷān's commentary in detail in John B. Carman and Vasudha Narayanan, *The Tamil Veda: Piḷḷān's Interpretation of the Tiruvāymoḻi* (Chicago: University of Chicago Press, 1989).

6. The later commentaries are also believed to be as long as certain Sanskrit works. The *Onpatināyirappaṭi* (*The Nine Thousand paṭi*) was the commentary of Nānjīyar and was rewritten by Nampillai, who is said to have lost the original work of his teacher. This work is said to be numerically equivalent to the *Śrī Bhāṣya* of Rāmānuja. The *Iṛupatinālāyirappaṭi* (*The Twenty-four Thousand paṭi*), written in the thirteenth century by Periyavāccān Piḻḻai, was said to be as long as the *Rāmāyaṇa*; the *Īṭu-Muppattāṛayirappaṭi* (*The Thirty-six Thousand paṭi*), written by Vaṭakku Tirvīti Piḻḻāi, a contemporary of Periyavāccān Piḻḻai, is thought to be as long as the *Śrutaprakāśika*, the commentary on Rāmānuja's *Śrī Bhāsya.*

7. S. Venkataraman, *Araiyar Cēvai* (Madras: Tamilputtakālāyam, 1985), pp. 4–5, 167–71.

8. Ibid., pp. 29–30.

9. *Ayarvu aṛum*. The *ayarvu* may be translated as "fatigue," "forgetfulness," or "sorrow." All these meanings are given by Uttamur Virarahgavacariar in his commentary on this verse.

10. Commentary on 3.10.5, pp. 79–80. Tirukkōnēri Dāsyai, Tiruvāymoḻi Vācakamālai. Tanjore: Saraswati Mahal Library Publications, 1950.

11. Commentary on 2.6.2, p. 34.

12. Commentary on TVM 5.4.9, p. 117.

13. The phrase *nirhetuka krpa* becomes characteristic of the later Śrīvaiṣnava subsect known as Teṅkalai.

14. Commentary on TVM 3.9.9, p. 77.

15. Women are allowed to comment on the *Tiruvāymoḻi*, but I have not known anyone to do so. However, I was recently informed about an eighty-year-old woman near Madras who had formally studied both poems of Nammāḻvār and the later commentaries on them, fifteen times under a certain (male) teacher. She is reported to have given brilliant oral commentaries on the *Tiruvāymoḻi.*

16. For a full account of this festival, see my book *The Vernacular Veda: Revelation, Recitation and Ritual* (Columbia: University of South Carolina Press, 1994).

17. TVM 2.4.11, pp. 29–30.

18. Commentary on TVM 3.3.1, p. 57.

19. TVM 5.6.1, p. 122.

20. TVM 5.8.1, p. 128.

21. Commentary on 10.2.5, p. 290.

22. Commentary on 10.7.5, p. 314.

23. Commentary on TVM 3.3.1, p. 55.

24. See commentary on 3.1.1, p. 55; also 7.5.10 for *carama sloka.*

25. Commentary on 3.4.10, p. 60. The divine auspicious form is also explained in 3.1.8, p. 50, and immediately after that, she quotes *Ṛg Veda.*

26. Commentary on 3.5.10, p. 62.

27. See commentary on 3.5.10, p. 62.

28. Commentary on 2.8.1, p. 42.

29. See commentary on TVM 6.10.10.

30. I have discussed this incident in "Oral and Written Comments on the *Tiruvāymoḻi,*" in *Texts in Context: Traditional Hermeneutics in South Asia*, Jeffrey Timm, Ed. (Albany: State University of New York Press, 1992).

Part III

Reform and Contemporary Arguments

7

By What Authority?

Hindu Women and the Legitimization of Reform in the Nineteenth Century

NANCY AUER FALK

The nineteenth century is a period especially crucial for understanding both the dilemmas and the distinctive opportunities that have emerged for Indian women. As is well known, the so-called "women's question" was one of its focal issues, and repercussions from the way that question was addressed continue to affect the lives of Indian women today. The women's question was the great nineteenth-century controversy over a series of customs that had restricted the lives of high-caste women and had prompted criticism from India's British rulers. These customs had been cited to justify England's argument that Indians—especially Hindus—were barbarians and therefore much in need of England's "civilizing mission." They were, moreover, much quoted by missionaries both in England and in the United States to justify evangelistic work in India.

What were the offending customs? An overview of the more well-known customs might be helpful here. *Satī*, a widow's death by burning on her husband's funeral pyre, was probably the most notorious. *Kulin* marriage, in which a single high-caste brahmin male might marry as many as twenty or thirty brahmin girls just to help their families achieve a hypergamous union for them, was a much-criticized practice in Bengal. *Child marriage*, in which a girl as young as four or five might be wed to another child or to a much older widower, was challenged in part because it so often led to early widowhood, and widowhood itself was problematic because high-caste widows could not remarry. If they did not perform *satī*–which had been banned early in the century—they were expected to spend the rest of their lives in ascetic self-discipline. *Purdah*, seclusion of women, was another target of criticism in the regions of India where it was practiced. And finally, there was the practice of keeping women illiterate so that they would remain docile and would not challenge the customs and discipline of families into which they married.

Many readers of this volume will be aware that several groups formed by nineteenth-century Hindus that promoted religious reform were also deeply engaged in challenge to these same customs. At various points during the century, they took up a series of projects intended to alter the status and roles of Hindu women. The two groups most active in this effort were the Brahmo Samaj, based in Bengal, and the Prarthana Samaj, based in the western province of Maharashtra. These two groups will be the focus of this chapter.

The leadership of the reform groups was male, and hence descriptions of the groups' goals were decidedly androcentric. Leaders justified working for women's education, for example, by saying that it would bring men more companionable wives and better mothers for their children. Nonetheless, the groups made a stringent effort to engage women in the project of their own emancipation. This often had unintended consequences, for the newly educated and active women turned out to have minds and viewpoints of their own. Among the most fascinating research going on in India today is the effort to recover those expressions by unearthing and studying autobiographies, diaries, letters, works of fiction, and essays published in women's periodicals.

Much of this work thus far has focused on the reform project's effects on women—the changes it introduced into their lives and their understanding of its purposes and benefits.[1] The present chapter has begun with a somewhat different question, asking what authority the reform groups drew on to legitimize such changes. The question of authority was particularly important to the movements, as many of the customs they challenged claimed the sanction of religion. To challenge them was to take on India's pandits and the weight of authority of Hinduism's many sacred texts. To do this, in turn, one had to cite some authority of one's own. Elsewhere in this volume, Paola Bacchetta asks a similar question about the authority invoked by the women active in the RSS Samhiti. In a similar vein, Ann Gold juxtaposes male and female uses of authority in a contemporary Rajasthani village.

Comparing respective approaches to the problem of authority in the writings of men and women in the movements is a central dilemma that is explored in this volume, and it points to a central dilemma that confronted the nineteenth-century male members of the movement. Although the emancipation project had begun with an attempt by male supporters to seize the authority of scripture and hence turn the pandits' own chief source of authority against them, the appeal to scripture had not lasted. Many would-be reformers left this demanding and cumbersome course to claim alternate sources of legitimization. When they did so they inadvertently also abandoned the very structures that had upheld their own authority over women. Yet the women's writings show how greatly the men had relied on women's acceptance of this male authority to secure women recruits for the emancipation efforts. What would happen as women began to take their movements' teachings seriously and began to think and act in ways that were genuinely free? Might they move in directions that the men were unable to tolerate? Some men in the movements found this possibility disquieting.

In the remaining pages of this chapter, I will document this dilemma and then will attempt to show what came of it. What effect did it have on the movements themselves? What effect did it have on the movements' women? I believe that it was a significant and too often overlooked factor in the backlash that overtook the movements during the last two decades of the century.

To understand the men's problem and its aftermath, it is necessary to survey briefly three male approaches to authority that underlay early phases of the emancipation movement. Most readers will be aware that the movement began with an appeal to the authority of the Hindu canon, especially to Vedic authority. Founder Ram Mohan Roy's campaign against *satī* was grounded in an argument put forth in two tracts: "Conference Between an Advocate for, and an Opponent of the Practice of Burning Widows Alive," published in 1818, and "On Concremation: A Second Conference Between an

Advocate and an Opponent of That Practice," published in 1820.[2] In both, he used the same weapon, a classical precept of *mīmāṃsā*: "Where variance is observed between the Veda, the Smriti, and the Purana, there the Veda is the supreme authority; when the Smriti and the Puranas contradict each other, the Smriti is the superior authority."[3]

Although the other precepts of *mīmāṃsā* are discussed at length elsewhere in this volume by Mary McGee, it is important to note that *mīmāṃsā* remained an important interpretive tool in the colonial, as well as the ancient, context. Using the maxim from *mīmāṃsā* cited above, Roy was able to discredit the *Purāṇic* teachings often cited in defense of *satī* while framing an argument based largely on appeals to passages in Manu and the Upaniṣads. He claimed essentially that Manu had charged widows to follow a path of spiritual discipline, and the Upaniṣads honored such paths above the rites "leading to fruition," which were entailed in *satī*.

This was a daring initiative because Roy had challenged the authority of traditional brahmin pandits[4] who had previously claimed the sole right to use the texts and the tools of argument on which he drew. His tracts caused a furor, much of which was provoked more by the fact of the challenge than by support for *satī* itself.[5] But his technique would prove to be highly effective, not the least because it offered the British rulers a rationale for banning *satī* that was based on indigenous texts and teachings. Roy's success would later inspire several distinguished imitators, most notably Ishwarchandra Vidyasagara, whose two treatises on widows' remarriage were constructed on a similar model.[6]

However, appeals to canon were cumbersome, and many who supported reform had neither the expertise nor the inclination to search through sacred texts to prove the legitimacy of their efforts. Many of Roy's successors in the emancipation movement, in fact, took a second radical step, locating their effort outside canonic authority altogether. The first to do so appealed to the authority of logical reasoning, models for which had been furnished by the works of contemporary Western philosophers. A wide range of Western works had already been available in India by the time of Roy, who is said to have been familiar with the writings of at least Francis Bacon, John Locke, David Hume, Edward Gibbon, Voltaire, Tom Paine, Jeremy Bentham, James Stewart Mill, and Robert Owen.[7] The new English-language schools included the study of such works in their curricula, apparently with some intention of thereby promoting reform efforts. In Calcutta, this had born fruit in the movement of avid young rationalists known as Young Bengal, whose denunciations of Hinduism scandalized the orthodox during the 1830s and 1840s. A somewhat calmer Bombay parallel was the Bombay Students Literary and Scientific Society, founded in 1848.[8] These young rationalist social critics used a language of natural rights and natural law to back their own pleas for improvement of women's status.[9]

It is significant that several members of the Young Bengal movement followed Debendranath Tagore from his early organization, the Tattvabodhini Sabha, into the Brahmo Samaj, when Tagore made his decision to take over and rejuvenate Roy's religious reform group.[10] A purely secular rationalism had proved too extreme to gain the Young Bengal movement much of a following. Many rationalists therefore made common cause with later Samaj leaders, who defended their own efforts by appealing to yet a third authority, that which Anantanand Rambachan has called the "authority of intuition."[11] This voice of Brahm, or God, speaking within the human heart, was first invoked by Debendranath to justify his convictions when he found that Vedic texts could not fully do so. Showing traces of the Upaniṣad teachings in which the early reform groups were steeped, the appeal to an authority of intuition posited a direct internal link between an individual human and God. Honed by a proper faith and course of spiritual discipline, a devotee would know God's path directly, and hence would choose the right course of action when the time came to take it. That is, it is God's own authority that stands behind the human conscience and the human moral instinct. Evidence for such divine guidance is found in the history of great men, whose inner convictions drive them to effect reformations despite the opposition of entrenched establishments. Debendranath's protégé and later rival, Keshab Chander Sen, was to work out the best-known version of this teaching, but it is also found in writings of the Prarthana Samaj leader, M. G. Ranade.

Combination of this belief in internal divine guidance with the dictates of reason had become a central creed for both Brahmo Samaj and Prarthana Samaj membership by the final third of the nineteenth century, when both groups were most actively promoting the women's emancipation effort. The two groups differed principally in how much credence they were willing to give to words of scripture. Keshab Sen's Brahmo Samaj, always more radical, rejected all external authorities: "The Samaj was free from teachers, priests, books, ceremonies and rites."[12] The more cautious Prarthana Samaj indulged in astute waffling: "No book shall be acknowledged or revered as the infallible word of God; yet no book which has been or may hereafter be acknowledged by any sect to be infallible shall be ridiculed or condemned."[13] This position allowed Prarthana Samajists to cite scripture in their defense when scripture was amenable. It also helped them avoid duplicating the Brahmo Samaj's total break with the orthodox community.

Whether reformers broke with scripture entirely or only partially, the implications were clear. They had jettisoned much, if not all, of the traditional Hindu authority system. Yet there was one place where they nonetheless continued to rely on it. Ironically, this was in their relationships with the women whom they were trying to emancipate. It is the women's writings, more than the men's, that allow us to see how thoroughly the men presupposed their own authority to turn upside down the worlds of their own mothers, aunts, sisters, wives, and daughters. They rarely asked for permission from the women of their own families when they decided to send a daughter to school, teach a young wife to read, take her to Samaj meetings, or arrange a new marriage for a widowed sister. As a result, they sometimes plunged the women being thus "emancipated" into undesired and painful conflict with their families.

Our most eloquent testimony to such enforced emancipation is found in Ramabai Ranade's account of her own education by her distinguished husband M. G. Ranade, long-time leader of the Prarthana Samaj.[14] Ramabai was married at the age of eleven, at the insistence of Ranade's father and over Ranade's stringent objections; Ranade himself was thirty-one and a widower, and he wished to marry a widow, not a child bride. Unsuccessful in his battle, he determined that his very young wife would grow up to meet his progressive standards. So he set about to teach Ramabai to read and write.

Although other women of his household had also acquired some literacy, they stringently resisted this effort by Ranade. They put pressure not on him but on the girl herself, telling her to "play dumb" so he would give up his efforts. This put her in a quandary. Her father had told her before her marriage that she was to hold her tongue, listen to her new in-laws, and endure—standard instructions for a Maharashtrian brahman bride. But no one had taught her what to do if her husband and his family made conflicting demands on her. Still, by old brahman standards of *pativrat*, commitment to one's husband, Ranade had priority. Ramabai, moreover, prized the times that she spent with her husband during her lessons. So she did her best to endure the taunting of the other women. Often, however, it left her in tears.

Ranade taught Ramabai English as well as Marathi, and was rewarded with a bride who was able to travel with him when responsibilities of his judgeship transferred him from Pune to other posts. Here he encouraged Ramabai to organize women's gatherings paralleling the Prarthana Samaj chapters that he himself was founding. He also persuaded her to begin making brief speeches in public in support of women's education. The first time she did this he wrote the speech for her. Soon she was confident enough to organize and conduct meetings on her own.

Each time she returned to the family home in Pune, however, the older women resumed their attacks. Her responses to these show her full acceptance of Ranade's authority. Recalling one summer, when the women had been trying to dissuade her from her friendship with the woman reformer Pandita Ramabai, she later wrote:

> When they spoke to me like this, I used to be greatly affected and I sometimes felt that I should heed their advice. I would half-heartedly agree to do as they suggested. But, when the time came, I would somehow do exactly what my husband wanted me to. I knew full well that everything my husband wished must be carried out; that otherwise he would be displeased. So I never failed to do what he wanted me to.[15]

Ramabai nonetheless did at one point manage to anger her husband, slipping away from a public meeting on pretense of illness rather than taking a conspicuous seat among attending reformists. Learning what she had done, Ranade refused to speak to her for an entire day. His response after she apologized shows that he fully recognized his authority over her and presumed this to be his husband's right:

> First, you behave stupidly. You yourself suffer because of it and make me suffer too. Who would like it if his own one didn't behave according to his will? Once you know the direction of my thoughts, you should always try to follow the same path so that neither of us suffers. Don't ever do such things again.[16]

I do not mean to suggest that the Ranades' relationship was totally authoritarian. It is clear from Ramabai's book that they developed a deep affection for one another.[17] But it is also clear that Ramabai engaged in reform projects almost wholly because her husband wished her to do so.

Ramabai Ranade was not the only woman "'emancipated" by a husband who was relying on authority given to him by the very Hindu system that he was challenging. Keshab Chander Sen's wife broke with purdah to attend a Brahmo Samaj service at her husband's instigation. She, too, did so in the face of resistance from Sen's relatives, who immediately banned both of them from the Sen joint family household.[18] Kailasbasini Debi, married to Brahmo Samaj member Durga Charan Das, not only was illiterate at the time of her marriage but also opposed the whole idea of women's education. He insisted that she should study, and she went on to become India's first woman author to publish a book of essays.

Ghulam Murshid has told her story and those of other Bengali women hauled into the movement by male family members in his *Reluctant Debutante: Response of Bengali Women to Modernization, 1849–1905*.[19] None questioned their men's authority to decide the course of their lives. In fact, some whose writings Murshid collected explicitly defended the old Hindu ideal of feminine submission.[20]

It was Sen himself who first seems to have recognized the risk that the movement had taken in removing women from the strictures of the traditional system. After an initial period of vigorous calls to end child marriage and purdah, support widows' remarriage, and promote education for girls and women, he began to sound warnings about the dangers of letting women become *too* liberated:

> The Native woman has made herself troublesome to her parents, and on the other hand troublesome to her husband. She has given up reading the Ramayana and Mahabharat, but she has not shown any special proclivities for Shakespeare and Milton. She does not sympathize with the elderly women in her family in the matter of domestic management. In fact, she does not seem to possess sufficient knowledge and domestic economy. . . . On the other hand she cannot sympathize with her husband.[21]

One solution that Sen would offer over the years was for pious Brahmo husbands to take wives in hand and offer them proper spiritual guidance:

> Let him remember that the wife has a soul, which the Lord has committed to his care, and which he must improve and enrich in the best way he can. If he is devout, let him make his wife as devout. If he is an ascetic, let him make his wife also take the vow of poverty. If he is a *yogi* he is bound his best to make his wife a *yogini*. If he rejoices in a lonely hermitage to share the joys of the retreat. According to the Hindu scriptures the wife is the husband's *sahadharmani*, partner in faith. So may she be![22]

Still another step Brahmos had to take was to design a proper system for female education, one that had to be somewhat different from the men's: "Women will not only be trained up in intellectual knowledge, but will also be able to learn domestic economy and receive a sound moral training."[23] Geometry, logic, science, and history were to be excluded. Here Sen parted company with his more rationalist followers, who seem to have been far less inclined to fear the prospect of sharing their world with independent women, as long as those women had well-trained minds. When an opportunity arose to found Sen's much longed-for school for women, he quarreled over its curriculum with the rationalist contingent led by Sivanath Shastri.[24] This quarrel opened a rift in the Brahmo community later made unbridgeable by Sen's decision to give away his daughter in the Kuch Behar marriage.[25] In 1878, a new Sadharan Brahmo Samaj seceded from Sen's Brahmo Samaj of India. Sen himself died of diabetes less than five years later. Neither the Sadharans nor the remnants of Sen's following ever recovered the membership or the influence that the Brahmos had had during the time of Sen's leadership.

Ironically, Sen's fear that the Brahmo Samaj might lose control of its women was misplaced. The Bengali women have been the group most studied by those who have tried to determine responses to the emancipation effort. The vast majority shared their menfolk's goals. They, too, expected that they would spend most of their lives as wives and mothers. They welcomed the new companionate ideal of marriage and the education that helped them become friends and helpers to their husbands. They wrote far less about the social struggle going on around them than about the need to maintain proper modesty and decorum and to take proper care of their families and their housework. Radicalism for them was taking a paying professional job or asking parents to delay a marriage until they had completed their education or found a husband who was a proper match for their own attainments. Ghulam Murshid has concluded sadly about his findings from their writings: "Thus, by freedom, Bengali women understood only a partial improvement in their degraded social position; [real] emancipation was still inconceivable."[26]

In Maharashtra, however, women had begun by the 1880s to strike out in ways that became more problematic for male leaders. They did not intimidate the male reformers themselves; for the most part, the latter were sympathetic. But newly activist women did awaken a backlash well exploited by other male leaders who were striving to discredit the reformers. Much of the problem here arose from the difference in political strategy utilized by Bengali and Maharashtrian reformers. The Bengalis, by and large, had simply cut their ties to the orthodox community, counting for strength on their own numbers and their ability to establish economic independence of their families through their access to jobs in the British civil service. Maharashtrian reformers, or at least the more moderate, such as Ranade, had tried to avoid making a formal break with orthodox practice. Unlike Brahmo Samajists, for example, Prarthana Samajists did not burn sacred threads, eat in public with Muslims, or declare their group to be no longer Hindu. In return, they won cautious acceptance and even backing for their measures from some of the more progressive orthodox leaders.

Three well-publicized crises centering on women provided the means by which this fragile detente was broken and orthodox tolerance of reform shifted into more rigid resistance. The first was a lawsuit, the so-called *Rakhmabai-Dadaji* case of 1884–1888; the second was the controversy of 1985–1991 over the reformer-backed Age of Consent Bill; and the third was the clamor of 1990–1992 over Christian conversions at the widows' school founded by Pandita Ramabai, Maharashtra's most famous woman reformer. We shall take these up in the order of their occurrence.

The chief protagonist of the *Rakhmabai* case was the young woman named Rakhmabai, born in Bombay in 1864 and a member of a so-called "carpenter" caste.[27] Although this caste was normally of fairly low standing, some of its members had gained wealth and prominence in Bombay by taking advantage of the city's commercial boom. Among these were Rakhmabai's father and maternal relatives. Rakhmabai's father, a building contractor, died when she was three; Rakhmabai had been his only child. When she was six, her mother remarried a prominent doctor, remarriage being allowable in their caste. This man, a strong reform supporter, made sure that his bright young ward received a fine education.

Nonetheless, Rakhmabai's mother and maternal grandfather insisted that she be married at the age of eleven to Dadaji Bhikaji, a somewhat less prosperous member of their caste whose education they planned to further. Unfortunately, Dadaji turned out to be a lazy wastrel who was suspected of being infected with tuberculosis. Rakhmabai's family therefore observed her wishes to stay in her own household rather than sending her after her puberty to Dadaji's family.

In 1884, when she was nineteen, Dadaji sued for restoration of his conjugal rights, attempting to force Rakhmabai to move in with him and his relatives. There is some reason to suspect that he was motivated by money, for Rakhmabai herself had just been awarded sole claim to the estate of her late father.[28] The first judge to hear the case held in Rakhmabai's favor, but an appellate court reversed him, and the Bombay High Court subsequently held for Dadaji also, imposing a six-month jail sentence if she failed to move to his home. Rakhmabai opted for jail, mobilizing so much public support that the courts backed off from enforcing her sentence. After one more attempt at a lawsuit against her family for defaming his character, Dadaji gave up his claims on Rakhmabai and took a financial settlement.

All of these developments received generous coverage in the Maharashtrian newspapers, with heated arguments both for and against Rakhmabai's position. She herself contributed to this publicity, publishing two letters in the *Times of India* in 1885 about the evils of child marriage and enforced[29] widowhood. Her language was scathing, charging that Hindu women were "treated worse than beasts,"[30] and that child marriage was intended to make a young bride "as submissive as a slave."[31]

Much of the controversy over Rakhmabai focused on legal points of the case: the first judge had ruled that her marriage was not valid because it was not consummated and she herself had never consented to it. However, critics also turned on Rakhmabai's calls for women's education, charging that her own education had left her feeling that she was too good for Dadaji. In the words of one writer, she had become "Rakhmabai, the Bombay young lady,—who, inspired with fine notions of independence and freedom which Western education has instilled into her, rebelled against the authority of her husband."[32]

Among the several newspapers that published pieces critical of Rakhmabai's position was the new English-language weekly *Mahratta*, and the Mahratti-language weekly *Keshari*, both founded only in 1881. These two publications were started by a pair of recent graduates of Deccan College, Chitpavan brahmans Bal Gangadhar Tilak and Gopal Ganesh Agarkar, with Tilak editing *Mahratta* and Agarkar, *Keshari*. The two had established the papers as part of a more ambitious project to bring renewal to their homeland via inexpensive English-language education that was to be structured and controlled by Indians. With several friends, they had founded the New English School in 1880, followed by the two newspapers, and then the Deccan Education Society in 1883, which in turn had raised funds for and founded Ferguson College in January 1885.

It had been a strange partnership from the beginning. Although both Tilak and Agarkar were both enthusiasts for the new Western secular moral philosophies, Tilak was more orthodox in practice than Agarkar and more brusque and impatient personally. Moreover the two men differed in priorities: Agarkar felt, as did most reformers, that social reform had to precede other efforts by Indians to win more control over their own destinies; Tilak believed that young India's first effort should be to find a means of gaining political independence from the British. By 1887, Tilak was quarreling with Deccan Education Society member Gopal Krishna Gokhale, who was also Agarkar's friend and a great deal more like him. Over the next three years, Tilak began to distance himself from the social reformers and to use both *Mahratta* and *Keshari* to build public support for his own nationalist convictions. In December 1890, Tilak resigned from the schools and society of which he had been cofounder, and Agarkar resigned from *Keshari*, letting Tilak become its new editor.

Tilak had meanwhile learned that he could build support for his political agenda by appealing to the mistrust that many orthodox Hindu males had for the programs and methods of the social reformers. Women's education was one point about which mistrust seemed justified, as exemplified by the *Rakhmabai* case. Tilak, with his gift for inflammatory overstatement, was to assert at one time during this case that founding a high school for girls would cause women to run away from home.[33] His *Mahratta*, moreover, furnished ample space to other voices raised in criticism.[34]

However, Tilak was not yet fully independent during the *Rakhmabai* case. It was the two controversies immediately following that most helped him to end the detente between the orthodox and the reformers. The controversy over the Age of Consent Bill was very complex, and we cannot discuss the whole of it here.[35] At base, however, the bill was a proposal put forth in January 1891 before India's supreme legislative council to make twelve the legal age at which a girl would be presumed mature enough to consent to sexual intercourse. This bill was technically an amendment to an earlier provision in the Indian Penal Code that had set the age of consent at ten. However, all its attackers and defenders knew it to be also a first attempt at limiting child marriage, against which the Maharashtrian reformer Behramji Malabari had been waging a campaign throughout the 1880s. One reason why the *Rakhmabai* case had gained so much publicity had been its bearing on this larger campaign.

The British government had not responded to Malabari's early initiatives, in large measure because of reluctance to take legal steps that could be construed as interfering with religious practice. This reluctance had been affirmed as official policy in Queen Victoria's Proclamation of 1858:

> We declare it to be our royal will and pleasure that none be in any wise favoured, none molested or disquieted by reason of their religious faith or observance, but that all shall alike enjoy the equal and impartial protection of the law; and we do strictly charge and enjoin all those who may be in authority under us, that they abstain from all interference with the religious belief or worship of any of our subjects on pain of our highest displeasure.[36]

This principle had nonetheless been violated on a number of previous occasions, most notably the 1829 abolition of *satī*, the 1856 Widow Remarriage Bill, and the Brahmo Marriage Act of 1872. In all these cases, reformers had argued that overriding principles of morality legitimized passage of the bills they advocated. The government, while sympathizing with Malabari's similar argument, feared a widespread public revolt if it tried to raise the age of marriage per se. But it eventually proved willing to take the far more cautious step of raising the age at which a child marriage could be consummated.

This provoked a widespread storm among Hindus. Pandits argued that the rite of *garbhadhan* ("giving an embryo"), which entailed intercourse, had to be completed immediately following a girl's first menstrual period. Hindu marriage had in effect been a two-staged affair, with the initial rites of commitment occurring during a girl's childhood but cohabitation beginning only with this *garbhadhan* ritual. According to the pundits, the *garbhadhan's* timing was a Śāstric requirement. The new law would mean that this requirement could not be met at its proper time if a bride happened to menstruate before reaching the age of twelve.

Male reformers cited countering arguments that were also based on Śāstric prescriptions, as well as assembling medical evidence on the damage done to young girls and their babies by premature copulation. Voices of women offered important new support for the reform position, most coming from groups in Maharashtra. The women's approach was somewhat different from the men's, and potentially much more disquieting, since women tended to argue that early marriage and sex resulted in loveless and bickering unions. One member of the Arya Mahila Samāj claimed that 99 percent of all child marriages were unhappy. Another, writing in the Prarthana Samaj's official journal, was more restrained, asserting that perhaps four or five marriages in one hundred might bring a couple to love and harmony.[37] Moreover, the women did not restrict their support to mere writing. Like the male reformers, they proved able to launch petition drives and organize mass public meetings. These were still much smaller than the men's, but they showed that women, too, could exercise political muscle—which, of course, was also potentially threatening.

Let us recall that Bal Gangadhar Tilak had made his last break with his reformist friends in the month just before the Age of Consent Bill was placed before the high council. With little to lose, and two newspapers to work with, he used his writing skills to convert controversy and masculine fears into political space for his own ambitions. He claimed the middle ground between the reformers and the pundits. Reformers were right, he claimed, to want change in an institution that had caused a great deal of human suffering. But they were wrong in their methods. They should not trust the government to make needed changes for them or do anything to increase the power of the state machinery that was used to limit and suppress them. By doing so, they put their own culture and religion in danger. It would be much better, and far more effective, to use education to achieve the desired ends. With this argument, in effect, Tilak could present himself as a moderate and much better ally for the orthodox than Ranade and his friends, who were among the bill's supporters.

Meanwhile Tilak had found still another source of controversy that helped him to discredit the old reformers. This was a series of actions taken by the famous Pandita Ramabai, the first woman in India to become a major emancipationist leader in her own right. This story is told elsewhere in this volume, but we must nonetheless recall here a few salient points to show why an attack on Ramabai could have so much power. Ramabai was the daughter of a pious and learned Chitpavan Brahman named Anant Shastri Dongre, whose ancestors moved from Maharashtra to Karnataka in the sixteenth century. As a young man, Dongre returned to Pune to study, and he was impressed to learn that the wife of the Peshwa was learning to read Sanskrit. Dongre decided that he would teach women of his own family to read the Purāṇas, and he successfully defended his decision to do so before a court of pandits. Dongre himself taught only his second wife and their older daughter, Krishnabai; his wife, Ambabai, taught the younger daughter, Ramabai. By this time the family had suffered financial reverses and was wandering through India, earning a scanty income by giving public readings from the Puranas.

Unlike most Brahman girls of her time, Ramabai did not marry young. Her father had suffered a bad experience with the marriage he had arranged for Krishnabai and, moreover, had no dowry to give for his younger daughter. Then both parents and Ramabai's sister died of famine and disease during the Maharashtrian famine of 1874–1876. Ramabai and her only brother continued to live a life of constant pilgrimage and Purāṇa readings, but they became increasingly disillusioned with religion when their purity and austerities failed to result in improvements to their harsh life. Then, in 1878, they came to Calcutta, where the learned young woman caught the attention of local pandits. Testing Ramabai's achievements, they awarded her the two titles of Pandita and Saraswati. Some of the city's pandits then asked her to lecture to women in purdah about Śāstric teachings on women's duties. Studying the Śāstras increased her discomfort with orthodox Hinduism; later in life she would write: "There were contradictory statements about almost everything."[38]

Meanwhile, Ramabai and her brother had become friendly with Brahmo Samaj leaders. Sen himself invited them to his home and gave Ramabai a copy of the Vedas, advising her to study it, together with the Upaniṣads. She had not done so previously, accepting orthodox belief that Vedic study was forbidden to women. Now she took Sen's advice, and here, too, she made disquieting discoveries.[39] Her brother, meanwhile, had become especially friendly with Samajist Bipin Behari Das Medhavi, a Kayastha lawyer from Sylhet. Falling critically ill, Dongre convinced his sister to marry Medhavi, despite the mismatch in their castes. But soon Medhavi, too, was dead, leaving Ramabai—never accepted by his family—to care for their baby daughter alone.

By now Ramabai's fame had begun to spread throughout India, and soon the Pune Chitpavan reformers had invited this woman of their caste to come and help their own reform efforts. Ramabai did move to Pune after her husband's death, attracting as much public notice there as she had in Calcutta. She gave well-attended lectures, organized the women's society called Arya Mahila Samaj, published a book on women's advancement, and offered testimony before the British Education Commission that was to have a long-term effect on British policy. She also met and became friends with young Ramabai Ranade, whose husband was one of her more enthusiastic supporters.

Despite such friendships and her increasing influence and visibility, all may not have been totally well in Ramabai's relationship with the reform community. Later in life, when estranged from this community, she complained about the hypocrisy of some reformers and their predilection to substitute talk for action.[40] It is certain, at least, that her would-be mentors tried to dissuade her when she proposed to travel to England to study medicine. A group of Anglican nuns at Pune had offered to sponsor her and to defray her expenses. Ramabai had met Christian women as early as her stay in Calcutta and was impressed by their work to relieve social suffering. Now she accepted the nuns' invitation.

In England, Ramabai experienced a double tragedy. An Indian woman with whom she had traveled committed suicide, and Ramabai was told that her own poor hearing would make medical study impossible. A long distance from home and cut off from the driving purpose of her life, she converted to Christianity. Three years later, by then on further travels in the United States, she compounded this rejection of her Hindu roots by writing *The High-Caste Hindu Woman*, a stinging attack on Hindu teachings and customs concerning women.[41]

Ramabai wrote this book in part to help her earn money for the project that was giving new direction to her life. She had decided to open a home and school for Hindu widows in Maharashtra that would help them escape from their dependence on in-laws' families. Using her Christian contacts and the fame she had acquired through her dramatic personal history, she had traveled throughout the United States, organizing Ramabai Circles pledged to raise money for this undertaking.

The conversion that brought her friends and support in the West, however, soon became an obstacle to her Hindu friends. Most were initially inclined to forgive it in their eagerness to help her get her widows' school started. When she returned to Maharashtra in 1889, Ramabai still found a number of Hindu reformers, including

Ranade, who were willing to list their names as her school's supporters and to serve on its advisory board. But she had placed these friends in an awkward situation. Her conversion had made her something of a traitor to the orthodox, who charged that her school was a covert Christian mission.[42] Both she and her board attempted to offset this fear by insisting that the school's program would avoid all religious propaganda. Ramabai, however, felt that this should not prevent her from allowing students to share in her private devotions or from helping students acquire Christian instruction if they wished it. Soon the inevitable happened. Two girls asked for instruction. Ramabai referred them to a missionary, and a Christian newspaper in New York boasted—incorrectly—that she had won two Christian converts. Tilak's paper *Keshari* soon got wind of the story. In February 1990 it charged that Ramabai's school was proselytizing and that her Hindu reformer friends were acting as colluders. Again and again, the *Keshari* hammered away at the issue:

> We consider the Christian women, who try to make inroads into our society under the garb of female education, and the organizers—no matter how learned and honoured by Government they may be—who assist them, to be the enemies of our society, of Hinduism, and even of female education![43]

Ramabai fought the charges, and Ranade and reformist newspapers at first defended her.[44] But the defense only let Tilak gain more and more political capital. He continued to hound the school for two more years, until Ranade and other board members notified Ramabai's American backers that they could no longer maintain connections with it. Families wishing to preserve their own respectability swiftly withdrew kinswomen from the school, leaving behind only students who were destitute and friendless.

Ramabai herself did not break. She regrouped and continued her work, turning her efforts toward the desperate women who would have her. Eventually she began working in famine relief for women, and she gathered together many in a large community known as Mukti Mission. But she ran this as an openly Christian enterprise, and she sought no further support among her onetime Hindu allies. Tilak's newspaper kept up attacks on her for twelve more years.[45]

The reformers, however, were badly hurt, for they had lost credibility at a time when support for the Age of Consent Bill had already done them serious damage. Backlash from both these factors turned public support toward Tilak. After the *Ramabai* case, Tilak won most political battles in the state, whereas reformers were humiliated by a series of defeats. By 1895 Tilak managed to seize control of the Sarvajanik Sabha, Ranade's political base in the city of Pune. Very soon his skillful maneuverings on a national level would remove the reformers' Indian Social Conference from the protection of the Indian National Congress.

The split in the Brahmo Samaj in the east and the rise of Tilak in the west marked a turning point in the emancipation movement. From this point on, raising the status of women was no longer a focal concern of groups that were working for change in the life of the nation. If anything, it became a bit unpatriotic to charge that women's condition needed improving—at least for Hindu men, whose attention and energies were now thoroughly captured by the nationalist movement. Reform efforts did survive, however, in two forms distinguished by supporters' gender and by their methods of legitimization.

The first, a true women's movement, evolved from the remnants of the older reform societies. As has been noted previously, both the Brahmo and Prarthana Samajes had promoted the formation of subsidiary women's organizations. Sen's Brahmo Samaj of India, for example, had founded a Brahmika Samaj as early as 1865, principally for religious instruction of women. This would be followed in 1871 by a Bama Hitaisini Sabha, oriented more toward promoting women's social welfare. Out of it, in turn, sometime before 1878, came a breakaway group called Nari Hitasadhini Sabha, mirroring the fission that was developing in the greater Brahmo Samaj group. After the 1878 Brahmo Samaj split, each branch had a woman's organization: the Arya Nari Samaj for Sen's group, the Banga Mahila Samaj for Sadharans–replaced in 1895 by the Bhārat Mahila Samiti–and the Sakhi Samiti, founded in 1886 in connection with Debendranath Tagore's Adi Brahmo Samaj.[46]

At first, such organizations had been highly unstable and much dependent on male mentoring. However, by the 1890s, most were working entirely under female leadership. They were also increasingly emphasizing social, rather than religious, concerns. Those surviving the political traumas that shook Bengal during the first decade of the twentieth century emerged as movements that were fully secular in rationale and orientation. Thus Saroj Nalini Gupta, a remarkable woman who founded at least five Bharat Mahila Samitis in rural areas of Bengal, justified her groups principally by the claim that they would be good for their country, for neighborhoods, and for families. Their purpose, she said, was to disseminate knowledge about such issues as sanitation, to aid in improving hospitals, to promote homes and classes for widows, to establish zenana (harem) schools, award prizes to girls' schools, train midwives, and found child-welfare centers.[47] It was local organizations such as these and those surviving in Maharashtra that coalesced in 1927 into the All India Women's Conference, India's first lasting nationwide women's organization.[48]

The second form in which the reform effort survived had both male and female supporters and was located, ironically, within the nationalist movement itself. It is tempting to conclude that nationalist leaders were simply reactionary sexists when confronted by such initiatives as the trashing of Pandita Ramabai or Tilak's battle against the Age of Consent Bill. But, as is also implied by Paola Bacchetta's chapter elsewhere in this volume, it is more accurate to say that the nationalists were opposed to forcing issues that held potential for alienating the orthodox Hindu community, whose political cooperation they sought to attract. Nationalist leaders in general arose from the same social milieu, had the same heavily Westernized educations, and admired the same Western thinkers as did the reformers. Many had no personal objections to change in women's status per se–Tilak himself had educated his two daughters. They simply did not find defense of such change to be politically expedient.

Most, therefore, at least tacitly accepted continuation of the change in women's status that had been set in process. They justified this by utilizing a new model of authority that drew on the prestige of scripture while escaping classic constraints of scriptural interpretation. This was the authority of the lost and golden Aryan age, when Indians ruled themselves, women were educated and free, and all lived in accordance with true Vedic dicta. Although trading on the authority of Vedic teachings and example, this vision of the Aryan past was essentially a brand-new construct, introduced through the discipline of Indological history. Historian Uma Chakravarti has traced the process by which the image of the Aryan golden age evolved, from its initial creation by Western Orientalists, through adaption by figures as disparate as Young Bengal enthusiast Peary Chand Mitra and Arya Samaj founder Dayananda Sarasvati, to its final appropriation by the nationalist cause.[49] By 1889 nationalist historian Romesh Chunder Dutt was able to assert with confidence that in the Aryan age women composed hymns, assisted at Soma sacrifices, moved about freely in society, chose their own husbands, could marry again when widowed, and had full access to education. They had done all this while serving as "intellectual companions of their husbands, affectionate helpers in their journey of life, and as inseparable partners in their religious duties."[50]

The implications of such a view of history were clear. Customs appropriate for Aryan ancestors were surely appropriate for Hindus themselves. The changes made in the past century had not been antagonistic to Hindu culture. They were a simple restoration of past practice, corrupted in subsequent eras. Although perhaps done badly and rudely, they could be considered an initial step toward India's recovery of her freedom. Women could and should be educated, especially about their Hindu religion. They could and should move about freely and assume public roles, even serve as ritualists and religious teachers. The strictures of marital custom could be eased: girls might complete their educations and wait for adulthood to be married; widows could train for roles that would make their lives more constructive and useful. Most importantly, all women could and should work for the national effort. Yet it would still be clear to all who accepted this paradigm that women's roles were supportive and complementary to men's. Like all roles of the classical Hindu teachings on *dharma*, these would support the social fabric and would not shake it.

Other chapters in this volume also emphasize the compromises of traditional Hindu thought about women in the midst of historical change. Katherine Young has focused on this accommodation in her discussion of women's participation in the Vaiṣṇava tradition, and Mary McGee has discussed this compromise perspective on women in the evolution of the *Mīmāṃsā* tradition. But although others have written of the Aryan movement, the present chapter shows its unique role in the evolution of the debate about women: it acted as a solution to a particular debate about authority, similar to the Mīmāṃsakas and the Śrīvaiṣṇava's debates in earlier centuries.

The authority of the Aryas' example offered not only acceptable grounds for compromise between the goals of nationalists and reformers but also a way to resolve the male reformers' dilemma. Women inspired by it would be able to become all that the reformers hoped for them to be. But they would not strike out on their own or ask troubling questions about the patriarchal structures that held them subordinate and preserved other inequalities of caste and class. In addition, many women also found the example of the Vedic golden age attractive. It gave them space in which to grow and the possibility of at least a limited partnership in the restoration of both their religion and their nation. It is no wonder that it had become by the end of the century, in Chakravarti's words, "so deeply embedded in the consciousness of the middle classes that [its] ideas about the past have assumed the status of revealed truths."[51] Not until a hundred years later would critics, carrying on the heritage of India's secular women's movement, begin to call its implications into question.

Notes

1. See, for example, Aparna Basu, "A Century's Journey: Women's Education in Western India," *Socialisation, Education, and Women: Explorations in Gender Identity* (New Delhi: Sangham Books, 1988); Meredith Borthwick, *The Changing Role of Women in Bengal 1849–1905* (Princeton, N.J.: Princeton University Press, 1984); Malavika Karleka, *Voices from Within: Early Personal Narratives of Bengali Women* (Delhi: Oxford University Press, 1991); Meera Kosambi, "The Meeting of the Twain: The Cultural Confrontation of Three Women in Nineteenth Century Maharashtra," *Indian Journal of Gender Studies* 1, no. 1 (1994), 1–22; Ghulam Murshid, *Reluctant Debutante: Responses of Bengali Women to Modernization, 1849–1905* (Rajshahi and Bangladesh: Sahitya Samsad and Rajshahi University, 1983); Srabashi Ghosh, "Birds in a Cage: Changes in Bengali Social Life as Recorded in Autobiographies by Women," *Economic and Political Weekly* 21, no. 43 (October 25, 1986), WS88–96; and Geraldine Forbes: "Caged Tigers: First Wave Feminists in India," *Womens Studies International Forum* 5, no. 6 (1982), 526–36.

2. Reissued in one volume as *Satī: A Writeup of Raja Ram Mohan Roy About Burning of Widows Alive* (Delhi: B. R. Publishing, 1989).

3. As translated from Vedavyasa and cited in Ishwarchandra Vidyasagar, *Marriage of Hindu Widows*, Arabinda Podder, Ed. (Calcutta: K. P. Bagchi, 1976), p. 15. Roy himself does not quote the rule but states it more diffusely.

4. Roy was a Brahman but did not have the classical Brahman's training that would have qualified him as a pandit. By the time he published the *satī* tracts, he had already embroiled himself in controversy with pandits for publishing translations from the Upaniṣads and Vedanta Sūtras, thus making them available for study by other householder Hindus.

5. Or at least by the fact of the challenge combined with the fact that Roy was appealing to the British to abolish the custom.

6. Vidyasagar, *Marriage of Hindu Widows*.

7. Nemi Sadhan Bose, *The Indian Awakening in Bengal* (Calcutta: K. L. Mukhopadhyay, 1969), p. 50.

8. For a brief sketch of its activities, see Richard P. Tucker, *Ranade and the Roots of Indian Nationalism* (Chicago: University of Chicago Press, 1972), pp. 78–79.

9. As well as a number of other political and social issues. Few reformers were concerned only with the status of women, although virtually none ignored it.

10. One such, Shibchandra Deb, eventually survived both splits in the Samaj to become the first secretary and later president of the Sadharan Brahmo Samaj. See Shivanath Sastri, *History of the Brahmo Samaj* (Calcutta: Sadharan Brahmo Samaj, 1912), vol. 2, p. 278.

11. See "Redefining the Authority of Scripture: The Rejection of Vedic Infallibility by the Brahmo Samaj," in *Authority, Anxiety, and Canon: Essays in Vedic Interpretation*, Laurie L. Patton, Ed. (Albany: State University of New York Press, 1994), pp. 259–69. The first part of this article is very much indebted to Rambachand's typology.

12. Ibid., p. 266, summarizing Sen's sermon "The Living God in England and India," delivered in Leeds on August 28, 1870.

13. From a Prarthana Samaj creed drawn up in 1874, written by Ranade and others, as cited in Richard Tucker, *Ranade and the Roots of Indian Nationalism*, pp. 62–63.

14. Translated into English by Katherine van Akin Gates as *Himself: The Autobiography of a Hindu Lady* (Toronto: Longmans, Green, 1938), and by Kusumavati Deshpande as *Ranade: His Wife's Reminiscences* (Government of India: Publications Division, 1963). Selections translated by Maya Pandit are included in the anthology *Women Writing in India: 600 B.C. to the Present*, Susie Tharu and K. Lalita, Eds. (Delhi: Oxford University Press, 1991), pp. 281–90. Where possible, I have followed the Pandit translation for quotations.

15. Pandit, *Ranade*, p. 84.

16. Ibid., p. 108. Deshpande's translation (*Ranade*, p. xx) makes Ranade appear less harsh: "You do something silly to begin with, and then get agitated. It upsets me too. Can one be happy to see one's dear one behave contrary to one's inclination? Once the direction is clear, you should try to keep to it firmly. That will save both of us from such agitation. Please don't do this again."

17. When she became ill and needed surgery shortly before Ranade's own final illness, he became so anxious that Ramabai castigated herself for causing him grief.

18. Their daughter Sunity Devi preserved the story in her own memoirs, *The Autobiography of an Indian Princess* (London: John Murray, 1921), pp. 3–6. For her, it was a story about the triumph of love, but it seems more to portray a triumph of wifely loyalty. Sen showed little interest of any kind in his wife during the earlier years of their marriage. Unlike Ranade, Sen did not educate his wife; nor did he push her into a leadership role among Brahmo Samaj women. He did, however, insist on his daughters' education. The banishment had not been permanent, but it was Sen's family, not Sen, that relented.

19. Murshid, *Reluctant Debutante*, pp. 38–39.

20. Ibid., especially pp. 120–23. This was not a simple phenomenon. Murshid notes increasing reluctance toward women's full equality with men after the mid-1870s. This coincides with the much broader disillusion with colonial influence that produced the Indian nationalist movement.

21. "The Reconstruction of Native Society," *Keshub Chunder Sen's Lectures in India* (London: Cassell, 1904), p. 314.

22. "Where is the Yogi Wife?" in *The New Dispensation*, 2nd. ed. (Calcutta: Brahmo Tract Society, 1915), vol. 1.

23. Sen, "Reconstruction of Native Society," p. 317.

24. And with British feminist Annette Akroyd, who had come to Bengal explicitly to help the Brahmos found their school. Dismayed with Sen's concept of proper female education, Akroyd instead founded her own school, supported by Shastri and the rationalist Brahmo contingent. The quarrel is described in David Kopf, *The Brahmo Samaj and the Shaping of the Modem Indian Mind* (Princeton, N.J.: Princeton University Press, 1979), pp. 31–41.

25. This marriage had been requested by the British government, hoping to settle the young Maharaja firmly in a progressive camp by finding him an acceptable educated bride. Sen's problem was that his fourteen-year-old daughter was underage by Brahmo standards, established in the Brahmo Marriage Act, for whose enactment Sen himself had worked. Moreover, the community had come to learn that Hindu rituals repudiated by Brahmos had been performed during the wedding. Sen offered no explanation to his bewildered followers except to say that God had told him to do this.

26. Murshid, *Reluctant Debutante*, p. 25, and see his chapter "In Their Master's Footsteps: The Dependent Nature of Women's Attitudes to Social Reform," pp. 167–99. Murshid does cite a few women who challenged women's conventional roles, or at least argued that they should not be the whole preoccupation of women. Moreover, one must remember in analyzing his conclusions that his book is based on women's writing for public consumption. Malavika Karlekar, examining more private writings such as memoirs and letters, has found a higher degree of independent thinking; see her *Voices from Within*.

27. The Pathkalshi subcaste of Pathares, according to Meera Kosambi, whose writings on this case I have used most extensively. See Kosambi's "Gender Reform and Competing State Controls Over Women," *Contributions to Indian Sociology* 29, nos. 1–2 (1995), 265–90; also her "Meeting of the Twain," pp. 1–22.

28. As cited in Padma Anagol-McGinn, "The Age of Consent Act (1991) Reconsidered: Women's Perspectives and Participation in the Child-Marriage Controversy in India," *South Asia Research* 12, no. 2 (November 1992), 102 n. 9; Kosambi ("Gender Reform," p. 288) has also noted how preoccupied Dadadji seems to have been with Rakhmabai's inheritance.

29. She initially signed herself "a Hindu Lady," but the *Times* later published her identity; for summaries of the contents of these letters, see Kosambi, "Gender Reform," pp. 103–105, and Anagol-McGinn, "Age of Consent Act," pp. 271–72.

30. "Infant Marriage and Enforced Widowhood," *Times of India*, June 26, 1885, p. 4; cited Kosambi, "Gender Reform," p. 271.

31. "Infant Marriage"; cited in Anagol-McGinn, "Age of Consent Act," p. 104.

32. *The Hindoo Patriot*, March 14, 1887, p. 127; cited in Kosambi, "Gender Reform," pp. 280–81.

33. From Tilak's fourth editorial on "Educational Course in the Female High School," *Keshari* 7, no. 42 (October 25, 1887), 2; cited in Stanley A. Wolpert, *Tilak and Gokhal: Revolution and Reform in the Making of Modem India* (Berkeley: University of California Press, 1962).

34. As sampled in Kosambi, "Gender Reform," pp. 280–81. *Keshari*, still under Agarkar's control, seems to have been more cautious about the case, advising mostly that Dadaji should reject a wife who did not want him (p. 284).

35. For a clear overview of its history and issues, see Meera Kosambi, "Girl-Brides and Socio-Legal Change: Age of Consent Bill (1891) Controversy," *Economic and Political Weekly* 36 (August 3–10, 1991), 1857–68. Anagol-McGinn, "Age of Consent Act," adds to this an important analysis of the differences between men's and women's perceptions of issues raised by the act in Maharashtra. Bengali responses to the bill are discussed in Dagmar Engels, "The Age of Consent Act of 1891: Colonial Ideology in Bengal," *South Asia Research* 3, no. 2 (1983), 107–33; Tanika Sarkar, "Rhetoric Against Age of Consent: Resisting Colonial Reason and the Death of a Child-Wife, *Economic and Political Weekly* 28, no. 36 (September 4, 1993), 1869–78; and Mrinalini Sinha, "The Age of Consent Act: the Ideal of Masculinity and Colonial Ideology in Nineteenth Century Bengal," in *Shaping Bengali Worlds: Public and Private*, T. K. Stewart, Ed. (East Lansing, Mich.: Asian Studies Center, 1989), pp. 99–127; and also her *Colonial Masculinity: the 'Manly Englishman' and the 'Effeminate Bengali' in the Late Nineteenth Century* (Manchester: Manchester University Press, 1995), pp. 138–80.

36. Cited in Kosambi, "Girl-Brides," p. 1864.

37. Both are cited in Anagol-McGinn, "Age of Consent Act," pp. 111–12.

38. Meera Kosambi, *Pandita Ramabai's Feminist and Christian Conversions*, RCWS Gender Series, *Gender and History/Social Change*, Book 2 (Bombay: Research Centre for Women's Studies, 1995), p. 39; cited from Ramabai's *A Testimony* (Kedgaon: Ramabai Mukti Mission, 1907), p. 18. Most of my summary of Ramabai's life is based on Kosambi's careful and well-researched account.

39. As reported in *A Testimony*, published near the end of her life. *Pandita Ramabai's Feminist and Christian Conversions*, p. 39. Kosambi has cautioned that these claims of early disillusion with the sacred texts may have been a case of hindsight.

40. She called this "talking-much-but-do-nothingness." The letter in which she used this harsh phrase was written during her time of crisis, when some reformers were already backing away from support of her school, so the anger of this phrase is understandable. But she tosses it out as if she had long familiarity with the problem. See Sister Geraldine, *The Letters and Correspondence of Pandita Ramabai*, A. B. Shah, Ed. (Bombay: Maharashtra State Board for Literature and Culture, 1977), p. 284.

41. Pandita Ramabai, *The High-Caste Hindu Woman* (Philadelphia: Jas. B. Rogers, 1887).

42. The sense of betrayal that Ramabai's conversion generated especially among nationalist Hindus is most sharply seen in Swami Vivekananda's attacks on her in the United States. He went so far as to charge that she had lied in her portrayals of Indian women's suffering. The ensuing battle with leaders of the Ramabai Circles is described in Marie Louise Burke, *Swami Vivekananda in the West, New Discoveries; Part II: The Prophetic Mission*, 3rd ed. (Calcutta: Advaita Ashram, 1984), pp. 276–328.

43. *Keshari*, June 16, 1891, p. 3; cited in Kosambi, *Pandita Ramabai*, pp. 161-62.

44. Ibid., p. 162. Others on her board, however, seem to have given her more trouble over this, demanding restrictions on her activities that annoyed and frustrated her; see her letter of September 15, 1891, about her problems with the board (actually, with two boards, as she had moved her school from Bombay to Pune in the interim and acquired at least a partially new one): Geraldine, *Letters and Correspondence*, pp. 263–70.

45. Kosambi, *Pandita Ramabai*, p. 163.

46. For a more extensive summary of their histories and activities, see Borthwick, *Changing Role of Women*, pp. 271-92; Borthwick's work in based extensively on information from Sastri, *History of the Brahmo Samaj*, vol. 2.

47. G. S. Dutt, *A Woman of India: Being the Life of Saroj Nalini (Founder of the Women's Institute Movement in India)* (London: Hogarth Press, 1929), pp. 94-97.

48. See Apama Basu and Bharati Ray, *Women's Struggle: A History of the All India Women's Conference 1927–1990* (New Delhi: Manohar, 1990).

49. "Whatever Happened to the Vedic *Dasi*? Orientalism, Nationalism, and a Script for the Past," *Recasting Women: Essays in Colonial History*, Kumkum Sangari and Sudesh Vaid, Eds. (New Delhi: Kali for Women, 1989). I have discussed Chakravarti's findings at great length in my article "Gender and the Contest over the Indian Past," *Religion* 28, no. 4 (1998), 309–18.

50. *A History of Civilisation in Ancient India* (Calcutta: Thacker, Spink, 1889), vol. 1, pp. 170-71; cited in Chakravarti, "Whatever Happened to the Vedic *Dasi*?" p. 51; see, in general, Dutt, *History of Civilization*, pp. 66–71.

51. "Whatever Happened to the Vedic *Dasi*?" p. 28.

8

Hindu Nationalist Women

On the Use of the Feminine Symbolic to (Temporarily) Displace Male Authority

PAOLA BACCHETTA

In most scholarship on right-wing women, there is an underlying assumption that right-wing women adhere rather directly to the ideology of their male counterparts.[1] However, the Rashtra Sevika Samiti (hereafter Samiti), the women's wing of India's most extensive all-male Hindu nationalist organization, the Rashtriya Swayamsevak Sangh (RSS), provides a striking oppositional example, for it has produced its own ideology. The Samiti was established in a gender separatist, homosocial setting, and it has developed in a somewhat autonomous manner from the RSS. While both organizations strive to establish in (otherwise secular) India a specifically Hindu nation, there are vast zones of differences, sometimes incompatible, between the Samiti and the RSS.[2] One of the starkest points of disagreement is on the models each organization puts forth for the gendered identities of the Hindu nation's ideal citizens.

In what follows, I will contend that the Samiti's models for Hindu women's identity operate in the lives of Hindu nationalist women as reference points for the displacement, albeit temporary, of male authority over real women. In the first section, I explore the models themselves, as they appear in the Samiti's own publications from 1954 to present. In the second section, I examine the operability of the Samiti's models in public space.[3] That is, I trace the mode in which the models inform and guide Hindu nationalist women's participation in a major national event in India: the 1992 Hindu nationalist demolition of the Babri mosque. But first, a few words on Hindu nationalism and on the Samiti as an organization are in order.

Hindu Nationalism

Hindu nationalism inscribes itself within the current global phenomenon of identity politics as what I shall call *an extremist religious micronationalism of elites*. It is a *micronationalism* insofar as its "imagined community," in Benedict Andersen's sense, is restricted to only a part of the nation in which it emerged.[4] Indeed, India is officially a secular state, made up of people adhering to a wide range of faiths. Of its 903 million inhabitants, 82.6 percent are classified as Hindu, 11.4 percent as Muslim, 2.4 percent as Christian, 2.0 percent as Sikh, as well as a smaller percentagte of Buddhists, Jains, and so on.[5] Hindu nationalism is expressly a *religious* micronationalism in that instead of "forgetting" its basis in religion (as what Anderson calls "official nationalisms" in the West do) or incorporating religious pluralism into its concept of secularism (as Indian nationalism does),[6] it constructs and establishes adherence to its own notion of Hinduism as a criteria for citizenship. It qualifies as *extremist* because its anti-other tenants—it is specifically anti-Muslim but generally opposed to all non-Hindu citizens—have been pushed to the extreme in its ideology and practice. It is a religious micronationalism of *elites* insofar as it is produced by individuals from the dominating caste, brahmins, who make up about 4 percent of the Hindu population.[7] Not all brahmins, of course, are Hindu nationalists. Indeed, many have been leaders of its most fervent oppositional organizations. Hindu nationalism proper was born with the first theorization of a Hindu nation-state, in 1923, with Vinayak Damodar Savarkar's treatise *Hindutva* (or "Hinduness"). Its rise occurred in the 1920s and 1930s, when the general notion of nationalism itself spread in India to become, in the words of Gyan Prakash, "a mass phenomenon."[8]

The Samiti: Historical Elements

The Samiti was established in 1936, in Wardha, Maharashtra, just eleven years after the founding of the RSS and in relatively close geographical proximity.[9] The period is characterized by the escalating activism of the Indian Women's Movement (IWM), made up largely of autonomous groups and whose roots are in the social reform movements of the 1800s (discussed by Nancy Falk elsewhere in this volume). Concurrently, women began to come to the fore in nearly every other political organization with the potential to challenge Hindu nationalism: the Indian National Congress, Communist Party, Bengal-based "terrorist" groups, and the movement for the rights of "backward classes" led by Dr. Ambedkar. In this period, the IWM began to forge links with the Indian National Congress, which had, in the 1920s and 1930s, mobilized women massively in the non-cooperation and civil disobedience movements led by Mahatma Gandhi.[10] The IWM also collaborated with the Communist party of India (formed in 1921).[11] Finally, 1936 was also the year in which Dr. Ambedkar's efforts to unite the various peoples that were designated "backward classes" culminated in the founding of his Labour party. Certainly this visible expansion of potential rivals and the increasing mobilization of women contributed to opening the minds of Hindu nationalist males to the idea of creating a women's wing in their movement, too.

The Samiti's founders were Dr. Hedgevar, the *sarsanghchalak* (supreme leader) of the RSS, and Lakshmibai Kelkar, a widowed mother of eight who had formerly been a Gandhian activist. They endowed the Samiti with the same goal as the RSS: the "renaissance" of the Hindu nation. Elsewhere, I have explored the different, even incompatible, modes in which they define that entity.[12] To reach their "common" goal, the Samiti was conceptualized to function separately and independently, so that it and the RSS would be "just like parallel lines which go in the same direction, but never meet, maintaining a certain distance."[13]

The "parallel" relationship is reflected in nearly every domain, from the material to the symbolic, from the beginning of the Samiti until today. For example, the two organizations share the same inauguration day but interpret its meaning in different ways. The day corresponds to the popular multisemic Hindu festival Vijaya Dashmi Day, drawn from the epic *Ramāyāna*. For the RSS, it is the day of the god Rāma's victory over his enemy Ravana, who kidnapped his wife, Sītā. For the Samiti, it is the day of the victory of the goddess Durgā, of whom Rāma is a devotee, over the demons. Indeed, the *Ramāyāna* contains both meanings; in the episode in question Rāma calls on Durga to give him the strength to overcome Ravana. In their respective readings, however, the male RSS selectively emphasizes exclusive male agency (Rāma's), whereas the Samiti selectively emphasizes exclusive feminine symbolic agency (that of the goddess).

Notwithstanding their "parallel" nature, the Samiti is a formal offshoot of the RSS and is structurally subordinate. This relationship is rendered visible in the terms used to describe the leaders. The director of the Samiti is called *pramukh sanchalika* (intellectual leader), a position that also exists in the RSS but is secondary to the *sarsanghchalak.*

Its parallel but subordinate nature is further reflected in the Samiti's name. The founders chose to retain the initials RSS; seemingly, the abbreviated signifier is intended to evoke similarity. However, in content there are some important differences. The literal translation of *Rashtra* ("National") *Sevika* ("Worker," in the feminine) *Samiti* ("Group") includes all the terms in the male group's name transposed into the feminine gender, except *swayam* (in Skt., *svayam*), or the "empirical self-acting-in-the-world." In Samiti publications that explain the origin of its name, there is no mention of the absence of *swayam*. This absence acts to repress but not to abolish the signifier *swayam* altogether. On the one hand, the Samiti constructs models for an autonomous feminine self-acting in-the-world, thus allowing for women's existence independent of men. On the other hand, in certain publications it defines the feminine self as inclusive of a number of other entities (the "family, society, nation, religion, and culture"), thereby rendering women's identities contingent on entities that include men.[14] The absence of the signifier *swayam* simultaneously permits the Samiti to operate a certain nonconcession (women as independent) and a certain concession (women as contingent) to the RSS at the level of the signified.

The Samiti has had only three national leaders to date: Lakshmibai Kelkar was succeeded in 1978 by Tai Apte, the niece of noted nationalist leader Lokamanya Tilak and Apte was succeeded in 1994 by Usha Chati. Today, it has about 1.5 million members (in contrast to about 2.5 million for the RSS) located mainly in urban centers across India and in several foreign countries in which the RSS also exists. The membership is largely upper-caste and middle-class, although attempts to recruit lower caste and rural women from 1973 onward have been increasingly successful.

The Samiti's internal structure and technique are modeled after those of the RSS. It is rigidly hierarchical, with power flowing from the national to regional to state to departmental to city to neighborhood level. From its beginning, the Samiti's most widespread activity in its *śākhās* (neighborhood "cells") were paramilitary and ideological training, much on a par with that of the RSS.[15] It has added more activities over the years: various courses for women, including Sanskrit, yoga, cooking, "Hindu history," and art, as well as boycotts against Muslim businesses and demonstrations on issues of gender and religion.

Ideology and Ideological Apparatus

The Samiti founded its own press in Nagpur, Maharashtra, in 1954. Its publications consist of an extensive array of genres: essays, journalism, song and game manuals, a hagiography of the founder, and lectures on sacred texts. Its thought was developed with specific, gendered addressees in mind. From its inception, the Samiti was not in this domain to be an exact "imitation" of its male counterpart.[16] Dr. Hedgevar maintained that he "knew nothing" about women,[17] and he left Lakshmibai Kelkar to determine "the basic principles and philosophy of women's life in Bharat."[18] The Samiti's discourse was to reflect "women's world view, her nature, her life ideals,"[19] which "in Bharat is quite different than that of men."[20] The early recognition and affirmation of separate gendered concerns has contributed to the Samiti's relative discursive autonomy. In constructing women's identities, Samiti ideologues draw from sources different from those of their male counterparts (the *Devī Mahātmyā*, for example, discussed below) and assign dissimilar meanings to the same sources (as above in the case of the *Ramāyāna*).

Hindu Women According to the Samiti

The Samiti puts forth a wide range of models for Hindu women. Consistently, upper-caste, middle-class Hindu women are the central subjects on which they are based, regardless of the connotations of the models in question and the genres in which they are constructed. Each model contains symbolic references drawn from upper-caste Hinduism or middle-class nationalist-inspired Indian history, in the form of goddesses, feminine principles such as *śakti* (feminine energy) and *prākṛtī* (eternal substance), or feminine historical figures mythified.

To make sense of the models, one of the axes along which they can be divided is their place in what I shall call a *series of metonymic configurations of "woman"/"femininity."* By that phrase I mean relatively self-contained *subsets* of social positions to which symbolic elements are attached. The positions in question are mother, daughter, elder sister, younger sister, wife, mother-in-law, widow, single woman, and female citizen. These positions include but extend far beyond the usual ones conceptualized within the upper-caste Hindu theory of *āśrama* (stages of life). In the latter, women are generally dependent on male counterparts and are confined to the context of the *garh* (home): as daughters, wives, mothers, and perhaps widows. Furthermore, the figure of the upper-caste widow is usually connoted negatively in the context of the *āśrama*; however, all three of the Samiti's own leaders, who function as supreme models for Hindu women, were widows.

Each *subset* in the series can be further divided into a range of smaller units, that is, the individual models, which are ethically connoted. The axis that seems most relevant here is the Samiti's own: its "conscious"/"unconscious" binary. In Samiti terminology, this split signifies that there are, on the one hand, Hindu women who are "conscious" of themselves as Hindu nationalists and, on the other hand, Hindu women who are "unconscious" of themselves as Hindu nationalists. The models are arranged into one or the other category, not so much according to their insertion into the temporal periods of *kāliyuga* (age of downfall of the Hindu nation) or *satyayuga* (golden age of its "resurrection"), as RSS models are, but rather according to the degree of "Hindu-ness" or of "westernization" assigned to them. Indeed, in the Samiti's scheme of things, individual women embody upper-caste Hindu concepts of eternal time and space. Thus, models for "conscious" women exist in both *satyayuga* and *kāliyuga*.

Each model functions as its own frame, or to extend a Bakhtinian concept, a *chronotope*, a space/time wherein a constructed social position and the symbolic referents assigned to it interact to create meaning.[21] Each model has its own depths and limitations for what can be expressed within it and what it is able to mean. The models for "conscious" Hindu women are central and are linked directly to the renaissance of the ideal Hindu nation, whereas the "unconscious" ones are marginal.

Each model contains elements located both in the *garh* and *babir* (the world). For the Samiti, all Hindu women are citizens, and thus can potentially invest the space of the *babir*, regardless of their other positions. Women's positions as citizens often constitute extensions of their positions in the private space into the public space. In that sense, the dichotomy posited between public space and private space in feminist writings on situations outside India is virtually collapsed. The one exception is the *pracharak* (full-time celibate Samiti worker or "preacher," the counterpart to the RSS's *pracharak*), who renounces family life and exists solely in the *babir*.

General Qualities of All "Conscious" Hindu Women

All "conscious" Hindu women, regardless of their particular location in the Samiti's series of metonymic configurations of "woman"/"femininity," share certain characteristics. Quite specifically, they are to embody "the seven qualities of women" as propounded in the *Bhāgavad Gītā*.[22] These include "fame or reputation of character"; "wealth combined with generosity"; "power of speech"; "memory"; "power to conceive, understand, synchronize, logical reason"; "patience, courage"; and "forgiveness."[23]

In addition, three central symbolic referents are found in various forms in nearly all the subsets in the series: Bhāratmātā, the territorial goddess of the Hindu nation; Aśṭabhūja (literally "Eight Armed"), a goddess created by Lakshmibai Kelkar specifically for the Samiti; and Sītā of the *Ramāyāna*. Often they function in a complementary fashion to emphasize qualities that might be desirable in one context or another.

For the Samiti, Bhāratmātā, although literally the territory of the Hindu nation as substance (nature), is extended to represent culture: "The qualities of the mother are reflected in the daughters—we are the daughters of Bhāratmātā. We are brought up and cultured. Our minds are to be refined to the maximum extent."[24] Bhāratmātā is also "affectionate" to her children,[25] "produces things that make our life prosperous and comfortable,"[26] and gives everyone a sense of peace and tranquility.[27] She is a "superpower."[28]

The Samiti describes Aśṭabhūja as a model of "the quintessence of feminine qualities to remind women of their own qualities."[29] Aśṭabhūja is "the creator of the world," and the "symbol of motherhood."[30] She is "an integral combination of Mahakali, Mahasaraswati and Mahalakshmi," and accordingly represents "Strength, Intellect, and

Wealth."[31] She holds "weapons in her eight hands" that "symbolize the qualities necessary for an ideal Hindu woman."[32] These are the saffron flag, the lotus, the *Bhāgavad Gītā*, a bell, fire, a sword, and a rosary; the eighth hand remains bare and is held in the traditional position used for conferring blessings.[33] Aśṭabhūja is subject to a range of personal interpretations by members who worship her. Most significantly, she reinforces fierce qualities of femininity.

Linked to women's potentially fierce qualities are those of vulnerability. This is where the referent Sītā enters. Sītā is the primary symbolic element for the model of the "conscious" wife, but she also traverses all other models in her aspect as the abducted woman of the *Ramāyāna*. The Samiti regards all Hindu women as the potential victims of "unconscious" Hindu men and all Muslim men. Samiti ideologues maintain: "Due to the make up of a woman's body her power to produce is made use of by abduction. This has been in popular use sometimes and sometimes rare. History is witness to it."[34] Potential vulnerability provides the rationale for military training and the use of violence; the Samiti claims they are necessary for women's self-defense.

Now, let us explore the specific models.

Mothers of Sons and Mother Warriors

A host of anthropologists, sociologists, and psychologists have observed that motherhood is a dominant paradigm for women in upper-caste Hindu social systems.[35] In general, the mother in question is a mother of sons. Also, for the Samiti, "the role of mother is the most important role a woman has to perform."[36] However, she is a mother of both sons and daughters. Furthermore, whereas social scientists maintain that the upper-caste Hindu mother is characterized by a general ambiguity (good, protective mother versus bad, aggressive, or withholding mother), the Samiti selectively deletes negative qualities from her altogether. Instead, the Samiti divides the mother into two personalities along a very different axis: a domesticated mother of Hindu nationalist children of both sexes; and a mother warrior who by her own power protects the Hindu nation.

The domesticated mother is the most recurring mother figure in the Samiti literature. She is "the pivot of the family, and the family is the pivot of the nation. It is on the organization of the family that the nation depends."[37] She provides the Hindu nation with "good citizens, in the form of doctors, artists, learned men and women, soldiers, leaders from each home, for its progress."[38] She is supposed to teach her children to be unselfish and to know about Hindu unity.[39] She is responsible for maintaining "pure Blood, genetics and tradition which are the crux of human life."[40] She was "created by God" for that purpose.[41] The Hindu mother is "a symbol of love, sacrifice, dedication, fearlessness, sanctity, devotion."[42] However, she should be able to sacrifice her own children "for the welfare" of Hindu society or the people.[43]

A multitude of symbolic references for the domesticated mother is available in Indian history and in the upper-caste Hindu symbolic world; the Samiti extracts a number of them as illustrative of this positionality. Most of the historical figures are local, upper-caste Maharashtrian ones, a fact that calls to mind the geographical and caste origins of the organization itself. Two important recurring referents are Ahalyābai Holkar and Jijabai. The former is an eighteenth-century figure from a Maratha family that ruled Indore and its region until 1948, when the area became part of the Indian Union. In popular versions, the male members of the family are remembered for their victories over local Moghul rulers and later over the British. Because her husband was deceased and her son died in the same year he ascended to the throne of Indore, Ahalyābhai Holkar herself ruled, with great success, for a number of years. In the Samiti version, in which Ahalyābhai's maternal qualities in relation to her son are emphasized, the implication is a collapsing of motherly and ruler qualities into one. The Samiti speaks of Jijabai as a mother who "trained her son Shivaji for fighting against foreign rulers."[44] Shivaji Bhonsla (1627–1680) was a Maratha ruler, widely known for having reconquered considerable territory held by Moghul rulers. The RSS has reconstructed him as a Hindu nationalist hero. In popular, non-Samiti versions, he is remembered as having been raised by a nurse and the renown guru Ramdas. Here, the Samiti selectively rewrites feminine history, emphasizing what is most meaningful to Hindu nationalist women.

Another recurring referent is Adītī, a goddess from the *Ṛg Veda*, who is the object of a number of mythologies, including those in the *Mahābhārata* and the *Purāṇas*. The Samiti's version draws from her presentation in the *Ṛg Veda* but then constructs her as the mother of a valorous Hindu nationalist son: "She came to the sage Kaśyapa and asked for a son who could free the motherland from the shackles of bondage. She was blessed with a valorous son called Vaman, who organized an army of youth and established his dominion over the three worlds. This great mother became the object of worship and emulation."[45] In the myth involving Kaśyapa, Adītī is his wife, who gives birth to Viṣṇu in his midget form. Another referent drawn from Sanskrit literature is Draupadī, from the epic *Mahābhārata*. The Samiti's version stresses her compassion and identification with other mothers. After her five sons were unjustly killed, she did not ask for revenge against the killer, Aśvatthaman. She felt that "her sufferings because of her sons' death should not be extended to Kripi (Aśvatthaman's mother). Motherhood is the virtue which gives completeness to a woman. Through it she overcomes crude force. It is the ultimate fulfillment for a woman."[46] Embedded in all these referents are a number of transreferents to additional characteristics: motherhood thus implies rulership, protection, divinity, and compassion.

Whereas all these symbolic referents involve mother-son relations, for that is indeed what dominates the upper-caste Hindu symbolic world from which they are drawn, the Samiti invents its own symbolic mother-daughter paradigm. It conceptualizes Aśṭabhūja and Bhāratmātā in their aspects as symbolic mothers to all Hindu women. It associates Aśṭabhūja with the mother's capacity to "mold the family,"[47] and conceptualizes Bhāratmātā as the all-giving, all-powerful, omnipotent mother of Hindus. Both divinities are invested with qualities of protectiveness, specifically in their relations to Hindu women as daughters. Here, the Samiti constructs as *presence* what has been perhaps repressed to some degree in the upper-caste Hindu symbolic world of its own members' milieux.[48]

The second model, the fierce, warrior-like mother, recurs less often in the Samiti literature than the domesticated mother and exists almost solely at the symbolic level. The threat she could pose to masculinity—and thus to the RSS—is striking. The fierce mother is, indeed, always more powerful than masculinity in any form, for she is both *śaktī* (feminine energy, without which the male is reduced to a corpse, to unanimation) and feminine form. She is unmarried, and her children—of both sexes—are not conceptualized as her biological offspring. As the work of Indologists, Sanskritists and anthropologists has demonstrated, from their historical genealogy as Devī, independent goddesses (unmarried and uncontrolled by male counterparts) who provide the symbolic referents for fierceness have been progressively domesticated, often through spousification, in most upper-caste Hindu contexts.[49] However, in the Samiti's symbolic, she is revived as a referent for Hindu women to emulate, and is connected specifically to the figure of the Hindu woman/ mother as citizen.

The Samiti's fierce mother is protective. She is most repeatedly exemplified by the goddess Kalī, whom the RSS largely eliminates from its discourse. The Samiti maintains that

> The slayer of the buffalo demon is a slayer of other demons. . . . Looking at her astride the lion who will dare to call the woman helpless. By slaying the corrupt, the mother goddess protects her devotees. Those who do not know the real meaning of non-violence take her to be violent. Rather she is the manifestation of non-violence in her slaying of the corrupt demons. Let the Bharatiya woman become like Kalī.[50]

The source for the Samiti's Kalī is the *Devī Mahatmya*, a sixth-century Sanskrit text in which the goddess is central, and which also forms part of the *Mārkaṇḍeya Purāṇa* (chapters 81–93). Of its three episodes, the Samiti emphasizes the last. Unlike the first two, the third is widely considered by Sanskritists, from Charlotte Vaudeville to Thomas Coburn, to be directly of pre-Aryan origin.[51] Two demons, Sumbha and Niṣumbha, conquer the world, and the male gods are incapable of defeating them. They call on the Devī, and she, by multiplying her forms during a ferocious battle, destroys them and their entire armies. She is presented as wounding, killing, and devouring the demons while retaining the maternal aim to protect her devotees.

Wives

Guidelines for the personality and behavior of upper-caste Hindu wives have been most elaborated in the context of the Dharma Śāstras (Rules of Conduct, or Hindu law books). These were composed from the Vedic period to today and number more than 7000. As Susan Wadley points out, a dominant theme is that men are to control women and their *śaktī*.[52] In the literature, women as wives are loosely polarized along a continuum into good-benevolent-controlled (by their husbands) and bad-malevolent-uncontrolled. In the Samiti's version, however, this scheme is circumvented. Again it is primarily the "conscious" versus "unconscious" binary that is operative.

The Samiti posits two models for the "conscious" wife. The first seems to conform to the good wife of the Dharmaśāstras: she is domesticated, self-sacrificing, and personally responsible first and foremost to her husband's will and duty. The second, however, is the wife who is active outside the home. She sacrifices herself for the larger goals of the Hindu nation, to which she is more dedicated than to her husband. Although they seem at first glance to be in contradiction, both models can coexist in the same person, being simply different aspects of her personality and duties (to the husband and to the nation). The existence of the second model and the potential coexistence of both in one wife mark significant ruptures with the normative, non-Samiti upper-caste model. Furthermore, the coexistence of the models in the Samiti discourse itself operates to allow the Samiti to present itself in conformity with the normative when necessary.

Before discussing the separate models, a few words about commonalities in the trajectory of the wife are in order. Regardless of the model in question, the perfect marriage is arranged. The major symbolic referent here is the marriage of Rāma and Sītā in the *Ramāyāna*:

> Family priests studied the birth documents and found that the bride and groom were made for each other. Suitable, the word has been used in a sense which should be kept in mind today. We look for suitable matches for our children. We see only the superficial characteristics. What would be the definition of suitable then? A practical example is given to illustrate the meaning. Sugar kept in different types of containers when mixed is hard to discriminate. This is homogeneity, not suitability. One more example: when lemon and sugar from different types of containers are mixed, the sugar dissolves. This merges the independent existence of both of them. If tasted the mixture will have the taste of both. Besides, the mixing has produced a third substance. The suitable living of man and wife creates a third human. In this view, the life of a man is external, and the life of a wife manifests itself from within him. Man and wife together make up the whole. It is their duty to support each other in all walks of life and guide each other. We see this wholesomeness of life in Rāma and Sītā.[53]

This description diverges from normative upper-caste marriage in the Samiti leaders' milieu, where the wife is supposed to take on the characteristics of the male family line and to support the husband while he guides her.

Now, let us turn to the models. The "conscious," domesticated wife is proud to be a housewife. She should "discard the feeling of inferiority in this and think of her housewifely duties as a great responsibility."[54] The "role of the housewife is important in every family and the smooth running of the country depends upon a well-managed family. If the family disintegrates, the state disintegrates too."[55] Furthermore, the "housewife is the equivalent of the Home Minister" in the domestic realm.[56] Thus, although the domesticated wife is located in the home, she is fundamentally linked to the Hindu nation. Her relation to her husband is in conformity with the Dharmaśāstras: "Man is as a god, and his wife is energy."[57] She knows how to "arouse the manliness, dutifulness, and brilliance of her husband."[58] She sacrifices everything for him to play his rightful role as a citizen of the Hindu nation.

The Samiti's major symbolic referent for the domesticated, controlled wife is Sītā of the *Ramāyāna*. Here, its ideologues simply draw directly from the normative, non Hindu nationalist milieu, where Sītā is generally conceptualized as an ideal for wives to emulate.[59] Most of the Samiti's discourse on Sītā is drawn from *Pathadarshini Sriramakatha*, Lakshmibai Kelkar's essays on the *Ramāyāna*. For the Samiti, Sītā's greatness resides in her sacrifice, devotion, and chastity. She accepts trial by fire and banishment to safeguard her husband's reputation. Although "some people consider her weak in character or too docile, she has combined devotion and love and played the role of the all-sacrificing woman for Rāma and the subjects. Her greatness lies in her readiness to sacrifice and her intense devotion to Rāma. A Hindu woman lives for her reputation of chastity. She struggles for it and also dies for the same."[60]

A particular event now a part of the annals of history reinforces this theme of chastity: "To preserve their purity of character, the women of Chittor offered themselves to the funeral pyre."[61] This refers to an incident in 1564, during Akbar's attack on the town of Chittor in Rajasthan. The local Rajputs understood that they would be overpowered, but instead of submitting they committed *johar* (suicide by throwing themselves onto a fire). The women of Chittor followed suit and won renown for their sacrifice.

Finally, the theme of sacrificial devotion to the husband is supported by mythology, for example, Tara, the wife of King Hariścandra, who is a subject of discussion in two texts the Samiti often draws from, the *Mārkaṇḍeya Purāṇa* and the *Mahābhārata*. King Hariścandra had to give up his kingdom to prove his devotion to Viśvāmitra. The Samiti states that Tara followed him to destitution "with a smile" and "inspired her husband to the path of duty whenever he was faltering."[62] When he had not means left to survive, she asked him "to sell her and her son to slavery."[63] Here, the wife subordinates her freedom to her husband's happiness.

In the second model, the Samiti breaks from normative upper-caste conceptions of the wife:

> Women and men are equal parts of the nation. The responsibility for the nation rests equally on both of them. Half the nation's power rests with the women. If a woman thinks that she is a normal housewife and has nothing to do with the society or the nation then her thoughts are not only baseless but they can destroy her soul.[64]

The Samiti's model for the wife who puts the nation first conserves the normative terms associated with the wife but gives them new meanings. The most pertinent and spectacular example of reconstituted meaning is the Samiti's reinterpretation of the notion of *patīvratā* (the wife as the husband's devotee). According to upper-caste norms, in theory the wife as *patīvratā* is to consider her husband a god, to worship and obey him regardless of his behavior. The Samiti divides the wife's loyalties, however, thereby curbing the husband's primacy, by maintaining that not only her husband but also the nation is her god.[65] It also allows the wife to resist unconditional devotion to her husband, stating that the husband is divine only if he is "conscious" of himself as a Hindu nationalist. Thus, it endows the wife with the right to evaluate her husband and eventually, to distance herself from him. There are no symbolic supports for such a model, however, and the Samiti opposes divorce. Furthermore, the Samiti institutionalizes this reinterpretation by rewriting the rituals of normative *patīvratā*. In theory, the wife is expected to fast to ensure the well-being of her husband. The Samiti, in contrast, recommends "fasting on the eleventh day for society" because "God is in society."[66] Insofar as society comprises both women and men, Samiti members are actually fasting for themselves, women and men, on that day.

The two "conscious" models appear largely in the same genre (essays) and in the same languages, and they coexist in time. They allow women of all political persuasions to relate to positionality of the wife, for they take into consideration a range of possible characteristics.

A model for an "unconscious" wife exists, but she is marginal and is located exclusively at the symbolic level. She is a woman who fights with other women and causes her husband's downfall. Prime examples are Shivaji's uncontrolled wives. Shivaji "was able to control the spies of his state by stern discipline. But he was not able to control the disintegrity at home. If the housewife herself lights the flame of family feuds, then how can a husband remain happy?"[67] Because of the arguing among his wives and "dissatisfaction at home," Shivaji "collapsed."[68] He had only a "short life" because of his wives."[69] The "unconscious" wife is posited as the direct opposite of the model for the domesticated, controlled wife.

Mothers-in-Law

The Samiti rarely discusses mothers-in-law and has not developed models by which to characterize them. In one passage, the Samiti states that mothers-in-law should take care of their daughters-in-law "more carefully than their own child."[70] No symbolic referents are attached.

Citizens

The woman as citizen is a figure who has been largely left by the wayside in Hindu sacred texts. In contrast, for the Samiti, the "conscious" Hindu woman as a citizen of the Hindu nation is a central figure. Three models take her into account: one is located in the *garh*, a second in both the *garh* and the *babir*, and the third exclusively in the *babir*. No model exists for the "unconscious" woman as citizen.

In the home, the domesticated female citizen is responsible for creating children, who will provide the nation with future citizens, and for raising them to be good Hindus. She should also inspire positive qualities in her husband. Here, her duties are connected to nurturing others. Throughout the literature, the Samiti quotes the *Manusmṛti* on how women are to be protected by their fathers, brothers, and sons, but it has developed its own interpretation of the relevant *ślokas*. In return for fulfilling her duty toward the family and the nation, insofar as the family is the vital unit of the nation, "a woman is to be protected in the same sense as a commander is protected in the war. . . . When the commander dies the whole army may get disturbed, therefore it is necessary to protect the commander."[71]

In contrast, the woman as citizen in both *garh* and *babir* is partly dependent upon and partly independent of male family members. She can carry out political campaigns in public space, engage in warfare in her own right, and be a political leader (discussed below). Samiti housewives have organized boycotts of Muslim-owned stores, struggled for "anti-Hindu" books to be banned, and campaigned against Muslim personal law. There are, however, no concrete symbolic supports for these activities.

Finally, the third model for women, located exclusively in the *babir*, concerns women as warriors. The Samiti points to the fact that during each of India's wars, Samiti members "were trained in rifle shooting and first aid" and used these skills.[72] The symbolic supports are drawn from relatively recent Indian history: the revolutionary "terrorist" women in Bengal from 1928 to 1934.[73] A major referent is Veena M. Das,

> younger sister of Kalyani Das, the great freedom fighter. Veena followed her sister's path. She participated actively in the civil disobedience movement. She was jailed and released. She attempted the shooting of Governor Mr. Staley Jackson. . . . She was punished with thirteen years in prison.[74]

Another is Pritilata, who

> left home to join the Indian Republican Army. She participated in a bombing at a European club in Chittagong on September 24, 1932. Two bombs exploded leaving an old woman dead and many others injured. The revolutionaries had got away. However, the police discovered Pritilata's body, who had taken her life herself.[75]

Here, the Samiti appropriates the history of Bengali Indian nationalist women by selectively inserting it into the Hindu nationalist framework.

As with other points in the "woman"/"femininity" series, women can conform to the models in their pure form or combine aspects of each of them in their personalities.

Political Leaders

Whereas the RSS has sporadically debated the question and never officially reached a conclusion, the Samiti has always provided a model (only one) for women as "conscious" Hindu nationalist political leaders. Such women are to be the exception, not the rule: "Everybody can not take over the responsibility of the state but they can cooperate in this by managing their homes well."[76] Still, the organization has trained the two women who have become the most prominent women Bharatiya Janata Party (BJP) representatives in Parliament: Uma Bharati and Sadhvi Rithambara (discussed below).

The major characteristics assigned to political leaders are fairness, determination, capacity to organize, and knowledge of how to incite the best qualities in their followers. This model is supported by several symbolic referents. The earlier literature, under the influence of Lakshmibai Kelkar, pointed to Mahatma Gandhi's belief that women should lead in the political realm.[77] Other referents include Ahalyābai Holkar, Queen of Indore, discussed above. The Samiti erected a statue to her, and its literature describes her as "an excellent example of efficient administration" because of her "contribution to encourage free trade," her "concept of the welfare state," the effectiveness of "her practices for maintaining integral nationality," and "her impartial justice."[78] Rani Laxmibai of Jhansi also provides a model of leadership. In the war of 1857, she "fought successfully against the British" and exhibited "inherent qualities of leadership such as boldness, patriotism, and qualities of generalship."[79]

Daughters

Although included as a position in the *garhaśthya aśrama* (householder stage), the Samiti does not generally locate the figure of the daughter within the domestic space of the family. Instead, such women are portrayed primarily in public space, as *sevikas*, citizens who are "the daughters of Bhāratmātā."[80] Bhāratmātā's "divine touch . . . has enlightened" their "lives" so that they are "not common human beings indulging in selfish affairs."[81] They are "molded" like her, as her "prototype" and her "miniature."[82] In this sense, the daughter occupies an autonomous space in relation to the family.

Sisters

The sister also is rarely discussed in relation to the family. Instead, she is conceptualized mainly as a *sevika*, the younger sibling of the RSS members, or *swayamsevaks*. In this sense, the Samiti constructs the public domain in terms of consanguinity. This framework includes the *pramukh sanchalika*. Lakshmibai Kelkar was described, and described herself, as the younger sister of Dr. Hedgevar. This relational mode demonstrates again the parallel but subordinate relationship between the RSS and the Samiti. As in the normative uppercaste Hindu family, the brother's position is structurally higher than the sister's. At the same time, internally in the Samiti, Lakshmibai Kelkar was considered to be the maternal aunt (and called Mausiji, or mother's sister) of the Samiti members. She could be in such a role in relation to women but not in relation to men.

Celibate, Single Women

One of the most striking features of the Samiti is that it allots a place for "conscious" celibate, single women,[83] who exist exclusively in public space, as *pracharikas* ("preachers" or full-time Samiti workers). However, the *pracharikas* are not discussed in the literature at all—probably because the Samiti is aware that such a positionality could be misinterpreted by the public as indicative of loose morals. A woman who is unattached to a male family member (father, husband, or brother) is an object of suspicion in normative upper-caste Hindu society, unless she can be constructed as a religious devotee or a saint.

Resembling some Indian feminists from its earliest moments onward, the Samiti openly took a stand in favor of celibate, single women.[84] As mentioned earlier, the Samiti used symbolic references. For example, Lakshmibai Kelkar wrote that in the Vedic period, some girls who went through the sacred thread ceremony married afterward, whereas some did not:

> Some girls who did not marry and who spent their time in the study of the Vedas, Vedāntas, were called "Brahmavādinī." Nobody used to put the evil eye on these girls who studied Vedas for a long period of time. Some parents used to pray and give offerings to have such a daughter. Brahmavādinī used to study the Vedas. But how difficult it is to state this here.[85]

Indeed, the Samiti is well aware that society is not ready to accept unmarried women. Lakshmibai Kelkar further states that educated women who "practiced abstinence used to take up teaching work."[86] The Samiti defends these women, although not all members agree with the position.[87]

"Unconscious" Hindu Women

The "unconscious" Hindu woman, in addition to those mentioned above in connection with specific points in the series of metonymic configurations of "woman"/"femininity," is one who is not a good Hindu nationalist, or one who is aligned (mentally or otherwise) with foreigners. She fails in the role of mother, wife, and citizen. She "creates conflict among her children" by encouraging individualism and selfishness"[88] and does not "cooperate" with her husband.[89] She is selfish and indulges in "personal development and pleasures."[90] She engages in "unnecessary competition for equality with men."[91] She has "adopted . . . ideals from the West" and belongs to the "women's liberation movement," which "is aimed against men."[92] "Like a poor maidservant wears an old sari, given to her by a rich lady, with immense pride, we are adopting the western style and culture with the same pomp and pride no matter how idiotic or unsuited they are in our situation."[93] The "unconscious" Hindu woman is unchaste. She dresses and behaves "in such a manner as to attract . . . eve-teasers."[94] The Samiti believes that if she is raped, it is at least partially her own fault.[95] Here, a woman's failure to be a good Hindu nationalist is linked to the proper fulfillment of her gender position and to the control of her sexuality.

Other than those discussed above, there are few symbolic referents for the "unconscious" Hindu woman. A recurring one, however, is Ahalyā, wife of Gautam, in a certain initial phase of her life. According to the *Ramāyāna*, Ahalyā was the first woman created by Brahma. The god Indra approached her sexually in the form of her husband. She could not tell the difference between them, and thus was seduced by Indra. Afterward, she was to do penance until Rāma came to touch her feet, for only his purity could free her from the stigma. She performed the penance, Rāma came, and she was freed. The Samiti maintains that Ahalyā would not have been raped by Indra had she known "how to protect her soul."[96] The selection of this myth and its interpretation provide symbolic support for the Samiti's practice of absorption and reeducation of "unconscious" Hindu women.[97] Indeed, it is interested not in excluding them but rather in rehabilitating them and bringing them into the Hindu nationalist fold.

The Models, Nodal Narratives, and the Ramjanmabhoomi-Babri Masjid Affair

These identitary models are not just ideal theoretical constructs, nor do they operate directly through a simple process of translation of discourse into action. Instead, they function as signposts in the Samiti's construction of territories of thought that provoke, structure, and guide its members' actions.

The models constitute a pool of identities available for selective insertion into a wider, but contextually specific, construction of what elsewhere I have called *nodal narratives of Hindu nationalism*.[98] By that term, I mean narratives in which a constellation of identitary models, a series of objects, and a plot are created, tied together like strands into a knot, assigned a meaning, evoked and reevoked, fixed, and finally essentialized. Indeed, nodal narratives of Hindu nationalism constitute one modality by which Hindu nationalism comes to be extended in real persons, in time, and in space. They make a place for themselves in the public discursive arena, in the private realm, and in the inner space of individuals. They are operational at an unconscious level, where they "play" themselves out (the persons "become" the models they contain), or at a conscious level when they are translated into real events (the persons "act them out") or into the interpretation of an otherwise arbitrary event (which is assigned a Hindu nationalist, gendered meaning).

In what follows I will give some background to the Ramjanmabhoomi–Babri Masjid event, trace the Samiti's discourse and actions in light of the particular nodal narrative operable therein and finally conclude with the place of the models in temporarily displacing male authority over Hindu nationalist women.

Ramjanmabhoomi–Babri Masjid

The Ramjanmabhoomi–Babri Masjid affair concerns the Hindu nationalist destruction of the Babri Masjid, a sixteenth-century mosque, in Ayodhya, on December 6, 1992, during a demonstration that drew 1200,000 people, mostly men. Hindu nationalists uniformly claim that the Babri Masjid was built by the "Muslim invader Barbar" on the ruins of a temple to the god Rāma, of the epic *Ramāyāna*, which Barbar himself had ordered destroyed, all points that non-Hindu-nationalist historians dispute.

The Samiti participated at every level of the action, from its provocation to the mosque's physical destruction. Throughout, at the surface, the nodal narrative that was operable was as follows: Muslim male invaders destroyed Hindu temples and built mosques in their place. They thereby violated the chastity of the nation's territory, Bhāratmātā. The Hindus must fight to regain her integrity and Hindu dignity. This narrative, however, took on many forms and various elements became attached to its significance throughout the different stages of the event. To make sense of it all, I will make use of some Irigarayan advice, that is, to "regress in order to progress."[99] Indeed, the historical place of the figures of Rāma and Sītā in the Samiti's discourse, the Samiti's construction of Bhāratmātā, the issue of mosques supposedly converted into temples, and Samiti activities leading up to the demolition certainly constitute stages in the turn of events.

Much before the Ramjanmabhoomi–Babri Masjid affair, the Samiti had claimed a link between Lakshmibai Kelkar and Rāma and Sītā: Kelkar was born in Ramnagar (town of Rāma); her coming into "consciousness" as a Hindu nationalist woman was preceeded by listening to Mahatma Gandhi's lectures on Sītā; from the 1940s until her death, she traveled throughout the country delivering her own interpretations of the *Ramāyāna*. These were published by the Samiti, finally, in 1977, under the title *Pathadarshini Shriramakatha*. The Samiti reedited the small book in 1988 when the Babri Masjid issue was becoming increasingly important. It also corresponded to the massive diffusion of the television serial of the *Ramāyāna*. The 1988 *Pathadarshini Shriramakatha* refers to the atmosphere in the streets when the television version was broadcast:

> All streets, markets, cinema halls and roads wore a deserted look. If not so much then at least at home all religious and social programs were cancelled or left aside during the transmission of *Ramāyāna*. There was no exception to this regarding language, sect, caste, etc. After thousands of years today *Ramāyāna* is imprinted on people's mind with the same intensity. The story of Shri Rāma has been the ideal and a subject of great respect and devotion in the life of Reverend Mausiji because our nation's history has been shaped by this epic and it is the best ideal of our life even today.[100]

In conformity with other Hindu nationalist organizations, the Samiti concerned itself with the issue of temples turned into mosques. In the 1977 version of *Pratadarshini Sriramakatha*, Lakshmibai Kelkar wrote:

> When I went to Kashi (Benaras) I was instructed by the priests to worship a well. When I asked why, they told me that when foreigners attacked the king of Kashi jumped into this well to protect himself. So one who should have protected others jumped into the well and to this day he has not been liberated. . . . Even today we can not visit or worship the birth places of Rāma or Krishna. Many years have passed since independence and even when the Supreme Court has declared them to be Hindu sites. Even then, we are forbidden. This shows the capability of the *sevikas*. What I mean is that one who keeps his eyes open will have real knowledge of things as they are.[101]

In the 1988 version of *Pratadarshini Sriramakatha*, the Samiti added the following comment: "What was mentioned by Mausiji twenty five years ago, this work has been left unfinished (Ramjanmabhoomi)." In these passages, several figures emerge: aggressive Muslim males; an "unconscious" Hindu male leader (the Kashi king) who preferred to drown himself rather than fight; the vulnerability of Hindu space/temple/Bhāratmātā; the responsibility and courage of Samiti members, who understand that a violation has taken place and are willing to fight. These all refer to the vulnerability assigned to all women and the potential fierceness contained within many of the specific models for women.

The demolition of the Babri Masjid was preceded by a highly visible Hindu nationalist campaign to drum up popular support for the cause. Women participated at every stage. When the RSS and its affiliate, the Vishwa Hindu Parishad (VHP, founded in 1964 by the RSS), requested bricks from villages to "rebuild" the Rāma temple, they used contacts groomed by the Samiti since the 1970s. The Samiti had, at that time, infiltrated villages around the country as part of the RSS mass expansion program under the leadership of *sarsanghchalak* Balasaheb Deoras. The Samiti contacted the women and set up free courses in "Sanskritization," cooking, yoga, health care, and so on as a means to introduce Hindu nationalist thought into the areas in question. Later, the RSS would follow up by gathering the youths into *śākhās*, with the express approval of their mothers, who had been reached by the Samiti. According to the Samiti, the bricks, made of earth, recall the sturdiness of the territorial goddess Bhāratmātā. The use of earthen bricks to reconstruct a temple supposedly destroyed by Muslim "enemies" evokes the protective, healing capacities of Bhāratmātā.

During the demonstration that resulted in the demolition of the mosque, women played an important role. The crowd included women, although men were certainly the overwhelming majority. Two of the most inciting speeches were given by women members of Parliament from the RSS-affiliated Bharatiya Janata Party: Uma Bharati and Sadhvi Rithambara.[102] Both women had been trained earlier in the Samiti. In several ways they constitute exceptions to the usual Samiti membership, while embodying many of its most treasured ideals. Unlike the majority of Samiti leaders, they are from relatively disadvantaged, lower-caste, rural milieux. They are, indeed, products of the Samiti's relatively recent expansion. Their personalities coincide with the model for the *pracharika*: they are relatively young, single, celibate, self-sacrificing, renouncing figures. They also directly embody the model for women as political leaders. Unlike most South Asian women leaders (including the symbolic referents for the Samiti's model, Ahalyābai and Rani of Jhansi), Uma Bharati's and Sadhvi Rithambara's ascensions to power have been due to their own efforts, via Samiti discipline, instead of to biological or marital connections to powerful males.

Uma Bharati and Sadhvi Rithambara spoke to the majority at the rally, the males. They criticized the men harshly for not being virile enough to prevent such an insult to their nation. They claimed that those who do not protect the Mother(land) are cowards, eunuchs, effeminate, and not fit to be called her sons.[103] The hidden referents are the Kashi king's cowardice, the potential "unconsciousness" of all men, the potential vulnerability of women, and femininity (real women, the temple as sacred space, and Bhāratmātā). The underlying models are the fierce mother (with Kalī and the fierce aspects of Aṣṭabhūja as symbolic referents) who protects her son (Rāma was sporadically represented as a child in the discourse of the Samiti during the event); the "conscious" wife who inspires her husband to battle; the dutiful daughters who have the responsibility of protecting Bhāratmātā, the chaste mother/land (the mosque stands for a phallus that is violating her body); the Hindu woman as citizen who takes the fate of the nation into her own hands. Finally, in the Samiti's discourse, women's agency is actually justified on the basis of women's supposed vulnerability combined with their supposed ethical superiority over men.

Concluding Remarks

I would like to return to the question of the Samiti's temporary displacement of male authority and to point out some of the ways in which this occurs. Unlike women in other right-wing organizations across the globe, the Samiti deemphasizes male discourse and male identities by constructing its own. Furthermore, the series of metonymic configurations of "woman/femininity" the Samiti has created includes at least two models for women's potential autonomy from men, which do not currently exist as such in the non–Hindu nationalist, upper-caste milieu of the Samiti ideologues themselves (*pracharika* and learned, religious celibate).

In practice, in the Ramjanmabhoomi–Babri Masjid affair, the Samiti called on models that base women's political leadership on their supposed ethical superiority over men. Uma Bharati and Sadhvi Rithambara were able to criticize and berate Hindu males on this basis. Furthermore, any Hindu nationalist woman was able to enter into the bigendered public space of the demonstration as a responsible citizen in contrast to male counterparts largely constructed as irresponsible. The Samiti encouraged women's violent actions (participation in the demolition of the mosque) and justified them as the revival of repressed fierce motherly qualities (symbolic Kalī) in the defense of the violated feminine (Bhāratmātā) and the violated son (Rāma). In all of these instances, the Samiti displaced male authority: as political leaders, as activists, as fundamentally connected in a gendered mode to the object of the Ramjanmabhoomi–Babri Masjid dispute, and even as the righters of wrongs through violence.

It is significant that this publicly visible displacement occurred in the midst of a particular *moment* of extreme conflict in the history of Hindu nationalism. In less conflictual times it is the Samiti's more domesticated versions of femininity that surface most visibly. Further, in both crisis moments and less conflictual ones alike, regardless of whether the Samiti produces ideal femininity as powerful, fierce, domesticated or victimized, the Samiti as an organization (and thus its membership) remains disjointedly "parallel" but ultimately subordinated to the RSS. It is in this sense, then, that the Samiti's displacement of male authority in certain aspects of its discourse and actions, in certain key moments, is always only temporary.

Notes

1. For a detailed overview of these studies see Paola Bacchetta, *La construction des identités dans les discours nationalistes hindous* (Paris: Presses Universitaires de France, in press).

2. See, for example, Paola Bacchetta, "Hindu Nationalist Women as Ideologists: The Sangh, the Samiti and their Differential Concepts of the Hindu Nation," in *Embodied Violence: Communalizing Women's Sexuality in South Asia*, Kumari Jayawardena, Ed. (New Delhi: Kali for Women, 1996).

3. This was inspired by a discussion about moving beyond structure into the realm of operability (the *comment ça marche*) in Gilles Deleuze and Félix Guattari, *l'Anti-Oedipe* (Paris: Minuit, 1972), pp. 124, 129–30.

4. Benedict Anderson, *Imagined Communities: Reflections on the Origin and Spread of Nations* (London: Verso, 1991), pp. 6–7.

5. John C. Wright, *The Universal Almanac 1995* (Kansas City: Andrews McMeel, 1995), p. 436.

6. Ashish Nandy, "The Politics of Secularism and the Recovery of Religious Tolerance," in *Mirrors of Violence: Communities, Riots and Survivors in South Asia*, Veena Das, Ed. (Delhi: Oxford University Press, 1990), pp. 69–93.

7. The state's definition of Hindu, it must be mentioned, is an object of contention by some low-caste intellectuals and activists, who feel that those outside the *varṇa* (caste) system have been unjustly lumped into the category of Hindu for political purposes.

8. Gyan Prakash, "Writing Post-Orientalist Histories of the Third World: Indian Historiography Is Good to Think," in *Colonialism and Culture*, Nicholas B. Dirks, Ed. (Ann Arbor: University of Michigan Press, 1995), p. 358.

9. The Samiti's history is discussed in depth in Bacchetta, *La construction des identités* and in Bacchetta, *The RSS and the Nation: Gendered Discourse/Gendered Practice* (New Delhi: Kali for Women, forthcoming).

10. Nandita Gandhi and Nandita Shah, *The Issues at Stake: Theory and Practice in the Contemporary Women's Movement in India* (Delhi: Kali for Women, 1991), p. 17.

11. Kumari Jayawardena, *Feminism and Nationalism in the Third World* (London: Zed Books, 1986), p. 106.

12. Bacchetta, "Hindu Nationalist Women as Ideologists."

13. Samiti, *Preface to Rashtra Sevika Samiti: Organisation of Hindu Women* (Nagpur: Sevika Prakashan, 1988), p. 14.

14. Ibid., p. 6.

15. Samiti, *Deep Stambh: Akhil Bharatiya Trayodesh Traivarshik Sammelan* (Pune: Hindusthan Mudranalay, November 7, 1986).

16. Samiti, *Shrimati Lakshmibai Kelkar Ki Jivani* (Nagpur: Sevika Prakashan, 1989), chap. 4.

17. Ibid., chap. 5.

18. Ibid., chap. 4; Samiti, *Preface*, p. 15.

19. Samiti, *Shrimati Lakshmibai Kelkar*, chap. 4.

20. Samiti, *Preface*, p. 15.

21. For Bakhtin, "each genre possesses definite principles of selection, definite forms for seeing and conceptualizing reality, and a definite scope of depth and penetration." See Mikhail Bakhtin and P. N. Medvedev, *The Formal Method in Literary Scholarship*, A. J. Wehrle, Trans. (Baltimore: Johns Hopkins University Press, 1978), p. 131.

22. Samiti, *Shrimati Lakshmibai Kelkar*, chap. 5.

23. Ibid.

24. Samiti, *Preface*, p. 50.

25. Ibid.

26. Ibid., p. 51.

27. Ibid.

28. Ibid., p. 53.

29. Samiti, *Shrimati Lakshmibai Kelkar*, chap. 5.

30. Ibid.

31. Samiti, *Preface*, p. 4.

32. Ibid.

33. Samiti, *Shrimati Lakshmibai Kelkar*, chap. 5.

34. Kakshmibai Kelkar, *Stri-Ek Urja Kendra: Strivishayak Vicharon Ka Sankalan* (Nagpur: Sevika Prakashan, n.d.), chap. 3.

35. For two examples, see Sudhir Kakar, "Feminine Identity in India," in *Women in Indian Society*, Rehana Ghadially, Ed. (New Delhi: Sage, 1988), pp. 67–68; and Ashish Nandy, "Women Versus Womanliness in India," in *Women in Indian Society*, ibid., p. 75.

36. Kelkar, *Stri-Ek Urja Kendra*, chap. 6.

37. Ibid.

38. Ibid., chap. 2.

39. Ibid., chap. 4.

40. Ibid., chap. 3.

41. Ibid.

42. Samiti, *Preface*, p. 4.

43. Kelkar, *Stri-Ek Urja Kendra*, chap. 6.

44. Samiti, *Preface*, p. 4.

45. Samiti, *Pratah: Smaraniya Mabilaen* (Nagpur: Sevika Prakashan, 1990), chap. 3.

46. Ibid.

47. Samiti, *Preface*, p. 4.

48. On the repression of the mother-daughter relation elsewhere and its consequences for women's identity, see Luce Irigaray, *Sexes et Parentés* (Paris: Les Editions de Minuit, 1987), pp. 69–102.

49. See, for example, Wendy Donniger O'Flaherty, *Sexual Metaphores and Animal Symbols in Hindu Mythology* (Delhi: Motilal Banarsidass, 1981); Lynn Gatwood, *Devi and the Spouse Goddess* (New Delhi: Manohar, 1985); and David Kinsley, *Hindu Goddesses* (Delhi: Motilal Banarsidass, 1986).

50. Samiti, *Pratah*, chap. 5.

51. Thomas Coburn, *Encountering the Goddess* (Albany: State University of New York Press, 1991), p. 24.

52. Susan Wadley, "Women and the Hindu Tradition," in *Women in the Hindu Tradition*, Renana Ghadially, Ed. (New Delhi: Sage, 1988), p. 29.

53. Lakshmibai Kelkar, *Pathadarshini Shriramakatha* (Nagpur: Sevika Prakashan, 1988), discourse 4.

54. Kelkar, *Stri-Ek Urja Kendra*, chap. 4.

55. Samiti, *Deep Stambh*, p. 42.

56. Kelkar, *Stri-Ek Urja Kendra*, chap. 4.

57. Ibid.

58. Samiti, *Pratah*, chap. 5.

59. Kakar, "Feminine Identity," p. 52.

60. Samiti, *Pratah*, chap. 4.

61. Ibid.

62. Ibid., chap. 1.

63. Ibid.

64. Kelkar, *Stri-Ek Urja Kendra*, chap. 6.

65. Ibid., chap. 5.

66. Ibid., chap. 4.

67. Lakshmibai Kelkar, *Pathadarshini Shriramakatha*, with a forward by Rashtra Sevika Samiti (n.d.).

68. Ibid.

69. Ibid.

70. Ibid., discourse 4.

71. Kelkar, *Stri-Ek Urja Kendra*, chap. 4.

72. Samiti, *Deep Stambh*, p. 26.

73. Geraldine Forbes, "Goddesses or Rebels? The Women Revolutionaries of Bengal," *The Oracle* (Netaji Research Bureau, Calcutta) 2, no. 2 (April 1980).

74. Samiti, *Pratah*, chap. 2.

75. Ibid.

76. Kelkar, *Stri-Ek Urja Kendra*, chap. 2.

77. Ibid., chap. 4.

78. Samiti, *Preface*, p. 5.

79. Ibid., pp. 4–5.

80. Ibid., p. 50.

81. Ibid.

82. Ibid.

83. For an account of the life of one such Samiti member, see Paola Bacchetta, "All Our Goddesses Are Armed: Religion, Resistance and Revenge in the Life of a Militant Hindu Nationalist Woman," in *Against All Odds: Essays on Women, Religion and Development from India and Pakistan*, Kamla Bhasin, Ritu Menon, and Nighat Said Khan, Eds. (Delhi: Kali for Women, 1994), pp. 133–56; condensed version in *Bulletin of Concerned Asian Scholars* (Boulder, Colorado) 25, no. 4 (October–December 1993), 38–51.

84. For insightful, critical discussions on parallels and relations between Indian feminism and Hindu nationalist women's organizations, see Patricia Jeffery and Amrita Basu, Eds., *Appropriating Gender: Women's Activism and Politicized Religion in South Asia* (New York: Routledge, 1998).

85. Kelkar, *Stri-Ek Urja Kendra*, chap. 1.

86. Ibid.

87. See Paola Bacchetta, "Militant Hindu Nationalist Women Re-imagine Themselves: Notes on Mechanisms of Expansion/Adjustment," *Journal of Women's History* 10, no. 4 (1999), pp. 125–147.

88. Kelkar, *Stri-Ek Urja Kendra*, chap. 4.

89. Kelkar, *Pratadarshini*, discourse 1.

90. Kelkar, *Stri-Ek Urja Kendra*, chap. 4.

91. Ibid.

92. Ibid.

93. Ibid.

94. Kelkar, *Pratadarshini*, discourse 8.

95. Ibid., discourse 4.

96. Ibid.

97. On the RSS modes of absorption of non-Hindu women, see Paola Bacchetta, "Communal Property/Sexual Property: On Representations of Muslim Women in a Hindu Nationalist Discourse," in *Forging Identities: Gender, Communities and Nations*, Z. Hasan, Ed. (New Delhi: Kali for Women, 1994), pp. 188–225; also published in the United States by Westview Press.

98. Bacchetta, *La construction des identités*.

99. Luce Irigaray, *Ethique de la différence sexuelle* (Paris: Les Editions de Minuit, 1984), and *Speculum de l'autre femme* (Paris: Les Editions de Minuit, 1974).

100. Kelkar, *Pathadarshini*, intro.

101. Ibid., discourse 3.

102. For an insightful analysis of the two women, see Amrita Basu, "Feminism Inverted: The Real and Gendered Imagery of Hindu Nationalism," *Bulletin of Concerned Asian Scholars* 25, no. 4 (1993), 25–37.

103. Ibid.

9

Counterpoint Authority in Women's Ritual Expressions

A View from the Village

ANN GRODZINS GOLD

Strong Words, Subtle Powers

A Rajasthani woman, Shobhag Kanvar, taught me much about women's religion. In an earlier work, I described her as someone who, although totally illiterate, "possesses more knowledge about rituals and traditional lore than most women in her large multicaste village, giving her a certain status there as a religious expert." I noted further that her repertoire included stories, songs, healing spells, and massage.[1] That published portrait of Shobhag Kanvar did not mention that she possessed the "subtle Veda" (*sukṣma ved*)—an orally transmitted corpus of powerful words and inner practices. The good reason for my reticence in this regard was simply that my mentor understood this particular branch of knowledge as esoteric; she gave it an aura of mystery. Anticipating that I would be rebuffed, I had always been hesitant to probe this subject. Shobhag Kanvar's claim to wield the subtle Veda serves as an opaque emblem to introduce this chapter on women's counterpoint ritual authorities.

Whereas some chapters in this volume focus on textual debates about women (McGee, Patton, Jamison, Findly, and Young), this one joins others (Falk, Narayanan, and Bacchetta) in considering texts produced by women and women's relationship to male textual authority. In the body of this chapter, I shall present other claims by women to knowledge and power in ritual media that are more publicly performed, readily articulated, and regularly transmitted.

As far as I understand it, Shobhag Kanvar learned her subtle Vedic art from a male, non-Brahmin priest with whom she shared many other devotional endeavors.[2] He had brought this teaching to the village from a guru he had met in his youthful wanderings. It consisted of meditative practice (*dhyān*) and spells (*mantra-tantra*) in combination. The details of both were secret, accessible only to initiates. When Shobhag Kanvar employed the subtle Veda—and this I have witnessed—she would stare at the inside of her right wrist, her eyes clouded and intent. I believe she was soundlessly reciting mantras, and from their efficacy she would eventually receive some kind of vision or insight.

As far as I could ascertain, Shobhag Kanvar's subtle Vedic practice was pragmatic: to obtain helpful clues about the future or the unknown—and this is not, of course, out of keeping with large portions of the ancient Vedic corpus.[3] For example, she has used the subtle Veda to locate lost objects or to predict the possibilities of their recovery. After the brief wrist gazing, she might pronounce: "You will find it in two days or not at all" or "It is still in the village" or "The person who took it belongs to your own family." This divinatory technique, as I've indicated, is only one among many ritual skills in Shobhag Kanvar's repertoire. It is, in village views, somewhat outlandish. Whereas many of her other specialties are female arts, she learned the subtle Veda from a man who learned it from a man. Regarding her status as a ritual expert and devotee, she declared to me once that she and her male instructor and ritual collaborator were equals.

What do I wish to make of Shobhag Kanvar's practice, given its elusive quality, its slippery subtlety? I will merely argue that it is one from among many examples available in the Rajasthan village where I have lived, on and off, over the past two decades, where women enact and sometimes verbally claim an authority that counters the male-authored, textually rooted brahminical story. Other chapters in this volume argue for subtler readings of the brahminical master narrative of gender in North Indian Hinduism. In this instance that narrative would say that women are unfit vessels for the sacred speech and eternal, superior knowledge that make up the Vedas. Here, I argue that women frankly express alternatives to the master narrative.[4] Shobhag Kanvar's counterpoint says: woman's capacity for ritual knowledge and concentration is no less than men's, or that in some cases gender is irrelevant.

In this chapter I shall explore other "counterpoints"—both blunt and subtle—performatively expressed in village women's ritual action and in the conceptualizations of gender that inform these actions. I shall argue that some rural Rajasthani women, while celebrating some calendrical festivals, counter with their words and acts a devaluation of female existence perceptible and pervasive in their social worlds. Most of my evidence is drawn from stories, songs, prayers, and elicited exegesis, as well as from visual arts and ritual actions. Those readers who would customarily understand all such behaviors to be epiphenominal and therefore of little account will probably want to stop here.

For those concerned with debating gender and women's responses and reimaginings of male-authored textual authority, what is at stake in highlighting such materials? I shall first introduce the issues, as I see them, using strong words to talk about strong words and more subtle powers. In doing so I resume a debate that seems to haunt gender studies in and beyond South Asia and that appears to be curiously rooted in the very muck we would like to shake from our shoes. Next I describe three festivals, pointing out as I go along various elements in their pageantry and narratives that speak of female and male identities in mutual relationship, and thus of gendered aspects of religious and social visions. My conclusion loosely weaves the preceding descriptions and preliminary argument into a message couched as soft claims.

Scholarship on gender configurations in South Asia (thus to limit our scope for the time being) and on the closely related subject of women's roles in South Asian society often appears divided. For the sake of rhetoric, and with advance apologies to all concerned, I shall use type 1 and type 2 (without naming names) to label two kinds of approaches.

Type 1 authors include those who highlight endemic, systemic, unmitigated devaluation, and consequent disempowerment of women at every level, from social and economic to cosmological and psychological. As Patton has also remarked of early scholarship on women and India in her introduction, such authors tend to look from elsewhere and above or, if they do case studies, to generalize bleakly from them.[5]

Type 2 writers, by contrast, tend to write from situated experiences and to portray women's multiple modes of living, negotiating, and imagining gender identities. Whether claiming that these modes demonstrate resistance, subversion, ironic insight, or merely spunk, type 2 scholars universally insist that women's actual voiced views and lived efforts demand attention.

Type 1 analysis will ultimately be doubly grounded in quantifiable, material, economic, and political data, fortified by the apparently unabashed misogyny of male-authored Sanskritic texts.

Type 2 exposition usually finds support in daily routines, gossip, vernacular expressive traditions, and domestic religious practice.

Type 1 approaches rarely fail to credit women with some voiced protest or capacity for reflexive cultural critique. However, they tend to conclude that any moves women do make against their gender-determined fates are fairly futile and ultimately insignificant, given the overweening structural circumstances by which women's lives are circumscribed.

Type 2 approaches usually recognize women's numerous disadvantages, as revealed in myths and statistics, but they also find it worthwhile to listen to women's own varied interpretations of their own plights; to recognize rebellious moments, as well as passive ones; to consider subversive speech, however contextually constrained, as possessing actual acute potency in particular situations and the further potential to alter existing power structures.

I acknowledge readily the crudity of my artifice here; these types of approach, in reality, may be less two visions with a gulf between them and more spectrum or continuum. There are, moreover, some bridging moves. Recent works by Bagwe and the Jefferys, for example, are among those that—although ultimately stressing rural Indian women's very difficult situations with a type 1 certitude—have nevertheless portrayed with care and sensitivity many of the elements from which type 2 approaches are built. They are prone, however, to hedge their recognition of these elements with cautionary verbs and adverbs. Bagwe, for example, writes: "It appears that there is much to be salvaged from the farm women's experience, which is directly strengthening, empowering and self-affirming."[6] The Jefferys, discussing women's songs, are still more excessively careful:

> If women's songs sometimes provided glimmerings of an alternative world of inverted hierarchies, the resistance seemingly implied by them was often "unthinkable." . . . Crucially, women generally differ from other subalterns in having rather greater stakes in the system, at least in the long term.[7]

Note the use of "if," "sometimes," "glimmerings," and "seemingly" within a single sentence that is itself dubious.

Raheja and Gold, who celebrate rural women's words in type 2 fashion, acknowledge repeatedly very real limitations on these words' effectiveness. In their afterword, concerned with issues of "potency," they directly question their book's implications beyond the expressive traditions that are its main subject: do these words interact with everyday realities and transform them, or does their power reside only in the imagination, only in the telling?[8] The answer is a highly qualified yes to efficacy.

Tharu and Lalita, who are concerned not with women's performances but with women's writings are boldly type 2 in framing their enterprise. In their landmark anthologies they have mustered many powerful, eloquent testimonies in women's words, recounting centuries of active struggle and accomplishment but nonetheless avoiding, as one reviewer points out, a "sentimental narrative of progress as the nexus between themes."[9] Tharu and Lalita's leading questions about women's words ring out:

> With what cunning did they press into service objects coded into cultural significations indifferent or hostile to them? How did they tread their oblique paths across competing ideological grids, or obdurately hang on to illegitimate pleasure? What forms did their dreams of integrity or selfhood take?[10]

Self-consciously, they have only been able to help answer these questions and accomplish their major work by dint of combing a literary history diminished by just those conditions pointed to in type 1 analyses.

Why bother, then, to make this discrimination? I believe it is helpful to lay the two approaches side by side to see where and how they diverge and converge and where the crucial disagreement ultimately lies.[11] Although few type 2 authors are so romantic as to deny the problems faced by women, a few extreme type 1 believers grant scant credence to any type 2 argument. They exhibit a strange deafness that is troubling in its implications, in that it dismisses at once both impact and substance of women's expressive and ritual traditions. This response says: what can songs, stories, and rituals matter if in the end the hegemonic system of male dominance allows women's actual disempowerment and abuse?[12] Aren't women just fooling themselves, letting off steam, and in the process only reinforcing their own bondage? Such a dismissal of human voice and consciousness troubles me.

The Jefferys' (1996) point that many women have a stake in the system is evidently valid and worth further consideration. But if the system is one that deprives them economically and politically, in what, then, does their stake consist?[13] Surely we who presume to write about South Asian women ought to make every effort to comprehend their motivations, rather than label them limited in their vision, complicit in their attitudes.

Why it is so difficult to understand from our scholarly vantage point what most Indian women grasp readily enough in their daily lives: that both things might be true? that South Asian women may well, on the one hand, submit to social conditions prescribed by what Nita Kumar cleverly calls "repressive 'malestream' discourse," while on the other hand, they not only defy these conditions psychologically but also manipulate them materially.[14]

Sherry Ortner, in an article entitled "Gender Hegemonies" (note the plural), expresses what to me is a sensible and realistic stance toward these complexities:

> The most interesting thing about any given case is precisely the multiplicity of logics operating, of discourses being spoken, of practices of prestige and power in play. Some of these are dominant–"hegemonic." Some are explicitly counterhegemonic–subversive, challenging. Others are simply . . . present because they are products of imagination that did not seem to threaten any particular set of arrangements.[15]

Following Ortner, we could think of South Asian women's tactical subversions and radical voiced imaginings as sometimes contesting, sometimes threatening, sometimes squelched should their threat be perceived to empower, sometimes empowering to the point of overturning. All processes would be understood to be simultaneously at work.

For me theory came after the fact. My attitude toward South Asian women is the result of living among them. As I have described elsewhere in greater detail, I arrived in rural India in 1979, having, I confess, read little of feminism and thought almost nothing about gender.[16] What could it have to do with the ineffable religious values I sought to understand? Living on rather intimate terms with village women for many months, I observed them to be not merely smart and manipulative—in "weapons of the weak" fashion—but also vocal, proud, defiant, and often in control of household finances as well as domestic rituals.[17] Women's exercise of power as I observed it extended well beyond the covert.[18]

In sum, nothing I learned of or from rural women during my initial twenty-one month research period in India made it possible for me to see them as crushed by misogyny, whether at the level of cosmology, social structure, or daily life. The words of women's songs and stories, performed in the context of worship, were part of the impression I received so strongly, but the initial impact was based on personal demeanor and the fabric of daily life, long before I was able to understand any but the most banal and conventional words. This does not mean, of course, that while living in Ghatiyali, I did not know a number of unhappy women, trapped in difficult and sometimes extremely oppressive situations that were in part a result of culturally posed gender structures; so I do while living in Ithaca, New York. Rather it means that I would not see these women as bound under some absolute regime of gender hierarchy that they could neither penetrate nor protest; nor would I think this of Ithaca women.

It may illuminate my foreigner's experience to look more closely at Bagwe's description of her impressions when—urban-raised and trained at Berkeley—she does anthropological fieldwork in a village that happens to be her ancestral home. Bagwe honestly portrays her own double perceptions of rural women's celebrations in southern Maharashtra. She finds it difficult indeed to reconcile village men's casual disregard for women's dignity (including her own, much of the time) with the women's energetic pleasures. Similarly she has trouble fitting her firsthand experiences of infragender female jealousies with the counterpoised collective solidarity she notes on occasions of festivity. She writes of song sessions:

> City and town women and girls watch with mouths agape the sheer energy that village women bring to the dancing. . . . It is a curious twist, then, that in such songs all women transcend their respective roles to find an uncommon solidarity against the mythical mother-in-law. It is to be acknowledged in any event that the songs provide a sharply subversive element of release in the face of an oppressive reality of grinding poverty, exhaustion from overwork, loneliness, sexual and emotional repression, and petty conflicts, bickering and jealousies among all the women in a household. It is no wonder then, that all women, young and old, look forward with undisguised eagerness to these sessions, which have a cherished place in Malvani folklore.[19]

Bagwe's conclusion—which veers startlingly in the type 1 direction—notes a similar paradox surrounding women's sexual freedom: "Another surprising observation concerns the prevalence of pre-marital and extramarital alliances. . . . Relatively mellow attitudes towards such undercover affairs exist despite rigid cultural injunctions emphasizing female 'virtue' and 'honour.'"[20] I found things exactly so in Ghatiyali and was equally surprised, initially even dismayed, to encounter this virtually incredible contradiction to all I had learned from anthropological literature (in the 1970s) to expect of Hindu women.

Having been thus overwhelmed by Rajasthani women's personal power and high spirits, their frank sexuality and clear visions of self-worth, I wish to argue against a discourse that has grossly or subtly portrayed rural Indian women as powerless, as perceiving their own bodies to be shame-laden and disgusting; as doomed to repress their sexuality into overbearing maternal love or to be labeled uncontrollable and dangerous, and as compliant with a system that allows them to exercise power only over one another. I have never argued that these negative conditions do not exist but merely that there are alternative views, experiences, and possibilities; that even when women acquiesce—as they often do—and play out their scripted roles, they do so self-consciously, with a sense of irony. I have certainly not been alone in making such arguments about South Asian women's expressive traditions, ritual worlds, or self-images.[21] Within the broader field of gender studies there exists a still vaster literature.[22] Nonetheless, extreme dismissive responses persist both in print and at academic meetings.

A number of recent studies have acknowledged the potency of ritual and religious teachings in subaltern strategies—for unmarked and thus presumably male subalterns.[23] Dirks's essay on "Ritual and Resistance" suggests that power in rural communities is and has been free floating and that rituals may express political fray as much as moral order:

> But if order can be seen as an effect of power rather than its condition, then resistance, too, can be freed from the (teleological) requirement that it establish a new order in order to be recognized as significant. Power need not be seen as either a cause or a first principle. Power is, rather, a relation, or, more precisely, an endless series of relations, characterized—we now emphasize—by struggle.

Dirks concludes: "Ritual now appears not only as a powerful way to produce the reality effect of the natural, but also as a way to contest and even appropriate that reality itself."[24]

It strikes me as suspicious, from a feminist perspective, that insights such as Dirks offers into male subaltern struggles in the guise of ritual are rarely subject to the same kinds of dismissive critiques frequently leveled at work on women's religious actions as struggle.

Substance: Counterpoints in Three Annual Celebrations

I will now focus on expressive traditions connected with three festivals that take place annually in rural Rajasthan: Holī, Sītalā Mātā, and Baṛī Tīj. Each holiday has immediate associations with female beings. Holī is Holikā, demon aunt to the great Vaishnavite devotee Prahlād. Sītalā Mātā is literally "Cool Mother," known as the smallpox goddess, but in Rajasthan today she has power over children's fevers and rashes as well as their health and the fertility of newlyweds. On Baṛī Tīj—literally "Big Third"; "Important Third"; or as I shall call it, "Grand Third"—the deity addressed by women is simply Grand Third Mother, but she is identified by participants with Shiva's resolute spouse, Parvati.

In terms of how these festivals are celebrated, who participates, what motivates participation, and how important they are in the annual holiday round, the three days are not much alike. However, I find all three conceptually linked, revealing attitudes toward female power and ritually claimed authority. Holī and Sītalā take place during the month of Caitra, as the moon wanes, a busy ritual time. This is also the harvest season for crops planted in the winter, especially barley and wheat. Holī conventionally marks the beginning of the hot season.[25] In the calendar, Holī and Sītalā are continuous, overlapping, and understood by women as a linked sequence.[26] Baṛī Tīj is celebrated toward the end of the rainy season, half a year later, in the dark half of Bhādra. It is also situated within a very active period of festivals important to women and to the community as a whole. Five days after Grand Third is Janamāṣṭamī ("Birth Eighth"), Lord Krishna's birthday; and the following twelfth is Bach Bāhras ("Calf Twelfth"), also called the day of Cow Worship.[27]

Alone among these three festivals, Holī is a major national holiday in India, and in the village it is an inclusive community event in which men and women, young and old, high and low, participate. Sītalā's Day is also a community-wide festival; every household in the village participates, but it is totally in the hands of women. Grand Third contrasts with both of these in that although most households would cook a special meal, its major celebrants are women drawn only from those communities that forbid second marriages (*nātā*). For participants, Tīj worship is primarily a personal vow and fast, or *vrat*.[28] However, unlike some vows, it involves collective ritual action. Two or three dozen women, usually neighbors and fellow caste members, perform their Tīj worship together, with storytelling and songs.

Celebrations of Holī, Sītalā, and Tīj take place in many parts of India, with significant regional variations in associated activities, mythologies, and meanings. Ethnographic and textual scholarship exists on each.[29] My major focus in this chapter is on material drawn from my own fieldwork in a single Rajasthan village. I shall spend disproportionate time on Holī because it gives the most acute picture of how women's practices and voiced interpretations counter near simultaneous, male-dominated activities. Holī in Ghatiyali reveals the ways in which a myth from the Sanskrit Puranas is retained, yet refashioned, within women's ritual traditions.

Holī is the collective destruction of a demoness; Sītalā Seventh and Grand Third are worships of the goddess in different forms. Each festival presents distinctive visions of female power; nonetheless, a perceptible "intertextuality" emerges from their stories as pooled meanings.[30] In this chapter I shall loosely follow my own participation in the first two festivals in 1993—as house guest and ethnographer. I shall layer oral texts with interviews in which my collaborator, Bhoju Ram Gujar, and I attempt to gather exegesis of both ritual and textual meanings, both from women and from men. I have not witnessed Grand Third worship since 1980, and my description of that occasion relies heavily on field notes, photographs, and oral texts—recorded and transcribed.

In 1993—perhaps because I was staying with Bhoju Ram's family and participated in a series of festivals with that household's women—I was struck forcefully by the ways in which women's celebrations discuss, enact, create, and embody aspects of female power as demonic and domestic, dangerous and life giving, subservient and demanding. Yet I have recently critiqued a prevailing dichotomous view of Hindu femaleness, arguing that women's expressive traditions often present female nature as "more unified than split, more auspicious than dangerous, more creative than destructive."[31] Similarly, in the festivals on which I focus here, although both sides of dualistic characterizations emerge, the prevailing experience of female power as women portray and worship it is one in which positive and negative ultimately blur, adding up to creative force and authoritative voice.[32]

For example, there are songs for each of these festival days that talk about ornaments, pretty clothes, and tasty food. Holī, though she herself may be on the side of evil, is addressed with a kind of familiar affection, and her songs also speak of her adornment, if only with cow dung, and her grooming, if only to remove lice. The offerings that please female power connect visibly and substantially with women's desires: squares of bright cloth named as the epitomizing female garment in Rajasthan, the *oṛhnī*, or wrap; jewelry and kitchen utensils modeled from dung or clay; and special fried treats.

The performance of each festival includes open or barely veiled references to women's sexuality, desirability, and/or birth-giving capacities, as well as their devotional and/or ascetic capacities. All three acknowledge, directly or obliquely, some dangerous potential in female nature, but it is shown as coexisting with women's auspiciousness rather than opposing it. Holī's valued nephew—whose birth from the destructive flames is ritually in the hands of women—was taught to love God by a fearless female devotee. Sītalā Mother, even as she gives people the pox, protects children's health and causes marital and agricultural fertility: all her traits are evoked simultaneously. In the Tīj story told in Ghatiyali, a stubborn woman's determination to fast brings first disaster but ultimately, happiness to her husband and his household.

My argument is not that women deny an identification of femaleness with dangerous power but rather that they situate the dangerous and the beneficent in close proximity, thereby diffusing dichotomy. Each holiday, it seems to me, addresses traditions of male superiority and authority, both to correct and to appropriate them. Thus, each denies some of the disadvantages Hindu patriarchal systems impose on women, both in ritual and in social life.[33] I hope to show, then, that women in rituals that celebrate female power, demonic and divine, make claims for female worth that run counter to male-authored devaluations and fragmentations.

Holī

Holī takes place throughout North India on the full harvest moon (often early March). One month before, Holī's arrival in the village is signified by a dead tree or sizable tree branch that is staked in the ground. In 1993 in Ghatiyali, with its population close to 4000, several Holīs belonged to various neighborhoods or, in the case of the Malis ("gardeners") and Regars ("leatherworkers"), caste communities. Once Holī has been staked, certain taboos on the movements of women ensue. During this period, daughters are not sent to their marital homes nor are sons' wives called back. In other words, the perpetual traveling back and forth of women from parents' to husbands' villages is shut down for the entire month. Why? One woman said it was "because Holī has a bad reputation, because people are shouting behind her and throwing dust and singing dirty songs." This would make any traveling female subject to the contagion of Holī's bad name.

What is so bad about Holī? Here is the most articulate version of her story, which I recorded from a nonliterate male farmer in his forties, Mohan Mali:

It's like this, there was a King Harṇakuś,[34] and his sister was Holī. The king, Harṇakuś, didn't let anyone take the name of Rām [God]. If anyone took Rām's name he ground him in the oil press.

But there was a potter woman, and she fixed all the pots in the open kiln;[35] she put all the pots in place and lit the fire. At this moment, there came a cat with kittens, and they all slipped into the fire.

She saw that the cat had gone in and she couldn't put out the fire, she started to call "Hey Rām, hey *Bhagvān*, there is only you." [That is, no one else can save the cat and kittens.]

Then while she was doing this Prahlād [the son of King Harṇakuś] came along, and he asked the potter woman, "Why are you taking the name of Rām?"

She says, "There is nothing but Rām."

"What happened?"

"After I lit the fire the cat went into this kiln with its kittens and now only Rām is their master."

So Prahlād said, "Don't take Rām's name, if he [that is, his father the king] knows you are taking the name of Rām he will put you in the oil press and grind you."

"I'm not worried. Let him put me in the oil press." And again she started to say "Rām Rām."

Prahlād thought, "I would like to know about Rām." So he also sat down over there. So when all the pots cooked and it became cool she opened the kiln.

There were still three unfired clay pots, and in them were the cat and its kittens, and they were alive.

Then Prahlād thought, "Oh this is amazing, there is nothing but Rām."

So from that day Prahlād also started to take the name of Rām.

So then Harṇakuś found out about it, and he thought, "If my own son takes the name of Rām then I should kill him first."

[He tries to kill Prahlād in various ways, but they all fail because Rām/Viṣnū protects him.]

Then Harṇakuś thought of his sister, Holikā, who took a fire bath every day. And he told his sister, "You take Prahlād in your lap and take a fire bath and he will die and you will come out."

"Sure, brother, I'll kill him, no problem."

But when she began her bath then Holikā burned up and Prahlād was saved.

So from that day the Holī festival began.

Bhoju Ram asked Mohan:, "After burning Holī what is the sign of Prahlād?" He replied: "Just after we burn Holī we pull it out [of the fire] and put it in the well, and that is Prahlād."

This was the first I had heard of Prahlād's physical representation in the Holī festivities. His "sign" is a charred stump, "delivered" from the flames by women (in spite of Mohan's "we")—a custom that seems to echo the rescue not only of the devotee demon's good son but also of the innocent kittens.

Mohan Mali's knowledge of the Holī story came to him as an oral tradition, one coexisting with Sanskrit texts, with Hindi versions, and these days with media productions. Nevertheless, not everyone in the village has such detailed knowledge. Here is a fragment of a conversation we had with Nathi, a drummer's wife, about the chartering myth of Holī. We had sought her out, after a casual encounter, because she struck us as remarkably articulate about women's ritual practices surrounding Holī. But when I asked her about the story, I didn't learn much:

Ann: Who is Holī?

Nathi: . . . somebody's wife . . . was it Arjun's wife (*Arjun kī bū*)? [She gives up.]

Bhoju Ram: Why do we burn Holī?

Nathi: She was a bad whore.

Bhoju Ram: Why was she bad?

Nathi: You don't know? We saw it on TV. She took her nephew in her lap and sat in the fire. But he didn't burn and he jumped away in the water and that whore burned up. The boy was a darling (*lālyo*); the darling boy is Prahlād and the father's sister was Holī.

Nathi's seemingly casual attitude toward, or disinterest in, the mythology does not by any means reflect ignorance of the festival, its multiple rituals, and their meanings for her and other women. These focus not on Holī but on the *lālyo*, the "darling boy." The Sanskritic, textual narrative's role here seems to be neither a charter for ritual nor a model for reality. It is more like the potter woman's wet clay, out of which ritual and oral exegesis cook meanings.[36]

At dusk on the first night of Holī (March 6 in 1993), little girls initiate the festival by taking cow-dung ornaments they have fashioned and bedecking Holī with them. These will later fuel the flames, when Holī is burned by grown men. I went with Bhoju Ram's daughters and their cousins when they took their ornaments to the nearby schoolyard Holī and scampered home again. For a while, I watched the girls and young women of this household dance and color their hands with henna.

Bhoju Ram and I had decided to observe the Malis' Holī fire, because their community is reputed to be the most "traditionally" inclined, or resistant to social change, among Ghatiyali's major caste groups. The Malis' caste occupation is gardener, but most Mali families in Ghatiyali grow grain, as well as vegetables, and an entire branch are stone quarriers. As we wandered through their neighborhood, passing the time until the fire, we chanced on a cluster of girls who were singing with gusto of the demoness herself. She is not addressed with anger and scorn. She is an honored "lady-guest":

Play, play with the cow-dung ornaments (*barbūliyā*)[37]
Holī is just like a lady-guest (*pāvaṇī*), and she will leave, and so we should play a lot.

Balu Bhai [any girl's brother's name] shakes the berry tree and his sister picks up the berries:
Holī is just like a lady-guest, and she will leave, and so we should play a lot.
O brother go to the country of Lady Holī, seat her in a car, and bring her here.
O Holī, there are so many lice in your hair, so please come soon and I will pick them out.

Picking out lice is an intimate act of affection (although saying someone has lots of lice can be a teasing insult).

I am most struck by the way this song lingers on the comfortable brother-sister relationship—valued, cooperative, and loving. It thus juxtaposes Holī's relationship with her brother, the evil king whom she supports and protects, to the singers' bonds with their beloved brothers. It seems to suggest that Holī's attempt to destroy Prahlād was a way of serving her brother, as a good sister ought to do. It thus evokes identity with the demoness who shares with these girls not only the common affliction of lice but also valued sibling loyalty. Rather than revulsion, I heard a playful identification in their words.

After the song of Holī the same girls spontaneously broke into another very vigorous song of other perilous, but thrilling, possibilities for women:

> O innocent *Śivjī*, my younger sister is going to school while riding on a motor bike (*phaṭphaṭiyā*).
> O *Śivjī*, she studied to the sixteenth class and joined the army.
> She beat the policemen with four sticks and hurt them, and the police grabbed her and brought her.

The girls' song seems to be uncertain about where women's new educational and professional freedoms may lead, but it sounds a decidedly adventurous note.

Later that night, still passing the time until the bonfire, we interviewed a mature man of the same Mali caste as these girls. He sang some verses that describe the modern degenerate era as a time known through the shamelessness of its women.

> The Kali Yug has come while calling, openly.
> In this Kali Yug, ladies are wearing sheer clothing,
> They are walking in the market half-naked,
> They have given up wearing wraps,
> And they haven't the least bit of shame.
> Oh, the men have shaved their mustaches and their masculinity is gone.
> In the Kali Yug, women are smoking cigarettes,
> Their husbands bring them cigarettes to smoke.

In the late twentieth century, Kali Yug that it is, gender ideologies are certainly in flux, and both songs recognize this. Thus, the oral traditions again resound with messages from ancient scripts, reflecting fears of unruly women. But we encounter alternative and diverging interpretations in men's and women's performances.

The girls' song of educational advancement and the man's of shameless women present two strongly contrasting visions of changing sex roles performed on the same occasion in the same community. These visions seem rooted in the contrasting ritual roles of men and women on the night of Holī. Men will beat down the demonic female, whereas it is women's part to rescue the child—with all its potentiality.

Still later, close to midnight, men light the bonfire. At the Mali fire, drunken men sang and danced with abandon. Their songs were graphically sexual and of a genre they share with women—called *keśyā*.[38] A mild verse follows:

> Keśyā, if you want to play then play before Holī,
> Lover, if you want to play then play before Holī;
> Later the fierce sun beats down.

Women do not normally arrive at this scene until both the fire and the men's rowdy singing have died down. In 1993, I had decided that my gray hair and long-term relationships in the village would protect me—and I was determined to witness this festival moment.

Bhoju Ram, my dear friend, host, assistant, advisor, and guardian, seemed willing to go along with this until at the fire I found myself the center of attention from a group of drunken farmers who persistently demanded that I photograph their sexually suggestive dance motions. Bhoju Ram panicked and became enraged, hissing through his teeth in English: "I request you to go back!" Gripped by the scene, and frankly fearing to walk alone in the dark, I stayed put. Bhoju later apologized for his rage, explaining that because I was living in his home, he had to protect my honor as if I were a woman of his own family, and the drunken males' attentions were threatening it.

However, he well understood the passions of an anthropologist. When he saw I would not budge, he channeled his anger into brilliant mid-revelry interviews. Thrusting the recorder right into the heat of the men's action, as they beat the glowing embers with sticks, Bhoju asked them what they were doing. This also served to draw attention away from me:

> Bhoju Ram: Why are you beating Holī?
>
> Mali man: That's just what I was thinking.
>
> Second Mali man: We are not beating Holī we are beating the "darling boy" [*lālyo*].
>
> Bhoju Ram: The "darling boy" was good and took the name of God so why are you beating it?
>
> Gisar Lal Mali: No no no! We are beating Holī because she wanted to burn him.
>
> Shiv Ram Mali: Holī was a woman of bad character [*durāchārī*] and she didn't want anyone to take the name of Rām. . . . Holī is burning, but even so something is saved. . . .

Something is saved. Women, gathered in the street within hearing but not seeing distance, waited a long time for the male revelry to cease. Then, with their own high-spirited jokes and gestures, they set forth to rescue the darling boy.

A physically powerful woman whom I knew quite well, Tulsa Mali, claimed the charred log. Tulsa, proud of her strength, her family, and her skills, was a leader among her caste. She hefted the log to her shoulder and bore it to her house. Bhoju Ram and I trailed behind her:

> Bhoju Ram: Why did you bring this darling boy here?
>
> Tulsa: It is an omen [*sūn*]. If I don't take it then someone else will take it. It is women's work.
>
> Bhoju Ram: Of what is it an omen?
>
> Tulsa: From bringing it our family will grow. After the child is born, we will make a peg for the oxen from it.
>
> . . .
>
> Bhoju Ram: You have the darling boy in your house so your family will grow. Is it good for anything else, like crops, and so forth?
>
> Tulsa: Everything will increase, like grain, animals, people, agriculture, everything.
>
> . . .
>
> Tulsa: It is a matter of satisfying one's soul. It's like: even if the field is dry and there is just a little rain, we put the seeds in—not knowing if there will be rain or not, in the same way, we have the same kind of faith in the darling boy.

The next day, the second day of Holī (*Holī ko dūsro din*), is also called *dhūlendī*, which must derive from the word *dhūl*, for "dust." Men go through the streets in a noisy procession led by a false, mocked king (called *bādśāh*) and engage in all kinds of wild, sometimes violent, horseplay, including inversions of the social order. Women and children stay home or visit neighbors, themselves playing energetically with colored powder. At Bhoju and Bali's house I was vigorously engaged in Holī games. Women rub the powder hard in one another's faces, including teeth and gums. Moods are very high, and appearances are transformed; rose-colored dust fills the air.[39]

Sītalā

Some women do not bathe between *Dhūlendī* and Sītalā's day, seven days later. They may wash their arms and change their clothes, but they should not wash their bodies. Why is this? One person told us Sītalā is a "butcher's wife"; thus she is dirty. This deliberate storing up of women's bodily dirt for seven days makes an explicit link between the two festivals. In referring to "dirt" (*gandagī*), women probably include whatever secretions would accumulate in their private parts. This dirt seems to connect the destruction of Holī, followed immediately by the darling boy's rescue from the fire, with the worship of the Cool Mother—a ritual that explicitly saves children from the deadly fire of fever.[40] I also heard that Sītalā likes being worshipped by menstruating women, something many other deities find offensive and perhaps another sign of her affinity both with the demoness and with women's generative capacities, which are understood to reside in uterine blood. In this regard, the textual traditions themselves support the valuation of female fluids. O'Flaherty speaks of the "blood of defloration" in the *Rig Veda* as "resonant with expressions of fertility."[41] This motif of female blood as beneficently powerful rather than dangerously polluting is a countertheme in other local traditions, such as the popular myth in which the goddess as embodied power is creator of all life and its regenerative potential.[42]

On Sītalā Seventh, the Cool Mother, or "smallpox goddess," embodied in crystal rocks must be ritually persuaded to stay cool. She forbids the lighting of the cooking fire. The night before her festival, women cook double the amount: the evening's usual meal and the food to be eaten cold the next day. The holiday foods are fried breads and doughnuts, treats common to all festivals. Special for Sītalā, though, is *oliyā*, made of thin corn porridge mixed with buttermilk—a very cooling food.

Bali, my companion, prepared her tray carefully on the eve of Sītalā's worship. It included a piece of cloth for Sītalā's wrap, a brass jar that she would fill with water in the morning, henna powder, a colored string, and a pile of seeds. These included wheat, barley, millet, large millet, white beans, corn, and a seed valued for buffalo fodder. Bali had to go to the neighbors to borrow the corn, millet, and barley—déclassé grains that many no longer eat but without which the ritual offerings are lacking.

From ordinary bread dough made with wheat flour, Bali modeled small items to include in her offerings: a cooking hearth; a flour grinder; a pot with a lid and a spoon, representing a pot of *oliyā*; and jewelry. Bali and I waited in the street for the other women of her Gujar community. Each caste or neighborhood group goes together in prearranged order. Finally, a large group gathered, and we walked sedately to the shrine, singing a somber devotional song to Sītalā:

> Honored Mother, a pendent for your forehead, I'll bring.
> Honored Mother, a jewel in your forehead ornament, I'll set.
> Lady, my pox-remover, put pox behind,
> My giver of sweet feasts, Sītalā.

Fulfill me with a son, mother,
Give the other ladies four pox.
You who wraps me in yellow cloth, Sītalā,
Support my life, Sītalā, fulfill me with a son, Mother.

A yellow cloth is worn by a mother after giving birth. Sītalā deals not only in disease and death but also in birth and health. This song acknowledges both aspects, without setting up any striking contrast between them. Like all village women, the goddess desires "a pendant for her forehead."[43] Yet, the lines "Fulfill me with a son, Mother/Give the other ladies four pox" prevent us from imagining an undifferentiated or noncompetitive female solidarity.

Inside the temple, lamps burned before the altar. All the little molded dough models were set down in a jumble. Each worshiper bathed the goddess, put henna on her, stuck multicolored strings to the wet and muddy henna, and sprinkled grains on top of that until Sītalā's aniconic stones were smeared with countless layers of auspicious stuff. The colored squares of cloth, Sītalā Mother's "wraps," were also placed on the shrine. A male priest sat outside, well removed from the action, but collecting his due in cooked food and grain.

After completing their worship, women go behind the temple, and in the loose dirt they create "fields"—using their fingers to make furrows—an action they explicitly call plowing (*hānkno*). In these fields they sow all the seeds left on their trays, which prescriptively are the appropriate seeds for the coming agricultural cycle (to be planted several months later when the monsoon breaks). Although women often do the work of sowing, plowing is ordinarily a tabooed task for them (the situation throughout South Asia and in many other parts of the world as well). I often asked the reasons for this, and only a few claimed that the work was actually too hard for women. More common responses had to do with appropriateness and auspiciousness and decorum. Were a woman to drive the plow, people told me, it would be as if she were to sit on her husband's head. I find this a striking image.

In this ritual, merrily, women plow. Then one covers another's eyes from behind, and the woman whose eyes are covered says something such as "If I die then show this buried treasure to my children [naming them]." This was explained to me as a bequest. The term I translate "buried treasure" is *khāī kotā*: *khāī* refers to a large ditch, and *kotā* is a common household bin for storing grain. Apparently rulers of old sometimes placed large grain bins in the ground in case of future famine. Thus women ritually claim a concealed but vast grain treasure, as well as the right to pass it on to their children. This is contrary to normal inheritance practices, just as their plowing is contrary to the normal division of labor. Perhaps their claim is to the fertility of the earth itself, which is linked by the next move of the ritual to active sexuality.[44]

In this move from the symbolic fields to Bhairūṅjī's shrine and back to the main goddess temple in the village, women broke into the bawdy songs called *keśyā*—the same songs, virtually, that men were singing at the Holī fire. In these songs women laughingly attribute sexual voraciousness to one another.[45] One woman pantomimed the motions of sexual intercourse; another put her hand somewhat forcefully if briefly between my legs. "Its all a joke, don't mind," she smiled. When they reach the temple, five serious songs of the goddess are performed, and the frolic is over.

Bāṛī Tīj

Bāṛī Tīj, or Grand Third, is celebrated in Ghatiyali on the third day of the dark half of Bhādra, the fourth month of the rainy season. It is called "grand" to distinguish it from a lessor "small Tīj"—the bright third of Śrāvaṇ, in the preceding month. Small Third, ideally, finds married daughters returning to their homes and married women and girls swinging on swings and singing rainy season songs. Grand Third is perhaps less playful, more serious in its purpose. As Lalas describes it in his Rajasthani-Hindi dictionary, Grand Third in Rajasthan is a fast celebrated by women whose husbands are alive and a day on which clothes, sweets, and jewelry are sent to married daughters from their fathers' houses.[46] This pan-regional definition exactly pinpoints the chief features of Grand Third in Ghatiyali. It involves a day-long fast undertaken by wives for their husbands' well-being. Moreover, as the story will testify, gifts from natal homes are critical in the minds of participants. From their ascetic resolution on Tīj, women seem to gain authority. Tīj songs imperiously summon absent spouses home to their lonely brides.[47] In Ghatiyali's Grand Third story, a husband follows direct orders from his fasting wife.

On August 28, 1980, I joined a group of brahmin women who were performing Tīj worship. The rains were bad in 1980, and women had told me repeatedly that their festivals were not nearly as festive as they would have been were the crops better. Nonetheless, I taped their songs and stories; photographed the ritual; and asked my brahmin research assistant, Vajendra Kumar Sharma, a relative of several participants, to write detailed descriptive notes. My account of Grand Third is based on these materials, as the event is rather less vivid in my memory than Holī and Sītalā in 1993.

My own notes on Grand Third include the following discussion of the worship's focus, which clearly puzzled me:

> Tried to find out who/what Tīj is; photographed two figures drawn in red on the wall said to be Tīj; Tīj said to be like Gangaur, all are *rūps* [forms] of Parvati. The meaning is the same as Gangaur, to worship the condition? of the *suhāg* [auspiciously married woman] and pray for its immortality.[48] The women were saying as they sat around after the *pūjā* that *suhāg* was equal to *bhagvān* [the Lord].

A photograph reveals that the markings on the wall are rather nondescript, if not wholly aniconic. Before them, however, is set an arrangement of "*nīm* branches tied together into the form of a beautiful plant," as Vajendra admiringly wrote. *Nīm* has multiple religious meanings and multiple ritual and medicinal uses. I have not noted it elsewhere in such close association with the goddess. However, at Grand Third worship, these *nīm* branches seem a three-dimensional, organic extension of the blurry divinity on the wall. Women tie their ritual colored strings and hang their cloth offerings on this *nīm* branch structure.[49]

Whereas the ritual ingredients and actions of Tīj worship are structurally similar to those for many other women's worships, including that performed for Sītalā, Grand Third calls for special attention to the signs of auspicious wifehood: jewelry and *sindhūr* (vermilion)—the deep red powder married women use to mark their hair partings, conventionally interpreted as both active sexuality and fertility. Each woman who was worshiping Tīj arrived at the home of the hostess, Nagina Bai, carrying a platter that contained worship ingredients. The women set down their plates in front of the wall drawing and the *nīm* branches. They put auspicious marks on the wall painting and lit small oil lamps and incense. They then placed their cloth offerings on the *nīm* branches, tied colored strings to them, and made offerings of henna. They offered the special sweets for Grand Third worship, called *sātū*, to Tīj Mother, along with grain.

Each woman then mixed water and milk in her polished platter and looked five times at the reflection of her jewelry in it. Each woman held a bottle of vermilion to her forehead. Vajendra, slightly diffident in the face of women's ritual knowledge, wrote of this act: "Perhaps the meaning is that women are requesting Tīj to keep their vermilion (auspicious wifehood) immortal forever." Other manipulations of ornaments were performed, and mantras—of which I have no record—were spoken. After all the women had finished the ritual, they sang Tīj songs. Nagina Bai, the hostess, then told the story of Tīj and two others. After hearing the stories, all the women touched the feet of women senior to them and took blessings from them—acts of closure for many domestic rituals. All the women went up to the roof, happily, to look at the moon; each then returned to her own house to break her fast by eating *sātū*—blessed leftovers of the goddess.

In Ghatiyali, as elsewhere, songs and stories of Tīj are remarkable for women's authoritative voices—sometimes playful, sometimes dead serious. In one song, the wife demands that her husband leave his job and come home to her. Her authority derives both from her outspoken love and from the holiday's enduring traditions. Summoning these conjoined authorities, she devalues external considerations of money or the prestige of city employment. Here women's domestic power extends outward to city domains via the romantic love that binds husband to wife. The refrain is as follows:

> Whether your work's in Kishan Garh or Mukan Garh,
> husband-lord,
> Having heard [this song of] Tīj, come home.

Verses include these:

> Your job is beloved to you, husband-lord,
> Lord, you are beloved to me.
>
> I will make you leave your job, husband-lord,
> For the festival of Tīj has come.

Most extraordinary to me was the story Ghatiyali women told on Tīj. This oral tale has little in common with the published pamphlet versions of Tīj's story—all of which have to do with Parvati's ascetic feats. Although Ghatiyali's Tīj heroine also denies herself to manipulate her man, the entire tone is different. Even when I first translated it, in 1981, the Tīj story struck me as both comical and radical.

The protagonist of the story of Grand Third, as I recorded it in Ghatiyali, is one of seven daughters-in-law. On the holiday of Tīj, she alone does not receive any of the "fine cakes" (*sātū*) that women's natal families traditionally send to their daughters' marital homes for this festival. These fine cakes, offered in Tīj worship, are then consumed by participants to break their fasts, as we have just seen. The other six daughters-in-law do receive *sātū* and taunt the unlucky one. Disconsolate, the heroine declares her intention not to break her fast at all but rather to go to bed hungry. Her evidently doting husband hears her resolve in alarm, fearing for her delicate life should she go to bed without eating. She demands that he bring her fine cakes, and the besotted man breaks into a rich merchant's house to get them. Nabbed by the police, he explains his overriding concern for his wife's health. The merchant not only drops the charges but also promises always to supply the seventh daughter-in-law with sweets and other gifts at all future Tīj festivals.

Here is Ghatiyali's story of Grand Third as Nagina Bai told it in 1980:

The Story

There was once a shopkeeper who had seven sons and seven daughters-in-law. A few days before the holiday of Grand Third, six of the daughters-in-law received fine cakes from their parents' homes, but the seventh son's wife received none. Her family was very poor and they could not afford to send any cakes.

On the morning of Grand Third when all the women of the house were going to the well to fill their waterpots, the six older daughters-in-law were muttering angrily as they walked along: "We can never leave the cooking fire. We never have a holiday rest. *Our* families sent fine cakes for Grand Third but none have come for our husband's younger brother's wife and so we will be forced to work and prepare hers."

They were grumbling in this way when the youngest brother's wife heard them and said, "Leave off, it's my own trouble! Why are you complaining? Let it be, it's no business of yours." So she spoke. She had become very angry.

That night when it was time to perform the worship of Grand Third, the seventh daughter-in-law went angrily to lie down and sleep. All the other women did the worship, and after worshiping together they broke their fasts with the fine cakes sent by their families. But the youngest brother's wife had none, so she just stayed inside in anger.

Then her husband came and asked her, "Have you eaten or not?"

She replied, "Oh leave me alone. I am keeping a complete fast. I will take nothing but bitter leaves[50] tonight and I will eat no food until tomorrow."

Her husband said, "What do you mean? What's the matter?"

She said, "What can I do? Everyone else received fine cakes from their parents' homes and I received none, so what is there for me to eat? I cannot bear to take any of your brothers' wives' cakes so I will eat nothing."

Her husband asked her, "What do you need?"

She answered, "Even if you have to steal them, bring me fine cakes made of chickpea flour. If you don't bring them, then I will keep a total fast and eat nothing but bitter leaves and drink only water and I will not take any food until tomorrow."

Then her poor husband thought, "Where can I go?" It was the middle of the night. He hurried to the house of a rich merchant, crept into that rich man's house and immediately lit the cooking fire. Then he found chickpeas and ground them in the grinder. After that he took a clay pot full of butter and emptied it into a frying pan. He fried the ground chickpea flour in the butter, then he added a lot of sugar and made the mixture into round fine cakes.

Just as the husband was coming out of the merchant's house carrying the stolen cakes, the village watchman, making his rounds, was passing by. The watchman saw him, shouted "Thief! Thief! Thief!" and grabbed him. He took him straight to the police station and sat him down there. Soon a crowd of people gathered and began to taunt him: "What a place you picked to do your thieving." They mocked him and prodded him with sticks. They said, "Look, the son of a father of unblemished character has taken to thievery."

But then a few wise and gentle persons came and said, "Let us hear his story. Listen to what he has to say."

The husband said: "Look what's going on here. They grabbed me and put me in the police station but meanwhile I don't know if my woman will live or die. She is sitting alone in anger. For this reason I stole, for this reason I committed a crime. I went to that merchant's house and ground chickpeas and lit the fire and took out butter and sugar and made fine cakes. I stole one kilo of chickpeas and a half-kilo of sugar and as much butter as was in the pot, for she is a stubborn woman and she won't eat anything else. For this reason I was hurrying to bring her the cakes when the watchman came and shouted, 'Thief! Thief! Thief! and grabbed me and took me to the police station. Everyone is calling me a thief. And meanwhile I am sitting here and who knows if she will die or live, or if she will eat or won't eat."

Now the merchant whose house he had robbed heard this whole speech and immediately said, "You should take twice as much, right now, as you have already taken. And next year before Grand Third, I will send fine cakes to your wife. Let my home be her parents' home."

So they set the husband free and at once he hurried home and gave his wife the cakes and she ate and he also ate. Both the husband and his wife ate and went to sleep.

[Town gossips repeat the whole event.]

The next year, four days before Grand Third, the rich merchant sent a long skirt, a shawl, cosmetics, bangles and everything—a complete outfit for the seventh daughter-in-law as well as the fine cakes. He also sent a separate outfit for the mother-in-law and for the husband's sister. For the brothers' wives he sent blouses and shawls. So from that very day the younger brother's wife always received fine cakes from her parents' home.

Grand Third Mother, as you made her parents' home, so make the whole world's.

What are we to make of the young wife who puts her husband in danger for her own seemingly selfish ends? The fast of Tīj is ultimately a fast, like many others, intended to sustain the condition of auspicious wifehood. But the story might well be read as an ironic commentary on the many tales of self-sacrificing women who suppress their own needs and desires for the sake of their male kin. Why, it seems to ask in all simplicity, should men not sacrifice themselves too, to succor their wives? In the context of rainy season sexual longings, this tale—together with the song of Tīj, which also places the wife's needs for company above the family's for income—hints at a complex of cultural motifs that approve the fulfillment of women's desires.

The happy ending vindicates the husband's devotion: the burglarized victim not only drops the charges but also adopts the daughter-in-law and personally sends her sweets, as well as new clothes and other adornments—full vindication for the stubborn wife and her doting spouse. All of these fine outcomes are swept under the umbrella blessing of the mother goddess of Grand Third.

Anne Pearson, in her study of brahmin women's ritual fasts in the city of Banaras, reports on Tīj as performed at the home of a woman with a masters' degree in Sanskrit. In spite of the female participants' literacy, a male pandit comes to their house to read the story aloud from a pamphlet and explain it to them in colloquial Hindi. "The women remained silent throughout," Pearson notes. This is in striking contrast to the Rajasthani celebration, in which all ritual action, verbal and nonverbal, is done by women. Vajendra was present only on sufferance, for my sake.

Pearson tells us that the Tīj story used in Banaras "highlights the extreme asceticism Pārvatī underwent in order to win Śiva as her husband. The fasting women listening to the story are presumably meant to identify with Pārvatī's grueling austerities." Pearson concludes: "The lesson for women observing this *vrat* is clear: steadfastly adhering to the difficult fasting requirement will eventually result in the fruition of one's desire—for young girls, to get a good husband like Śiva, and for married women, to win or better preserve their *saubhāgyavatī* state"—the state, that is, of auspicious wifehood. Even so, Pearson observes, there may be more empowering lessons for women in the Tīj story: "By observing austerities one gets power not only to achieve one's goals but also to control one's own life, rather than be controlled by others (notably by men)."[51]

This underlying message becomes the whole story in Ghatiyali's version. What seems so refreshing in the vernacular telling is its light-hearted, nearly mocking approach to the whole business of women's asceticism. The Śiva-like husband is a love-struck fool, a rather inept if sincere slave to his wife's desires. Yet they are both richly rewarded—by the goddess of Grand Third.[52]

Conclusion: Soft Claims

These festivals offer a kaleidoscope of ritual and narrative imagery: envisionings and imaginings in words, icons, stories, and songs of what female power is and does. Taken together they may still seem as impermanent and unproductive as toy fields plowed with fingers. Yet piled up as they are in minds and days, in songs and stories and practices taught and shared from year to year, mother to daughter, mother-in-law to daughter-in-law, they possess weight. My attempt here has been in part to highlight claims made in these cultural performances for female authority in worship and knowledge and against female devaluation on biological or cosmological grounds. I have also tried to present women's views of female power—divine, demonic, and mortal—differing from those found in male-authored texts and male-dominated rituals. To summarize:

1. At Holī:

   Conceptually, the female demonic is humanized, her kinship acknowledged. Although complete identification is certainly avoided, complete horror is never posed.

   Ritually, it is men who vividly act out aggressive, demonic violence, whereas women take the part of rescuers and life givers.

2. On Sītalā's day:

   Conceptually, the goddess who afflicts children with disease and fever is the very goddess who is pleased with female body grime and menstrual pollution and who grants fertility to newlywed couples and protects children's health.

   Ritually, women transgress the taboo on plowing and claim the right to bequeath property—recognizing the intimate connection between these two.[53] Thus they assert opposition to these doubled ritual and economic disempowerments.

3. On Baṛī Tīj:

   Conceptually, women's self-determination in marriage arrangements and their capacity for ascetic feats are stressed. Grand Third is high-caste pageantry, explicitly defined as important only for those groups who forbid widows' remarriage or divorce. Tīj might appear to come closer than the other two festivals to a view of females as subservient half bodies. Yet, in song and story, women claim a romantic power to motivate doting husbands and through this, as Pearson also observes, to control situations that may otherwise seem squarely in the hands of men.

   Ritually, on Grand Third women worship auspicious wifehood as identical with God. In doing so, they link their own complex domestic struggles with those of the goddess Parvati, who pitted her will and spiritual strength against all male advice and resistance and won her heart's desire.

In this chapter I have attempted to highlight the claims women themselves make for female authority in worship and knowledge, beginning with Shobhag Kanvar's claim to possess the Subtle Veda and to wield its power. Elsewhere in this volume, Vasudha Narayanan explores the implicit authority of the female commentator Tirrukoneri Dāsyai. Here I have focused on village women's explicit conceptualizations. I have called conceptualizations of gender evident in women's celebrations "counterpoints." I find these offer both blunt and subtle denials of the female devaluation and subordination that exist in the dominant, male-authored discourse—whether on biological or on cosmological grounds. I have explored in detail the ways in which women, through narratives, worship, celebrations, and plastic and verbal arts, claim authority in contradistinction to male-authored prescriptions for their sex.

Neither I nor other writers sympathetic to the coexistence of multiple gender hegemonies—writers of what I have earlier called type 2 bent—have argued that women's counterpoint claims give them any significant advantages in economic or political realms. However, like the other authors in the volume (whether textual, historical, or ethnographic in their outlook), I cannot view women's words and acts as meaningless play or—worse—delusive hindrances to understanding their actual subordination.[54] All the Rajasthani women I know well understand the several apparent disadvantages of being female; nevertheless, they take great pleasure and satisfaction in ritually enacting expressions of female worth and power.

Notes

In writing and speaking on Rajasthani women for over a decade, my accumulated personal and intellectual debts are vast and must be acknowledged collectively. For knowledge featured in this particular chapter, first and deepest thanks go to Bali Gujar for sharing her home and her worship with me. I also thank Bhoju Ram Gujar, Lindsey Harlan, Shobhag Kanvar, Tulsa Mali, Gloria Raheja, Vajendra Kumar Sharma, Susan Wadley, and all members of the Working Group on Gender and Indic Traditions of Authority. Research trips to Rajasthan between 1979 and 1993 were enabled by fellowships from the American Institute of Indian Studies and a CIES (Council for International Exchange of Scholars) Fulbright Scholar Award for Research, and I am grateful for this support. This chapter was first proposed, and eventually composed for a seminar/workshop on Gender, Religion and Social Definition, sponsored by the Centre of South Asian Studies, SOAS (School for Oriental and African Studies), University of London, and organized by Julia Leslie. Some portions of text appearing here are identical with, or adapted from, my contribution to Julia Leslie and Mary McGee, Eds., *Invented Identities: The Interplay of Religion and Politics in India* (Delhi: Oxford University Press, 2000), the volume emerging from that conference. I thank both Julia Leslie and Laurie Patton not only for the ways in which their respective editorial labors improved my work but also for allowing me to participate in both their seminars and volumes. I am grateful as well to Oxford University Press, Delhi and New York.

1. Gloria Goodwin Raheja and Ann Grodzins Gold, *Listen to the Heron's Words: Reimagining Gender and Kinship in North India* (Berkeley: University of California Press, 1994), p. 165.

2. Ann Grodzins Gold, *Fruitful Journeys: The Ways of Rajasthani Pilgrims* (Berkeley: University of California Press, 1988), pp. 167–68.

3. See, for example, Wendy Doniger O'Flaherty, *The Rig Veda* (New York: Penguin Books, 1981); Patrick Olivelle, *Upaniṣads* (New York: Oxford University Press, 1996).

4. "Unbelievers and infidels, Untouchables and women, were forbidden to learn Sanskrit, the sacred language, because they might defile or injure the magic power of these words. If the

sacred chants were to be spoken by such people, it was believed, the words would be polluted like milk contained in the skin of a dog." Wendy Doniger O'Flaherty, *Other Peoples' Myths* (New York: Macmillan, 1988), p. 57.

5. For the "god trick" as an epistemological strategy, see Donna Haraway, *Simians, Cyborgs, and Women: The Reinvention of Nature* (New York: Routledge, 1991). Chandra T. Mohanty offers an acute critique of the literature on Indian women as passive victims that is relevant here; see her now classic "Under Western Eyes: Feminist Scholarship and Colonial Discourses," in *Third World Women and the Politics of Feminism*, Chandra T. Mohanty, Ann Russo and Lourdes Torres, Eds. (Bloomington: Indiana University Press, 1991), pp. 51–80; see also Raheja and Gold, *Heron's Words*, pp. 30–38.

6. Anjali Bagwe, *Of Woman Caste: The Experience of Gender in Rural India* (London: Zed Books, 1995), p. 208.

7. Patricia Jeffery and Roger Jeffery, *Don't Marry Me to a Plowman! Women's Everyday Lives in Rural North India* (Boulder, Colo.: Westview Press, 1996), pp. 17–18.

8. Raheja and Gold, *Heron's Words*, p. 182.

9. Anju Kapur, "Theorizing Women Writing in India," *South Asia Bulletin* 14, no. 1 (1994), 114-21, quote on 114.

10. Susie Tharu and K. Lalita, Eds., *Women Writing in India 600 B.C. to the Present* (New York: Feminist Press, 1991), pp. 1–37, quote on p. 36.

11. As Anju Kapur ("Theorizing Women Writing") points out in her review of Tharu and Lalita, theoretical stances that originated in Marxism, poststructuralism, and various forms of feminist criticism have influenced not only their particular treatment of Indian women's writings but also, undoubtedly, motivate many type 1 and type 2 authors. I choose here to focus not on the theories that drive these authors but on the results they present, the interpretations they offer, and the ways in which they handle descriptive material. This is of greater relevance to my project here, founded in ethnographic substance; to take the alternative route would be to write an entirely different chapter.

12. Declan Quigley provides a perfect example; he writes of Raheja and Gold's work: "There is an attempt to argue that behind their veils, or behind closed doors, women's defiance shows through. But it too often comes across as a hollow, tittering gesture, like that of the schoolchild who sticks up two fingers when the teacher's back is turned"; see his "Review of *Listen to the Heron's Words* by Gloria G. Raheja and Ann G. Gold," *Journal of the Royal Anthropological Institute* 2, no. 2 (1996), 391–92, quote on p. 392. Evidently, Quigley has failed to read the book carefully and failed to read the last two chapters entirely before dismissing Indian women's voices. His approach is symptomatic of an extreme type 1 perspective; he has no need to consider any evidence, having made up his mind and known the truth long before such evidence is set before him. For a male anthropologist's experience of similar dismissive responses to his presentations on a women's oral performance genre (Warao laments in eastern Venezuela) as socially powerful, see Charles Briggs, "'Since I Am a Woman, I Will Chastise My Relatives': Gender, Reported Speech, and the (Re)production of Social Relations in Warao Ritual Wailing," *American Ethnologist* 19, no. 2 (1992), 337–61.

13. As Bina Agarwal has documented so extensively, until recent years most systems of property inheritance in South Asia were disadvantageous to women; see *A Field of One's Own: Gender and Land Rights in South Asia* (Cambridge: Cambridge University Press, 1994). I make no claims that women's expressive traditions or their cultural critiques serve to put land titles in their names. In Ghatiyali I do know several cases in which independent women have defied the entire system of arranged patrilocal marriage and patrilineal inheritance and, in fact, hold and farm land in their natal village, but I shall not argue from exceptions here.

14. Nita Kumar, "Introduction," in Nita Kumar, Ed., *Women as Subjects* (Calcutta: Stree, 1994), pp. 1–25.

15. Sherry B. Ortner, "Gender Hegemonies," *Cultural Critique*, Winter 1990, pp. 35–80, quote on p. 45.

16. Raheja and Gold, *Heron's Words*, pp. xxvi–xxxiii.

17. James C. Scott, *Weapons of the Weak: Everyday Forms of Peasant Resistance* (New Haven, Conn.: Yale University Press, 1985).

18. See, for example, Gold, *Fruitful Journeys*, pp. 123–30; Raheja and Gold, *Heron's Words*.

19. Bagwe, *Woman Caste*, pp. 65–69.

20. Ibid., p. 200.

21. Selected examples would include Parita Mukta, *Upholding the Common Life: The Community of Mirabai* (Delhi: Oxford University Press, 1994); Kirin Narayan, "Songs Lodged in Some Hearts: Displacements of Women's Knowledge in Kangra," in *Displacement, Diaspora and Geographies of Identity*, S. Lavie and T. Swedenburg, Eds. (Durham, N.C.: Duke University Press, 1996), pp. 181–213; Kirin Narayan, "Women's Songs, Women's Lives," *Manushi*, No. 81 (1994), 2–10; Gloria Goodwin Raheja, "Crying When She's Born and Crying When She Goes Away: Marriage and the Idiom of the Gift in Pahansu Song Performances," in *Hindu Marriage from the Margins*, Lindsey Harlan and Paul Courtright, Eds. (New York: Oxford University Press, 1995), pp. 19–59; Debra Skinner, Dorothy Holland, and G. B. Adhikari, "The Songs of Tīj: A Genre of Critical Commentary for Women in Nepal," *Asian Folklore Studies* 53, no. 2 (1994), 259–305.

22. An entire bibliography is evoked here; some samples are Lila Abu-Lughod, *Veiled Sentiments: Honor and Poetry in a Bedouin Society* (Berkeley: University of California Press, 1986); Jill Dubisch, Ed., *Gender and Power in Rural Greece* (Princeton, N.J.: Princeton University Press, 1986), pp. 3–41; Laurel Kendall, *Shamans, Housewives, and Other Restless Spirits: Women in Korean Ritual Life* (Honolulu: University of Hawaii Press, 1985); Jane M. Young and Kay Turner "Challenging the Canon: Folklore Theory Reconsidered from Feminist Perspectives," in *Feminist Theory and the Study of Folklore*, Susan Tower Hollis, Linda Pershing, and M. Jane Young, Eds. (Urbana: University of Illinois Press, 1993), pp. 9–28.

23. See, for example, Saurabh Dube, "Myths, Symbols and Community: Satnampanth of Chhattisgarh," in *Subaltern Studies VII: Writings on South Asian History and Society*, P. Chatterjee and G. Pandey, Eds. (Delhi: Oxford University Press, 1992), pp. 121–58; Gyan Prakash, *Bonded Histories: Genealogies of Labor Servitude in Colonial India* (Cambridge: Cambridge University Press, 1990); Gyan Prakash, "Becoming a Bhuinya," in *Contesting Power*, D. Haynes and G. Prakash, Eds. (Berkeley: University of California Press, 1991), pp. 45–174.

24. Nicholas B. Dirks, "Ritual and Resistance: Subversion as a Social Fact," in *Culture/Power/History: A Reader in Contemporary Social Theory*, Nicholas B. Dirks, Geoff Eley, and Sherry B. Ortner, Eds. (Princeton, N.J.: Princeton University Press, 1994), pp. 483–503, quote on pp. 501–502. See also Lila Abu-Lughod, "The Romance of Resistance: Tracing Transformations of Power Through Bedouin Women," in *Beyond the Second Sex: New Directions in the Anthropology of Gender*, Peggy Reeves Sanday and Ruth G. Goodenough, Eds. (Philadelphia: University of Pennsylvania Press, 1990), pp. 313–37. Following Foucault, as does Dirks, Abu-Lughod also traces modes of resistance in relation to power. Her focus is on Bedouin women's words; she carefully recognizes the limitations on their potency without denying its existence.

25. I lack the space here for comparative ethnography; each village has its particular customs, but there is a region-wide character to most festivals, in part because of the circulation of women who carry the practices of their natal villages into their marital homes. For two accounts of the annual festival round in rural Rajasthan see Brij Raj Chauhan, *A Rajasthan Village* (New Delhi: Vir Publishing House, 1967), and S. L. Srivastava, *Folk Culture and Oral Tradition* (New Delhi: Abhinav Publications, 1974).

26. See Leona M. Anderson, *Vasantotsava: The Spring Festivals of India: Texts and Traditions* (New Delhi: D.K. Printworld, 1993), for a richly documented study of "spring festivals" in San-

skrit textual sources. Her discussion of the "demoness" associated with childhood diseases, obscenity, and fire is particularly relevant to Ghatiyali's ethnography.

27. I have discussed women's activities and expressive traditions on Calf Twelfth in considerable detail elsewhere, finding it to be an explicit performance of female power over death; see Gold, *Fruitful Journeys*, pp. 123–32.

28. For women's vows, see Anne M. Pearson, "*Because It Gives Me Peace of Mind*": *Ritual Fasts in the Religious Lives of Hindu Women* (Albany: State University of New York Press, 1996), and Susan S. Wadley, "*Vrats*: Transformers of Destiny," in *Karma: An Anthropological Inquiry*, Charles F. Keyes and E. Valentine Daniel, Eds. (Berkeley: University of California Press, 1983), pp. 147–62.

29. Considerable material exists on Holī and Sītalā in rural North India. Holī is most often treated for its carnivalesque reversals of social hierarchies, including gender hierarchies; see McKim Marriott, "The Feast of Love," in *Krishna: Myths, Rites, and Attitudes*, Milton B. Singer, Eds. (Chicago: University of Chicago Press, 1966), pp. 200–12; Susan S. Wadley, *Struggling with Destiny in Karimpur, 1925–1984* (Berkeley: University of California Press, 1994), pp. 227–30. For considerations of Sītalā's figure in offering insights into constructions of femaleness, see Edward C. Dimock, "A Theology of the Repulsive: The Myth of the Goddess Sītalā," in *The Divine Consort: Radha and the Goddesses of India*, J. S. Hawley and D. M. Wulff, Eds. (Berkeley, Cal.: Graduate Theological Union, 1982), pp. 184–203; Pauline Kolenda, "Pox and the Terror of Childlessness: Images and Ideas of the Smallpox Goddess in a North Indian Village," in *Mother Worship: Theme and Variations*, James J. Preston, Ed. (Chapel Hill: University of North Carolina Press, 1982), pp. 227–50; and Susan S. Wadley, "Sītalā," *Asian Folklore Studies* 39, no. 1 (1980), 33–62. For Tīj in India, see Pearson, *Ritual Fasts*, pp. 158–63, 239–44, and Raheja and Gold, *Heron's Words*, pp. 131–32, 142–45. For Tīj in Nepal, see Dorothy C. Holland and Debra G. Skinner, "Contested Ritual, Contested Feminities: (Re)forming Self and Society in a Nepali Women's Festival," *American Ethnologist* 22, no. 2 (1995), 279–305; and Dorothy Holland, William Lachicotte Jr., Debra Skinner, and Carole Cain, *Identity and Agency in Cultural Worlds* (Cambridge, Mass.: Harvard University Press, 1988), pp. 228–32, 254–69.

30. For intertextuality in oral performance genres, see Joyce Burkhalter Flueckiger, *Gender and Genre in the Folklore of Middle India* (Ithaca, N.Y.: Cornell University Press, 1996).

31. Raheja and Gold, *Heron's Words*, p. 71.

32. Other interpretations of South Asian women's experience of rituals, especially those dedicated to female power, include Kathleen M. Erndl, *Victory to the Mother: The Hindu Goddess of Northwest India in Myth, Ritual, and Symbol* (New York: Oxford University Press, 1993); Lindsey Harlan, *Religion and Rajput Women: The Ethic of Protection in Contemporary Narratives* (Berkeley: University of California Press, 1991); Sasheej Hegde and Seemanthini Niranjana, "Of the Religious and the (Non)feminine: Open Questions," *Contributions to Indian Sociology* 28, no. 1 (1994), 107–22; Leslie and McGee, *Invented Identities*; Pearson, *Ritual Fasts*; William Sax, *Mountain Goddess: Religion and Politics in the Central Himalayas* (New York: Oxford University Press, 1991).

33. For Vedic sources of women's ritual disadvantages, see Frederick M. Smith, "Indra's Curse, Varuna's Noose, and the Suppression of the Woman in the Vedic Srauta Ritual," in *Roles and Rituals for Hindu Women*, Julia Leslie, Ed. (Delhi: Motilal Banarsidass, 1992), pp. 17–45.

34. Sanskrit, Hiraṇyakaśipu; for his story in the *Purāṇas*, see Cornelia Dimmitt and J. A. B. van Buitenen, Eds. and Trans., *Classical Hindu Mythology* (Philadelphia: Temple University Press, 1978), pp. 76–79.

35. Picture not an oven but an open-air pile of cow-dung fuel in which the unfired pots are nested, with more cow-dung patties layered on top and crowned with broken pots (*āv*).

36. For the ways in which similar processes have worked on the epic *Ramayana*, see Paula Richman, Ed., *Many Rāmāyaṇas: The Diversity of a Narrative Tradition in South Asia* (Berkeley: University of California Press, 1991).

37. This is a special term, used, as far as I know, only for the ornaments crafted by girls to decorate Holī.

38. For *keśyā*, see Raheja and Gold, *Heron's Words*, pp. 45–47, 62–66.

39. The day after Holī, also a ritually busy one for Rajasthani women, is the prescribed occasion for Brother Second (*Bhāī Doj*), for the first Dasā Mātā story, and for *ḍhūṇḍanā*—a protective ritual for first sons born during the preceding year. For more details, see Raheja and Gold, *Heron's Words*, p. 152.

40. Speculatively, I might connect this with the still common practice for women not to bathe for a ritually prescribed series of days after childbirth (nine but often reduced to seven or even three).

41. Wendy Doniger O'Flaherty, *Women, Androgynes, and Other Mythical Beasts* (Chicago: University of Chicago Press, 1980), p. 20.

42. Ann Grodzins Gold, "Gender, Violence and Power: Rajasthani Stories of Shakti," in *Women as Subjects: South Asian Histories*, Nita Kumar, Ed. (Charlottesville: University Press of Virginia, 1994), pp. 26–48. For complexities of menstrual pollution from different categories of Hindu textual sources, see Julia Leslie, "Some Traditional Indian Views on Menstruation and Female Sexuality," in *Sexual Knowledge, Sexual Science: The History of Attitudes to Sexuality*, Roy Porter and Mikulas Teich, Eds. (Cambridge: Cambridge University Press, 1994), pp. 63–81. For other positive associations with vaginal blood in Indian ritual contexts, see Frederique Marglin, "Gender and the Unitary Self: Looking for the Subaltern in Coastal Orissa," *South Asia Research* 15, no. 1 (1995), 78–130; Frederique Apffel Marglin and Purna Chandra Mishra, "Sacred Groves: Regenerating the Body, the Land, the Community," in *Global Ecology: A New Arena of Political Conflict*, Wolfgang Sachs, Ed. (London: Zed Books, 1993), pp. 197–207. For other female sexual fluids, see Frederique Marglin, "Refining the Body: Transformative Emotion in Ritual Dance," in *Divine Passions: The Social Construction of Emotion in India*, Owen Lynch, Ed. (Berkeley: University of California Press, 1990), pp. 212–36; O'Flaherty, *Women, Androgynes*, p. 43.

43. For women's desires expressed in songs, see Ann Grodzins Gold, "Outspoken Women: Representations of Female Voices in a Rajasthani Folklore Community," *Oral Tradition* 12, no. 1 (1997), 103–33.

44. No one has more eloquently summed up the symbolic force of the seed and field complex in Hindu gender constructions than Leela Dube; she documents at length the reproductive metaphor of male seed and female field and sums up its implications: "The symbolism is utilized by the culture to underplay the significance of woman's contribution to biological reproduction." Dube connects this metaphor to patrilineal agrarian economy, and hence to male ownership of both land and progeny; see her masterful germinal article, "Seed and Earth: The Symbolism of Biological Reproduction and Sexual Relations of Production," in *Visibility and Power: Essays on Women in Society and Development*, Leela Dube, Eleanor Leacock, and Shirley Ardener, Eds. (Delhi: Oxford University Press, 1986), pp. 22–53, quote on p. 38. See also Wendy Doniger, "Playing the Field: Adultery as Claim Jumping," in *The Sense of Adharma*, Ariel Glucklich, Ed. (New York: Oxford University Press, 1994), pp. 169–88. For evocative associations between women and water, more positive than those between women and earth, see Anne Feldhaus, *Water and Womanhood: Religious Meanings of Rivers in Maharashtra* (New York: Oxford University Press, 1995).

45. See Raheja and Gold, *Heron's Words*, pp. 63–65.

46. Sitaram Lalas, *Rajasthani Sabad Kos*, 9 vols. (Jodhpur: Rajasthani Shodh Sansthan, 1962–1978), vol. 2, p. 1531.

47. Note that Tīj takes place in the rainy season—a season which, according to Charlotte Vaudeville, "almost all folk-poetry in India" connects with "sexual frustration"; see her *Bārahmāsā in Indian Literatures* (Delhi: Motilal Banarsidass, 1986), p. 28.

48. Gangaur in Ghatiyali has much in common with Tīj; it, too, is a celebration of Parvati's ascetic practice. For Gangaur, see Ann Grodzins Gold, "From Demon Aunt to Gorgeous Bride: Women Portray Female Power in a North Indian Festival Cycle," in Leslie and McGee, *Invented Identities*, pp. 203–30.

49. For *nīm* (*Melia azadirachta* or *Azadirachta indica*) in Rajasthani religious and medical lore, see Prabhakar Joshi, *Ethnobotany of the Primitive Tribes in Rajasthan* (Jaipur: Printwell, 1995), p. 199.

50. These are *nīm* leaves; thus the story makes a connection with the physical ritual.

51. See Pearson, *Ritual Fasts*, pp. 160–61.

52. Some of the most interesting work on Tīj comes from Nepal, where a Tīj festival appears to be more public and more important. Here again the chartering myth is that same story of Parvati's austerities, but the songs are of women's sorrow (*dukha*). In these songs, Debra Skinner, Dorothy Holland, and G. B. Adhikari point out, women offer "a critical commentary on gender relations and on the wider political situation that has dominated them both as females and as poor villagers"; moreover, Tīj songs in Nepal are distinctly "incongruent with the rituals that bracket their performance." See "Songs of Tīj," pp. 259–305, quote on p. 261.

53. Bina Agarwal offers a powerful discussion of this link: "But it is the taboo against women plowing, found in most cultures, and, to my knowledge, certainly in all communities of South Asia, which presents perhaps the biggest obstacle. . . . This taboo makes dependence on men unavoidable under settled cultivation, and severely constrains women's ability to farm independently"; (*Field of One's Own*, pp. 212–13).

54. See Raheja and Gold, *Heron's Words*, pp. 182–93.

Afterword

LAURIE L. PATTON

One of the emergent metaphors in this book has been that of the jewel: how it authorizes and constrains women at the same time, how it provides a metaphor to create and comment alongside male textualists, and how it provides an impetus to that creativity. Whereas the historical material that depicts the ambivalent role of jewelry in women's lives is abundant, the contemporary material is equally rich and relevant. One ethnographer of religion[1] observed recently that young, educated Keralite women, arriving in Hyderabad to conduct research at the American Social Research Council, simply refused to wear any kind of gold, even small earrings. As they saw it, gold acted as the sole measure of a woman's worth in the more traditional parts of Keralite society (which nonetheless enjoys its reputation as the most literate state in India). "A woman is worth her weight in gold" is the traditional Hindu view against which they were arguing. And yet, taken in another context, that very same statement could be a liberating rallying cry about the near priceless value of a woman in contemporary society. Once again, in this most postmodern of contexts, we see the glittering ambivalence of the image of jewelry in women's lives.

This small anecdote, as well as many of the chapters in this volume, raise both direct and indirect questions about how ancient texts and contemporary enthnographies can be used to improve the lives of women in India today. Some (Findly and Jamison) advocate a subtler reading of presently available texts so that Indian history can be used in a realistic way. Some (McGee, Patton, and Narayanan) advocate new interpretive practices that utilize traditional Sanskrit and Tamil categories. Some (Falk and Bacchetta) open the way for an ongoing ideological critique of reform and nationalist movements' perspectives on women. Others (Young and Gold) imply more indirectly that the emphasis on the constructive details of women's lives can go a long way toward uncovering strategies for their flourishing.

Whatever the strategies, and whatever the individual scholar's opinions about the role of activism within the academic field of Indology, a new era is opening up for textual practices by and about women. First, we can envision a new role for textual studies in a myriad of traditional Hindu topics: women in the Gṛhya Sūtras, the "domestic" manuals of the Vedic period; women in the plays of Kālidāsa; the role of women in religious commentarial work, particularly that in Tamil, Hindi, Marathi, Gujurati, Telugu, Punjabi, Bengali, and other vernacular languages, emerging in the past two centuries; a careful and thorough history of women's participation in sacrificial rituals; women and Vedāntan textual traditions; and so on. The list is endless, once the lens has become as finely focused as a jeweler's lens must be.

Second, of particular interest is the growing number of Hindu women in the role of textual elites. Many Sanskrit departments at Indian universities find increasing enrollments of women—sometimes even outnumbering that of men, as the men look for more prestigious work in science, engineering, and computer technology. Moreover, increasing numbers of women are becoming ritual leaders in roles traditionally reserved for brahmin men. What are their textual practices, and how do they differ from men's in the same role? There are, of course, rare institutions geared toward the education of women as *pujāris* and as reciters of mantras. These institutions deal with households that find the services of women equal to that of men.[2] And then there are the small and impoverished temples, where there is no man left to perform the rites. As one woman *pujāri* in a small temple in Pune said to me: "You do the Sanskrit parts, and I'll do the Marathi. Then we can learn from each other. That's all we can do for now since we have no one else to guide us." Ethnography of these temples and women, as well as a careful study of their textual practices, would be invaluable.

Third, it is clear from the suggestions of Falk and Bacchetta that it is no longer sufficient to speak of "women and Indian nationalism"; rather, it is important at this stage, with the voluminous number of postcolonial studies on this topic, to begin to write a history of women and Indian nationalism. Clearly, there are continuities and differences to be traced in the ways in which different nationalist movements use images of women. Why, for instance, was there more of a place for the celibate female *samnyasinī* in the late twentieth-century RSS than there was in the colonial reform movements? Why could these women, as paramilitaries with weapons, protect other Hindu women's bodies and honor in a way that was not allowed to women in the late nineteenth century? Are the goddess figures, the Bhārat Mātas and the Kālīs of the colonial period, somehow differently configured in the Aṣṭabhūja or the Dūrga of the late twentieth-century Samiti?

Finally, there is the important question of Indian women, Western women, and the Hindu textual tradition in the information age. Our conference was able to support Indian and Western scholars working in North America and Europe, and it is a source of regret that more scholars working in India could not be present. The chance for Western and Indian scholars and feminists to work together occurs so rarely. There needs to be a companion volume to *Jewels of Authority*, published in India by Indian scholars, on these very same issues. Although many volumes of this kind already exist and are cited in this volume, in fact, one might argue that *Jewels of Authority* is simply a response to those works already produced in India. Another, equally valuable companion project might be a volume in which the two cultures of textual scholarship meet and interact.

This era of new textual practices also has an important practical corollary: the rapid and economical exchange of texts is still very much in the hands of Western economies. Textual scholars working on women in those countries can and should make a commitment to publishing their work in India, to reading Indian scholarship, and to buying Indian books.[3] Scholars and universities with the funds should organize support for libraries and documentation centers that are currently unable to exchange their valuable resources with centers of research outside of India. Scholarly book exchanges should be set up with Indian libraries. Scholars should actively promote fellowships for Indian scholars who are working on these topics to travel to the United States, as well as the other way around. Although the Internet gives us a kind of *saṃvāda*, or colloquy, which makes the possibility of exchange between Indian and Western scholarship on women all the more possible, these other forms of practice can also promote *saṃvāda* at the level of actual textual publication.

Such economic, as well as intellectual commitments, might give another, more textual meaning to the phrase "A woman is worth her weight in gold." It would mean that the garlands of our intellectual work about women could be a gift from one group of scholars to another, across both continents and generations in both directions.

Notes

1. I am grateful to Joyce Flueckiger, personal communication, for this observation.
2. See the work of Mary McGee, presentation to the Working Group on Gender and Authority in Indic Traditions, April 1994, and her forthcoming article on these institutions.
3. It is clear that the high price of Western books about India (including my own) and the difficulty of their purchase there, is one of the things that makes it extremely difficult for texts to be both widely disseminated and accounted for.

Bibliography

Primary Hindi, Sanskrit, and Tamil Sources

Aitareya Brāhmaṇa. Satyavrata Sāmaṣrami, Ed. Calcutta: Satya Press, 1895–1906.

Aṅguttaranikāya, vol. 1: Richard Morris Ed. (1885), rev. A. K.Warder (1961); vol. 2: Richard Morris, Ed. (1888); vol. 3: E. Hardy, Ed. (1897); vol. 4: E. Hardy, Ed. (1899); vol. 5: E. Hardy, Ed. (1900). Oxford: Pali Text Society.

Āpastamba Dharma Sūtra. Georg Blahler, Ed. Bombay: Education Society's Press, 1868–1871.

Āpastamba Dharma Sūtra. M. Winternitz, Ed. Vienna: A. Holder, 1887.

Āpastamba Śrauta Sūtra. Richard Garbe, Ed. Calcutta: Baptist Mission Press, 1882–1902.

Āpastambha Dharma Sūtra. 2nd ed. Umeschandra Pandey, Ed. Kasi Sanskrta Granthamala, 93. Varanasi: Chowkhamba Sanskrit Series Office, 1969.

Āśvalāyana Śrauta Sūtra. Rāmanārāyana Vidyāratna, Ed. Calcutta: Baptist Mission and V_lmiki Presses, 1868–1871.

Āśvalāyana Gṛhya Sūtra. Rāmanārāyana Vidyāratna and Anandachandra Vedāntāvāgīsa, Eds. Calcutta: Baptist Mission Press, 1869.

Atharva Veda. Śrīrāma Śarma, Ed. Delhi: Munshiram Manoharlal, 1962.

Atharva Veda Saṃhitā. 4 vols. V. Bandhu Hoshiarpur, Ed. Vishveshavaranand: Vedic Research Institute, 1960–1962.

Baudhāyana Dharma Sūtra. E. Hultzsch, Ed. Nendeln, Liechtenstein: Kraus Reprint, 1966.

Baudhāyana Dharma Sūtra, 2nd ed. Umeschandra Pandey, Ed. *Kasi Sanskrta Granthamala*, 104. Varanasi: Chowkhamba Sanskrit Series Office, 1972 (1934).

Bhāgavata Purāṇa, 1st edition. Samskarta Jagadisalala Sastri, Ed. Dilli: Motilala Banarasidasa, 1983.

Bhāskara, Laugākṣi. *Arthasaṃgraha*. A. B. Gajendragadkar and R. D. Karmarkar, Eds. Delhi: Motilal Banarsidass, [1934]/1984.

Bhaṭṭa, Kamalākara. *Nirṇayasindhu*. Sivadatta Dādhīca, Ed. Bombay: *Śrī* Veṅkateśvara Press, Saka [1815]/Vikrama 1950.

Bhaṭṭa, Nīlakaṇṭha. *Vyavahāra Mayūkha*. P. V. Kane, Ed. Poona: Bhandarkar Oriental Research Institute, 1926.

Brahmanda Purāṇa. J. L. Shastri, Ed. Delhi: Motilal Banarsidass, 1973.

Bṛhadāraṇyakopaniṣad. In *The Principal Upaniṣads*, S. Radhakrishnan, Ed. London: George Allen & Unwin, 1953.

Bṛhaddevatā, 2 vols. Arthur Anthony Macdonell, Ed. and Trans. *Harvard Oriental Series*. Cambridge: Harvard University Press, 1904.

Carudatta of Bhāsa. Em. J. Nanjundaradhya, Ed. n.p., 1962.

Chandogya Upaniṣad, 2nd edition. Upaniṣad Series. Swami Swahananda, Trans. Madras: Sri Ramakrishna Math, 1965.

Chāndogyopaniṣad. In *The Principal Upanisads*. S. Radhakrishnan, Ed. London: George Allen & Unwin, 1953.

The Dāyabhāga of Jimutavahana. A. Subrahmanya Sastri, Ed. Varanasi: A. Subrahmanya Sastri, 1973.

Dīghanikāya. vols. 1 and 2. T. W. Rhys Davids and J. Estlin Carpenter, Eds. (1890, 1903); vol. 3: J. Estlin Carpenter, Ed. London: Pali Text Society.

Dūrga Āchārya. *Yāska's Nirukta with Dūrga's Commentary*, 2 vols. H. M. Bhadkamkar, Ed. *Bombay Sanskrit and Prakrit Series*, nos. 73 and 85. Bombay: Government Central Press, 1918.

Encyclopaedia of Religion and Ethics. James Hastings, Ed. New York: Scribner's, 1917.

Gautama Dharma Sūtra. L. Srinivasacharya, Ed. Mysore: Government Branch Press, 1917.

Gautama Dharma Sūtra. Umeschandra Pandey, Ed. *Kasi Sanskrta Granthamala*, 172. Varanasir: Chowkhamba Sanskrit Series Office, 1966.

Gobhila Gṛhya Sūtra. Chandrakanta Tarkala-ftkara, Ed. Calcutta: Baptist Mission Press, 1880.

Hiraṇyakeśi Gṛhya Sūtra (or *Gṛhyasūtra of Hiraṇyakeśin)*. J. Kirste, Ed. Vienna: A. Holder, 1889.

Jayākhyasaṃhitā of Pāñcarātra Āgama. Embar Krishnamacharya, Ed. Baroda: Oriental Institute, 1967.

Kāśikā: A Commentary of Pāṇini's Grammar. Aryendra Sharma, Khanderao Despande, and D. G. Padhye, Eds. Sanskrit Academy Series: 17, 20, 23, 32. Hyderabad: Sanskrit Academy, Osmania University, 1969–.

Kāthaka Samhitā. Sripada Sarma Bhattacarya, Ed. Aundha, Bharata Mudranalya, 1943.

Kātyāyana Śrauta Sūtra. H. G. Ranade, Ed. Pune: H. G. Ranade and R. H. Ranade, 1978.

Kātyāyana Śrauta Sūtra and Other Vedic Texts. Lokesh Chandra, Ed. Sata-pitaka Series, vol. 304. Nẹw Delhi: International Academy of Indian Culture, 1982.

Kauṣītaki Brāhmaṇa. B. Lindner, Ed. Jena: H. Costenoble, 1887.

Kauṣītakibrāhmaṇopaniṣad. In *The Principal Upaniṣads*, S. Radhakrishnan, Ed. London: George Allen & Unwin, 1953.

Kauṭilya. *The Kauṭilya Arthaśāstra*, 2nd ed., 2 vols. R. P. Kangle, Ed. and Trans. Bombay: University of Bombay, 1969.

Kelkar, Lakshmibai. *Pathadarshini Shriramakatha*. Nagpur: Sevika Prakashan, 1988.

Kelkar, Kakshmibai. *Stri-Ek Urja Kendra: Strivishayak Vicharon Ka Sankalan*. Nagpur: Sevika Prakashan, n.d.

Khādira Gṛhya Sūtra. A. Mahadeva Sastri and L. Srinivasacharya, Eds. Mysore: Government Branch Press, 1913.

Kṛṣna Yajur Veda. Sripada Damodara, Ed. Paradi, Ji. Balasada: Svadhyaya-Mandala, 1983.

The Kumarasaṃbhava of Kālidāsa. Gautama Patela, Ed. Dilli: Bharatiya Buka Karporesana, 1996.

The Kumarasaṃbhava of Kālidāsa: With the Two Commentaries, Prakasika of Arunagirinatha and Vivarana of Narayanapandita. Trivandrum Sanskrit Series, vols. 27, 32, 36. T. Ganapati Sastri, Ed. Trivandrum: Travancore Govt. Press, 1913–1914.

Kṛṣṇamācāryar, Ed. Bhagavadviṣayam: *Commentaries on Nammāḻvār's* Tiruvāymoli. Madras: Nobel Press, 1925–1930.

Lalas, Sitaram. *Rajasthan Sabad Kos*, 9 vols. Jodhpur: Rajasthan Shodh Sansthan, 1962–1978.

Maitrāyaṇī Saṃhitā. Leopold von Schroeder, Ed. Leipzig: F. A. Brockhaus, 1881–1886.

Majjihimanikāya, vol. 1: V. Trenckner, Ed. (1888); vols. 2 and 3. Robert Chalmers, Ed. (1896, 1899). London: Pali Text Society.

The Mālatīmādhava. of Bhavabhuti. Michael Coulson and Roderick Sinclair, Eds. Delhi and New York: Oxford University Press, 1989.

The Mālavikāgnimitra of Kalidāsa. Poona: S. Seshadri Ayyar, 1896.

Manusmṛti. Mahdmahopidhyiya Canginitha, Ed. Calcutta: Royal Asiatic Society of Bengal, 1939.

Manusmṛti, with the Manubhāṣya of Medhātithi, 3 vols. Ganganatha Jha, Ed. Bibliotheca Indica, work 256, nos. 1516, 1522, 1533. Calcutta: Asiatic Society, 1932–1939.

The Mārkaṇḍeya Purāṇa. F. Eden Pargiter, Trans. Delhi: Indological Book House, 1969.

The Mārkaṇḍeyamahapurāṇam. Delhi: Nag Publishers, 1983.

Mīmāṃsā Sūtra, with the commentary of Śabara, 6 parts. V. G. Apte, Ed. *Ānandāśrama Sanskrit Series*, 97. Poona: Ānandāśrama Press, 1930–1932.

Miśra, Maṇḍana. *Vidhiviveka, with the commentary Nyāyakaṇikā of Vacaspati Miśra*. Mahaprabhu Lal Goswami, Ed. Varanasi: Tara Publications, 1978.

The Mitākṣara of Vijñaneśvara. Calcutta: Educational Press, 1832.

Mitramiśra. *Vīramitrodaya*. Benares: Chowkhamba Sanskrit Series Office, 1935.

Mṛcchakatika. Gangasagara Rayah, Ed. Varanasi: Caukhambha Samskrta Bhavana, 1997.

Mumukūpati. Sri. Kirusnasvami Ayyankar, Ed. Tirucci, Ktaikkumitam: S. Kirusnasvami Ayyankar, 1970.

Mutal Tiruvāntati of Poykaiy Ālvār. n.p.,1962.

Naradī Saṃhitā. Raghava Prasada Chaudhary, Ed. Tirupati: Kentiya Sanskrit Vidyapeetha, 1971.

Pāṇini. *Aṣṭādhyāyī of Pāṇini*. Austin: University of Texas, 1987.

Padma Saṃhitā, 2 vols., Pancaratra Parisodhanaparisatprakasanam, vols. 3–4. Seetha Padmanabhan and V. Varadachari, Eds. Madras: Pancaratra Parisodhana Parisat, 1974.

Parasara Bhaṭṭa, 1st edition. Srinivasa Visistadvaita granthamala, vol. 2. Svami Srikrsnacarya, Ed. Delhi: Indore Centre, Bharati Research Institute, 1971.

Pāraskara Gṛhya Sūtra. Adolf Friedrich Stenzler, Ed. Leipzig: F. A. Brockhaus, 1876–1878.

Patañjali. *Vyākaraṇa-Mahābhāṣya*, Âhnikas 1–3. K. V. Abhyankar and Jayadev Mohanlal Shukla, Eds. Poona: Bhandarkar Oriental Research Institute, 1975.

Pauśkara Saṃhitā. Tirupati-Rastriyasamskrtavidyapithagranthamala, vol. 54. Tirupatih: Rastriyasamskrtavidyapitham, 1991.

Pauśkara Saṃhitā. Yatiraja Sampathkumara, Ed. Bangalore: A Srinivasa Aiyangar and M. C. Thirumalachariar, 1934.

Periya Tirumoḻi. n.p., 1976.

Periyavaccānpiḷḷai Śrīsūktimālā. Ayankar R. Srinivas, Ed. Tirucci: n.p., n.d.

Raghunandana. *Smṛtitattva*. Calcutta: Pandit Jībānanda Vidyāsāgara, 1895.

Ṛgveda, 2 vols. Theodor Aufrecht, Ed. Bonn: Adolph Marcus, 1877.

Ṛg Veda Saṃhitā, together with the Commentary of Sāyaṇa Āchārya, 4 vols. F. Max Muller, Ed. Varanasi: Chowkhamba Sanskrit Series, 1966.

Śabarasvāmī. *Jaiminīya Mīmāṃsā Bhāṣyam*, vol. 5. Yudhisthira Mimamsaka, Ed. Bahalagarha: Ramalal Kapur Trust, 1977–1986.

Samiti. *Deep Stambh: Akhil Bharatiya Trayodesh Traivarshik Sammelan*. Pune: Hindusthan Mudranalay Nov. 7, 1986.

——. *Pratah: Smaraniya Mabilaen*. Nagpur: Sevika Prakashan, 1990.

——. *Shrimati Lakshmibai Kelkar Ki Jivani*. Nagpur: Sevika Prakashan, 1989.

Śamyuttanikāya, vols. 1–5. M. Leon Feer, Ed. London: Pali Text Society, 1884, 1888, 1890, 1894, 1898.

Śāṅkhāyana Gṛhya Sūtra. H. Oldenberg, Ed. Leipzig: F. A. Brockhaus, 1876.

Śatapatha Brāhmaṇa. Ācarya Satyavrata Sāmaśramī, Ed. Calcutta: Baptist Mission Press, 1903–1912.

The Ślokavārttika of Kumārila Bhaṭṭa. Trivandrum: CBH Publications, 1990.

Śiva Purāṇa, 2 vols. Bombay: Venkatesvara Press, 1900.

Skanda Purāṇa. K. Śrīkṛṣṇadāsa, Ed. Bombay: Veṅkateśvara Press, 1910.

Smṛticandrandrikā, 6 vols. R. Shamasastry and L. Srinivasachargya, Eds. Mysore: Government Branch Press, 1914–1921.

Śrīpraśna Saṃhitā. Edited by Seetha Padmanabhan. Tirupati: Kendriya Sanskrit Vidyapeetha, 1969.

Sriranganarayana, Jiyar, Ed. *Aṣṭadasarahasyam of Piḷḷailokācārya*. Madras: Ananta Press, 1911.

Srīviṣṇusahasranāma Bhāgavadguṇadarpanakhyam Śriviṣṇusahasra-nāmabhāṣyam. P. B. Annagaracarya, Ed. Kancipuram, 1964.

Taittirīya Āraṇyaka. A. Mahadeva Sastri and K. Rangacarya, Eds. Delhi: Motilal Banarsidass, n.d.

Taittirīya Brāhmaṇa, 4 vols. Delhi: Motilal Banarsidass, 1985.

Taittirīya Prātiśākhya. Madras University Sanskrit Series, no. 1. V. Venkatarama Sharma, Eds. Madras: University of Madras, 1930.

Taittirīya Saṃhitā. E. Roer and E. B. Cowell, Eds. Calcutta: Baptist Mission Press, 1860–1899.

Taittirīya Saṃhitā, 2 vols. Albrecht Weber, Ed. *Indische Studien*, 11, 12. Leipzig: F. A. Brockhaus, 1871–1872.

Taittirīya Upaniṣad. Swami Lokeswarananda, Trans. Calcutta: Ramakrishna Mission Institute of Culture, 1996.

The Tantravārtika of Kumarila Bhatta: A Gloss on Sabara Svami's Commentary on the Mimams Sūtras. 3 vols. Benares Sanskrit Series. Gangadhara Sastri, Ed. Benares: Braj Bushan Das, 1882–1903.

Tiruvāymoḻi. Pu. Ra. Purusottma Nayatu, Ed. Madras University Tamil Dept. publication no. 18, 1–10. 1959–72.

The Tuptīkā of Kumarila of Bhatta: A Gloss on Sabara Svami's Commentary on the Mimamsa Sūtras. Benares Sanskrit Series, no. 18. Gangadhara Sastri, Ed. Benares: Braj Bushan Das, 1904.

Upādhyāya, Kāśīnātha. *Dharmasindhu*. Vaśiṣtha Datta Miśra, Ed. *Kashi Sanskrit Series*, 183. Varanasi: Chowkhamba Sanskrit Series Office, 1968.

Vaikhāna Śrauta Sūtram. W. Caland, Ed. and Trans.. New Delhi: Ramanand Vidya Bhavan, n.d.

The Vajra-suci of Aṣvaghosa, 1st ed., Harajivanadas prachyavidya granthamala, vol. 3. Ramanayan Prasad Dwivedi, Ed. Varanasi, Bharata: Chaukhamba Amarabharati Prakashana, 1985.

Vāmana. *Kāśikā; Pāṇiniyavyākaraṇasūtravṛttiḥ*, 4th ed., 2 vols. *Kaśī Samskrta Granthamala*, 37. Varanasi: Chowkhamba Sanskrit Series Office, 1969–1972.

Vāsiṣṭha Dharma Sūtra. Alois Anton Fuhrer, Ed. Bombay: Government Central Book Depot, 1883.

Vasiṣṭha Dharma Sūtra. Śrīvasiṣṭha Dharmaśāstram; Aphorisms on the Sacred Laws of the Aryas, as Taught in the School of Vasiṣṭha. A. A. Fuhrer, Ed. Rpt. Delhi: Indological Book House, 1983.

The Veda of the Black Yajus School, 1st edition. Harvard Oriental Series, vols. 18–19. Arthur Berriedale Keith, Trans. Cambridge: Harvard University Press, 1914.

Venkataraman, S. *Araiyar Cēvai*. Madras: Tamilputtakālāyam, 1985.

The Vikramorvaśīya of Kālidāsa, Sanskrit Series, vol. 1. M. R. Kale, Ed. Bombay: Sharada Kridan Press, 1898.

Vinaya Piṭakam, 4 vols. Hermann Oldenberg, Ed. London: Pali Text Society, [1879]/1969, [1880]/1977, [1991]/1984, [1888]/1984.

The Vīramitrodaya of Mitramiśra. 12 Vols. Varanasi: Caukhamba Samskrta Sirija Aphisa: Pradhana Vitaraka Krshnadasa Akadami, 1987.

Viṣṇusaṃhitā. M. M. T. Ganapati Sastri, Ed. Delhi: Sri Satguru Publications, 1990.

Viṣṇu Smṛti, with commentary of Nandapaṇḍita. *Adyar Library Series*, 93. Madras: Adyar Library and Research Center, 1964.

Viśvāmitra Saṃhitā. Undemane Shankara Bhatta, Ed. Tirupati: Kentriya Sanskrit Vidyapeetha, 1970.

Viśveśvara. *Subodhinī*. Bombay: S. S. Setlur and J. R. Gharpure.

The Vyavahāra Mayūkha of Nilakantha. Vishwanath Narayan Mandlik, Ed. New Delhi: Asian Publication Services, 1982.

Yàjñavalkyasmṛti, with the commentary Mitākṣarā of Vijñāneśvara. Shastri Moghe, Ed. Nirnayasagar Press Edition, 1892; rpt. Delhi: Nag Publishers, 1985.

Secondary Sources and Translations

Abu-Lughod, Lila. "The Romance of Resistance: Tracing Transformations of Power Through Bedouin Women." In *Beyond the Second Sex: New Directions in the Anthropology of Gender*, Peggy Reeves Sanday and Ruth G. Goodenough, Eds., pp. 313–37. Philadelphia: University of Pennsylvania Press, 1990.

——. *Veiled Sentiments: Honor and Poetry in a Bedouin Society*. Berkeley: University of California Press, 1986.

Acharya, Kala. *Purāṇic Concept of Dāna*. Delhi: Nag Publishers, 1993.

Agarwal, Bina. *A Field of One's Own: Gender and Land Rights in South Asia*. Cambridge: Cambridge University Press, 1994.

Anagol-McGinn, Padma. "The Age of Consent Act (1991) Reconsidered: Women's Perspectives and Participation in the Child-Marriage Controversy in India." *South Asia Research* 12, no. 2 (November 1992), 78–99.

Anderson, Benedict. *Imagined Communities: Reflections on the Origin and Spread of Nations*. London: Verso, 1991.

Anderson, Leona M. *Vasantotsava: The Spring Festivals of India Texts and Traditions*. New Delhi: D. K. Printworld, 1993.

Ayyangar, Rajagopala, *Śrīmad Rahasyatrayasāra*, Ed. Kumbakonan: Agnihothram Ramanuja Thathachariar, 1956.

Bacchetta, Paola. "All Our Goddesses Are Armed: Religion, Resistance and Revenge in the Life of a Militant Hindu Nationalist Woman." In *Against All Odds: Essays on Women, Religion and Development from India and Pakistan*, Kamla Bhasin, Ritu Menon, and Nighat Said Khan, Eds., pp. 133–56. Delhi: Kali for Women, 1994; condensed version in *Bulletin of Concerned Asian Scholars* 25, no. 4 (October–December 1993), 38–51.

——. "Communal Property/Sexual Property: On Representations of Muslim Women in a Hindu Nationalist Discourse." In *Forging Identities: Gender, Communities and Nations*, Z. Hasan, Ed., 188–225. New Delhi: Kali for Women, 1994.

——. *La construction des identités dans les discours nationalistes hindous*. Paris: Presses Universitaires de France, in press.

——. "Hindu Nationalist Women as Ideologists: Rashtriya Swayamsevak Sangh, Rashtra Sevika Samiti, and Their Respective Projects for a Hindu Nation." In *Embodied Violence: Communalizing Women's Sexuality in South Asia*, Kumari Jayawardena, Ed. New Delhi: Kali for Women, 1996.

——. "Militant Hindu Nationalist Women Re-imagine Themselves: Notes on Mechanisms of Expansion/Adjustment." *Journal of Women's History* 10, no. 4 (1999), 125–47.

Bagwe, Anjali. *Of Woman Caste: The Experience of Gender in Rural India*. London: Zed Books, 1995.

Bakhtin, Mikhail, and P. N. Medvedev. *The Formal Method in Literary Scholarship*, A. J. Wehrle, Trans. Baltimore: Johns Hopkins University Press, 1978.

Basham, A. L. *History and Doctrines of the Ājīvikas: A Vanished Indian Religion*. London: Luzac & Company, 1951.

Basu, Amrita. "Feminism Inverted: The Real and Gendered Imagery of Hindu Nationalism." *Bulletin of Concerned Asian Scholars* 25, no. 4 (1993), 25–37.

Basu, Apama, and Bharati Ray. *Women's Struggle: A History of the All India Women's Conference 1927–1990*. New Delhi: Manohar, 1990.

Basu, Aparna. "A Century's Journey: Women's Education in Western India." In *Socialisation, Education, and Women: Explorations in Gender Identity*. New Delhi: Sangham Books, 1988.

Bayly, C. A. "Rallying Around the Subaltern," *Journal of Peasant Studies* 16.1 (1998), 110–120.
Bhat, M. S. *Vedic Tantrism: A Study of the Ṛg-Vidhāna of Śaunaka*. Delhi: Motilal Banarsidass, 1987.
Bloomfield, M. "On the Etymology of the Particle Om." *Journal of the American Oriental Society* 14 (1890), cl–clii.
Borthwick, Meredith. *The Changing Role of Women in Bengal* 1849–1905. Princeton, N.J.: Princeton University Press, 1984.
Bose, Nemi Sadhan. *The Indian Awakening in Bengal*. Calcutta: K. L. Mukhopadhyay, 1969.
Breckenridge, Carol A., and Peter Van Der Veer, Eds. *Orientalism and the Postcolonial Predicament: Perspectives on South Asia*. Philadelphia: University of Pennsylvania Press, 1993.
Briggs, Charles. "'Since I Am a Woman, I Will Chastise My Relatives': Gender, Reported Speech, and the (Re)production of Social Relations in Warao Ritual Wailing." *American Ethnologist* 19, no. 2 (1992), 337–61.
Buhler, Georg, Trans. *The Laws of Manu. Sacred Books of the East*, vol. 25. Oxford: Clarendon Press, 1886; rpt. New York: Dover Publications, 1969.
van Buitenen, J. A. B "Aksara." *Journal of the American Oriental Society* 79 (1959), 176 -87.
Burke, Marie Louise. *Swami Vivekananda in the West: New Discoveries*, 3rd ed. Vols. 1 & 2, *His Prophetic Mission*. Calcutta: Advaita Ashrama, 1983–1987.
Carman, John. *The Theology of Rāmānuja*. New Haven, Conn.: Yale University Press, 1974.
Carman, John, and Vasudha Narayanan. *The Tamil Veda: Piḷḷān's Interpretation of the Tiruvāymoḻi*. Chicago: University of Chicago Press, 1989.
Chakravarti, Uma. "Whatever Happened to the Vedic *Dasi*? Orientalism, Nationalism, and a Script for the Past." In *Recasting Women: Essays in Colonial History*, Kumkum Sangari and Sudesh Vaid, Eds. New Delhi: Kali for Women, 1989.
Chatterjee, Partha. "Colonialism, Nationalism and Colonized Women: The Contest in India." *American Ethnologist* 16.4 (1989), 634–60.
——. *The Nation and Its Fragments: Colonial and Postcolonial Histories*. Princeton: Princeton University Press, 1993.
Chauhan, Brij Raj. *A Rajasthan Village*. New Delhi: Vir Publishing House, 1967.
Clooney, Francis X. *Thinking Ritually: Rediscovering the Pūrva Mīmāṃsā of Jaimini*. Vienna: De Nobili Research Library, 1990.
Coburn, Thomas. *Encountering the Goddess*. Albany: State University of New York Press, 1991.
Cohn, Bernard. *An Anthropologist among the Historians and Other Essays*. Delhi and New York: Oxford University Press, 1991.
Coward, Harold G., Julius J. Lipner, and Katherine K. Young, Eds. *Hindu Ethics: Purity, Abortion, and Euthanasia*, McGill Studies in the History of Religions. Albany: State University of New York Press, 1989.
Dalmia, Vasudha, and Heinrich von Stietencron, Eds. *Representing Hinduisms: The Construction of Religious Traditions and National Identity*. New Delhi: Sage, 1995.
Damodaran, Gurusamy. *Ācārya Hrdayam: A Critical Study*, 1st ed. With a foreword by Sir C. P. Ramaswamy Aiyer. Tirupati: Tirumala Tirupati Devasthanams, 1976.
Deleuze, Gilles, and Félix Guattari. *l'Anti-Oedipe*. Paris: Minuit, 1972.
Deshpande, Kusumavati. *Ranade: His Wife's Reminiscences*. Government of India: Publications Division, 1963.
Deussen, Paul. *Sixty Upanisads of the Veda*, 2 parts. V. M. Bedekar and G. B. Palsule, Trans. Delhi: Motilal Banarsidass, 1980.
Devi, Sunity. *The Autobiography of an Indian Princess*. London: John Murray, 1921.
Dimmitt, Cornelia, and J. A. B. van Buitenen, Eds. and Trans. *Classical Hindu Mythology*. Philadelphia: Temple University Press, 1978.
Dimock, Edward C. "A Theology of the Repulsive: The Myth of the Goddess Sītalā." In *The*

Divine Consort: Radha and the Goddesses of India, J. S.Hawley and D. M. Wuff, Eds., pp. 184–203. , Cal.: Graduate Theological Union, 1982.

Dirks, Nicholas B. "Ritual and Resistance: Subversion as a Social Fact." In *Culture/Power/History: A Reader in Contemporary Social Theory*, Nicholas B. Dirks, Geoff Eley, and Sherry B. Ortner, Eds., pp. 483–503. Princeton, N.J.: Princeton University Press, 1994.

Doniger, Wendy. "Playing the Field: Adultery as Claim Jumping." In *The Sense of Adharma*, Ariel Glucklich, Ed., pp. 169–88. New York: Oxford University Press, 1994.

Doniger, Wendy, with Brian K. Smith. *Laws of Manu*. London: Penguin Books, 1991.

Dube, Leela. "Seed and Earth: The Symbolism of Biological Reproduction and Sexual Relations of Production." In *Visibility and Power: Essays on Women in Society and Development*, Leela Dube, Eleanor Leacock, and Shirley Ardener, Eds., pp. 22–53. Delhi: Oxford University Press, 1986.

Dube, Saurabh. "Myths, Symbols and Community: Satnampanth of Chhattisgarh." In *Subaltern Studies VII: Writings on South Asian History and Society*, P. Chatterjee and G. Pandey, Eds., pp. 121–58. Delhi: Oxford University Press, 1992.

Dubisch, Jill, Ed. *Gender and Power in Rural Greece*. Princeton,, N.J.: Princeton University Press, 1986.

Dutt, G. S. *A Woman of India: Being the Life of Saroj Nalini (Founder of the Women's Institute Movement in India)*. London: Hogarth Press, 1929.

Dutt, Romesh Chunder. *A History of Civilization in Ancient India*, vol. 1. Calcutta: Thacker, Spink, 1889.

Dutt, Sukumar. *Buddhist Monks and Monasteries of India: Their History and Their Contribution to Indian Culture*. London: George Allen & Unwin, 1962.

Edgerton, Franklin, Trans. and Ed. *Mīmāṃsa Nyāya Prakāśa*, 2nd ed. Delhi: Satguru Publications, 1986.

Eggeling, Julius, Trans. *The Śatapatha-Brāhmaṇa. Sacred Books of the East*, vols. 12, 26, 41, 43, 44. Delhi: Motilal Banarsidass, [1882, 1885, 1894, 1897, 1900]/1963.

Elizarenkova, Tatyana. *The Language and Style of the Vedic Ṛṣis*. Albany: State University of New York Press, 1994.

Engels, Dagmar. "The Age of Consent Act of 1891: Colonial Ideology in Bengal." *South Asia Research* 3, no. 2 (1983), 107–33.

Erdosy, George, Ed. *The Indo-Aryans of Ancient South Asia: Language, Material Culture and Ethnicity*. Berlin: Walter de Gruyter, 1995.

Erndl, Kathleen M. *Victory to the Mother: The Hindu Goddess of Northwest India in Myth, Ritual, and Symbol*. New York: Oxford University Press, 1993.

Falk, Nancy Auer. "Exemplary Donors of the Pāli Tradition." In *Ethics, Wealth, and Salvation: A Study in Buddhist Social Ethics*, Russell F. Sizemore and Donald K. Swearer, Eds., pp. 24–143. Columbia: University of South Carolina Press, 1990.

Feldhaus, Anne. *Water and Womanhood: Religious Meanings of Rivers in Maharashtra*. New York: Oxford University Press, 1995.

Findly, Ellison Banks. "Ananda's Case for Women." *International Journal of Hindu Studies*, July 1996.

——. "Forging a Balance: The Dynamics of Giving in Early Buddhism," *International Journal of Hindu Studies*, April 1996.

Flax, Jane. "Postmodernism and Gender Relations in Feminist Theory." *Signs* 12.4 (1987), 621–43.

Flueckiger, Joyce Burkhalter. *Gender and Genre in the Folklore of Middle India*. Ithaca, N.Y.: Cornell University Press, 1996.

Fontanille, Marie-Therese. *Avortement et Contraception dans la Medecine Greco-Romaine*. Paris: Laboratiore Searle, 1977.

Forbes, Geraldine. "Caged Tigers: First Wave Feminists in India." *Women's Studies International Forum* 5, no. 6 (1982), 526–36.

———. "Goddesses or Rebels? The Women Revolutionaries of Bengal." *The Oracle* (Netaji Research Bureau, Calcutta) 2, no. 2 (April 1980).
Frauwallner, Erich. *The Earliest Vinaya and the Beginnings of Buddhist Literature*, L. Petech, Trans. Roma: Is. M.E.O., 1956.
Fryckenberg, Robert. "The Emergence of Modern 'Hinduism' as a Concept and as an Institution: A Reappraisal with Special Reference to South India," in *Hinduism Reconsidered*, Gunther Sontheimer and Hermann Kulke, Eds. 1991, 29–50. See also *Subaltern Studies* 10: "Subaltern Identity," Ranajit Guha, Ed. (1989).
Gandhi, Nandita, and Nandita Shah. *The Issues at Stake: Theory and Practice in the Contemporary Women's Movement in India*. Delhi: Kali for Women, 1991.
Gates, Katherine van Akin, Trans. *Himself: The Autobiography of a Hindu Lady*. Toronto: Longmans, Green, 1938.
Gatwood, Lynn. *Devi and the Spouse Goddess*. New Delhi: Manohar, 1985.
Ghosh, Srabashi. "Birds in a Cage: Changes in Bengali Social Life as Recorded in Autobiographies by Women." *Economic and Political* Weekly 21, no. 43 (October 25, 1986), WS88–96.
Gitomer, D. "Urvaśī Won by Valor," *Theater of Memory: The Plays of Kālidāsa*, Barbara Stoler Miller, Ed.; Edwin Gerow, David Gitomer, and Barbara Stoler Miller, Trans. New York: Columbia University Press, 1984.
Gold, Ann Grodzins. "From Demon Aunt to Gorgeous Bride: Women Portray Female Power in a North Indian Festival Cycle." In *Gender Constructs in Indian Religion and Society*, Julia Leslie, Ed. Delhi: Oxford University Press, forthcoming.
———. *Fruitful Journeys: The Ways of Rajasthani Pilgrims*. Berkeley: University of California Press, 1988.
———. "Gender, Violence and Power: Rajasthani Stories of Shakti." In *Women as Subjects: South Asian Histories*, Nina Kumar, Ed., pp. 26–48. Charlottesville: University Press of Virginia, 1994.
———. "Outspoken Women: Representations of Female Voices in a Rajasthan Folklore Community." *Oral Tradition* 12, no. 1 (1997), 103–33.
Gombrich, Richard. *Theravāda Buddhism*. New York: Routledge, 1988.
Gonda, Jan. "The Indian Mantra." *Oriens* 16 (1000), 244–97.
Gupta, Sanjaktu. "The Pañcarātra Attitude to Mantra." In *Understanding Mantra*, Harvey P. Alper, Ed. Albany: State University of New York Press, 1989.
Halbfass, Wilhelm. *Tradition and Reflection: Explorations in Indian Thought*. Albany: State University of New York Press, 1991.
Haraway, Donna. *Simians, Cyborg, and Women: The Reinvention of Nature*. New York: Routledge, 1991.
Hardy, Friedhelm. "Mādhavendra Pūri: A Link Between Bengal Vaiṣṇavism and South Indian Bhakti." *Journal of the Royal Asiatic Society* 1 (1974), 23–41.
———. "The Tamil Veda of a *Śūdra* Saint: The Śrīvaiṣṇava Interpretation of Nammāḻvār." In *Contributions to South Asian Studies*, G. Krishna, Ed. Delhi: Oxford University Press, 1979.
Hari Rao, V. N., Ed. and Trans. *Koil Olugu: The Chronicle of the Śrirañgam Temple with Historical Notes*. Madras: Rochouse and Sons, 1961.
Harlan, Lindsey. *Religion and Rajput Women: The Ethic of Protection in Contemporary Narratives*. Berkeley: University of California Press, 1991.
Heesterman, J. C. *The Broken World of Sacrifice–An Essay in Ancient Indian Ritual*. Chicago: University of Chicago Press, 1993.
———.*The Inner Conflict of Tradition: Essays in Indian Ritual, Kingship, and Society*. Chicago: University of Chicago Press, 1985.
_____. "Reflections on the Significance of the Dākṣinā." *Indo-Iranian Journal* 4 (1959), 241–58.
Hegde, Sasheej, and Seemanthini Niranjana. "Of the Religious and the (Non)feminine: Open Questions." *Contributions to Indian Sociology* 28, no. 1 (1994), 107–22.

Hein, Norvin. "Kālayavana, A Key to Mathurā's Cultural Self-Perception." In *The Cultural Heritage*, Doris Meth Srinivasan, Ed., pp. 223–26. New Delhi: American Institute of India Studies, 1989.

Hellman, Eva. "Political Hinduism: The Challenge of the Viśva Hindu Pariṣad." Doctoral dissertation, Department of the History of Religions, Uppsala University, Uppsala, Sweden, 1993.

Hindoo Patriot. March 14, 1887, p. 127.

Hock, Hans Henrick. "On the Origin and Early Development of the Sacred Sanskrit Syllable *om*. Perspectives on Indo-European Language, Culture, and Religion." *Studies in Honor of Edgar C Polomé. Journal of Indo-European Studies Monographs* 1, no. 7 (1991), 89–110.

Holland, Dorothy, Carole Cain, William Lachicotte, Jr., and Debra Skinner. *Identity and Agency in Cultural Worlds*. Cambridge, Mass.: Harvard University Press, 1988.

Holland, Dorothy C., and Debra G. Skinner. "Contested Ritual, Contested Feminities: (Re)forming Self and Society in a Nepali Women's Festival." *American Ethnologist* 22, no. 2 (1995), 279–305.

Horner, I. B., Trans. *The Book of the Discipline, Vol. 5. Cullavagga*. Oxford: Pali Text Society, [1952]/1988.

——. *Women Under Primitive Buddhism: Laywomen and Almswomen*. London, 1930; rpt. Delhi: Motilal Banarsidass Publishers, 1989.

Hume, Robert Ernest. *The Thirteen Principal Upanishads*. Oxford: Oxford University Press, [1921]/1968.

Inden, Ronald. *Imagining India*. Oxford: Blackwell, 1990.

India Today. August 15 1994, p. 26.

"Infant Marriage and Enforced Widowhood." *Times of India*. June 26, 1885, p. 4.

Insler, Stanley. "On the Soma Ritual." Address to the Columbia University Seminar on the Veda and Its Interpretation, New York, November 9, 1995.

Irigaray, Luce. *Ethique de la différence sexuelle*. Paris: Les Editions de Minuit, 1984.

——. *Sexes et Parentés*. Paris: Les Editions de Minuit, 1987.

——. *Speculum de l'autre femme*. Paris: Les Editions de Minuit, 1974.

Jacobi, Hermann, Trans. Jaina *Sutras, Part 1. Sacred Books of the East*, vol. 22. Oxford University Press, 1884; rpt. Delhi: Motilal Banarsidass, 1964.

Jamison, Stephanie W. *The Ravenous Hyenas and the Wounded Sun: Myth and Ritual in Ancient India*. Ithaca, N.Y.: Cornell University Press, 1991.

——. *Sacrificed Wife /Sacrificer's Wife: Women, Ritual, and Hospitality in Ancient India*. New York: Oxford University Press, 1996.

Jayawardena, Kumari. *Feminism and Nationalism in the Third World*. London: Zed Books, 1986.

Jeffery, Patricia, and Amrita Basu, Eds. *Appropriating Gender: Women's Activism and Politicized Religion in South Asia*. New York: Routledge, 1998.

Jeffrey, Patricia, and Roger Jeffrey. *Don't Marry Me to a Plowman! Women's Everyday Lives in Rural North India*. Boulder, Col.: Westview Press, 1996.

Jha, Ganganath. *The Prābhākara School of Pūrva Mīmāṃsā*. Delhi: Motilal Banarsidass, 1978.

Johnson, Mark. *Moral Imagination: Implications of Cognitive Science for Ethics*. Chicago: University of Chicago Press, 1993.

Joshi, Prabhakar. *Ethnobotany of the Primitive Tribes in Rajasthan*. Jaipur: Printwell, 1995.

Kakar, Sudhir. "Feminine Identity in India." In *Women in Indian Society*, Rehana Ghadially, Ed. New Delhi: Sage, 1988.

Kane, Pandurang Vaman. *History of Dharmaśāstra: Ancient and Mediaeval Religious and Civil Law*. 2nd ed., 2 vols. Poona: Bhandarkar Oriental Research Institute, 1941, 1946, 1979.

Kapur, Anjur. "Theorizing Women Writing in India." *South Asia Bulletin* 14, no. 1 (1994), 114–21.

Karleka, Malavika. *Voices from Within: Early Personal Narratives of Bengali Women*. Delhi: Oxford University Press, 1991.

Keith, Arthur Berriedale. "Om." In *Encyclopedia of Religion and Ethics*, J. Hastings, Ed. (1917) 11.490–92.

——, Trans. *The Veda of the Black Yajus School Entitled* Taittirīya Saṃhitā. *Harvard Oriental Series*, vols. 18, 19. Delhi: Motilal Banarsidass, [1914]/1967.

Kendall, Laurel. *Shamans, Housewives, and Other Restless Spirits: Women in Korean Ritual Life.* Honolulu: University of Hawaii Press, 1985.

Kinsley, David. *Hindu Goddesses.* Delhi: Motilal Banarsidass, 1986.

Kishwar, Madhu, and Ruth Vanita. "Inheritance Rights for Women: A Response to Some Commonly Expressed Fears." *Manushi* 57 (March–April 1990), 3–15.

Klostermaier, Klaus K. *A Survey of Hinduism.* Albany: State University of New York, 1994.

Kolenda, Pauline. "Pox and the Terror of Childlessness: Images and Ideas of the Smallpox Goddess in a North Indian Village." In *Mother Worship: Theme and Variations*, James J. Preston, Ed., pp. 227–50. Chapel Hill: University of North Carolina Press, 1982.

Kopf, David. *The Brahmo Samaj and the Shaping of the Modem Indian Mind.* Princeton, N.J.: Princeton University Press, 1979.

Kosambi, Meera. "Gender Reform and Competing State Controls over Women." *Contributions to Indian Sociology* 29, no. 1-2 1 (995), 265–90.

——. "Girl-Brides and Socio-Legal Change: Age of Consent Bill (1891) Controversy." *Economic and Political Weekly* 36 (August 3–10, 1991), 1857–68.

——. "The Meeting of the Twain: the Cultural Confrontation of Three Women in Nineteenth Century Maharashtra." *Indian Journal of Gender Studies* 1, no. 1 (1994), 1–22.

——. *Pandita Ramabai's Feminist and Christian Conversions.* RCWS Gender Series, *Gender and History/Social Change*, book 2. Bombay: Research Centre for Women's Studies, 1995.

Kumar, Nina, Ed. *Women as Subjects: South Asian Histories.* Calcutta: Stree, 1994; and Charlottesville, Virginia: University Press of Virginia, 1994.

Kumārila Bhaṭṭa. *Ślokavārttika*, 2nd ed. Ganganath Jha, Trans. Delhi: Sri Satguru Publications, [1900]/1983.

LaFleur, William. *Liquid Life: Abortion and Buddhism in Japan.* Princeton, N.J.: Princeton University Press, 1992.

Lal, Shyam Kishore. *Female Divinities in Hindu Mythology and Ritual.* Pune: University of Pune, 1980.

Lariviere, Richard W. "Adhikāra–Right and Responsibility." In *Languages and Cultures: Studies in Honor of Edgar C. Polomé.* M. A. Jazayery and W. Winter, Eds., pp. 359–64. Amsterdam: Mouton de Gruyter, 1988.

Leslie, I. Julia. *The Perfect Wife. The Orthodox Hindu Woman According to the Strīdharmapaddhati of Tryambakayajvan.* Delhi: Oxford University Press, 1989.

——. "Some Traditional Indian Views on Menstruation and Female Sexuality." In *Sexual Knowledge, Sexual Science: The History of Attitudes to Sexuality*, Roy Porter and Mikulas Teich, Eds., pp. 63–81. Cambridge: Cambridge University Press, 1994.

Leslie, Julia, and Mary McGee, Eds., *Invented Identities: The Interplay of Religion and Politics in India.* Delhi: Oxford University Press, 2000.

Leslie, Julia, Ed. *Roles and Rituals for Hindu Women.* Rutherford: Fairleigh Dickinson University Press, 1991.

Mahadevan, Iravatham. "From Orality to Literacy: The Case of the Tamil Society." In *Journal of the Centre for Historical Studies.* New Delhi: Sage, 1995.

Marglin, Frederique. "Gender and the Unitary Self: Looking for the Subaltern in Coastal Orissa." *South Asia Research* 15, no. 1 (1195), 78–130.

——. "Sacred Groves: Regenerating the Body, the Land, the Community." In *Global Ecology: A New Arena of Political Conflict*, Wolfgang Sachs, Ed., pp. 197–207. London: Zed Books, 1993.

Marglin, Frederique, and Purna Chandra Misra. "Refining the Body: Transformative Emotion in Ritual Dance." In *Divine Passions: The Social Construction of Emotion in India*, Owen Lynch, Ed., pp. 212–36. Berkeley: University of California Press, 1990.

Marriott, McKim. "The Feast of Love." In *Krishna: Myths, Rites, and Attitudes*, Milton B. Singer, Ed., pp. 200–12. Chicago: University of Chicago Press, 1966.

Matsubara, Mitsunori. *Pañcarātra Saṃhitās and Early Vaiṣṇava Theology*. Delhi: Motilal Banarsidass, 1994.

Mohanty, Chandra T. "Under Western Eyes: Feminist Scholarship and Colonial Discourses." In *Third World Women and the Politics of Feminism*, Chandra T. Mohanty, Ann Russo, and Lourdes Torres, Eds., pp. 51–80. Bloomington: Indiana University Press, 1991.

Monier-Williams, Monier. *A Sanskrit-English Dictionary*. Oxford: Clarendon Press, [1899]/1970.

Morgenstierne, Georg. *Uber das verhaltnis zwischen Carudatta und Mrcchakatika*. Halle a.d.S., Buchdruckerei des Waisenhauses, 1920.

Mukta, Parita. *Upholding the Common Life: The Community of Mirabai*. Delhi: Oxford University Press, 1994.

Mumme, Patricia Y. *The Mumukṣuppati of Piḷḷai Lokācārya with Maṇavāḷamāmuni's Commentary*. Bombay: Ananthacharya Indological Research Institute, 1987.

Murshid, Ghulam. *Reluctant Debutante: Responses of Bengali Women to Modernization, 1849–1905*. Rajshahi and Bangladesh: Sahitya Samsad and Rajshahi University, 1983.

Nandy, Ashish. "The Politics of Secularism and the Recovery of Religious Tolerance." In *Mirrors of Violence: Communities, Riots and Survivors in South Asia*, Veena Das, Ed., pp. 69–93. Delhi: Oxford University Press, 1990.

——. "Women Versus Womanliness in India." In *Women in Indian Society*, Rehana Ghadially, Ed. New Delhi: Sage, 1988.

Narayan, Kirin. "Songs Lodged in Some Hearts: Displacements of Women's Knowledge in Kangra." In *Displacement, Diaspora and Geographies of Identity*, S. Lavie and T. Swedenburg, Eds., pp. 181–213. Durham, N.C.: Duke University Press, 1996.

——. "Women's Songs, Women's Lives." *Manushi*, no. 81 (1994), 2–10.

Narayanan, Vasudha. "Brimming with *Bhakti*, Embodiements of *Shakti*: Devotees, Deities, Performers, Reformers, and Other Women of Power in the Hindu Tradition." In *Feminism and World Religions*, Arvind Sharma and Katherine K. Young, Eds. Albany: State University of New York Press, 1999.

——. "Oral and Written Comments on the Tiruvāymoḻi." In *Texts in Context: Traditional Hermeneutics in South Asia*, Jeffrey Timm, Ed. Albany: State University of New York Press, 1992.

——. *The Tamil Veda: Piḷḷān's Interpretation of the Tiruvāymoḻi*. Chicago: University of Chicago Press, 1989.

——. *The Vernacular Veda: Revelation, Recitation and Ritual*. Columbia: University of South Carolina Press, 1994.

——. *The Way and the Goal: Expressions of Devotion in the Early Śrī Vaiṣṇava Tradition*. Cambridge, Mass.: Center for the Study of World Religions, Harvard University, 1987.

Nath, Vijay. *Dāna: Gift-System in Ancient India (c. 600* B.C.*–c.* A.D. *300)* A *Socio-Economic Perspective*. New Delhi: Munshiram Manoharlal Publishers, 1987.

Nathanson, Paul, and Katherine K. Young. *Beyond the Fall of Man: From Feminist Ideology to Intersexual Dialogue* (under review).

Nayar, Nancy Ann. "The 'Other' Āṇṭāḷ: Portrait of a 12th-Century Śrīvaiṣṇava Woman." *Journal of Vaiṣṇava Studies* 3 (1995), 149–72.

O'Flaherty, Wendy Doniger. "Introduction." In *Karma and Rebirth in Classical Indian Traditions*, Wendy Doniger O'Flaherty, Ed. Berkeley: University of California Press, 1980.

——. *Other's People's Myths*. New York: Macmillan, 1988.

——. *The Rig Veda*. New York: Penguin Books, 1981.

——. *Sexual Metaphores and Animal Symbols in Hindu Mythology*. Delhi: Motilal Banarsidass, 1981.

——. *Women, Androgynes, and Other Mythical Beasts*. Chicago: University of Chicago Press, 1980.

Oldenberg, Hermann, Trans. *The Gṛhyasūtras. Sacred Books of the East*, vols. 29, 30. Delhi: Motilal Banarsidass, [1886, 1892]/1964.

Olivelle, Patrick. "Introduction." in *Saṃnyāsa Upaniṣads*, pp. 3–112. New York: Oxford University Press, 1992.

——. *Upaniṣads*. New York: Oxford University Press, 1996.

Orr, Leslie C. "The Vaiṣṇava Community at Śrīraṅgam in the Early Medieval Period." *Journal of Vaiṣṇava Studies* 3, no. 3 (1995).

——. "Women of Medieval South India in Hindu Temple Ritual: Text and Practice." In *The Annual Review of Women in World Religions*, 3 vols., Arvind Sharma and Katherine K. Young, Eds. Albany: State University of New York Press, 1994.

Ortner, Sherry B. "Gender Hegemonies." *Cultural Critique*, Winter 1990, pp. 35–80.

Pandit, Maya, Trans. *Women Writing in India: 600 B.C. to the Present*. Susie Tharu and K. Lalita, Eds. Delhi: Oxford University Press, 1991.

Parpola, Asko. *Deciphering the Indus Script*. Cambridge: Cambridge University Press, 1994.

——. "On the Primary Meaning and Etymology of the Sacred Syllable Om." *Studia Orientalia* 50 (1981), 195–213.

Patel, Kartikeya. "Women, Earth, and the Goddess: A Shākta-Hindu Interpretation of Embodied Religion." *Hypatia* 9, no. 4 (Fall 1994), 69–87.

Patton, Laurie. "The Fate of the Female Ṛṣi." In *Myths and Mythmaking in India*, Julia Leslie, Ed. London: Curzon Press, 1996.

——. "Making the Canon Commonplace." *The Journal of Religion*. January 1997, pp. 1–19.

——. *Myth as Argument: The Bṛhaddevatā as Canonical Commentary* in *Religionsgeschichtliche Vorsuche und Vorarbeiten*, vol. 41. Berlin: Degruyter, 1996.

Pearson, Anne M. "*Because It Gives Me Peace of Mind*": *Ritual Fasts in the Religious Lives of Hindu Women*. Albany: State University of New York Press, 1996.

Prakash, Gyan. "Becoming a Bhuinya." In *Contesting Power*, D. Haynes and G. Prakash, Eds., pp. 45–174. Berkeley: University of California Press, 1991.

——. *Bonded Histories: Genealogies of Labor Servitude in Colonial India*. Cambridge: Cambridge University Press, 1990.

——. "Can the 'Subaltern' Ride? A Reply to O'Hanlon and Washbrook." *Comparative Studies in Society and History* 34.1 (1992), 168–84.

_____. "Writing Post-Orientalist Histories of the Third World: Indian Historiography is Good to Think." In *Colonialism and Culture*, Nicholas B. Dirks, Ed. Ann Arbor: University of Michigan Press, 1995.

Prakash, Gyan, Ed. *After Colonialism: Imperial Histories and Postcolonial Displacements*. Princeton: Princeton University Press, 1995.

Quigley, Declan. "Review of *Listen to the Heron's Words* by Gloria G. Raheja and Ann G. Gold." *Journal of the Royal Anthropological* Institute 2, no. 2 (1996), 391–92.

Raheja, Gloria Goodwin. "Crying When She's Born and Crying When She Goes Away: Marriage and the Idiom of Gift in Pahansu Song Performances." In *Hindu Marriage from the Margins*, Lindsey Harlan and Paul Courtright, Eds., pp. 19–59. New York: Oxford University Press, 1995.

Raheja, Gloria Goodwin and Ann Grodzins Gold. *Listen to the Heron's Words: Reimagining Gender and Kinship in North India*. Berkeley: University of California Press, 1994.

Rajan, K. V. Soundara. "The Typology of the Anantaṣāyi Icon." *Artibus Asiae* 29 (1967), 76–72.

Rajan, Rajeswari Sunder. *Signposts: Gender Issues in Post-Independence India*. New Delhi: Kali for Women, 1999.

Ramabai, Pandita. *A Testimony*. Kedgaon: Ramabai Mukti Mission, 1907.

Ramabai Sarasvati, Pandita. *The High-Caste Hindu Woman*, 3rd ed. With an introduction by Rachel L. Bodley. Philadelphia: Press of the J. B. Rodgers Print. Co., 1888.

Ramanujan, A. K. *The Interior Landscape: Love Poems from a Classical Tamil Anthology*. Bloomington: Indiana University Press, 1967.

Rambachan, Anantanand, "Redefining the Authority of Scripture: The Rejection of Vedic Infallibility by the Brahmo Samaj." In *Authority, Anxiety, and Canon: Essays in Vedic Interpretation*, Laurie L. Patton, Ed. Albany: State University of New York Press, 1994.

Reddiar, K. Venkatacami, ed. *Nālāyirativyappirapantam*. Tiruvenkatattan: Tirumantram, 1973.

Richman, Paula, Ed. *Many Rāmāyaṇas: The Diversity of a Narrative Tradition in South Asia*. Berkeley: University of California Press, 1991.

Rocher, Ludo. "Mantras in the *Śivapurāṇa*." In *Understanding Mantras*, Harvey P. Alper, Ed. Albany: State University of New York Press, 1989.

Roy, Ram Mohan. *Sati: A Writeup of Raja Ram Mohan Roy About Burning of Widows Alive*. Delhi: B. R. Publishing, 1989.

Rukmani, T. S. "A Critique of Om Based on Early Upaniṣadic Sources." *Journal of the Institute of Asian Studies*. (March 1998): 101–12.

Ryder, Arthur William, Trans. *The Little Clay Cart: A Hindu Drama*. Harvard Oriental Series, vol. 9. Cambridge, Mass: Harvard University Press, 1905.

Samiti. *Preface to Rashtra Sevika Samiti: Organisation of Hindu Women*. Nagpur: Sevika Prakashan, 1988.

Sarkar, Tanika. "Rhetoric against Age of Consent: Resisting Colonial Reason and the Death of a Child-Wife." *Economic and Political Weekly* 28, no. 36 (September 4, 1993), 1869–78.

Sastri, Shivanath. *History of the Brahmo Samaj*, 2 vols. Calcutta: Sadharan Brahmo Samaj, 1912.

Sax, William. *Mountain Goddess: Religion and Politics in the Central Himalayas*. New York: Oxford University Press, 1991.

Scharpe, A., Ed. *Kālidāsa-Lexicon*. Brugge: De Tempel, 1954–.

Schmidt, Hans-Peter. *Some Women's Rites and Rights in the Veda*. Poona: Bhandarkar Oriental Institute, 1987.

Schwarz, Henry. *Writing Cultural History in Colonial and Postcolonial India*. Philadelphia: University of Pennsylvania Press, 1997.

Scott, James C. *Weapons of the Weak: Everyday Forms of Peasant Resistance*. New Haven, Conn.: Yale University Press, 1995.

Selby, Martha. *The Color of Gender: On Embryology and Sex Determination in the Caraka and Susruta Samhitas*. Unpublished ms.

Sen, Keshab Chander. "The Reconstruction of Native Society," *Keshub Chunder Sen's Lectures in India*. London: Cassell, 1904.

——. "Where is the Yogi Wife?" In *The New Dispensation*, 2 vols., 2nd ed. Calcutta: Brahmo Tract Society, 1915.

Shastri, Madhu. *Status of Hindu Women: A Study of Legislative Trends and Judicial Behaviour*. Jaipur: RBSA Publishers, 1990.

Sinha, Mrinalini. "The Age of Consent Act: the Ideal of Masculinity and Colonial Ideology in Nineteenth Century Bengal." In *Shaping Bengali Worlds: Public and Private*, T. K. Stewart, Ed., pp. 99–127. East Lansing, Mich.: Asian Studies Center, 1989.

——. *Colonial Masculinity: the 'Manly Englishman' and the 'Effeminate Bengali' in the Late Nineteenth Century*. Manchester: Manchester University Press, 1995.

Sister Geraldine. *The Letters and Correspondence of Pandita Ramabai*, A. B. Shah, Ed. Bombay: Maharashtra State Board for Literature and Culture, 1977.

Skinner, Debra, Dorothy Holland, and G. B. Adhikari. "The Songs of Tīj: A Genre of Critical Commentary for Women in Nepal." *Asian Folklore Studies* 53, no. 2 (1994),259–305.

Smith, Frederick. "Indra's Curse, Varuna's Noose, and the Suppression of the Woman in the Vedic Śrauta Ritual." In *Roles and Rituals for Hindu Women*, Julia Leslie, Ed., pp. 17–45. Delhi: Motilal Banarsidass, 1992.

——. *The Vedic Sacrifice in Transition: A Translation and Study of the Trikāṇḍamaṇḍana of Bhaskara Miśra*. Pune: Bhandarkar Oriental Research Institute, 1987.

Srivastava, Sahab Lal. *Folk Culture and Oral Tradition:* A Comparative Study of Regions in Rajasthan and Eastern U.P. New Delhi: Abhinav Publications, 1974.

Sutton, Constance R., Ed. *Feminism, Nationalism, and Militarism.* Arlington, Va.: Association for Feminist Anthropology/American Anthropological Association, 1995.

Tamil Lexicon, 6 vols. Madras: University of Madras, 1982.

Tarkapañcānana, Jagannātha. A *Digest of Hindu Law, On Contracts and Successions; with a Commentary.* [Vivādabhaṅgārṇava.] London: J. Debrett, 1798–1801.

Tharu, Susie, and K. Lalita, Eds. *Women Writing in India 600* B.C. *to the Present.* New York: Feminist Press, 1991.

Thieme, Paul. "Agastya und Lopāmudrā." In *Kleine Schriften*, Teil 1. Wisebaden: Franz Steinder Verlag GMBH, 1971.

Thomson, Judith Jarvis. *Rights, Restitution and Risk: Essays in Moral Theory.* Cambridge, Mass.: Harvard University Press, 1986.

Tilak. "Educational Course in the Female High School." *Keshari*, nos. 7, 42 (October 25, 1887), 2

Tucker, Richard P. *Ranade and the Roots of Indian Nationalism.* Chicago: University of Chicago Press, 1972.

Vajpeyi, Kailash. *The Science of Mantras: A Manual for Happiness and Prosperity.* New Delhi: Arnold-Heinemann, 1979.

Vaudeville, Charlotte. *Bārahmāsā in Indian Literatures.* Delhi: Motilal Banarsidass, 1986.

Venkatachari, K. K. A. *The Manipravala Literature of the Śrīvaiṣṇava Ācāryas: 12th–15th Century* A.D. Bombay: Anantacharya Research Institute, 1980.

Vidyasagar, Ishwarchandra. *Marriage of Hindu Widows*, Arabinda Podder, Ed. Calcutta: K. P. Bagchi, 1976.

Wadley, Susan S. "Sītalā." *Asian Folklore Studies* 39, no.1 (1980), 33–62.

——. *Struggling with Destiny in Karimpur, 1925–1984.* Berkeley: University of California Press, 1994.

——. "*Vrats*: Transformers of Destiny." In *Karma: An Anthropological Inquiry*, Charles F. Keyes and E. Valentine Daniel, Eds., pp. 147–62. Berkeley: University of California Press, 1983.

——. "Women and the Hindu Tradition." In *Women in the Hindu Tradition*, Renana Ghadially, Ed. New Delhi: Sage, 1988.

Wezler, Albrecht. "A Note on Sanskrit Bhrūna, and Bhrūnahatyā," in *Festschrift Klaus Bruhn*, Nalini Balbir and Joachim K. Bautze, Eds. Reinbeck: Verlag für Orientalistische Fachpublikationen, 1994, pp. 623–48.

Wheelock, Wade T. "The Mantra in Vedic and Tantric Ritual." In *Understanding Mantras*, Harvey P. Alper, Ed. Albany: State University of New York Press, 1989.

Willis, Janice D. "Female Patronage in Indian Buddhism." In *The Powers of Art: Patronage in Indian Culture*, Barbara Stoler Miller, Ed., pp. 46–53. Delhi: Oxford University Press, 1992.

——. "Nuns and Benefactresses: The Role of Women in the Development of Buddhism." In *Women, Religion and Social Change*, Yvonne Yazbeck Haddad and Ellison Banks Findly, Eds. Albany: State University of New York Press, 1985.

Wolpert, Stanley A. *Tilak and Gokhal: Revolution and Reform in the Making of Modem India.* Berkeley: University of California Press, 1962.

Wright, John C. *The Universal Almanac* 1995. Kansas City: Andrews & McMeel, 1995.

Young, Jane M., and Kay Turner. "Challenging the Canon: Folklore Theory Reconsidered from Feminist Perspectives." In *Feminist Theory and the Study of Folklore*, Susan Tower Hollis, Linda Pershing, and Jane M. Young, Eds., pp. 9–28. Urbana: University of Illinois Press, 1993.

Young, Katherine K. "Theology Does Help Women's Liberation: Srīvaiṣṇavism, A Hindu Case Study." *Journal of Vaisnava Studies* 3, no. 4 (1995), 173–233.

Zysk, Ken. *Religious Medicine.* New Brunswick,, N.J.: Transaction Publishers, 1993.

Index